WordPerfect 6 for DOS
The Visual Learning Guide

Watch for these forthcoming titles in this series:

Quicken 3 for Windows: The Visual Learning Guide
1-2-3 for Windows: The Visual Learning Guide
WordPerfect for Windows: The Visual Learning Guide

Available Now!

Windows 3.1: The Visual Learning Guide
Excel 4 for Windows: The Visual Learning Guide
Word for Windows 2: The Visual Learning Guide
WordPerfect 6 for DOS: The Visual Learning Guide

How to Order:

Quantity discounts are available from the publisher, Prima Publishing, P.O. Box 1260BK, Rocklin, CA 95677; telephone (916) 786-0426. On your letterhead include information concerning the intended use of the books and the number of books you wish to purchase.

WordPerfect 6 for DOS
The Visual Learning Guide

Grace Joely Beatty, Ph.D.

David C. Gardner, Ph.D.

Prima Publishing
P.O. Box 1260EXC
Rocklin, CA 95677
(916) 786-0426

Copyright © 1993 by The Gardner Beatty Group

All rights reserved. No part of this book may be reproduced or transmitted in any form or by any means, electronic or mechanical, including photocopying, recording, or by any information storage or retrieval system without written permission from Prima Publishing, except for the inclusion of quotations in a review.

Library of Congress Catalog Card Number: 93-85008
ISBN: 1-55958-310-X

Executive Editor: Editor: Roger Stewart
Managing Editor: Neweleen A. Trebnik
Project Manager: Becky Freeman
Production and Copy Editing: Laurie Stewart
Production and Layout: Marian Hartsough Associates
Interior Design: Grace Joely Beatty, S. Linda Beatty, David C. Gardner,
   Laurie Stewart, and Kim Bartusch
Technical Editing: Linda Miles
Cover Design: Page Design, inc.
Color Separations: Ocean Quigley
Index: Katherine Stimson

Prima Publishing
Rocklin, CA 95677-1260

Every effort has been made to supply complete and accurate information. However, neither the publisher nor the authors assume any responsibility for its use, nor for any infringements of patents or other rights of third parties that would result.

93 94 95 96 RRD 10 9 8 7 6 5 4 3 2 1

Printed in the United States of America

Acknowledgments

We are deeply indebted to reviewers around the country who gave generously of their time to test every step in the manuscript. Raymon Holder, David Coburn, David Sauer, Jeannie Jones, Nora Bird, and Margaret Short cannot be thanked enough!

Carolyn Holder and Anne-Barbara Norris are our in-house production team, reviewers, proofreaders, screen capturers, and friends. They, along with Ray Holder and Margaret Short, keep us functioning.

We are personally and professionally delighted to work with everyone at Prima Publishing, especially Roger Stewart, executive editor, Neweleen Trebnik, managing editor, Becky Freeman, project manager, Debbie Parisi, publicity coordinator, and Kim Bartusch, production coordinator.

Linda Miles, technical editor, Laurie Stewart, production and copy editor, Ocean Quigley, color separator, Marian Hartsough and Barbara Lewis, interior layout, and Paul Page, cover design, contributed immensely to the final product.

Bill Gladstone and Matt Wagner of Waterside Productions created the idea for this series. Their faith in us has never wavered.

Joseph and Shirley Beatty made this series possible. We can never repay them.

Asher Shapiro has always been there when we needed him.

Paula Gardner Capaldo and David Capaldo have been terrific. Thanks, Joshua and Jessica, for being such wonderful kids! Our project humorist, Mike Bumgardner, always came through when we needed a boost!

We could not have met the deadlines without the technical support of Ray Holder, our electrical genius, Fred Harper of Blue Line Communications, Sandi Hetzel of WordPerfect Corporation and the outstanding WordPerfect technical support staff. Thank you all!

CONTENTS

Introduction xiii

Part I: Entering, Editing, and Printing Text......................1

Chapter 1: Changing Margins and Fonts and Entering Text 2
Opening WordPerfect for the First Time 2
Changing from Text Mode to Graphics Mode...3
Displaying the Button Bar and Ribbon..5
Displaying the Scroll Bars..6
Setting Margins 7
Changing the Font 8
    Changing the Font for the Current Document..8
    Changing the Font for All New Documents 10
Reading the Status Line 13
Entering Text..14
    Creating the Letterhead 14
    Entering the Date, Address, and Salutation 15
    Entering the Body of the Letter 16
Inserting Symbols and Finishing the Letter 18
    Inserting a Scissors Symbol...18
    Inserting Box Symbols 21

Chapter 2: Naming and Saving a Document 23
Naming and Saving a New Document...23
Saving While You Work 25
    Using the Save Command...25

Chapter 3: Previewing and Printing a Document..26
Viewing a Document Before Printing 26
    Changing Pages in Preview 27
    Viewing Multiple Pages in Preview 27
    Closing the Preview Screen...28
Printing a Document 29
    Printing the Current Page 29

CONTENTS

    Printing Selected Pages 30
    Printing the Entire Document 31

Chapter 4: Closing a File and Opening a Saved File 32
  Closing a File 32
    Closing After Changes 33
  Exiting WordPerfect 34
  Booting Up WordPerfect 35
  Opening a Saved File with the File Manager 35

Chapter 5: Using the Grammar Checker, Spelling Checker, and Thesaurus 37
  Using Grammatik 5 37
  Using Speller 42
    Adding a Word to the Dictionary 43
    Ignoring a Suggested Change 44
    Editing a Word in the Document 45
    Accepting a Suggested Change 46
  Using the Thesaurus 47
    Using Search 47
    Replacing a Word with the Thesaurus 48

Chapter 6: Editing a Document 50
  Inserting Text 50
  Deleting Text 51
  Undoing an Edit 52
    Undoing an Undo 52
  Combining Paragraphs 53
  Outwitting Text Wrap 54
    Inserting a Home Space 54
    Inserting a Hard Return 58
  Using the Replace Command 59
  A Note About Scrolling 60
  Drag-and-Drop Moving 61
  Inserting a Page Break 63
  Deleting a Page Break 64

Drag-and-Drop Copying	65
Copying and Pasting Text	68
Copying the Text	68
Using the Go To Command	69
Pasting the Text	70

Part II: Formatting a Document 71

Chapter 7: Customizing Text 72

Changing Type Size	72
Making Text Bold	73
Underlining Text	74
Centering Text	75
Using the Ribbon	75
Using the Layout Menu	77
Undoing Text Alignment	78
Adding a Border and Shading	80
Deleting Borders and Shading	83
Creating a Bulleted List	84
Creating a New Bullet Style	84
Applying the Bullet Style to Other Paragraphs	86
Deleting a Bullet	87
Saving Your Work	87

Chapter 8: Setting Tabs 88

Setting a Left-Aligned Tab with the Mouse	88
Resetting Tabs for a Bulleted List	89
Using a Pre-Set Tab	92
Inserting a Right-Aligned Tab	92
Making a Solid-Line Leader	94
Setting a Tab with the Set Tab Command	96
Deleting a Tab	99
Opening a New Document	100
Setting a Right-Aligned Tab	100
Setting a Center-Aligned Tab	101

Setting Decimal Tabs 102
Applying Tabs 103
Switching Between Open Documents 104
Closing Without Saving 105

Chapter 9: Adding a Header and a Page Number 106
Changing the Margin 106
Adding a Header 108
    Changing the Space Between the Header and the Text 109
    Creating the Header 109
Inserting a Page Number 111
Viewing the Header and Page Number 114
    Using Page Mode 114
    Using Print Preview 115

Part III: Mailing Lists, Form Letters, and Envelopes 117

Chapter 10: Printing an Envelope 118
Using the Envelope Button to Print 118
    Printing with a HP LaserJet II or III Series Printer 119
    Printing with a Dot-Matrix Printer 120
Printing the Return Address 121
    Omitting and Restoring the Standard Return Address 122
Customizing the Envelope Text 123
    Changing the Font and Point Size 123
    Making the First Line of the Address Bold 126
Printing a Letter with an Attached Envelope 128
    Attaching an Envelope to a Letter 128
    Printing a Letter with an Attached Envelope 129
Printing an Attached Envelope Without a Letter 130
Printing a Letter Without an Attached Envelope 132
Closing a Letter Without Saving an Attached Envelope 132

Chapter 11: Creating a Mailing List 133
Setting Up a Data Table 133
    Opening a Data Table 133
    Entering Field Names 135

Creating a Mailing List 137
Saving the Mailing List 141

Chapter 12: Editing a Mailing List 142
Adding Fields to the Mailing List 142
    Adjusting the Column Width 146
Entering More Data in a Mailing List Data Table 148
Saving the Edited Mailing List 150

Chapter 13: Setting Up a Form Letter for Merge Printing 151
Opening a List of Field Names 151
Inserting Merge Fields into a Form Letter 155
Copying and Pasting Merge Fields 161
Saving the Form Letter with the Save As Command 163

Chapter 14: Printing a Form Letter 164
Setting Up to Print a Form Letter 164
    Beginning the Merge Process 164
    Selecting the Form File and Data File to Merge Print 165
Printing the Letter 166
Closing the File 168

Chapter 15: Printing Envelopes for a Mailing List 169
Creating an Envelope to Print a Mailing List 169
    Entering Merge Fields for the Mailing Address 170
    Inserting the Mail Merge Envelope in the Document 173
Saving the Envelope 174
Printing Envelopes for a Mailing List 175
Setting Up WordPerfect to Print with an Envelope Tray 178
    Saving the Envelope Tray Setup 182
Printing a Specific Envelope from a Mailing List 183
    Marking an Envelope to Print 183
    Printing the Marked Envelope 187
Closing the Envelope File Without Saving 188

Chapter 16: Converting a Mailing List Created in Another Program 189
Converting a Mailing List 189

CONTENTS

Converting a File from a Specific Program..191
Adding Field Names to a Converted Mailing List.......................................192
    Changing the View...192
    Entering Field Names..193
Saving the Mailing List as a WordPerfect Data File....................................194

Part IV: Introducing Tables 197

Chapter 17: Creating a Table 198
Creating a Table..198
Joining Cells..200
Entering Text and Numbers in a Table 202

Chapter 18: Editing a Table 205
Sorting Data Alphabetically 205
Sorting Data Numerically 208
Undoing a Sort 210
Adding a Row...211
Deleting a Row...213
Changing Column Width 214
Formatting Text 216
    Increasing Type Size..216
    Changing Cell Formats..217
Changing Table Position 218
Saving the Table 220

Chapter 19: Formatting Numbers and Writing Formulas....................221
Formatting Numbers..221
    Formatting Numbers as Currency 221
    Centering Numbers in a Cell..224
Writing Formulas 225
    Writing a Multiplication Formula..225
    Copying a Formula 226
    Writing an Addition Formula...228
Deleting and Undeleting a Table 229

Part V: Introducing File Manager 231

Chapter 20: Opening and Printing Multiple Files 232
- Opening Several Files at the Same Time 232
  - Marking Files 232
  - Opening Marked Files 235
  - Switching to Another Open Document 235
- Printing Several Files 236
  - Marking Files to Print 236
  - Printing Marked Files 238
  - Closing All Marked Files 240

Chapter 21: Sorting, Moving, and Copying Files 241
- Sorting Files in a Directory 241
  - Sorting by Date and Time 241
  - Sorting by Size 243
  - Sorting Alphabetically 244
- Viewing the Contents of a File 245
- Creating a Directory 246
- Moving Files to Another Directory 248
  - Marking Files to Move 248
- Copying a File to a Disk 250
  - Changing the Directory 250
  - Copying a File to a Disk 251
  - Returning to the Original Directory 252
- Closing File Manager 252
- What Next? 252

Part VI: Appendix 253

Appendix: Installing WordPerfect 6 for DOS 254
- Installing WordPerfect 6 for DOS 254
  - Installing a Printer 258
  - Completing the Installation 260
  - Entering Your Registration Number 263

Index 265

Customize Your Learning

Prima *Visual Learning Guides* are not like any other computer books you have ever seen. They are based on our years in the classroom, our corporate consulting, and our research at Boston University on the best ways to teach technical information to nontechnical learners. Most important, this series is based on the feedback of a panel of reviewers from across the country who range in computer knowledge from "panicked at the thought" to sophisticated.

This is not an everything-you've-ever-wanted-to-know-about WordPerfect 6 for DOS-but-didn't-know-enough-to-ask book. It is designed to give you the information you need to perform basic (and some not so basic) functions with confidence and skill. It is a book that our reviewers claim makes it "really easy" for anyone to learn WordPerfect 6 for DOS quickly.

Each chapter is illustrated with full-color screens to guide you through every task. The combination of screens, step-by-step instructions, and pointers make it impossible for you to get lost or confused as you follow along on your own computer. You can either work through from beginning to end or skip around to master the skills you need. If you have a specific goal you want to accomplish now, choose it from the following section.

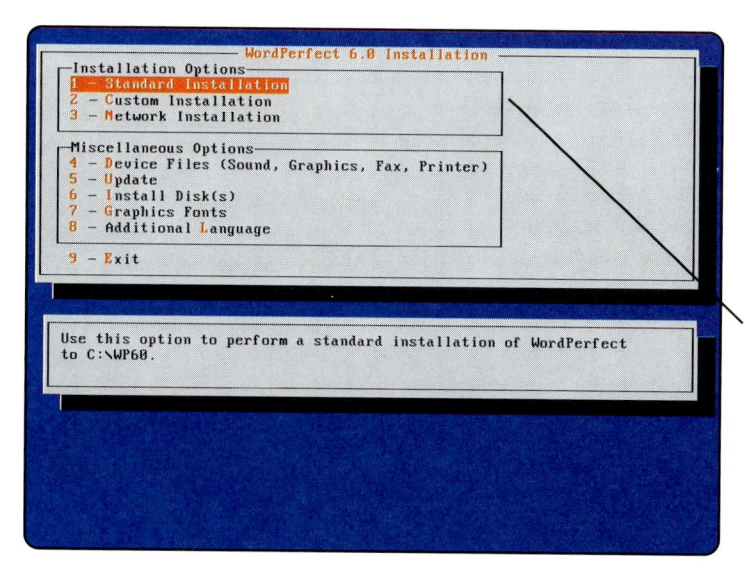

SELECT YOUR GOALS

From the list below, select your personal goals so you can start using WordPerfect 6 for DOS immediately.

❖ I would like help installing WordPerfect 6 for DOS.

Go to the Appendix, "Installing WordPerfect 6 for DOS."

WORDPERFECT 6 FOR DOS: THE VISUAL LEARNING GUIDE

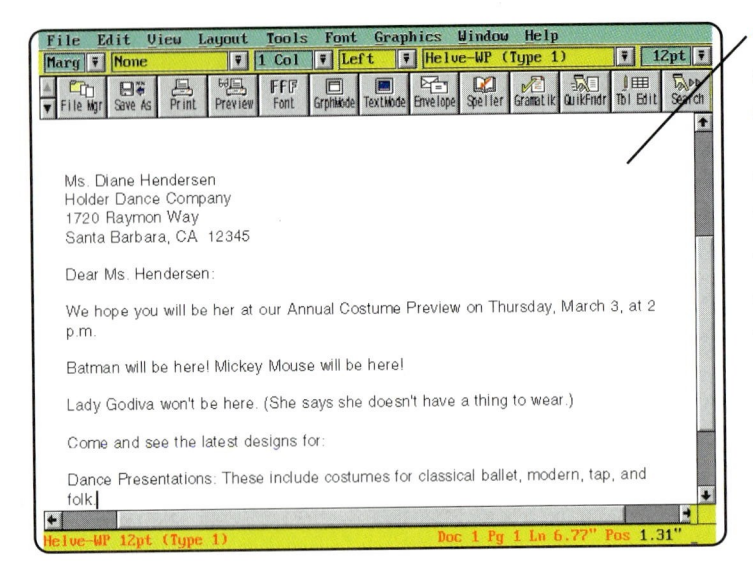

❖ I'm new to WordPerfect and I want to learn how to create and print a letter.

Turn to Part I, "Entering, Editing, and Printing Text," to learn how to set margins, change the font, and enter text. You'll also learn how to save, name, and print a document and use the spelling checker, grammar checker, and Thesaurus.

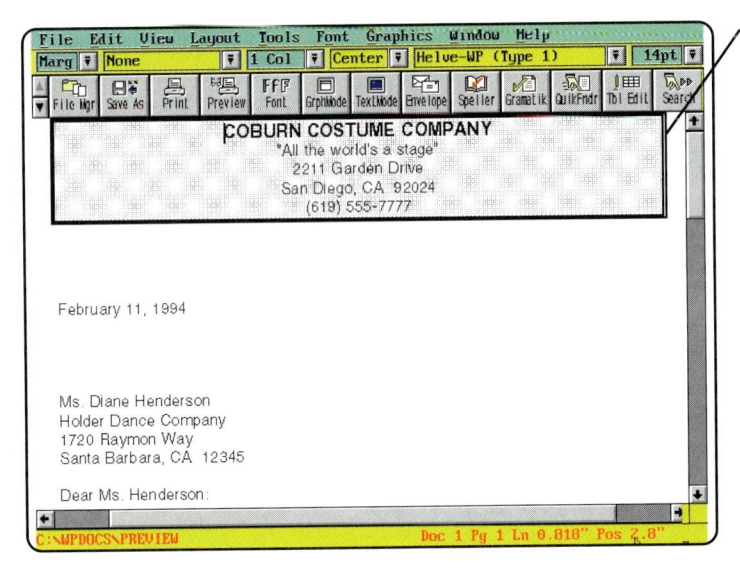

❖ I want to know how to customize a document.

Turn to Part II, "Formatting a Document," to learn how to customize text by changing the type style to bold, adding a page number, and setting tabs. You will also learn how to center text and create special effects, such as shaded borders.

INTRODUCTION

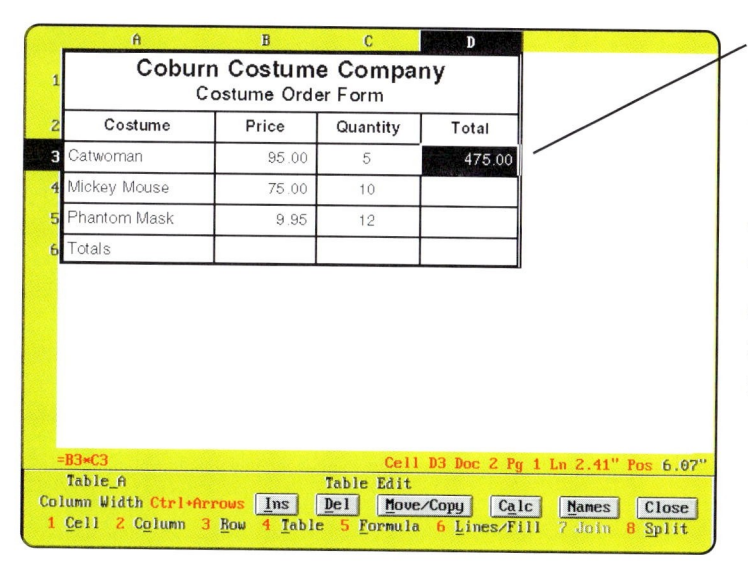

❖ I want to do special functions like setting up tables, formatting numbers, and writing formulas.

Turn to Part IV, "Introducing Tables," to learn how to create a table, edit a table, format numbers, and write formulas.

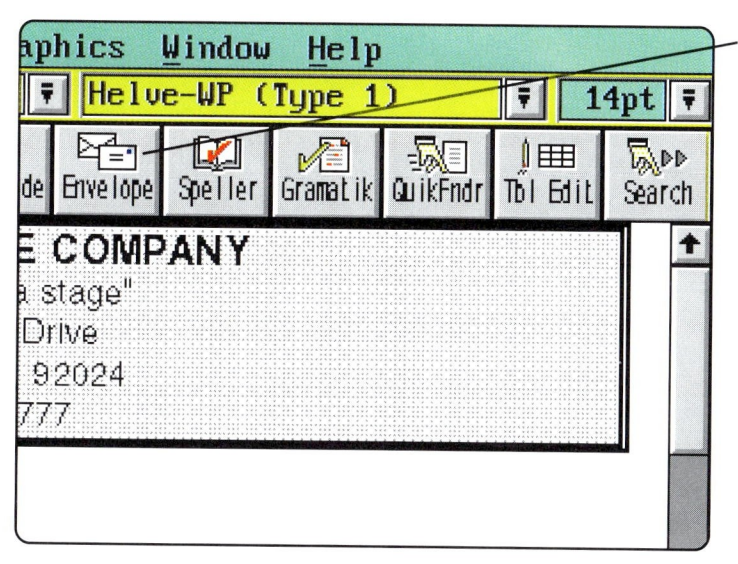

❖ I want to know how to use WordPerfect's special Envelope button.

Turn to Chapter 10, "Printing an Envelope," to learn how to print a single envelope.

Chapter 15, "Printing Envelopes for a Mailing List," covers how to print merge envelopes.

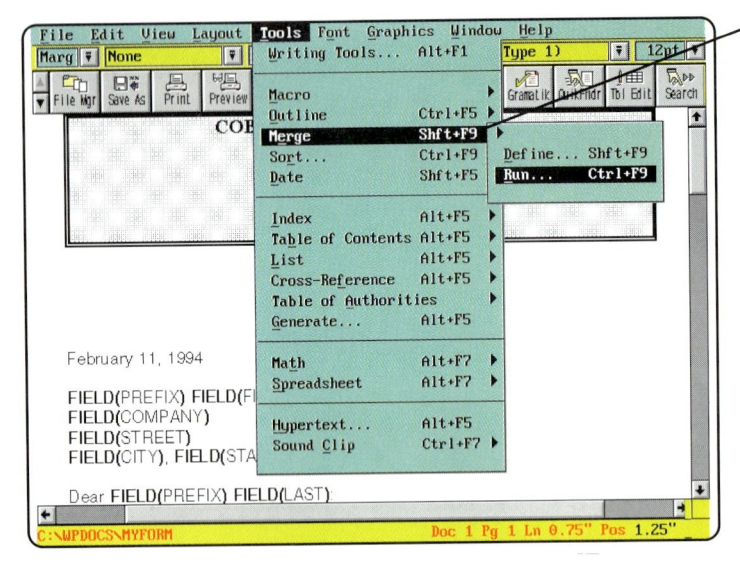

❖ I want to learn how to create and print a personalized version of a form letter for a list of people using WordPerfect 6's Merge feature.

In Chapter 11, you will learn how to create a mailing list. Chapter 12 teaches you how to edit a mailing list and Chapters 13 and 14 show you how to set up and print a personalized version of a form letter. Chapter 15 covers how to print envelopes for your mailing list.

If you are switching to WordPerfect 6 from another word-processing program, such as Word 2 or WordStar, see Chapter 16 in Part III to learn how to convert a mailing list from another program.

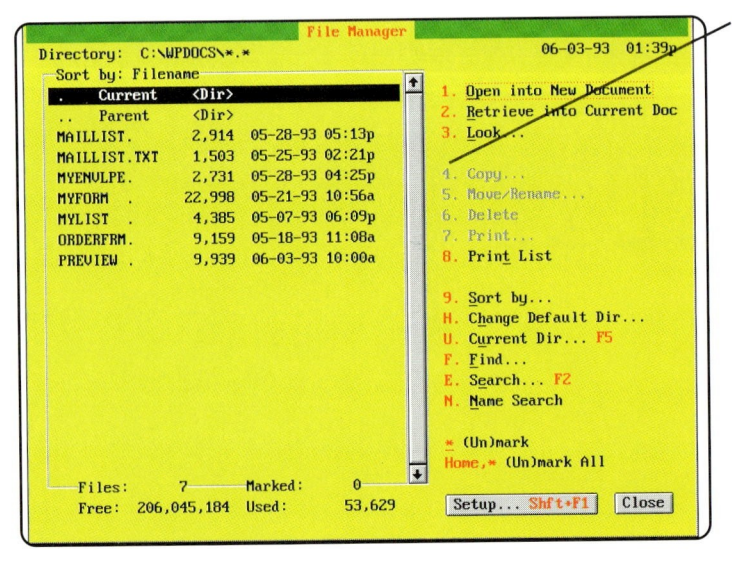

❖ I want to learn how to use WordPerfect's File Manager.

Turn to Part V, "Introducing File Manager." You will learn how to open and print multiple files at the same time. You will also learn how to sort, copy, move files and create a new directory.

File Manager

Part I   Entering, Editing, and Printing Text

Chapter 1: Changing Margins and Fonts and Entering Text	Page 2
Chapter 2: Naming and Saving a Document	Page 23
Chapter 3: Previewing and Printing a Document	Page 26
Chapter 4: Closing a File and Opening a Saved File	Page 32
Chapter 5: Using the Grammar Checker, Spelling Checker, and Thesaurus	Page 37
Chapter 6: Editing a Document	Page 50

Changing Margins and Fonts and Entering Text

WordPerfect 6 combines all the power of this extremely popular word-processing program with an easy-to-use graphical environment. Now you can learn WordPerfect without ever having to memorize keystroke commands! Just pull down a menu and select a command or simply click on a button. You'll love how easy it is to create documents and add exciting customized features. In this chapter you will do the following:

- Open a WordPerfect document
- Change your screen display to Graphics mode
- Display the button bar, ribbon, and scroll bars
- Set margins
- Change the font
- Learn to read the status line
- Enter text
- Use special fonts to insert symbols into the text

OPENING WORDPERFECT FOR THE FIRST TIME

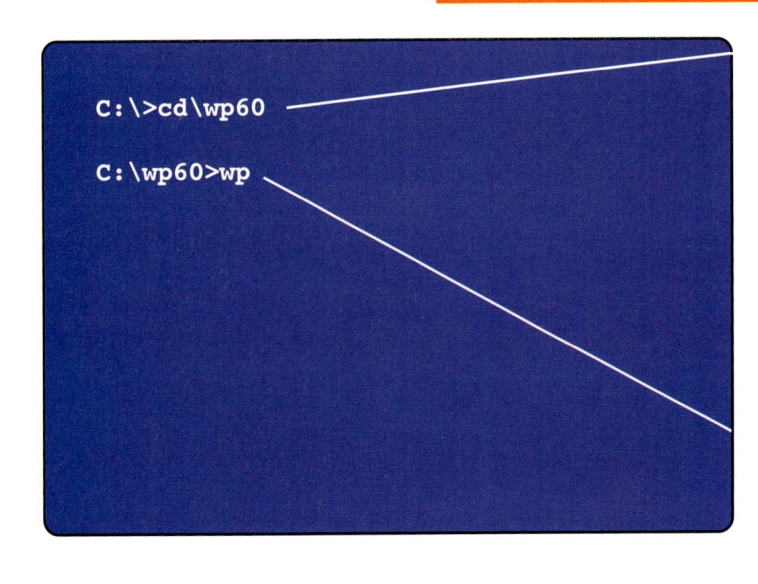

```
C:\>cd\wp60

C:\wp60>wp
```

1. Type cd\wp60 at the C:\> (C prompt) on your screen to change to the WordPerfect directory prompt. If you get an error message that says, "Invalid switch," you probably typed a forward slash (/) instead of a backward slash (\). Try it again.

2. Type wp at the C:\wp60> directory prompt to open, or *boot up*, WordPerfect 6.

CHAPTER 1: CHANGING MARGINS AND FONTS AND ENTERING TEXT

CHANGING FROM TEXT MODE TO GRAPHICS MODE

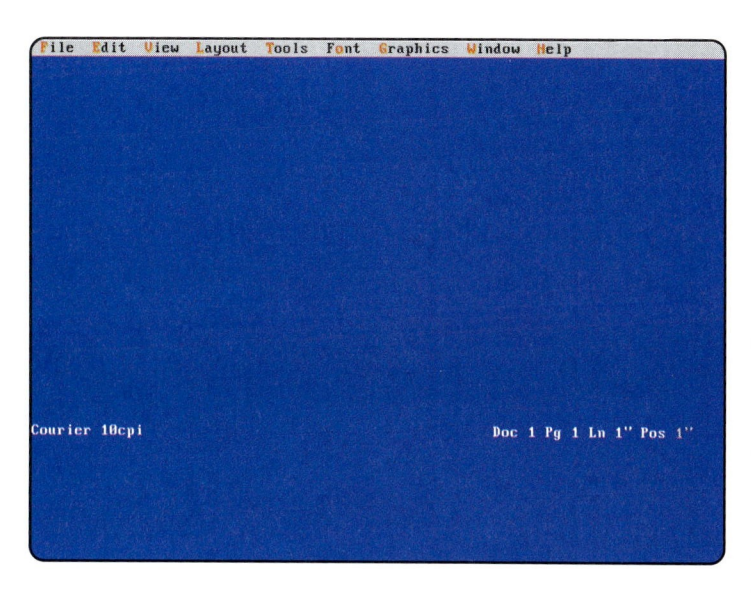

When the WordPerfect opening screen appears, it will look like this. This is the Text mode. WordPerfect provides another view, called the Graphics mode. You can work in either mode, but the Graphics mode lets you take full advantage of the new graphical environment in WordPerfect 6. The Graphics mode also displays text on the screen as it will appear when printed (called WYSIWYG, or "What You See Is What You Get"). Because of this, text displays slightly slower in Graphics mode than in Text mode, but the ease with which you can use it makes up for the small difference in speed. (If someone has used WordPerfect on your computer before you, the Graphics mode may already be selected. Go to the next section, "Displaying the Button Bar and Ribbon.")

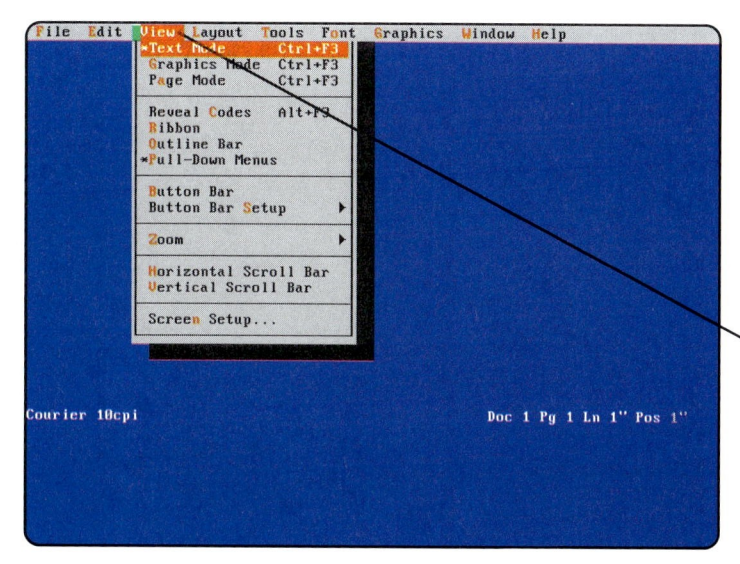

1. Move the mouse pointer to **View** in the menu bar and **click** the left mouse button. A pull-down menu will appear.

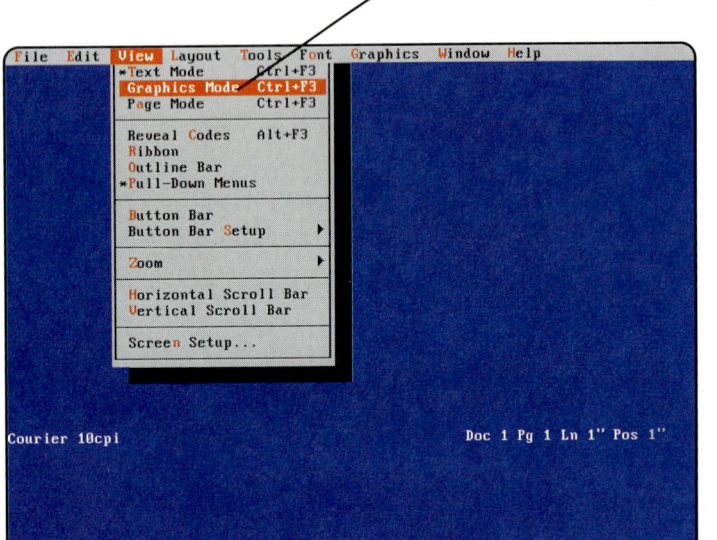

WORDPERFECT 6 FOR DOS: THE VISUAL LEARNING GUIDE

2. **Move** the mouse pointer to **Graphics Mode** and click the left mouse button. Your screen will change to the one in the following example.

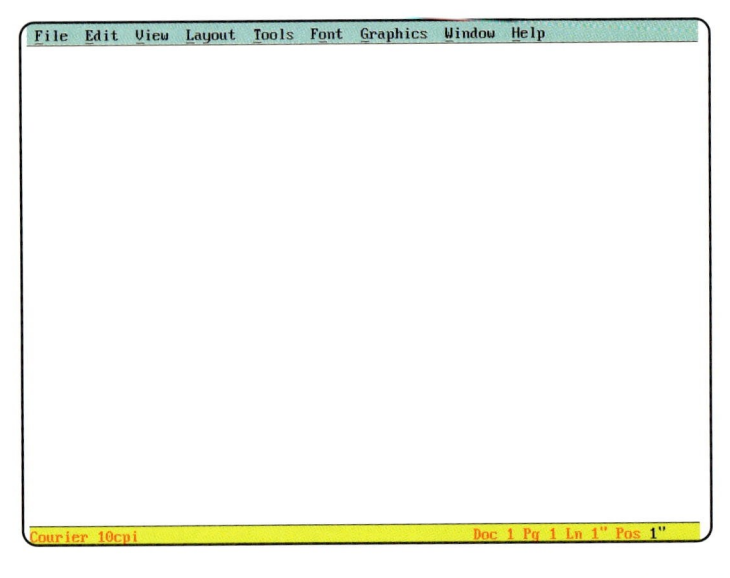

Your screen should now look like this.

If you haven't used a mouse before, trying to control it may make you a little crazy in the beginning. You may not believe us now, but you'll learn to love it.

We hope you are comfortable with the concept of moving the mouse pointer to the item you want to select and then clicking on it to select it. Because from now on, we will shorten the explanation to "**click on**."

CHAPTER 1: CHANGING MARGINS AND FONTS AND ENTERING TEXT

DISPLAYING THE BUTTON BAR AND RIBBON

To take full advantage of the Graphics mode, you need to display two of the new features of WordPerfect 6, the button bar and the ribbon. You will learn how to display them in this section and how to use them later in this chapter. If someone has used WordPerfect on your computer before you, these features may already be displayed.

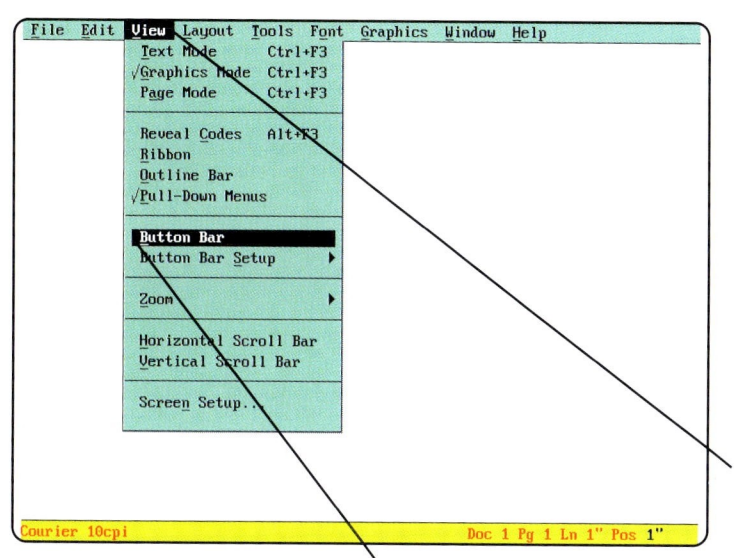

1. Click on **View** in the menu bar. A pull-down menu will appear.

2. Click on **Button Bar**. The pull-down menu will disappear and the button bar will appear on your screen.

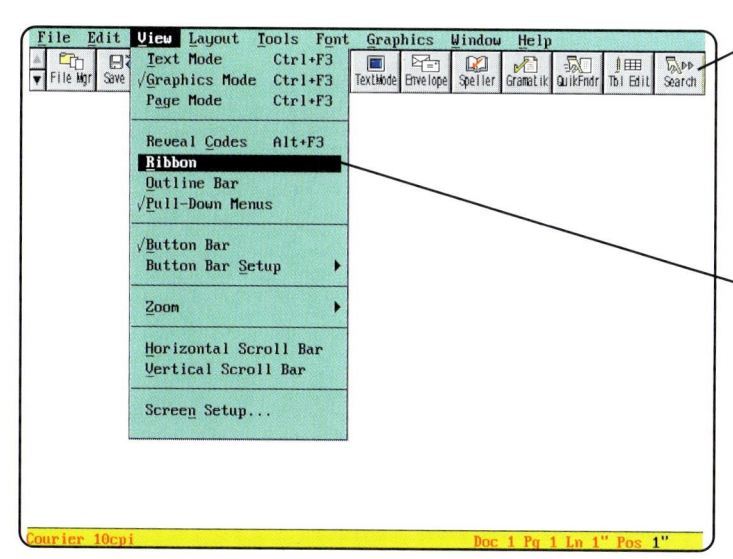

Notice the button bar that appears.

3. Repeat step 1. Notice that a check mark appears to the left of each selected feature.

4. Click on **Ribbon** in the pull-down menu. The pull-down menu will disappear and the ribbon will appear on your screen, as shown on the next page.

WORDPERFECT 6 FOR DOS: THE VISUAL LEARNING GUIDE

DISPLAYING THE SCROLL BARS

Scroll bars make it easy to move within a document. You will learn how to display scroll bars in this section. You will learn how to use them later.

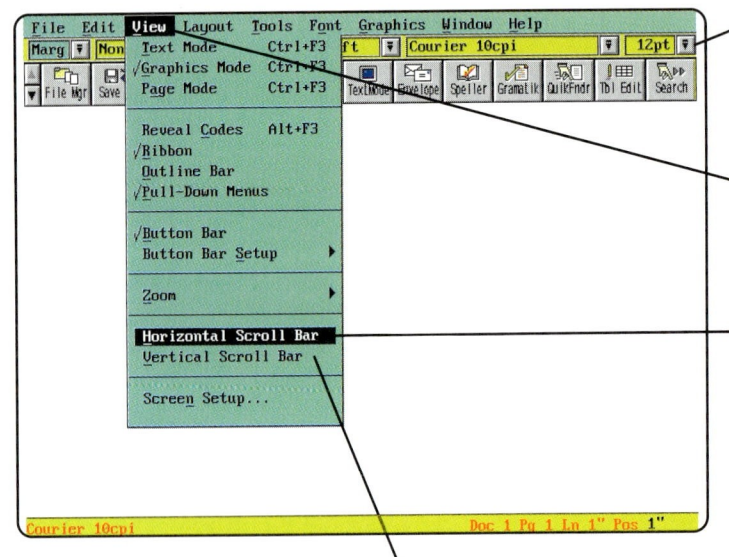

Notice the ribbon that you added in the previous section.

1. Click on **View** in the menu bar. A pull-down menu will appear.

2. Click on **Horizontal Scroll Bar**. The pull-down menu will disappear and a scroll bar will appear at the bottom of your screen, as shown on the next screen.

3. Repeat step 1, then **click** on **Vertical Scroll Bar** to display a scroll bar at the right edge of your screen, as shown on the next screen.

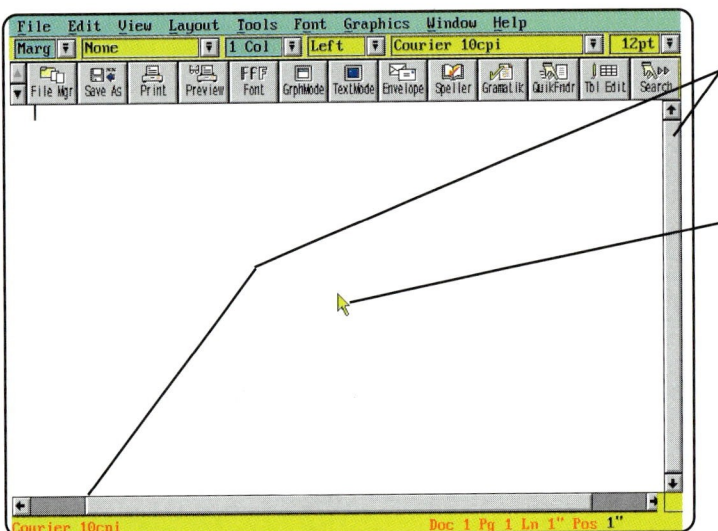

Notice the horizontal and vertical scroll bars that appear.

If your mouse pointer gets away from you occasionally and disappears from your screen, move your mouse in circles on your mouse pad until the pointer reappears.

CHAPTER 1: CHANGING MARGINS AND FONTS AND ENTERING TEXT

SETTING MARGINS

The standard (*default*) margins in WordPerfect are preset at 1 inch on the top and bottom and 1 inch on the left and right. You can change any or all of these settings as many times as you want within a document. Each time you make a change, the new margin applies in the document until you change it again. In this example you will change the top margin.

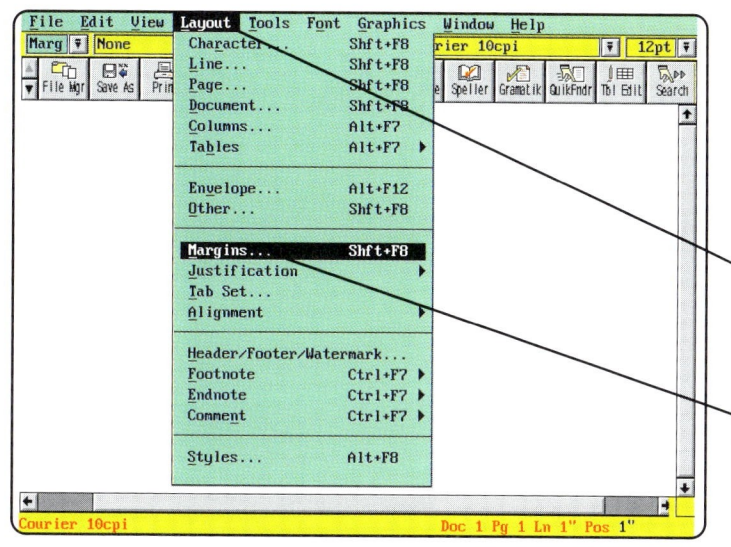

1. Click on **Layout** in the menu bar. A pull-down menu will appear.

2. Click on **Margins**. The Margin Format dialog box will appear.

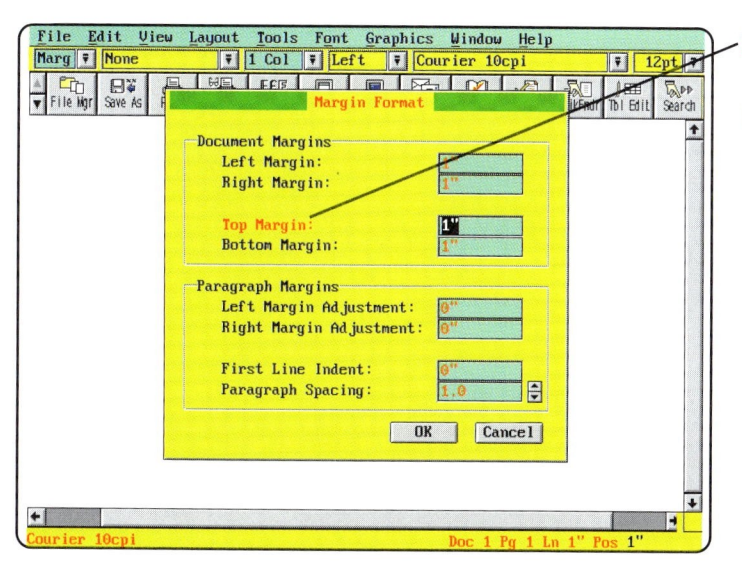

3. Click on **Top Margin**. The 1" in the box will be highlighted.

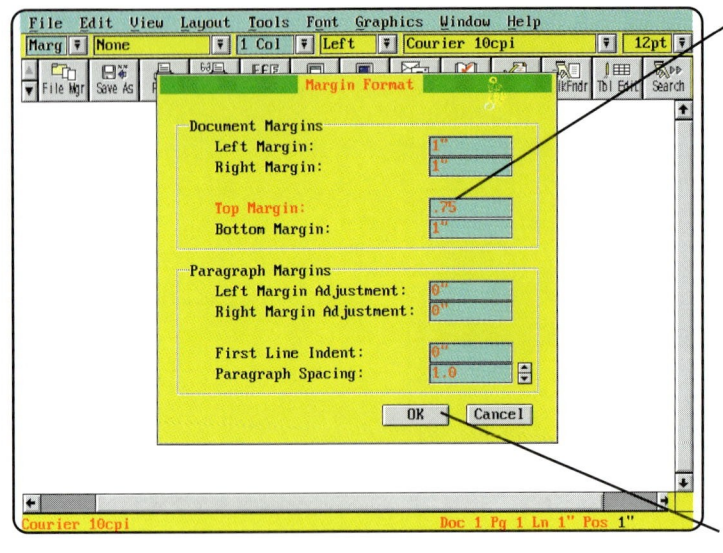

WORDPERFECT 6 FOR DOS: THE VISUAL LEARNING GUIDE

4. Type .75. It will replace 1". This will decrease the top margin to .75 inch. You are making the top margin smaller than standard to give yourself the extra room to create the letterhead in the example in this chapter. (If you are going to print on stationery that already has a letterhead, the top margin for a short-to-medium-length letter should be about 2.5 inches.)

5. Click on **OK**. The Margin Format dialog box will disappear.

CHANGING THE FONT

WordPerfect is set up to print with the Courier 10cpi (characters per inch) *font*, or type style.

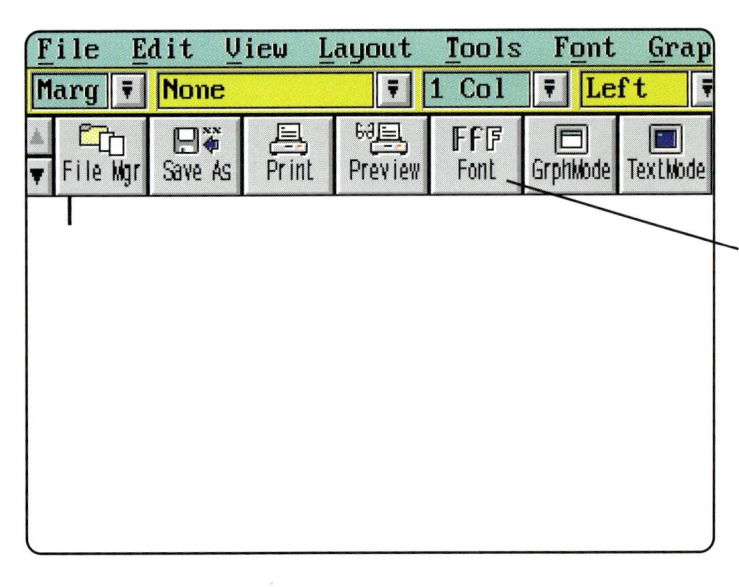

Changing the Font for the Current Document

1. Click on the **Font button** in the button bar. The Font dialog box will appear.

Notice that this is a magnified view of a portion of the screen. You will see both full-screen and magnified views throughout this book.

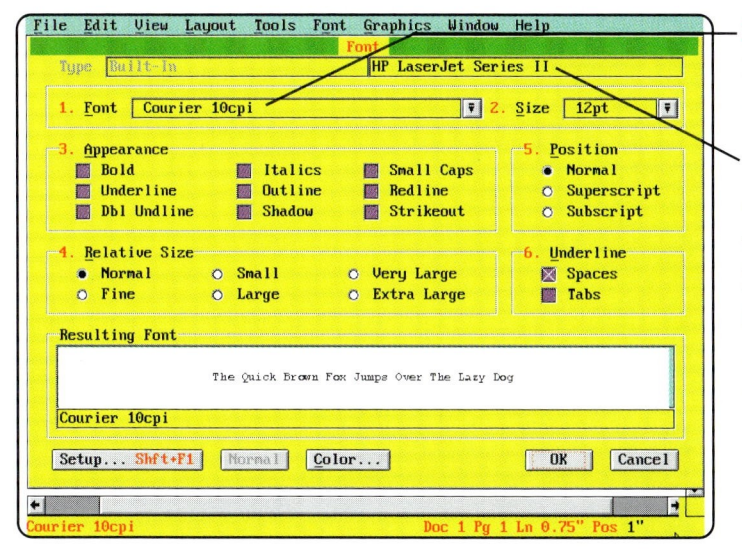

CHAPTER 1: CHANGING MARGINS AND FONTS AND ENTERING TEXT

2. **Click** anywhere on the **Font box**. A drop-down list of fonts will appear.

The fonts in the list depend on the selected printer. In this example the printer is HP LaserJet Series II. If you have a different printer selected, you will see different fonts in your list.

3. **Click repeatedly** on the **down arrow** on the scroll bar to scroll down the list of fonts until you highlight **Helve-WP (Type 1)**. This is the Helvetica font used in WordPerfect. If you go past Helve-WP, simply click on the **up arrow** to go back up the list.

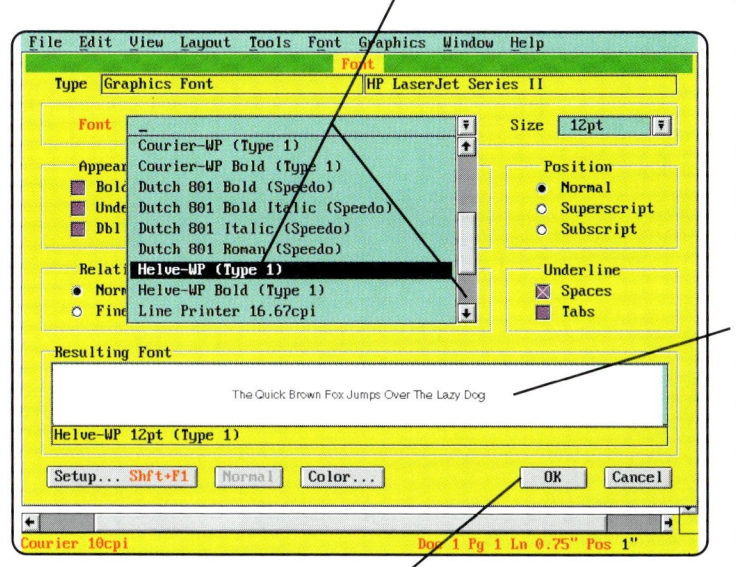

Notice that an example of the highlighted font shows in the Resulting Font box. It's fun to watch as you scroll through the list.

If you don't have Helve-WP or you prefer another font, it's okay to select something else. Just be aware that if you follow the examples in this book, your text may line up differently. Different fonts take up different amounts of space even when they are the same point size.

4. **Click** on **OK** to confirm the change and return to the document screen.

Changing the Font for All New Documents

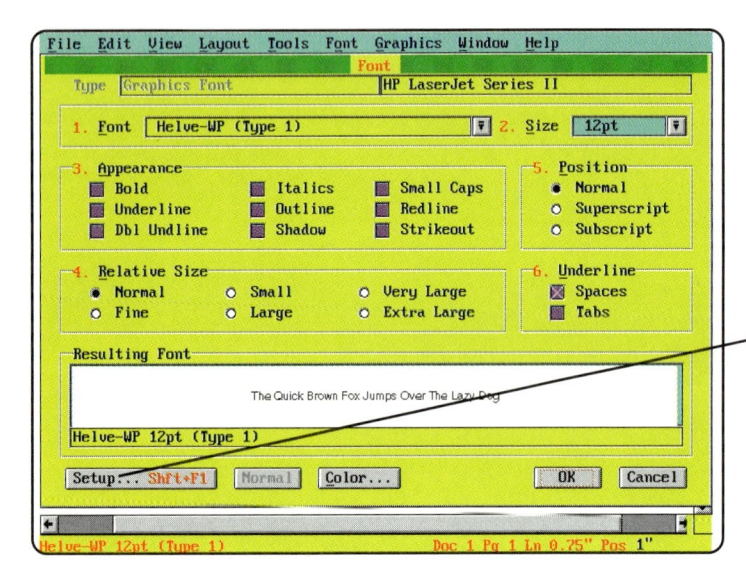

You can also select a font that will apply to *all* new documents.

1. Click on the **Font button** in the button bar. The Font dialog box will appear.

2. Click on **Setup** in the lower-left corner of the dialog box. The Font Setup dialog box will appear.

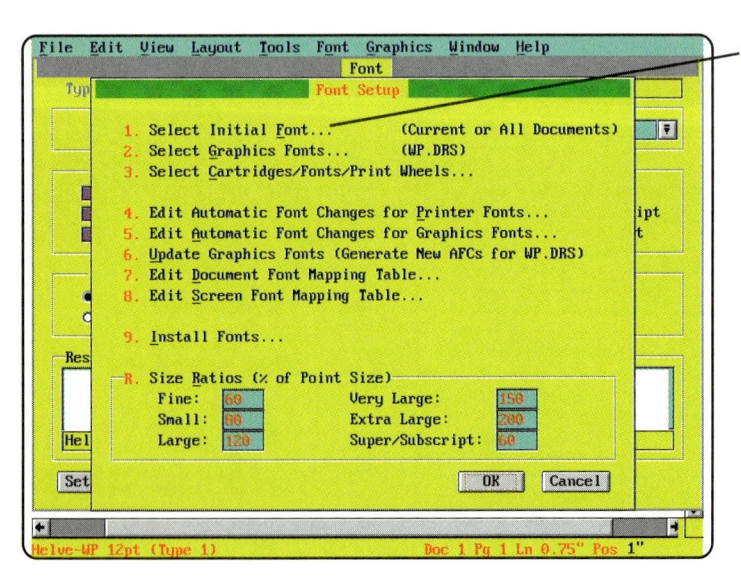

3. Click on **Select Initial Font**. The Initial Font dialog box will appear.

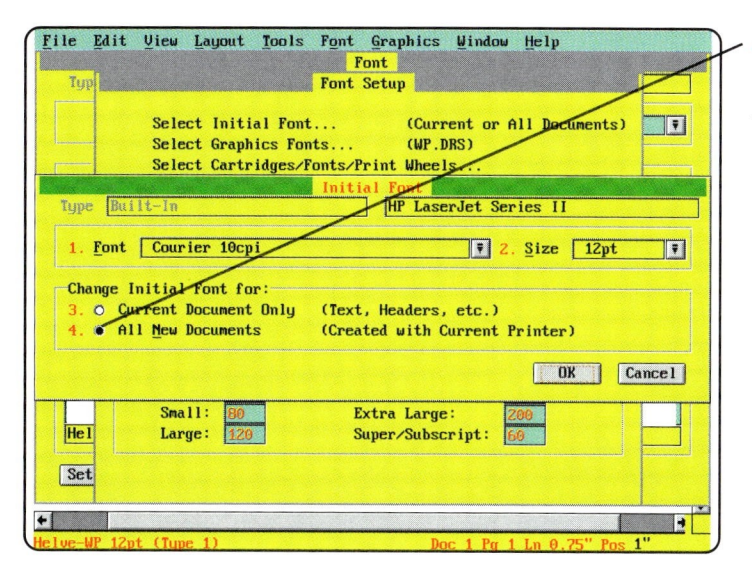

CHAPTER 1: CHANGING MARGINS AND FONTS AND ENTERING TEXT

4. Click on **All New Documents** to insert a dot in the circle.

5. Click anywhere on the **Font box**. A drop-down list of fonts will appear.

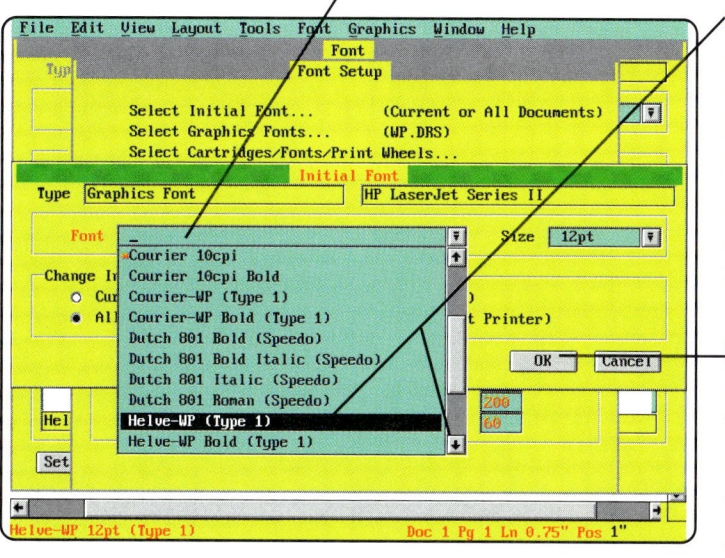

6. Click repeatedly on the **down arrow** on the scroll bar to scroll down the list of fonts until you highlight **Helve-WP (Type 1)**. If you go past Helve-WP, simply click on the **up arrow** to go back up the list.

7. Click on **OK** to confirm the changes. This will close both the font list and the Initial Font dialog box. You will return to the Font Setup dialog box.

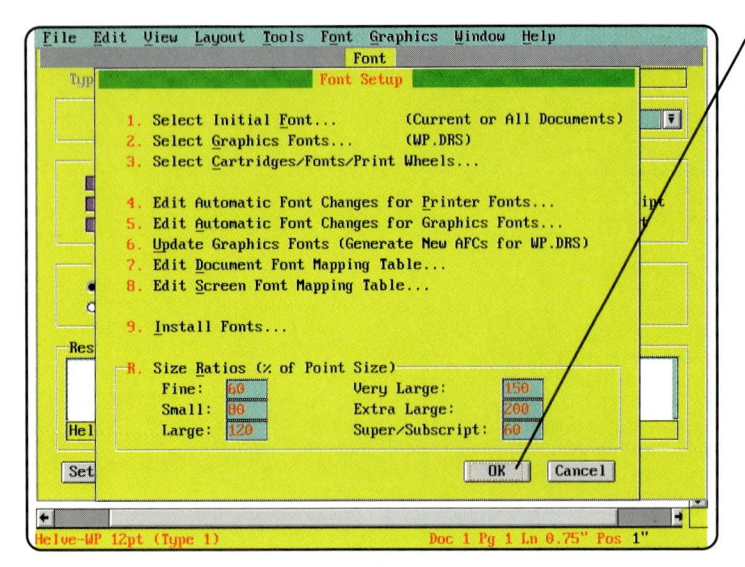

WORDPERFECT 6 FOR DOS: THE VISUAL LEARNING GUIDE

8. Click on **OK** to confirm the Font Setup. The Font dialog box will reappear.

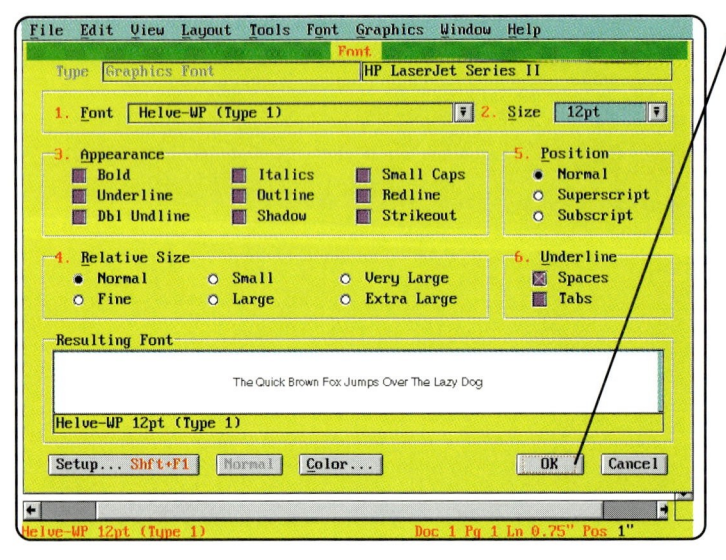

9. Click on **OK** to confirm the change and return to the document screen.

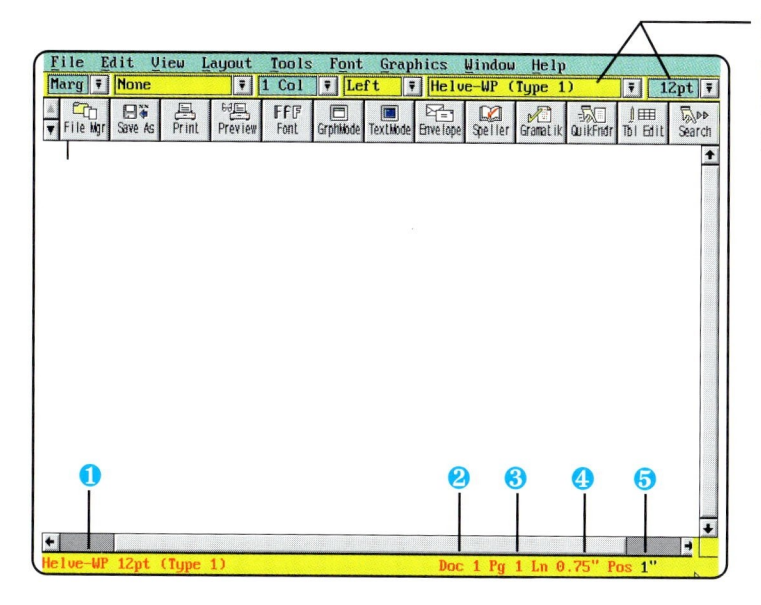

CHAPTER 1: CHANGING MARGINS AND FONTS AND ENTERING TEXT

Notice that the font and point size are indicated in the ribbon at the top of your screen.

READING THE STATUS LINE

Notice the status line at the bottom of your screen. The status line also contains information about your document.

❶ Helve-WP 12pt (Type 1) is the font and point size of the type in this document.

❷ Doc 1 means that this is the first document opened during this session.

❸ Pg 1 tells you that your cursor is on page 1 of the document.

❹ Ln 0.75" tells you that the cursor is .75 inch from the top of the page as it will print.

❺ Pos 1" tells you that the cursor is 1 inch from the left side of the paper as it will print.

WORDPERFECT 6 FOR DOS: THE VISUAL LEARNING GUIDE

ENTERING TEXT

You are now ready to type a letter. In the following examples you will type a letter from the Coburn Costume Company inviting a customer to come to the Annual Costume Preview.

Creating the Letterhead

The first thing you will type is the company name and return address. Notice that the insertion point is flashing at the beginning of the document. This means you can start typing and the text will begin at this point.

1. Press the **Caps Lock key** to turn on the capital letters feature so that the text you type will appear as capital letters.

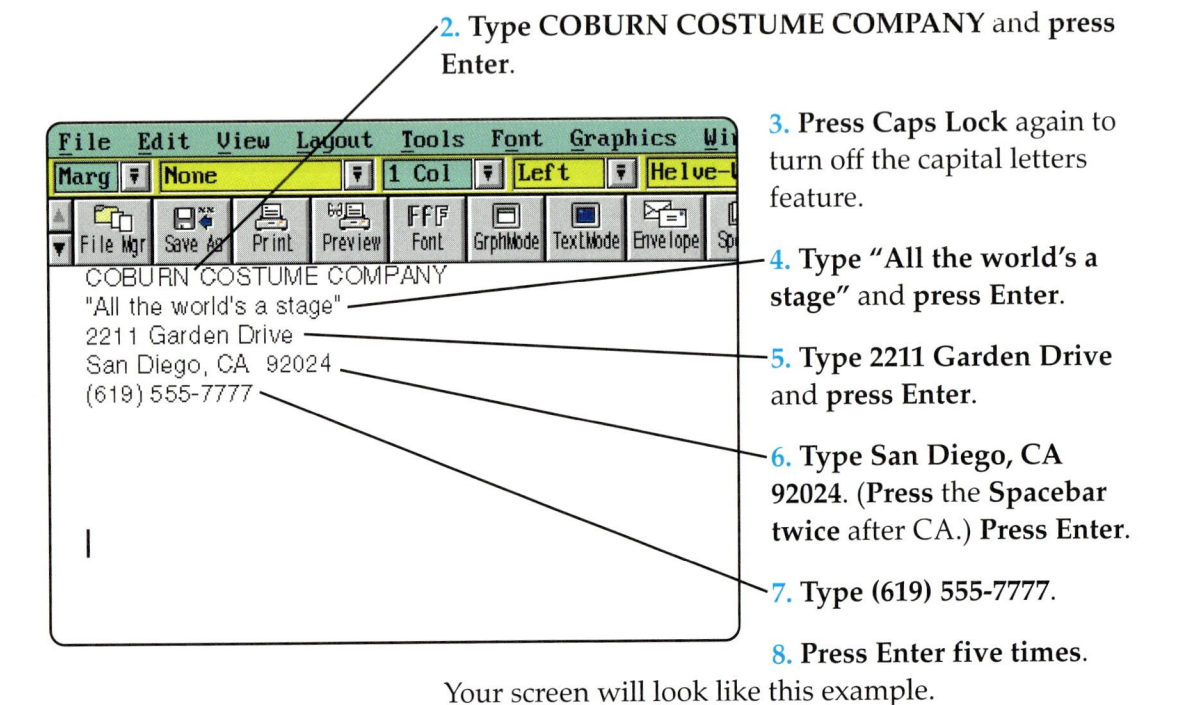

2. Type COBURN COSTUME COMPANY and **press Enter.**

3. Press Caps Lock again to turn off the capital letters feature.

4. Type "All the world's a stage" and **press Enter.**

5. Type 2211 Garden Drive and **press Enter.**

6. Type San Diego, CA 92024. (**Press** the **Spacebar twice** after CA.) **Press Enter.**

7. Type (619) 555-7777.

8. Press Enter five times.

Your screen will look like this example.

CHAPTER 1: CHANGING MARGINS AND FONTS AND ENTERING TEXT

Entering the Date, Address, and Salutation

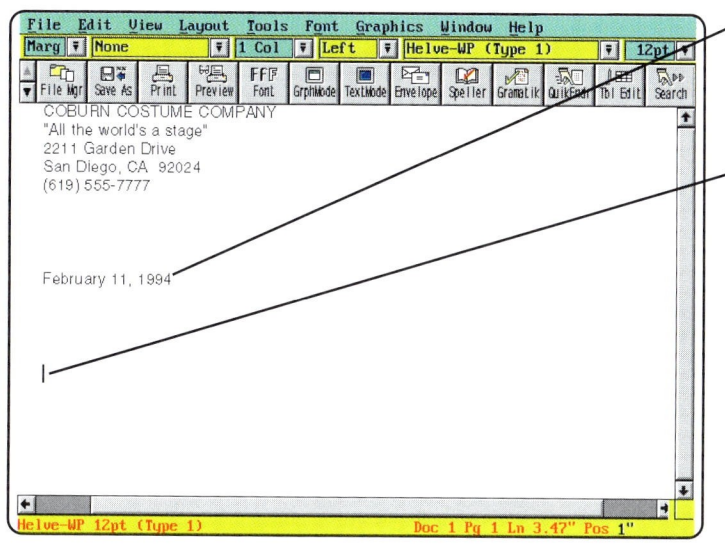

1. Type the date. Use today's date instead of the date you see in the example.

2. Press Enter five times.

3. Type the following lines (**press Enter** after each line):

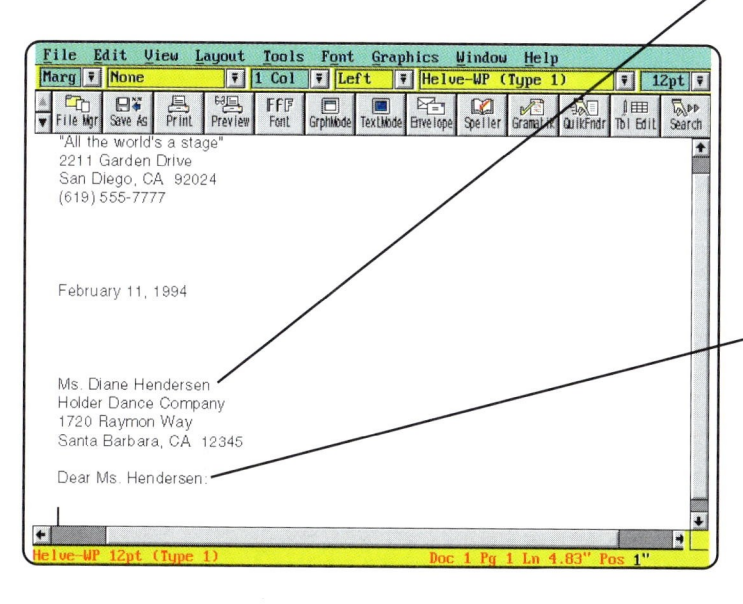

Ms. Diane Hendersen
Holder Dance Company
1720 Raymon Way
Santa Barbara, CA 12345
(**Press** the **Spacebar twice** after CA.)

4. Press Enter twice after the last line.

5. Type Dear Ms. Hendersen: (don't forget the colon).

6. Press Enter twice. The screen will automatically scroll (move up) to make room for the additional lines.

Entering the Body of the Letter

You are now ready to enter the body of the letter. Like all word-processing programs, you can type without worrying about your right margin. WordPerfect will wrap the text around to the next line automatically. In word-processing programs you press the Spacebar only *once* after the period at the end of a sentence.

1. Type the text below. It contains errors (shown in pink) that you will correct later, so include them if you want to follow along with these procedures. If you make an unintentional typing error, press Backspace and type the correct letters. Press Enter twice to create a new paragraph.

We hope you will be her at our Annual Costume Preview on Thursday, March 3, at 2 p.m.

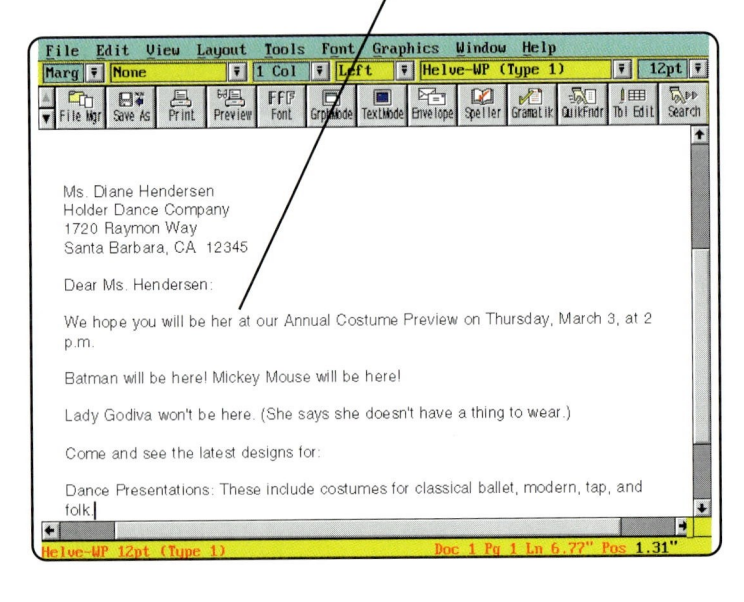

Batman will be here! Mickey Mouse will be here!

Lady Godiva won't be here. (She says she doesn't have a thing to wear.)

Come and see the latest designs for:

Dance Presentations: These include costumes for classical ballet, modern, tap, and folk.

CHAPTER 1: CHANGING MARGINS AND FONTS AND ENTERING TEXT

2. Continue typing the following text (remember, press the Enter key *only* at the end of a paragraph):

Theatrical Presentations: These include costumes for performances such as Cats, Les Miserables, and Phantom of the Opera.

Fantasy Costumes: These include childrens and adults' versions of characters such as Batman, Catwoman, and Disney characters such as Mickey Mouse.

Historical Figures: These include costumes for figures such as Napoleon and Josephine and masks for current political figures.

Because you are a valued customer, Ms. Hendersen, you will recieve a 20 percent discount on any order placed at the Preview.

Please return a copy of the reply form below by Wednesday, February 23.

3. Press Enter twice after the last line.

Notice the line that appears. This is the *automatic page break*. It indicates the end of the first page. You will learn how to change the location of the page break in Chapter 6, "Editing a Document."

The exact location of the automatic page break depends on the margins you set and the size of the font.

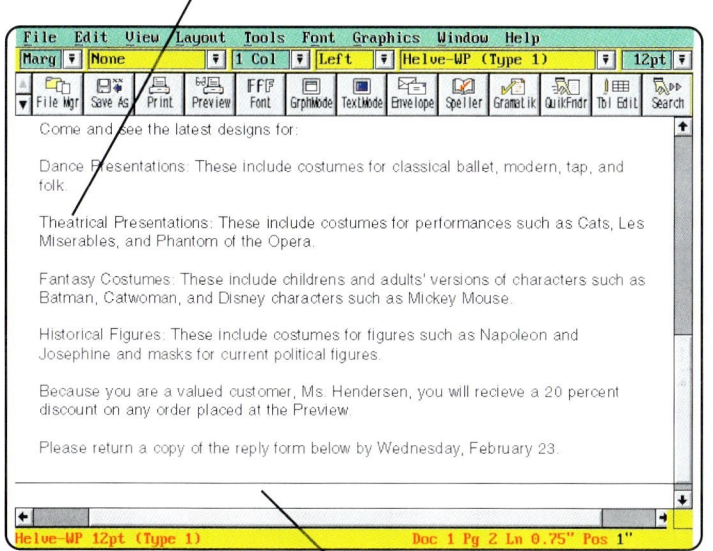

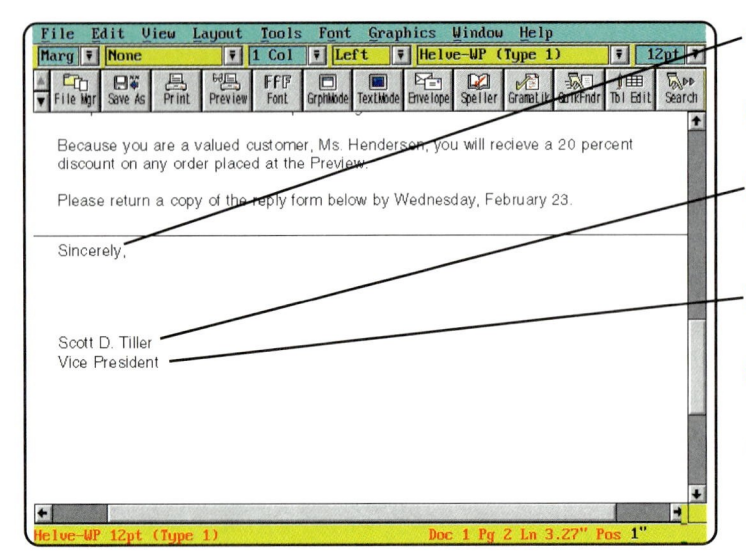

WORDPERFECT 6 FOR DOS: THE VISUAL LEARNING GUIDE

4. **Type Sincerely,**

5. **Press Enter five times.**

6. **Type Scott D. Tiller** and **press Enter.**

7. **Type Vice President.**

8. **Press Enter seven times.** Your screen will look like this example.

INSERTING SYMBOLS AND FINISHING THE LETTER

WordPerfect 6 comes with a variety of character sets that range from symbols to foreign language alphabets. In this section, you will insert two different symbols into the text.

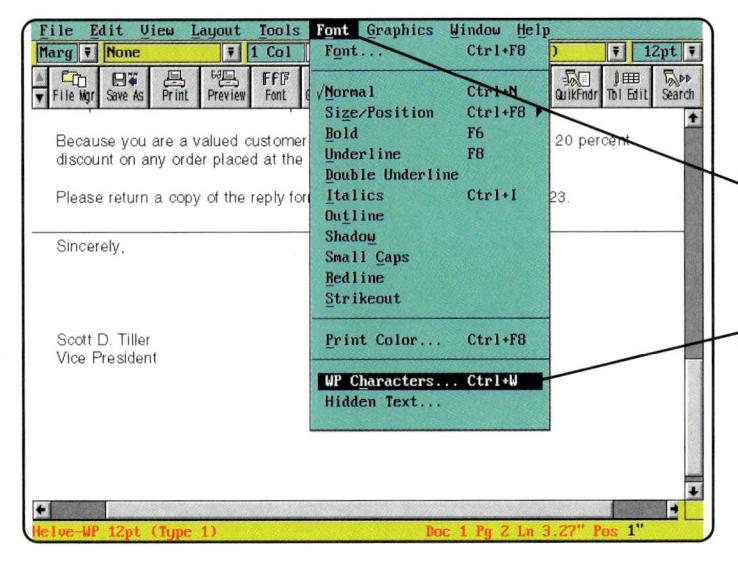

Inserting a Scissors Symbol

1. **Click** on **Font** in the menu bar. A pull-down menu will appear.

2. **Click** on **WP Characters**. The WordPerfect Characters dialog box will appear.

CHAPTER 1: CHANGING MARGINS AND FONTS AND ENTERING TEXT

3. Click on **Set**. A drop-down list of character sets will appear.

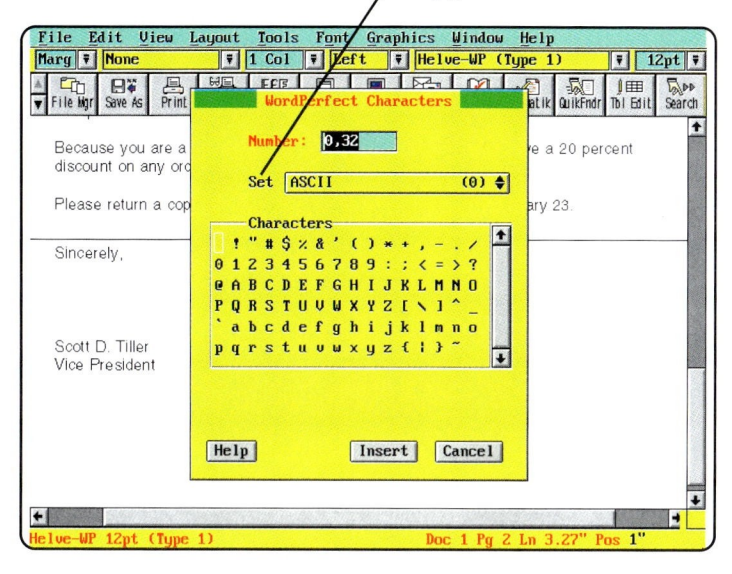

4. Click twice on **Iconic Symbols**. Iconic Symbols will appear in the Set box and the Iconic Symbols set will appear in the Characters box.

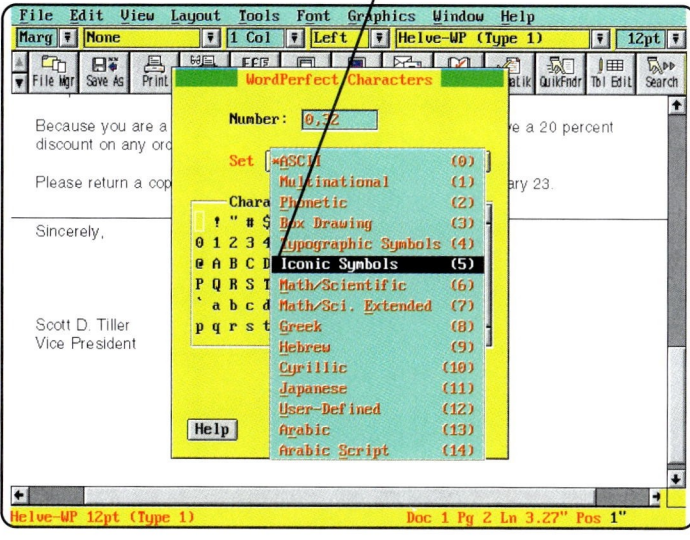

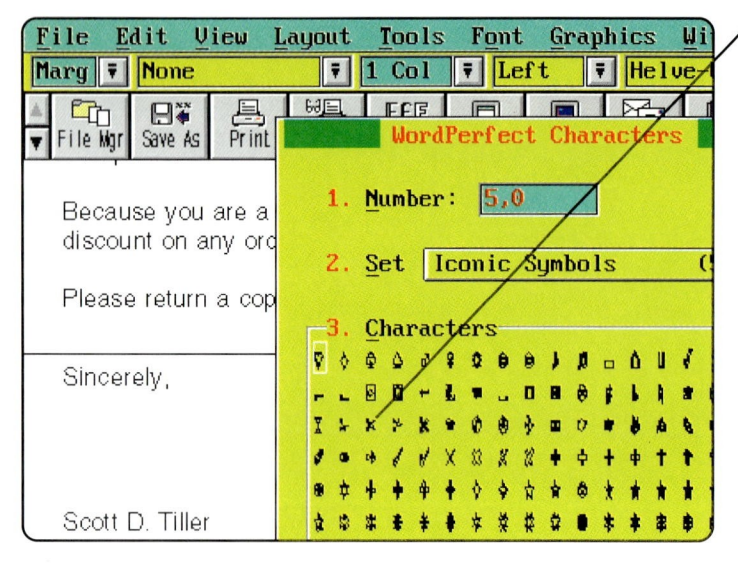

WORDPERFECT 6 FOR DOS: THE VISUAL LEARNING GUIDE

5. Place the mouse pointer on the **scissors symbol**, which is in the third column from the left in the third row.

You may feel like you need a magnifying glass to see the scissors. They will, however, be more visible to the naked eye when they are inserted into the document.

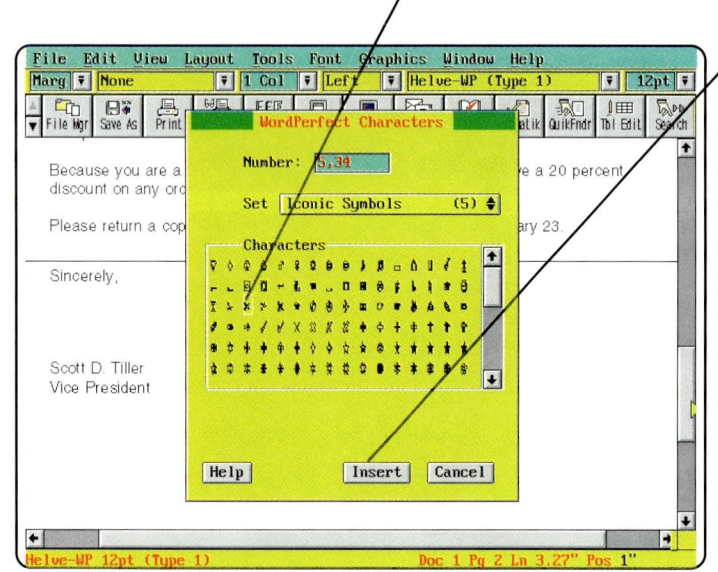

6. Click on the **scissors symbol**.

7. Click on **Insert**. The scissors symbol will be inserted into your letter.

If you mistakenly select the wrong character, backspace to erase the character and repeat steps 1 through 7.

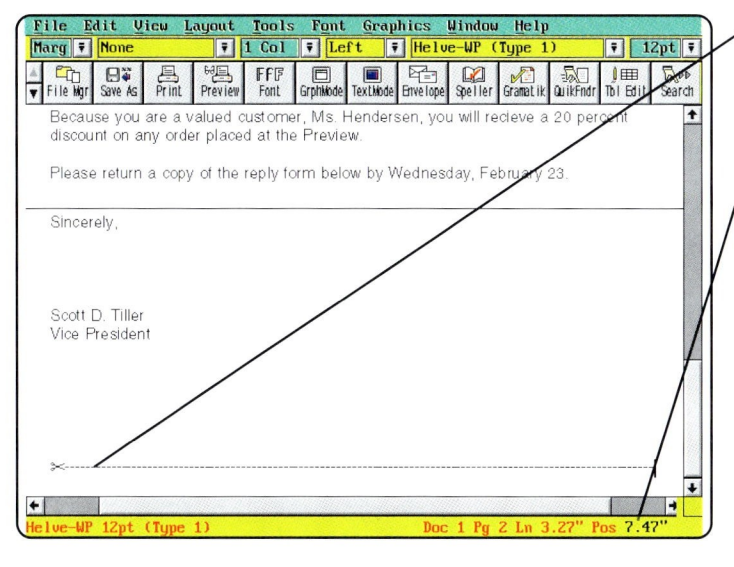

CHAPTER 1: CHANGING MARGINS AND FONTS AND ENTERING TEXT

8. Press and hold the **Hyphen key** on your keyboard to type the dotted line.

Continue to hold the Hyphen key until the position on the status line reads Pos = 7.47". If you go beyond 7.47 inches, the extra hyphens will wrap around to the next line. Simply press the Backspace key until the insertion point goes back to the previous line.

9. Press Enter twice.

Inserting Box Symbols

1. Repeat steps 1 and 2 in the previous section to open the WordPerfect Characters dialog box.

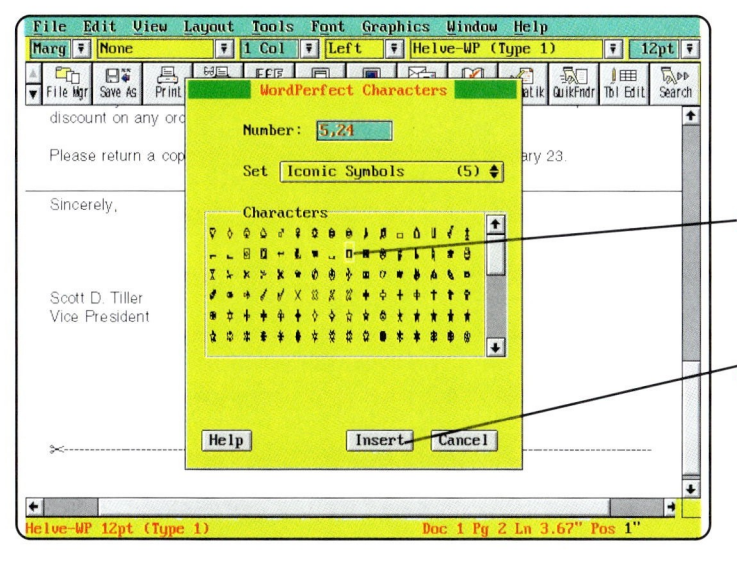

The Iconic Symbols set will show in the Characters box because it is the last character set that you used.

2. Click on the **square symbol** in the second row and the ninth column.

3. Click on **Insert**. The square symbol will be inserted into the letter.

WORDPERFECT 6 FOR DOS: THE VISUAL LEARNING GUIDE

4. **Press** the **Spacebar**.

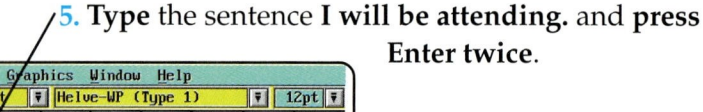

5. **Type** the sentence **I will be attending.** and **press Enter twice**.

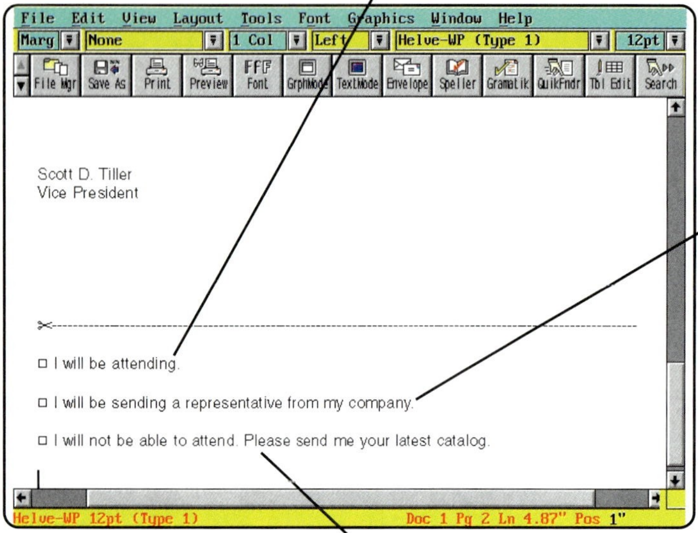

6. **Repeat steps 1 through 4** to insert another square into the text.

7. **Type** the sentence **I will be sending a representative from my company.** and **press Enter twice**.

8. **Repeat steps 1 through 4** to insert the square into the text a third time.

9. **Type** the following sentences: **I will not be able to attend. Please send me your latest catalog.** and **press Enter twice**.

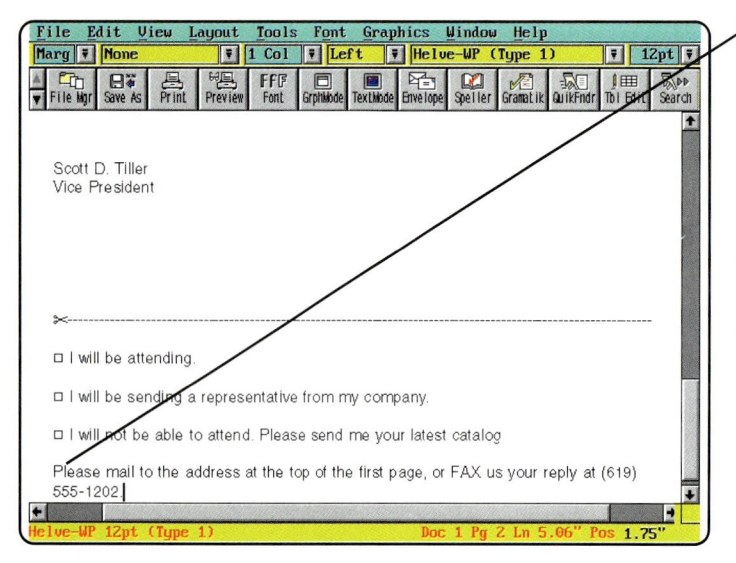

10. **Type** the sentence **Please mail to the address at the top of the first page, or FAX us your reply at (619) 555-1202.**

Congratulations! You just created a letter in WordPerfect. In Chapter 2, you will name the letter and save it.

Naming and Saving a Document

Saving a file is as easy as clicking your mouse in WordPerfect 6. And when you save a document, WordPerfect automatically saves it to the WPDOCS directory unless you specify otherwise. This way all of your working files are saved in one place. Once you've saved a file, WordPerfect allows you to save your changes as you work without exiting. There's even an automatic backup feature that protects you from losing your work in case of a power or equipment failure. WordPerfect has you covered! In this chapter you will do the following:

❖ Name and save a document
❖ Save while you work

NAMING AND SAVING A NEW DOCUMENT

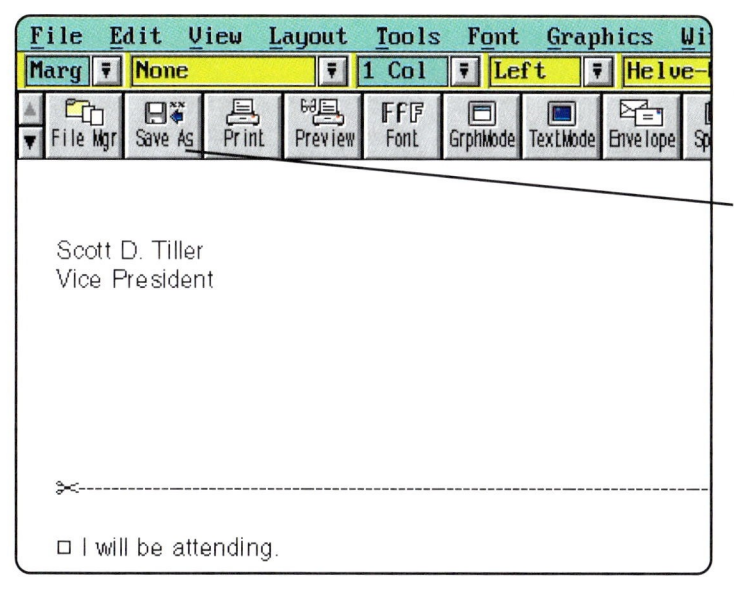

In this section you will name the document you typed in Chapter 1 and save the file to the WPDOCS directory.

1. Click on the **Save As button** in the button bar. The Save Document dialog box will appear.

WORDPERFECT 6 FOR DOS: THE VISUAL LEARNING GUIDE

2. Type preview in the Filename box. (A filename should have no more than eight characters.)

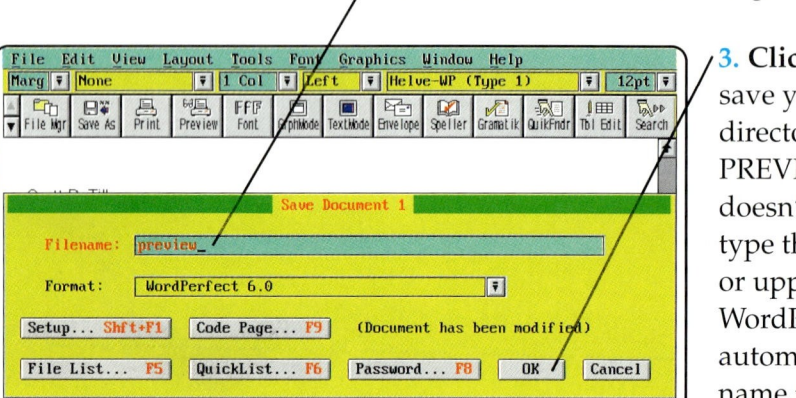

3. Click on **OK**. This will save your file to the directory WPDOCS with the PREVIEW filename. It doesn't matter whether you type the filename in lower- or uppercase letters. WordPerfect will automatically convert the name to all capital letters as you will see in the next screen.

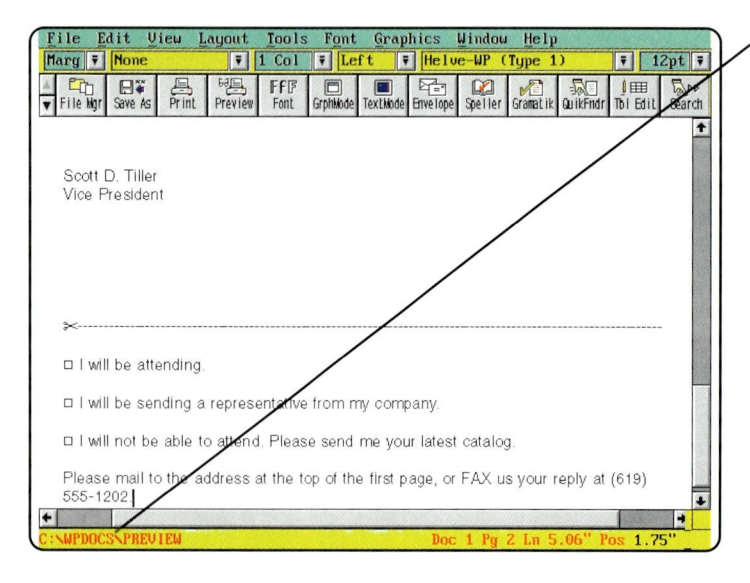

Notice that the status line now shows the drive (C:), the directory (WPDOCS), and the filename (PREVIEW) in all capital letters.

You can continue to work on the file. Once a file has been named and saved using the Save As command, use the Save command if you make any changes that you want to save. See the next section.

CHAPTER 2: NAMING AND SAVING A DOCUMENT

SAVING WHILE YOU WORK

It's a good idea (in fact it's a *great* idea) to develop the habit of saving your document intermittently as you work on it.

WordPerfect has a handy pre-set backup feature that makes a backup copy of your document every ten minutes as you work on it. (You may have noticed the message box flash on your screen as you typed the letter in Chapter 1.) This protects you from losing work due to a power or equipment failure. The backup feature saves your work to a backup file (in this case, PREVIEW.BK!), rather than to your current document (PREVIEW). The backup feature is, therefore, not a substitute for regularly saving your work.

Using the Save Command

If you've already named a file, use the Save command to save as you work.

1. **Click** on **File** in the menu bar. A pull-down menu will appear.

2. **Click** on **Save**. A message box will appear: "Saving: (C:\WPDOCS\PREVIEW)." WordPerfect will save and return you to your document.

Another quick way to save is to **press and hold** the **Ctrl key** and then **press F12** (Ctrl + F12).

Previewing and Printing a Document

There are several ways to print a document in WordPerfect 6. You can print the whole document, the current page, or selected pages. But before you actually print a file, you can take advantage of the Preview feature to see how the document will look on the printed page. In this chapter you will do the following:

❖ Preview a document before printing it
❖ Print a document

VIEWING A DOCUMENT BEFORE PRINTING

In this section you will use the Preview button in the button bar to view a document before printing. If you don't have the PREVIEW file open, open it now. If you have been following along with the previous chapter, you should have the PREVIEW file on your screen and your cursor is at the end of the file on page 2. If your cursor is not at this location, press the Home key twice, then press the ↓ key (Home, Home, ↓) to go to the end of the file.

1. **Click** on the **Preview button**. The Preview screen will appear showing you the page on which your cursor is located.

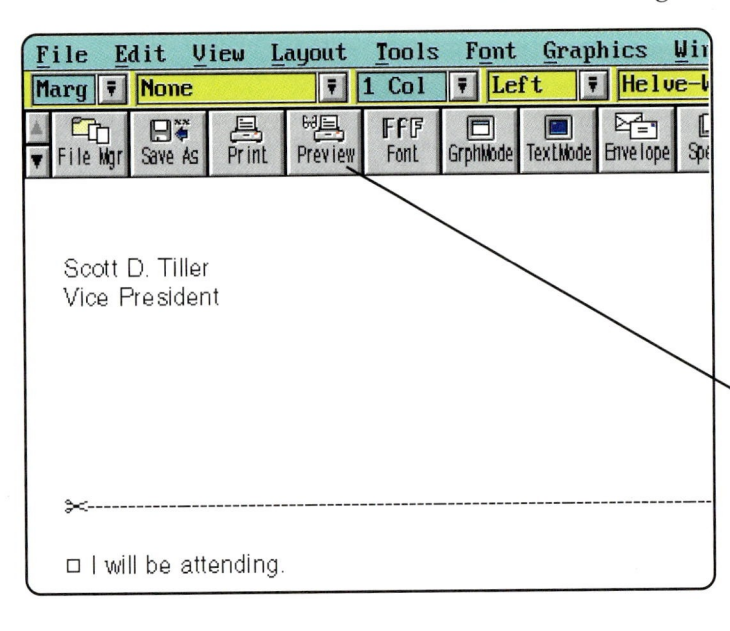

CHAPTER 3: PREVIEWING AND PRINTING A DOCUMENT

Changing Pages in Preview

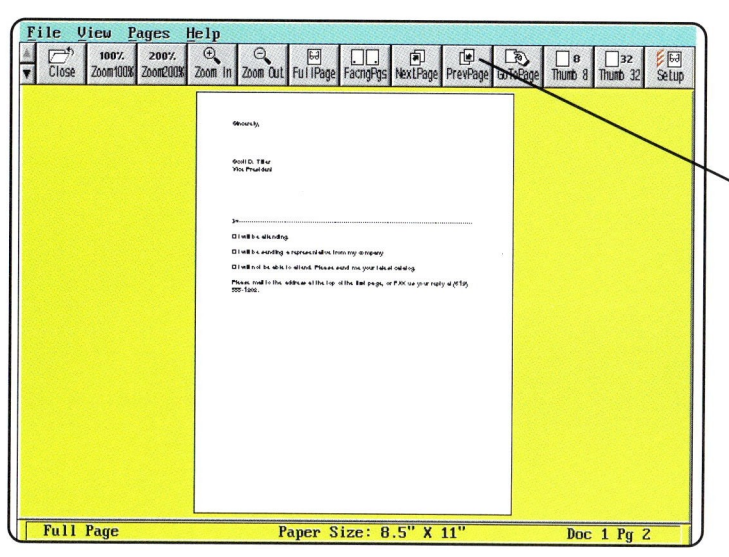

You can scroll through pages of your document very easily.

1. Click on the **PrevPage button**. This will show you the immediately preceding page in your document. In this case, you'll see page 1 of the PREVIEW document.

Viewing Multiple Pages in Preview

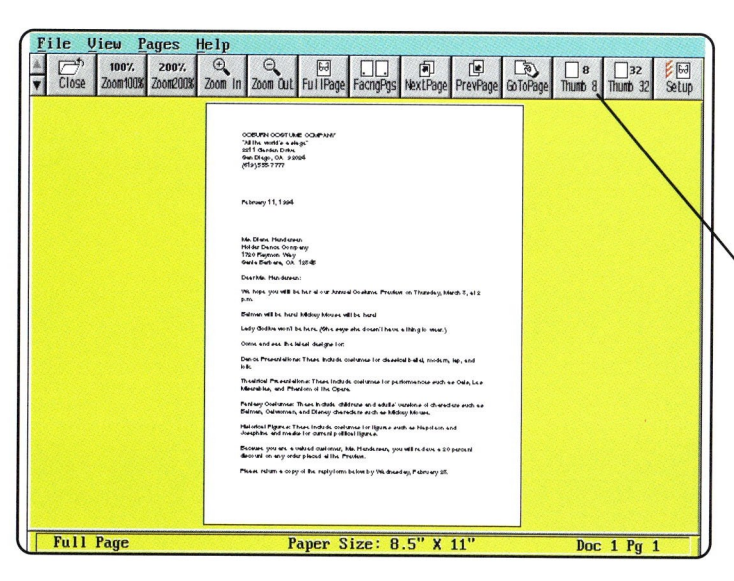

So far you have seen only one page at a time. With the Thumbnail 8 feature you can see up to eight pages at one time.

1. Click on the **Thumb 8 button**. Since there are only two pages in your document, both pages will be displayed side by side, as shown on the next page.

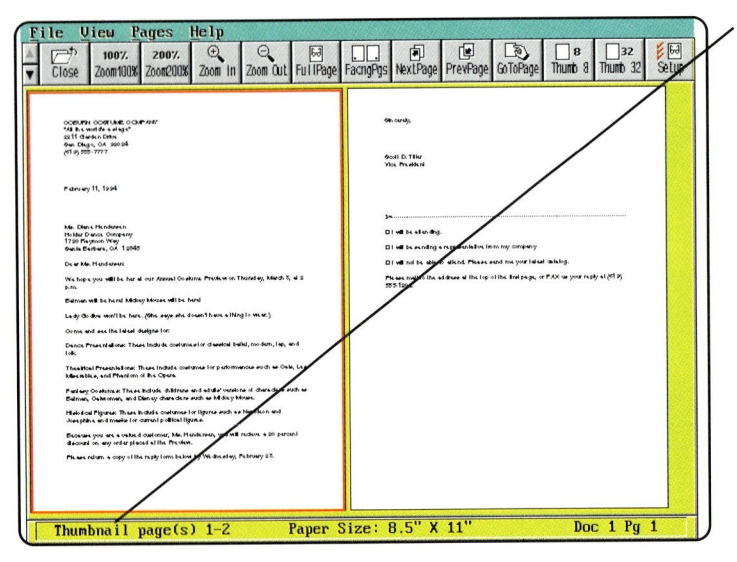

WORDPERFECT 6 FOR DOS: THE VISUAL LEARNING GUIDE

Notice that Thumbnail page(s) 1–2 shows at the bottom of your screen in the status line.

Closing the Preview Screen

Notice the various view options in the button bar. Try experimenting with the other buttons to see how they change the view of your document. Just remember to click on the Thumb 8 button when you're finished exploring so that the Preview screen will return to this view when you open it again.

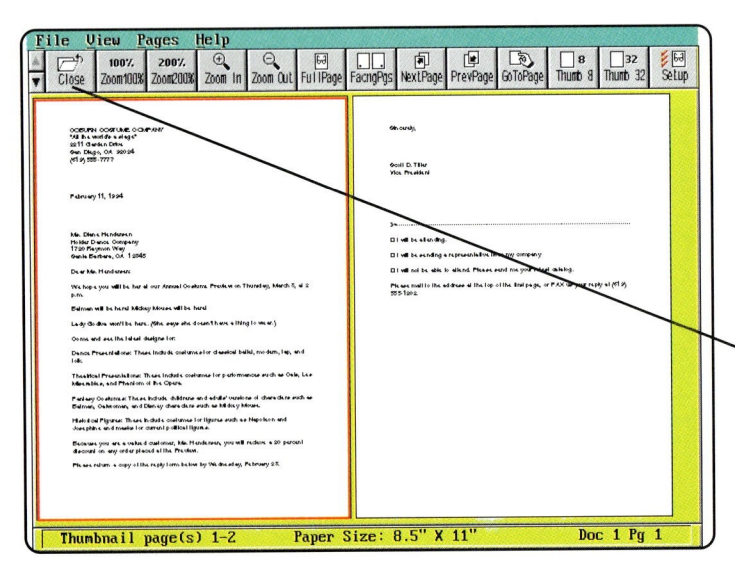

1. **Click** on **Close**. You will be returned to your document.

CHAPTER 3: PREVIEWING AND PRINTING A DOCUMENT

PRINTING A DOCUMENT

In this section you will use the Print button in the button bar to print a document. Again, if you do not have a file open, open one now. Also, make sure your printer is turned on or you will get an error message when you try to print.

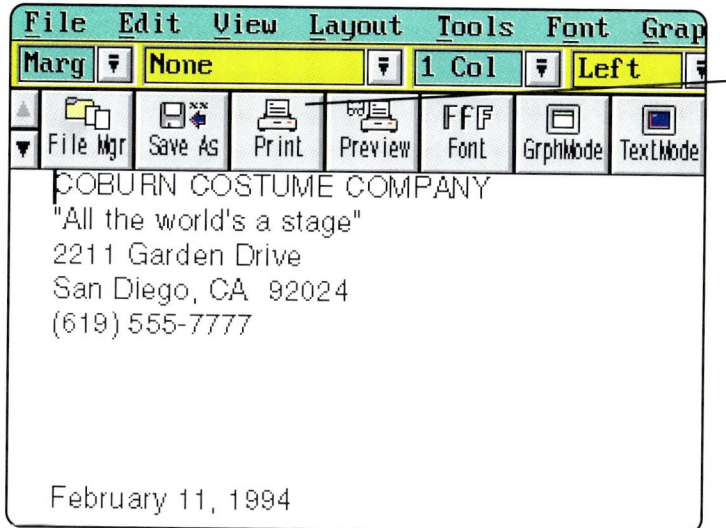

1. Click on the **Print button** in the button bar. (You could also **click** on **File** in the menu bar, and then **click** on **Print** in the pull-down menu.) The Print dialog box will appear.

From here you can either print the current page, a range of pages, or the entire document. The following examples show you how.

Printing the Current Page

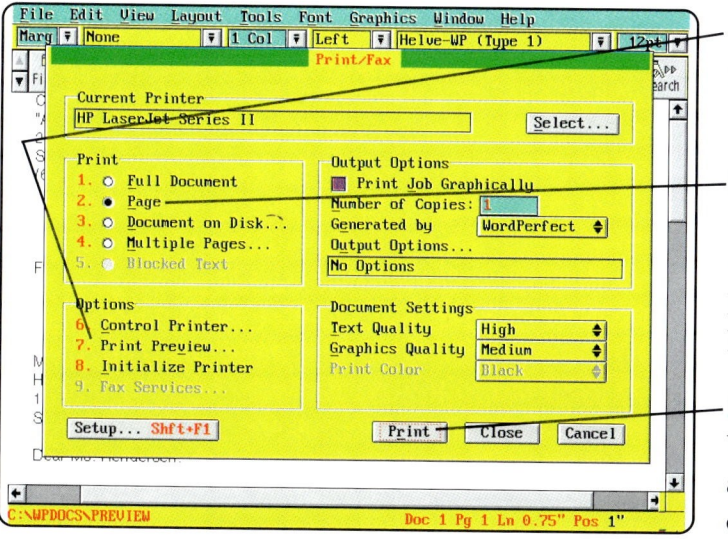

Notice that you can also preview your document from this menu.

1. Click on **Page** to insert a dot in the circle. This instructs WordPerfect to print only the page where your cursor is located.

2. Click on **Print**. A Please Wait message box will appear briefly. Then the current page will print.

Printing Selected Pages

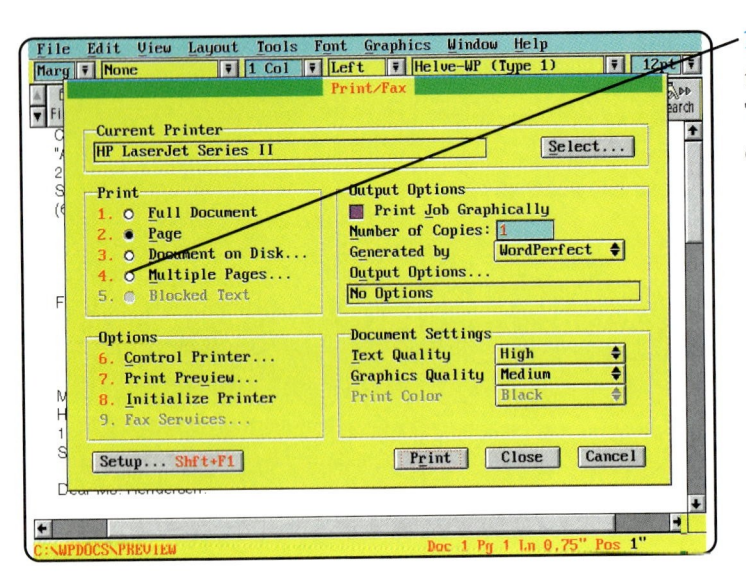

1. Click on **Multiple Pages** to insert a dot in the circle. The Print Multiple Pages dialog box will appear.

2. Click on **Page/Label Range**. The word "all" (in parentheses) will be highlighted in the box to the right.

3. Press the **Backspace key** to delete "(all)."

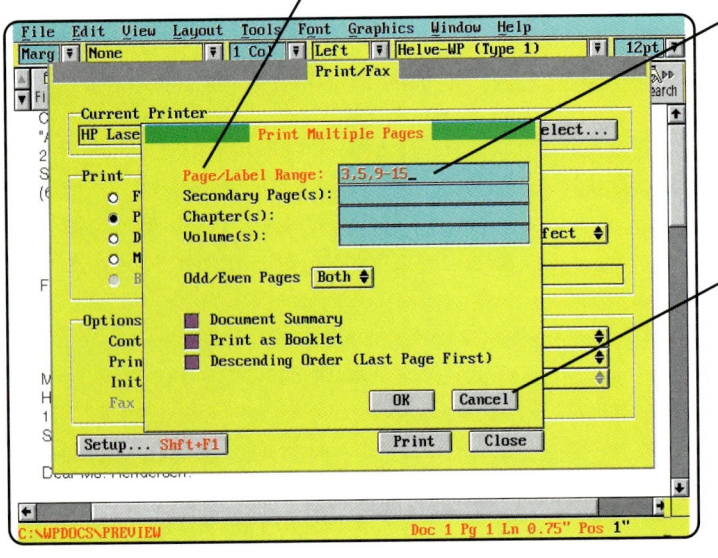

4. Type 3, 5, 9-15. This specifies that pages 3, 5, and 9 through 15 are to be printed. Since this document isn't that long, cancel out of this dialog box.

5. Click on **Cancel** (or **OK** if the document you have open is that long). The Print dialog box will reappear.

6. Click on **Close** (or **Print** to print the selected pages).

CHAPTER 3: PREVIEWING AND PRINTING A DOCUMENT

Printing the Entire Document

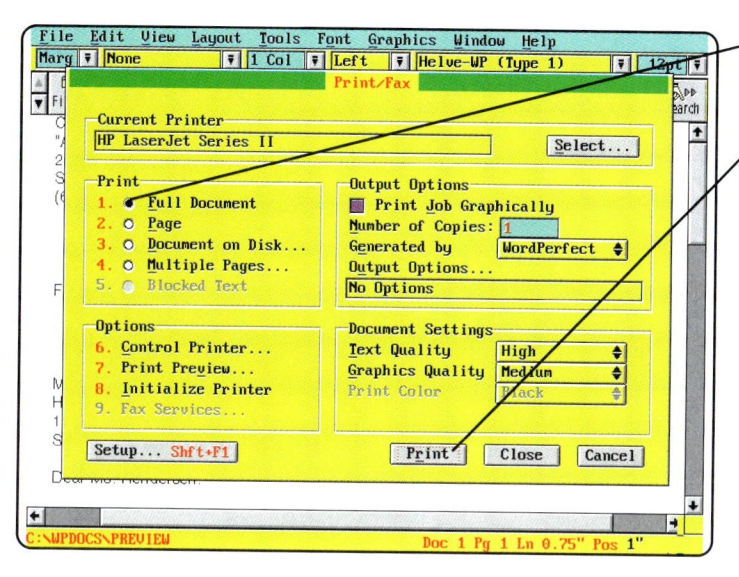

1. **Click** on **Full Document** to insert a dot into the circle.

2. **Click** on **Print**. A Please Wait message box will appear briefly. Then the entire document will print.

Closing a File and Opening a Saved File

When you close a file, WordPerfect 6 will always ask if you want to save any changes you've made since your last save. You can choose to save the changes to the original file or to a new file, leaving the original unchanged. Or you can close the file without saving any of the changes. Once a file is closed, there are several ways to open it, but by far the easiest is to use the File Manager. This way you also make the best use of your mouse and WordPerfect's new graphical environment. In this chapter you will do the following:

- Close a file
- Exit WordPerfect
- Boot up WordPerfect
- Open a saved file

CLOSING A FILE

In this section you will close the PREVIEW file you created in Chapter 1. Since WordPerfect will prompt you to save if you have made any changes since your last save, there is no need to worry about losing changes to your file.

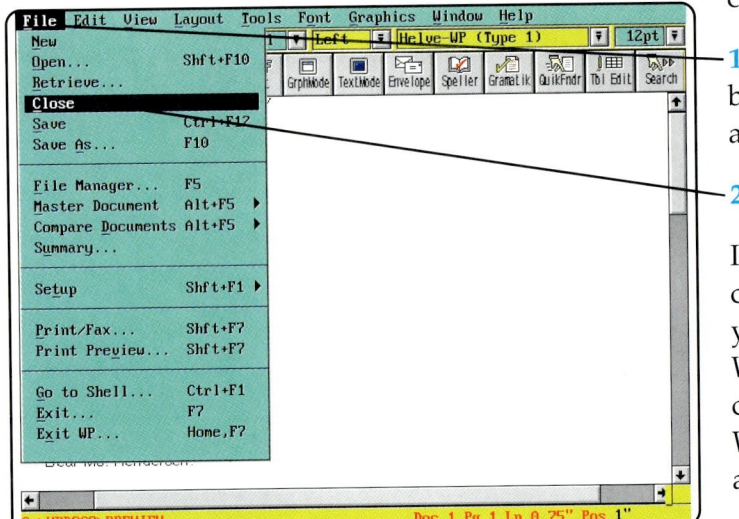

1. **Click** on **File** in the menu bar. A pull-down menu will appear.

2. **Click** on **Close**.

If you have not made any changes to PREVIEW since you saved in Chapter 2, WordPerfect will simply close the file and a blank WordPerfect screen will appear.

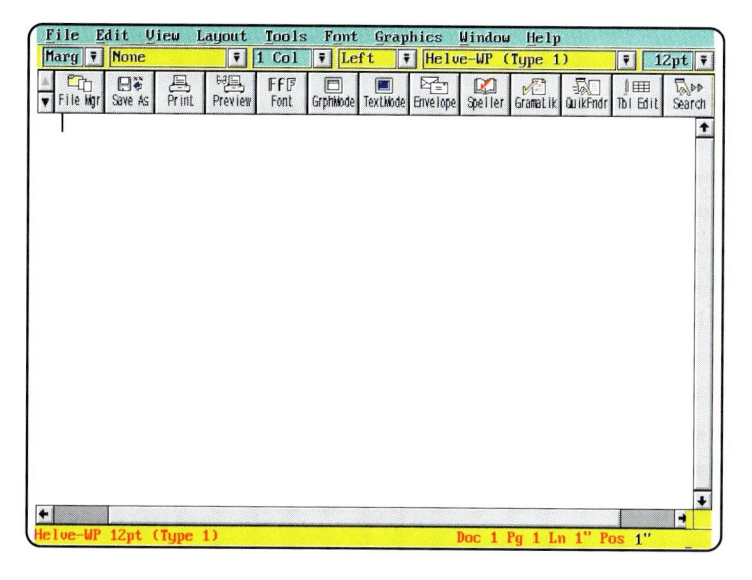

CHAPTER 4: CLOSING A FILE AND OPENING A SAVED FILE

Your screen will look like the example to the left.

Closing After Changes

Note: If you have been following along with the previous chapters, you won't see the screen in the following example because you saved your document before you exited the file.

If, however, you have made changes since the last time you saved, you will see the following screen when you try to close the file.

a. Click on **Save As** to save the changes as a new file and keep the original unchanged. You will use the Save As command in Chapter 13, "Setting Up a Form Letter for Merge Printing."

or

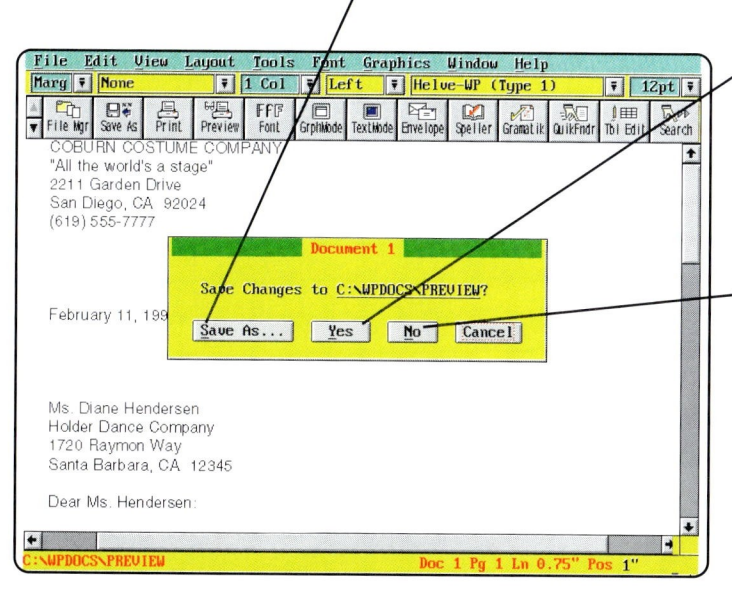

b. Click on **Yes** to save changes. A blank document screen like the one above will appear.

or

c. Click on **No**. The changes will not be saved and the file will return to what it was before the changes.

WORDPERFECT 6 FOR DOS: THE VISUAL LEARNING GUIDE

EXITING WORDPERFECT

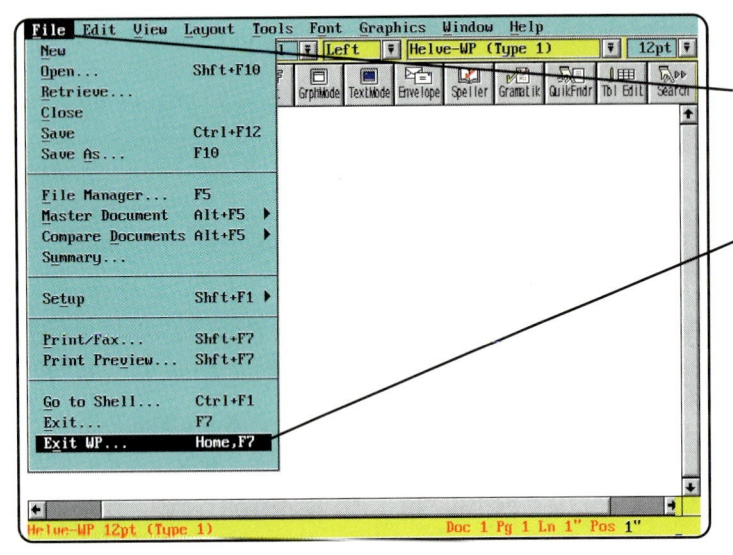

1. Click on **File** in the menu bar. A pull-down menu will appear.

2. Click on **Exit WP**. The Exit WordPerfect dialog box will appear.

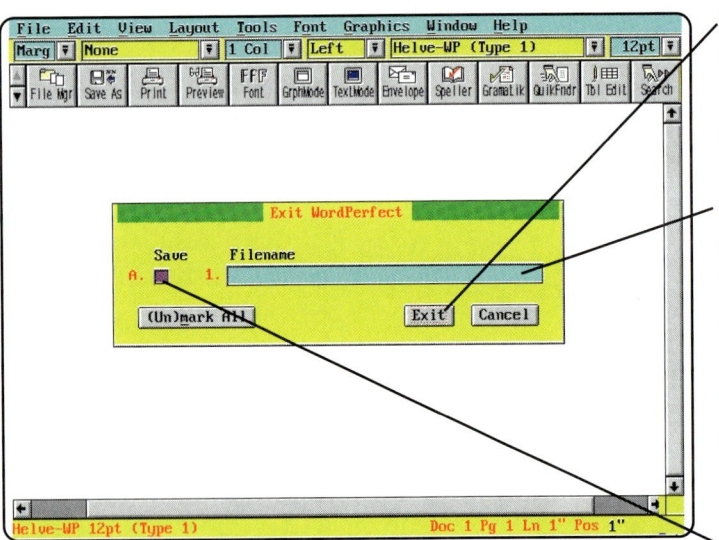

3. Click on **Exit**. The WordPerfect program will close and you will be returned to the DOS screen.

If you did not save your file before you clicked on Exit WP, the filename will appear in the Filename text box. If you have more than one file open, you will see a box for each file. (You can have up to nine files open at a time.)

There will be an ✕ in the Save box to the left of each filename. You can choose not to save changes in a specific file by clicking on the check box to remove the ✕. Then click on Exit.

CHAPTER 4: CLOSING A FILE AND OPENING A SAVED FILE

BOOTING UP WORDPERFECT

1. **Type cd\wp60** at the C:\> (C prompt) on your screen to change to the WordPerfect directory prompt.

2. **Type wp** at the C:\wp60> directory prompt to open, or boot up, WordPerfect 6. A blank WordPerfect screen will appear.

```
C:\>cd\wp60

C:\wp60>wp
```

OPENING A SAVED FILE WITH THE FILE MANAGER

1. **Click** on the **File Mgr button** in the button bar. The Specify File Manager List dialog box will appear.

Notice that C:\WPDOCS*.* is highlighted in the Directory text box. This is the directory where WordPerfect saves all the files you create. The *.* means all the files in the directory WPDOCS will be shown if you look in this directory.

2. **Click twice** (quickly) in the **Directory text box**. The File Manager dialog box will appear showing a list of files in the directory WPDOCS.

An alphabetic list of all files saved to this directory will appear on the left. In this example PREVIEW is the only file that has been saved to the WPDOCS directory. If others have used WordPerfect on your computer before you, you may see other files listed. Click on the **down arrow** on the scroll bar to scroll through the list until you see PREVIEW.

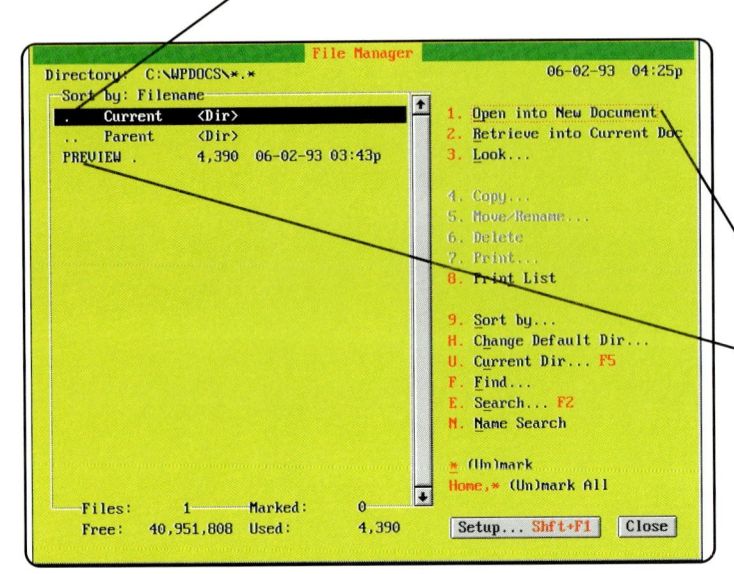

Notice that Open into New Document is selected.

3. Click twice on PREVIEW. (If nothing happens, try clicking twice again.) The letter you created in Chapter 1 will appear.

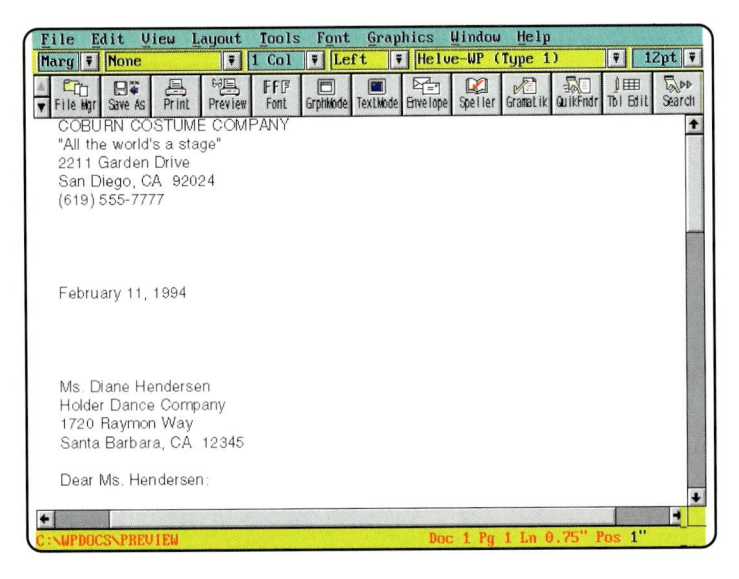

You are now ready to continue working on the PREVIEW document in the next chapter.

Using the Grammar Checker, Spelling Checker, and Thesaurus

WordPerfect 6 has two handy utilities that will check your grammar and spelling and make suggestions for changes. It also contains a Thesaurus that will offer a list of synonyms. Now, if it would only go out for coffee . . .

In this chapter you will do the following:

❖ Use the grammar checker—Grammatik 5
❖ Use the spelling checker—Speller
❖ Use the Thesaurus

USING GRAMMATIK 5

If you want to check an entire document, click at the beginning of the file. In this example, you will check only one sentence in the PREVIEW document.

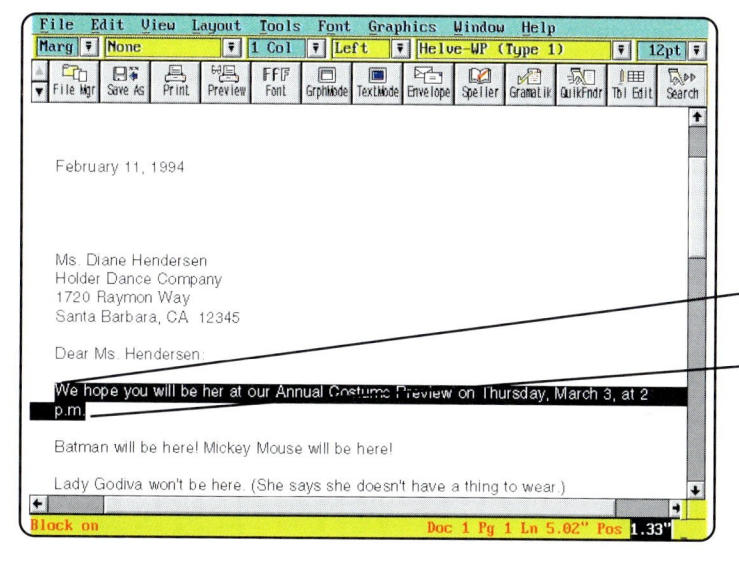

1. Click on the **down arrow** on the scroll bar until the first sentence in the letter **"We hope you will . . ."** can be seen in your document screen.

2. Click to the **left of "We."**

3. Press and hold the mouse button as you **drag** the highlight bar **over the first sentence**.

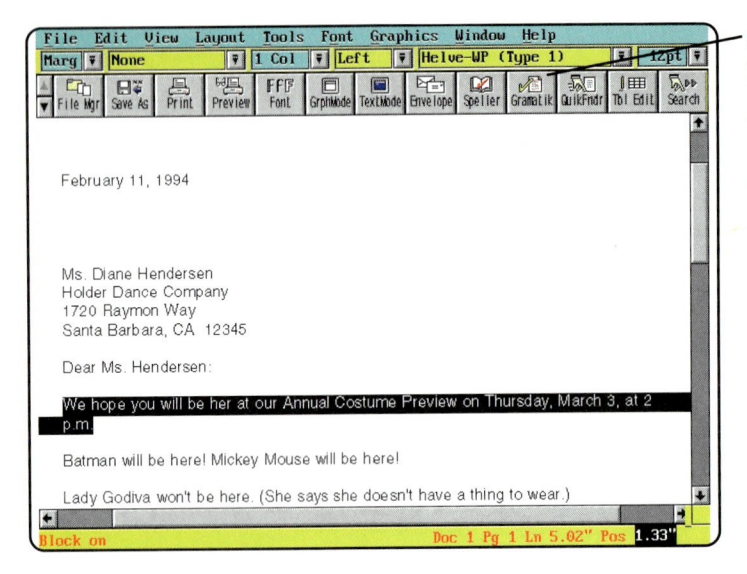

WORDPERFECT 6 FOR DOS: THE VISUAL LEARNING GUIDE

4. Click on the **Grammatik button** in the button bar. A message box will flash "Please Wait" and the Grammatik 5 screen will appear.

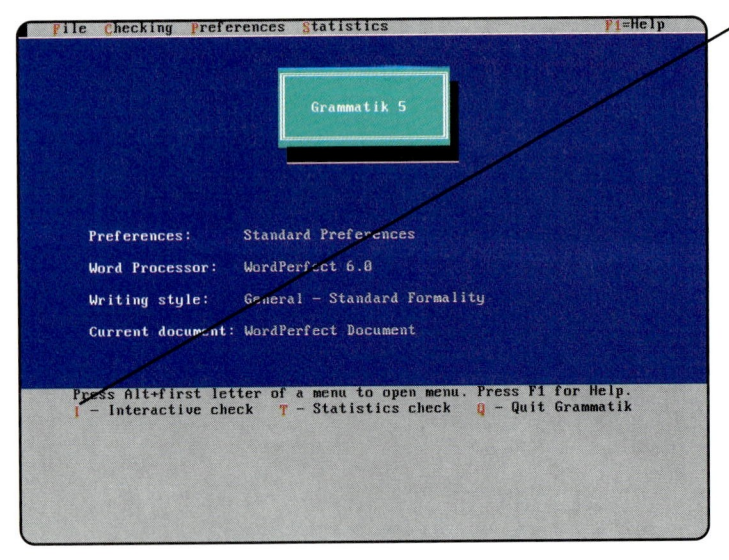

5. Click on **I** for Interactive check. The Scanning for first error . . . message will flash and the Grammatik 5 interactive screen will appear.

CHAPTER 5: USING THE GRAMMAR/SPELLING CHECKERS, AND THESAURUS

This is an example of a rule that does not apply in the context of this sentence. Since "2 p.m." indicates time, "2" is correctly written as a number.

6. **Click** on **Ignore rule class**. The highlight bar will indicate "her" as the next potential error.

Notice that WordPerfect has identified "her" as an error, but for the wrong reason. This is another example of why computers are not ready to rule the world. In this example the suggested replacement is not appropriate so you will have to edit the word directly.

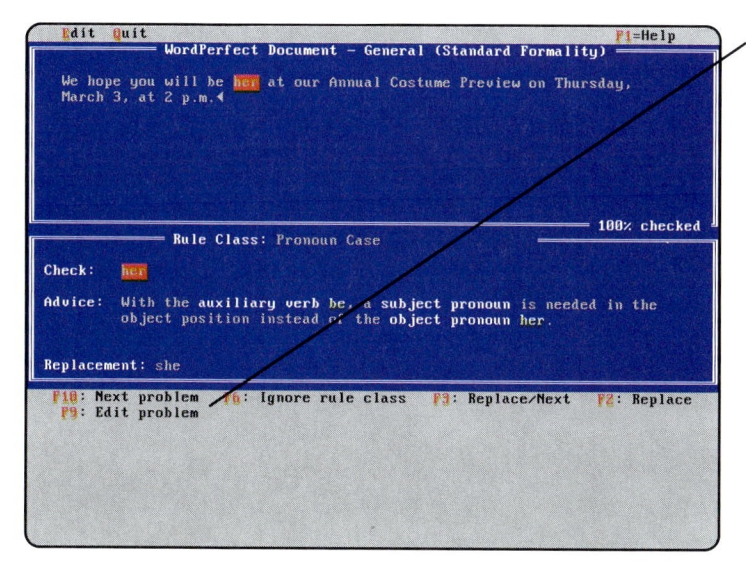

7. **Click** on **Edit problem**. The editing screen will appear and your cursor will be flashing in front of the word "her."

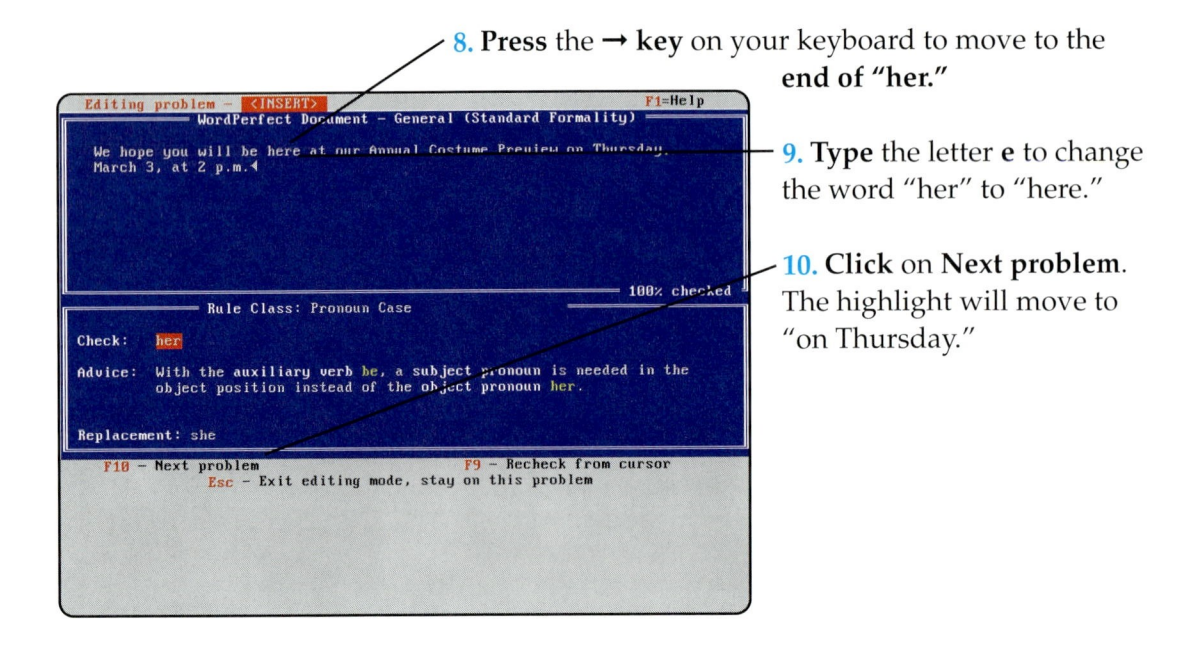

8. **Press** the → **key** on your keyboard to move to the **end of "her."**

9. **Type** the letter **e** to change the word "her" to "here."

10. **Click** on **Next problem**. The highlight will move to "on Thursday."

In this example Grammatik recommends that you simplify "on Thursday."

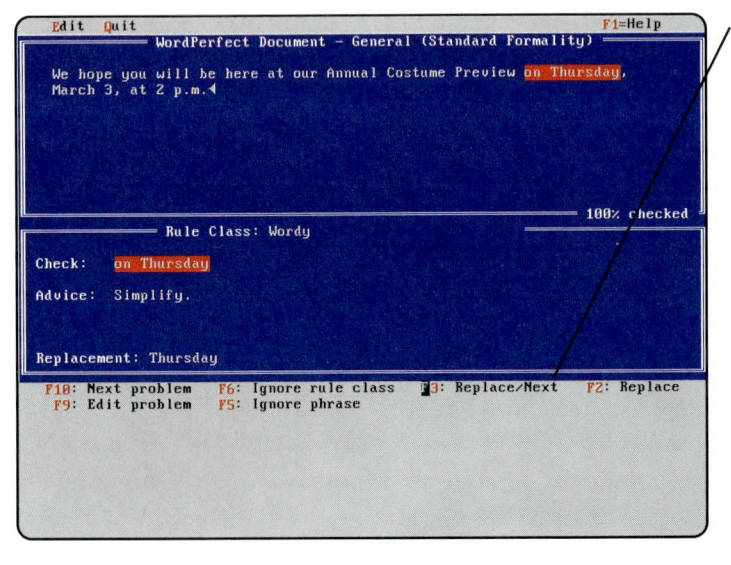

11. **Click** on **Replace/Next**. Grammatik will correct the error.

When Grammatik has completed checking the highlighted text, a dialog box will appear.

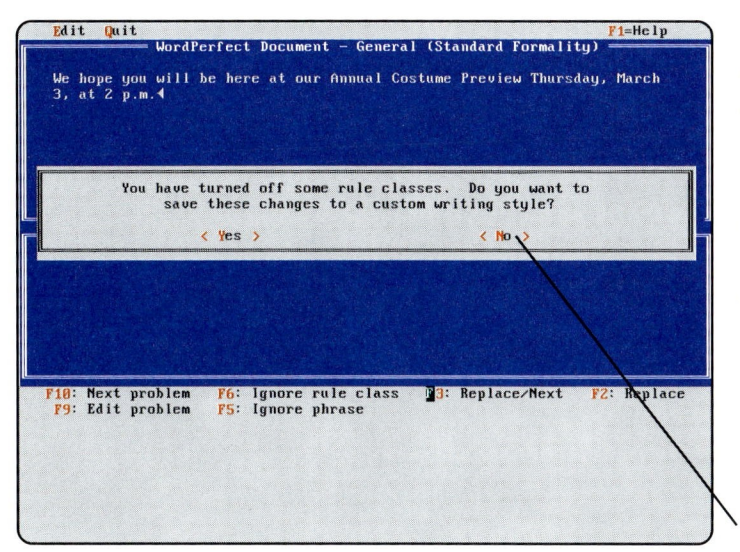

CHAPTER 5: USING THE GRAMMAR/SPELLING CHECKERS, AND THESAURUS

Because you ignored a Grammatik rule in step 6, Grammatik will ask if you want to save the instructions to override the rule to a custom writing style. Since it's preferable to keep Grammatik's standard rules turned on for future documents, don't save the changes to a custom writing style.

12. Click on **No**.

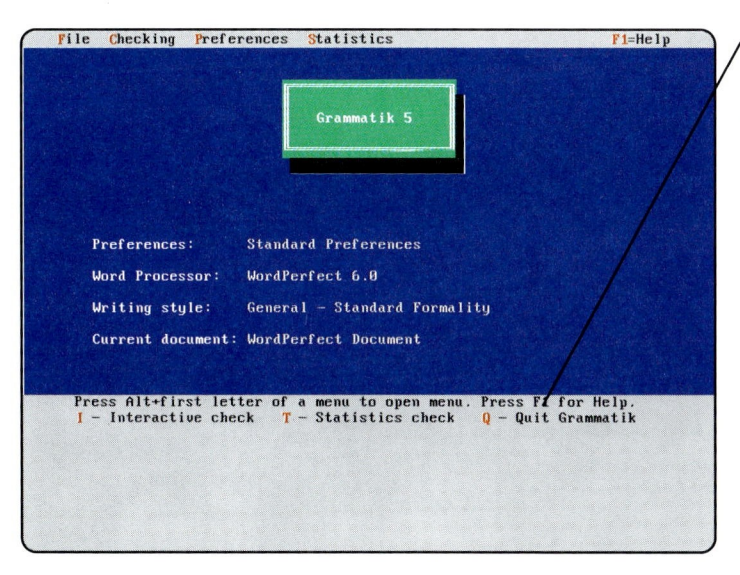

13. Click on **Quit Grammatik**. A Grammatik done message box will flash and you will be returned to the document screen.

USING SPELLER

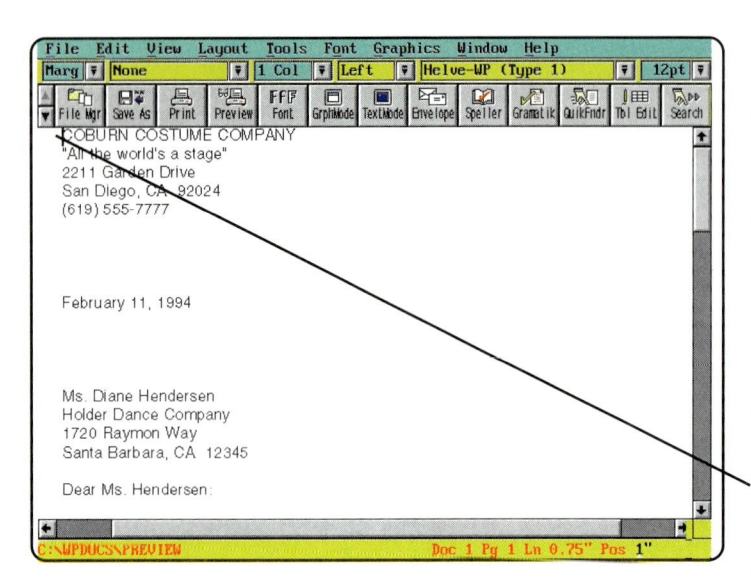

Speller will start a check at the point where your cursor is located. Once it reaches the end of the document, it wraps around to the beginning and then completes the check up to the cursor location. For this example you will check the PREVIEW document from the beginning.

1. **Press Home twice** then **press** ↑ (Home, Home, ↑) to go to the beginning of the PREVIEW file if you are not already there.

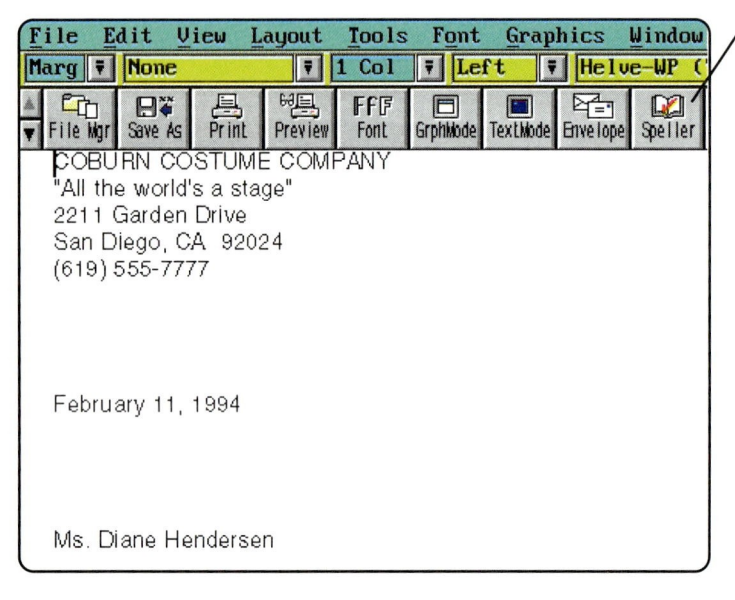

2. **Click** on the **Speller button** in the button bar. The Speller dialog box will appear.

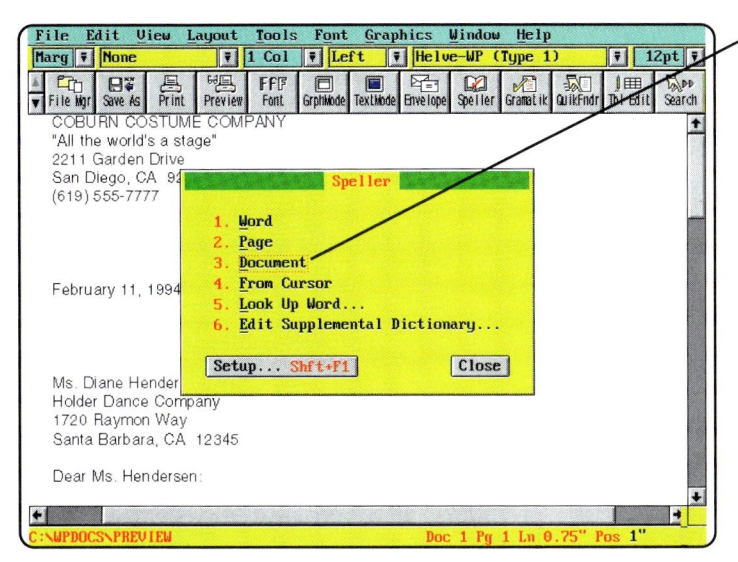

CHAPTER 5: USING THE GRAMMAR/SPELLING CHECKERS, AND THESAURUS

3. Click on **Document** to check the spelling in the entire letter. Speller will highlight your first misspelled word and the Word Not Found dialog box will appear.

Adding a Word to the Dictionary

In this example "COBURN" has been identified as a misspelled word. If you use a specific proper name often, you can add it to the dictionary so that WordPerfect will not continually identify it as a misspelled word.

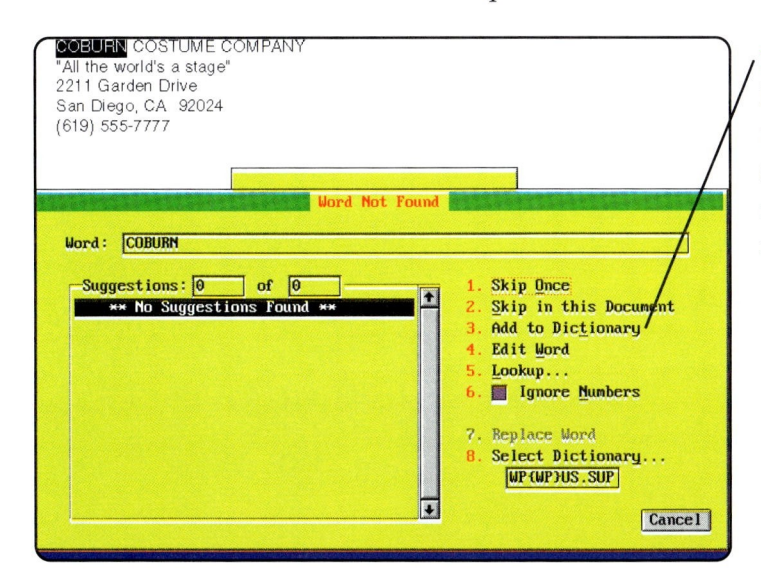

1. Click on **Add to Dictionary**. Speller will add the word to the supplemental dictionary and move on to the next misspelled word.

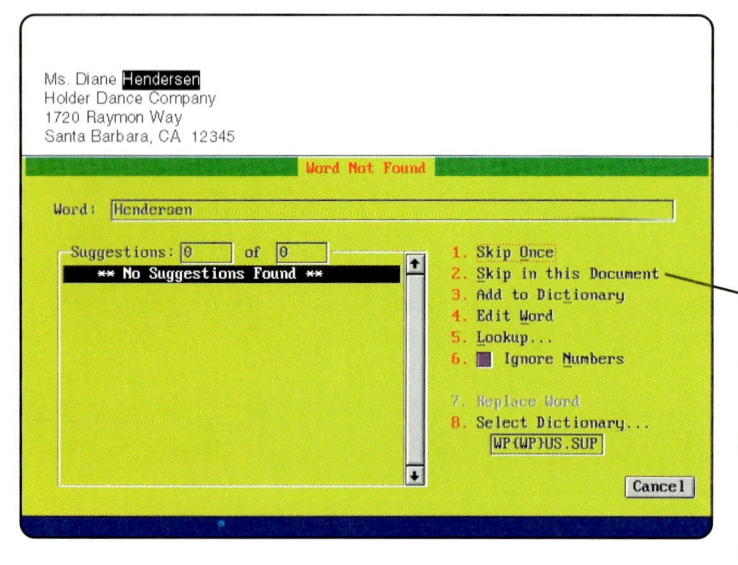

WORDPERFECT 6 FOR DOS: THE VISUAL LEARNING GUIDE

You can also choose to skip a word rather than add it to the dictionary. You can even tell WordPerfect to skip the word every time it occurs in this letter.

2. Click on **Skip in this Document** to skip every occurrence of "Hendersen."

3. Click on **Skip in this Document** when Speller identifies **"Raymon"** as a misspelled word. Speller will move on to the next word it suspects is misspelled.

Ignoring a Suggested Change

You probably learned, as we did, that "p.m." is correct. WordPerfect obviously has its own ideas about that. In this example you will ignore the suggestion to change "p.m." to "pm".

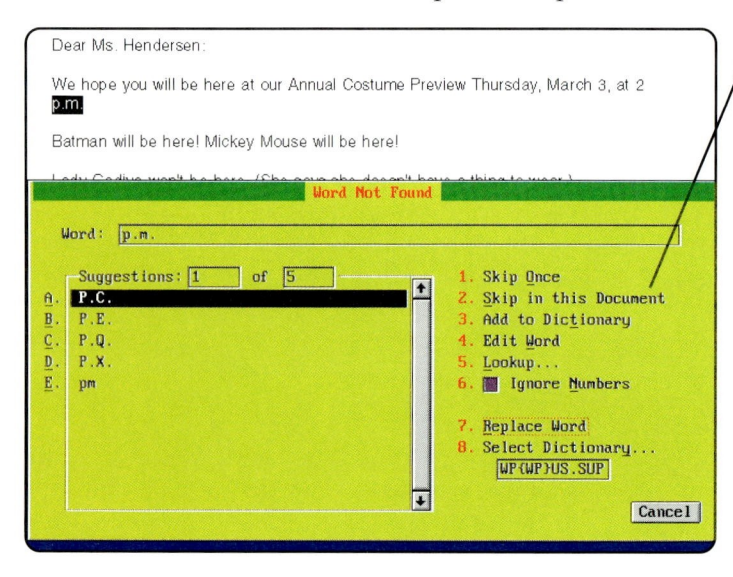

1. Click on **Skip in this Document**.

2. Click on **Skip in this Document** when WordPerfect identifies each of the following words as misspelled:

"Godiva"
"Les"
"Miserables"

CHAPTER 5: USING THE GRAMMAR/SPELLING CHECKERS, AND THESAURUS

Editing a Word in the Document

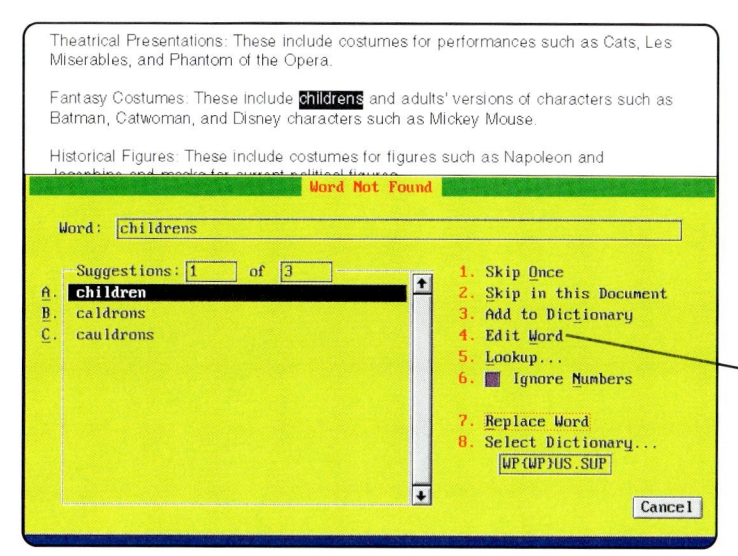

In this example WordPerfect has identified "childrens" as a misspelled word. Since Speller does not offer the possessive form of the noun as a suggested change, you can edit the word directly in the document.

1. Click on **Edit Word**. Your cursor will appear in the document on the upper-half of your screen.

2. Click after "n" in "childrens."

3. Type ' (an apostrophe).

4. Press Enter. You will exit the edit mode and the word "Catwoman" will be highlighted.

5. Click on **Skip in this Document** for the word **"Catwoman."**

Accepting a Suggested Change

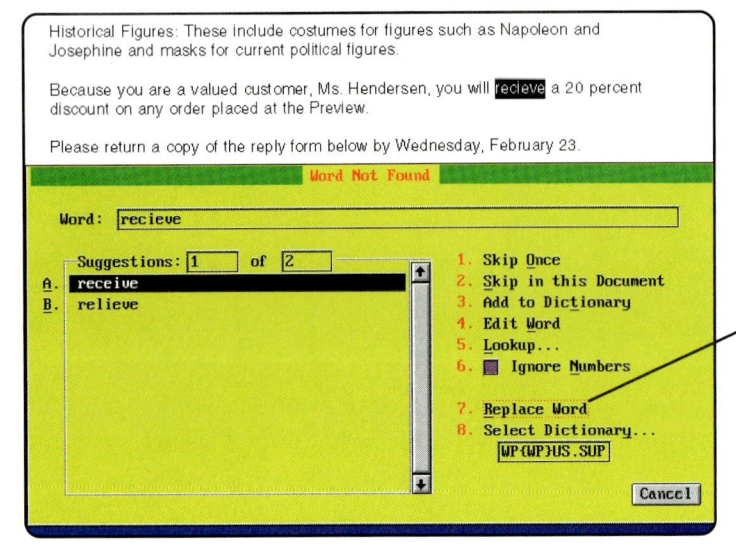

In this example WordPerfect has correctly identified "recieve" as a misspelled word. Since "receive" is already highlighted in the Suggestions list, do the following:

1. Click on **Replace Word**. WordPerfect will replace the word and the Spell Check Completed message box will appear.

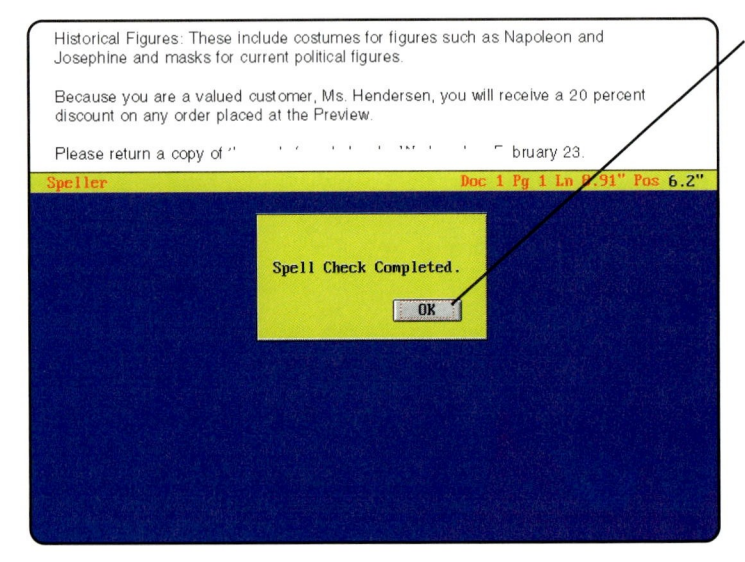

2. Click on **OK**. The Speller screen will disappear and the document screen will appear.

CHAPTER 5: USING THE GRAMMAR/SPELLING CHECKERS, AND THESAURUS

USING THE THESAURUS

In this section you will use the Thesaurus to view words that can replace "latest." First, however, you will use the Search button to locate the word.

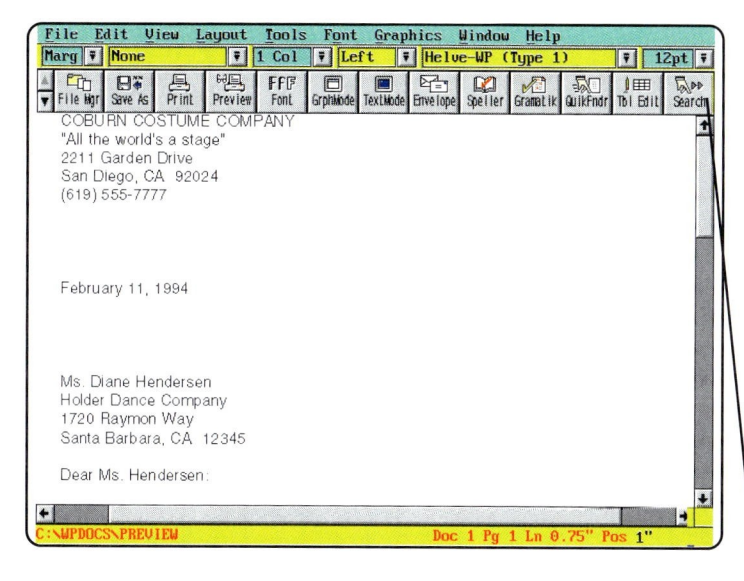

Using Search

You can search forward or backward in a document. In this example, you will go to the beginning of the file and search from that point.

1. Press the **Home key twice**, then **press** ↑ (Home, Home, ↑) to go to the beginning of the file.

2. Click on the **Search button** in the button bar. The Search dialog box will appear.

3. Type the word **latest**.

4. Click on **Search**. WordPerfect will search for the first occurrence of this word in your document.

The cursor will be flashing after the word "latest."

WORDPERFECT 6 FOR DOS: THE VISUAL LEARNING GUIDE

Replacing a Word with the Thesaurus

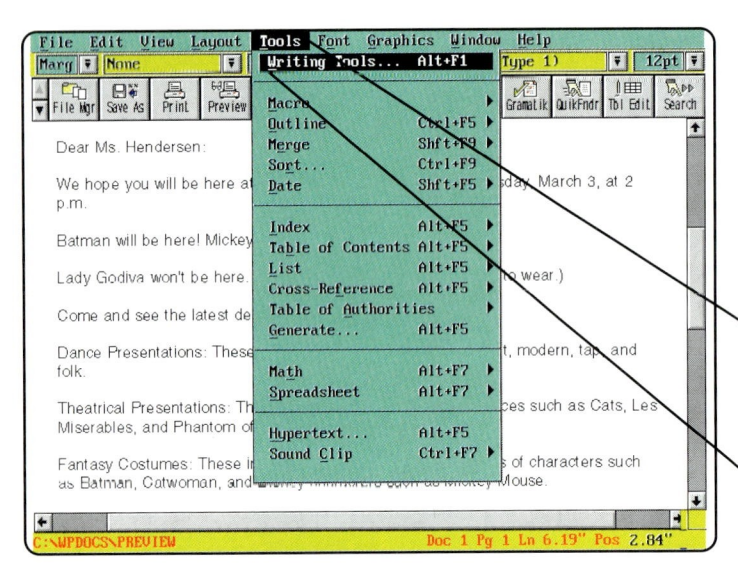

Place your cursor to the right of the word you want to replace with the Thesaurus. If you have been following these procedures, your cursor is already to the right of "latest."

1. Click on **Tools** in the menu bar. A pull-down menu will appear.

2. Click on **Writing Tools**. The Writing Tools dialog box will appear.

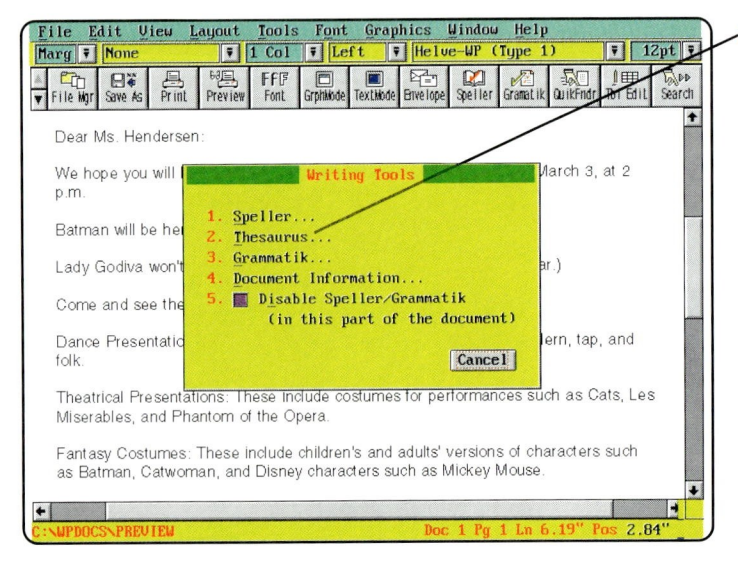

3. Click on **Thesaurus**. The Thesaurus dialog box will appear. A list of possible replacement words will appear in the Thesaurus dialog box.

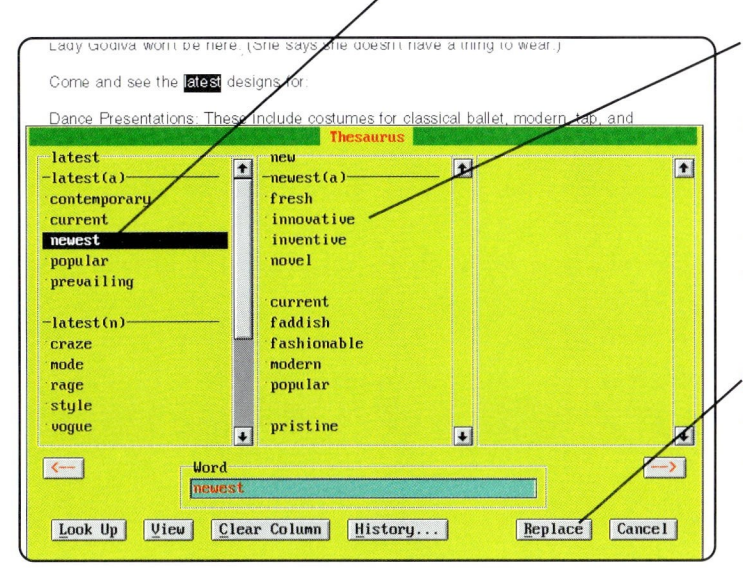

CHAPTER 5: USING THE GRAMMAR/SPELLING CHECKERS, AND THESAURUS

4. **Click** on **"newest"** in the first column.

If you click twice on "newest," a list of its synonyms appears in column 2. If you try this, make certain that you click on "newest" in the first column again before the next step.

5. **Click** on **Replace**. The document screen will appear.

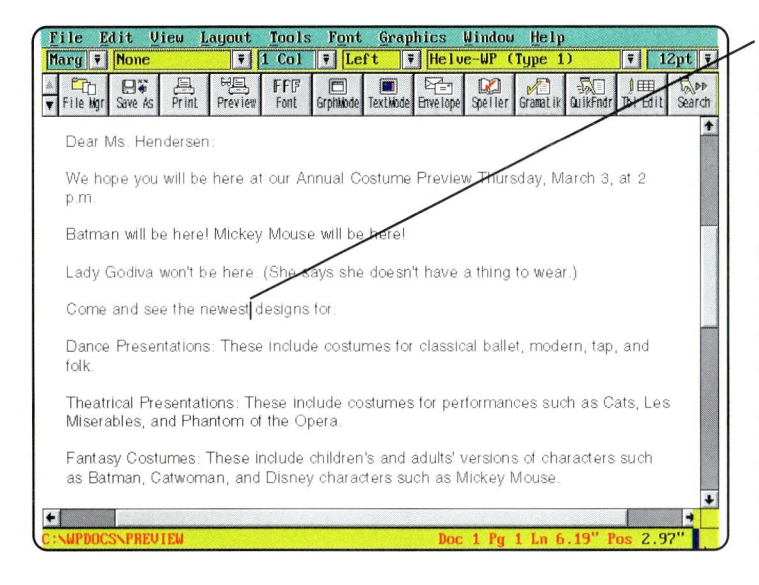

Notice that "latest" has been replaced by "newest" and that the cursor is in the same position.

You are now ready for Chapter 6, "Editing a Document," where you will learn how to make other changes in the letter.

Don't forget to save your changes as you work. See "Saving While You Work" in Chapter 2.

Editing a Document

WordPerfect 6 has a number of nifty editing features that, when combined with the mouse and scroll bars, make moving through and editing your document quite easy. You'll be delighted with the ease with which you can move and copy text by using the new drag-and-drop features. Deleting text has also never been easier to do. But when you find that you've changed your mind, you can use the Edit Undo feature and undo your change immediately. In this chapter you will do the following:

- Add and delete letters and words and combine paragraphs
- Use the Edit Undo feature
- Use the Replace command to correct an error that occurs in several places
- Move and copy text
- Insert and change the position of the page break

INSERTING TEXT

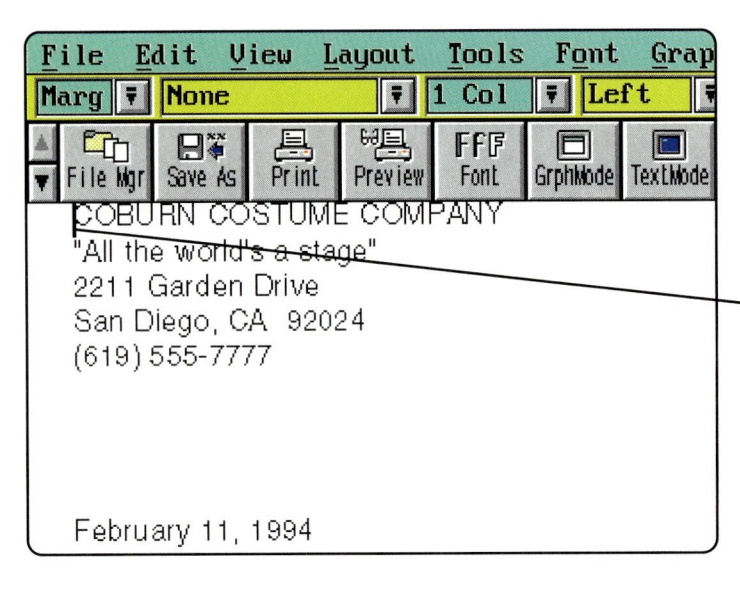

In this section you will add text to a paragraph in the PREVIEW document. As you do this, you will also learn how to move around in your document.

1. Press the **Home key twice**, then **press** ↑ (Home, Home, ↑). This will place the cursor at the beginning of the file.

CHAPTER 6: EDITING A DOCUMENT

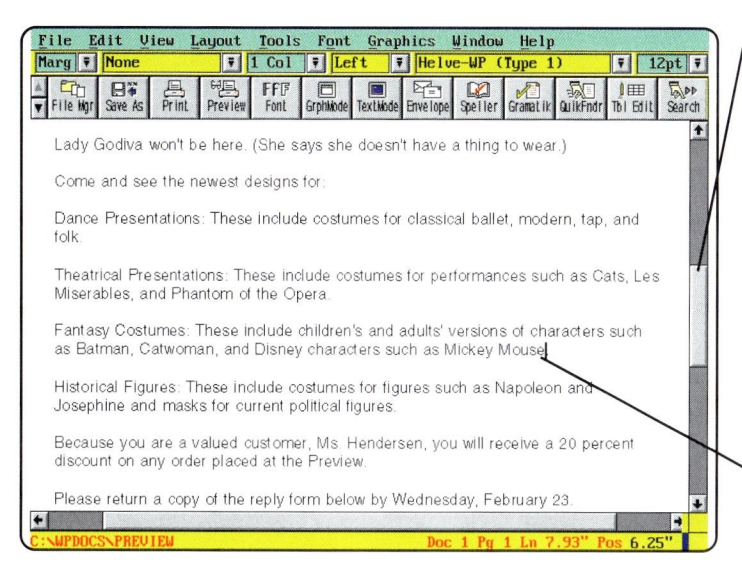

2. **Place** the mouse arrow **on top of the scroll button**. On your screen it will be at the top of the scroll bar.

3. **Click and hold** as you **drag** the scroll button **halfway down** the scroll bar. This will move you to about the middle of the first page of your document.

4. **Click between "Mouse" and the period** at the end of the "Fantasy Costumes" paragraph to place the cursor.

5. **Press** the **Spacebar** then **type** the phrase **and Donald Duck**. Notice that the period moves as you type and the text automatically wraps around to the next line.

DELETING TEXT

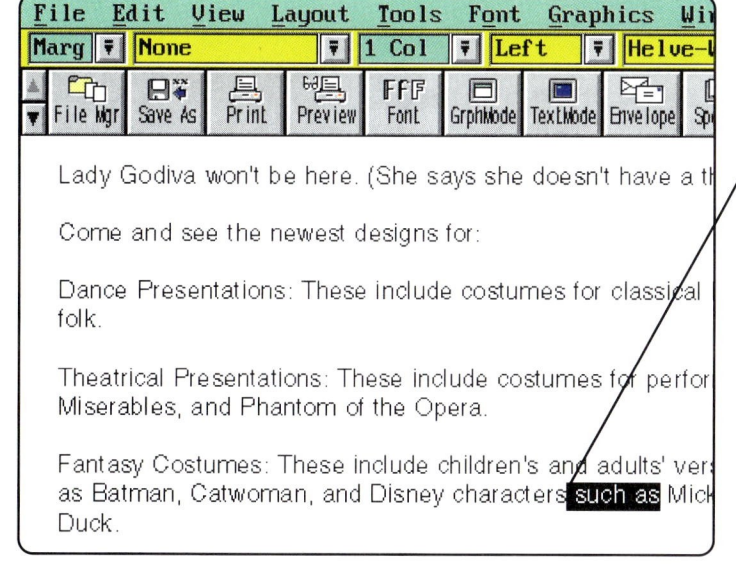

In this section you will delete text from the same paragraph you edited in the previous section.

1. **Click** to the **right of "Disney Characters"** in the "Fantasy Costumes" paragraph to place the cursor.

2. **Press and hold** the mouse button and **drag** the cursor **over "such as."** Be careful not to highlight the space after "as" or you will delete the space between the words.

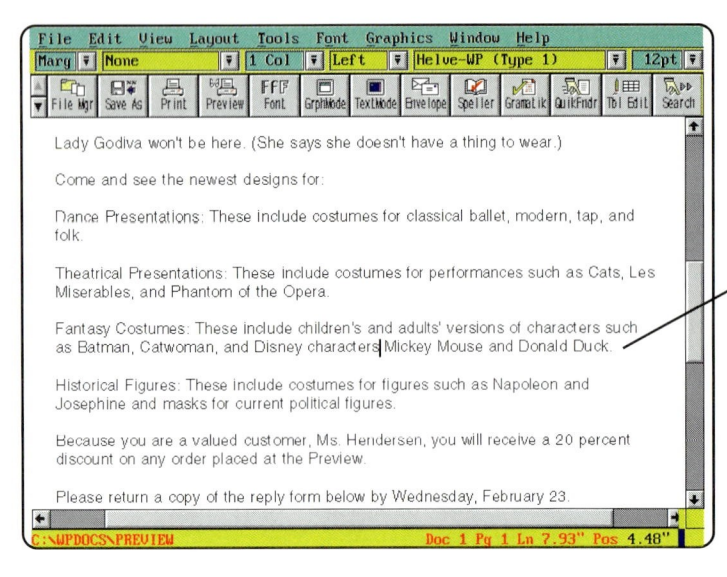

WORDPERFECT 6 FOR DOS: THE VISUAL LEARNING GUIDE

3. Press the **Del key** on your keyboard. The highlighted text will be deleted. Notice that the rest of the sentence is automatically repositioned.

The sentence will look like this.

UNDOING AN EDIT

If you have been following along with this chapter, you just deleted the phrase "such as." What if that was a mistake and you didn't really mean to delete those words? WordPerfect has a wonderfully forgiving feature called Edit Undo. This feature will undo your very last action as long as you don't perform any other function before you use the Undo feature.

1. Click on **Edit** in the menu bar. A pull-down menu will appear.

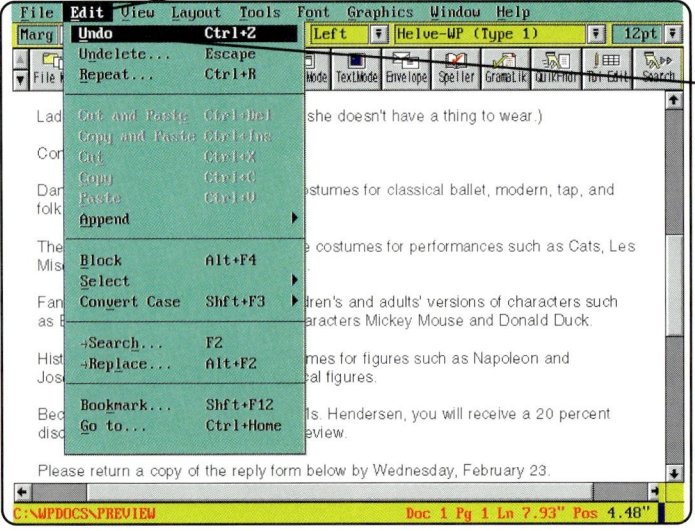

2. Click on **Undo**. The deleted text will be restored.

Undoing an Undo

You can even undo an undo.

1. Repeat steps 1 and 2 above to undo the undo, deleting the text once again.

CHAPTER 6: EDITING A DOCUMENT

COMBINING PARAGRAPHS

In this section you will combine the "Lady Godiva" paragraph with the preceding paragraph that has "Batman" and "Mickey Mouse" in it.

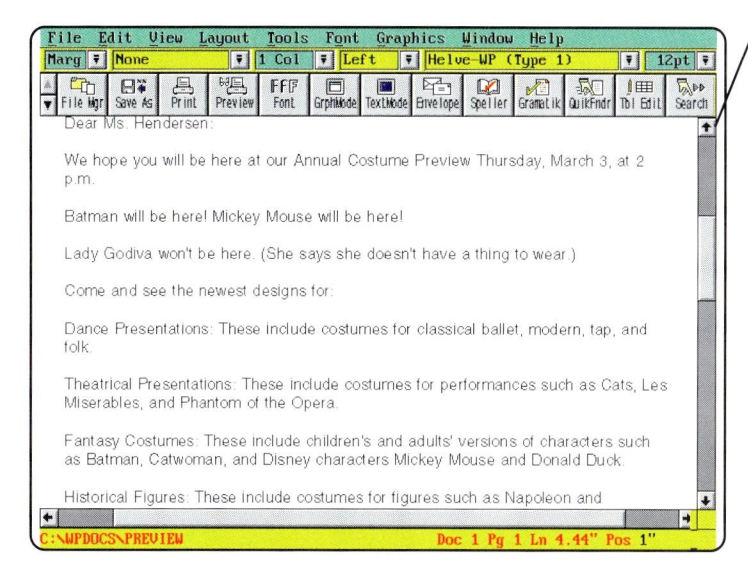

1. Click on the **up arrow** on the scroll bar to scroll up so that you can see "Dear Ms. Hendersen."

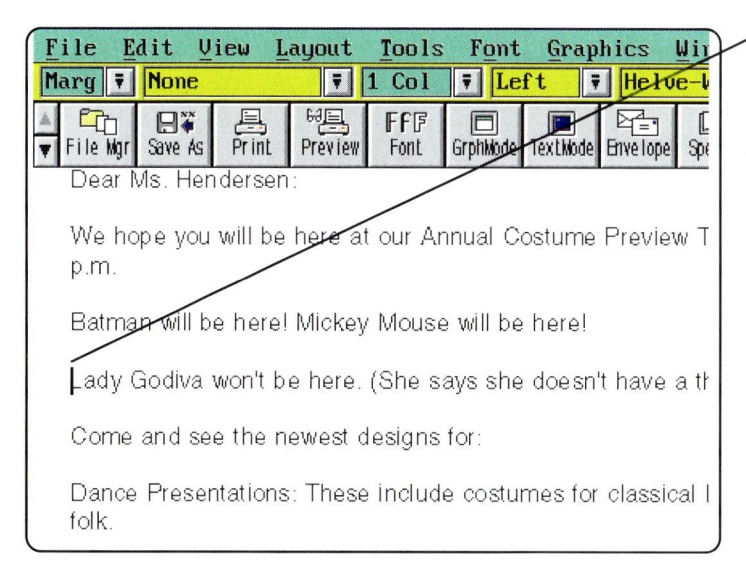

2. Place the mouse pointer at the **beginning of the "Lady Godiva" sentence**. **Click** to set the cursor in place.

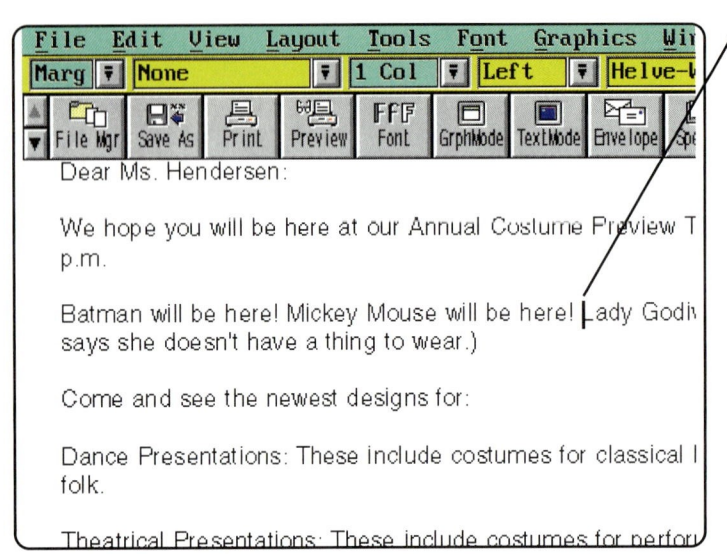

WORDPERFECT 6 FOR DOS: THE VISUAL LEARNING GUIDE

3. **Press** the **Backspace key twice**. Then **press** the **Spacebar**. This will bring the entire "Lady Godiva" paragraph up to the end of the "Mickey Mouse" sentence and put a space between the sentences.

OUTWITTING TEXT WRAP

Text wrap is the function within WordPerfect that automatically wraps long sentences to the next line. It does not always make the wrap in a place that makes sense.

Inserting a Home Space

In the example you see here, having "p.m." on a line all by itself does not look good. It would be more readable if "at 2 p.m." were together on the second line. If you press the Enter key, however, you will insert what is called a *hard return*. This means that this text will permanently stay as a separate line. It will not wrap back and forth between lines as you add and delete text. You can, however, move "at 2" to the next line by inserting a *Home Space*.

1. **Click** to the **left of "2"** to set the cursor.

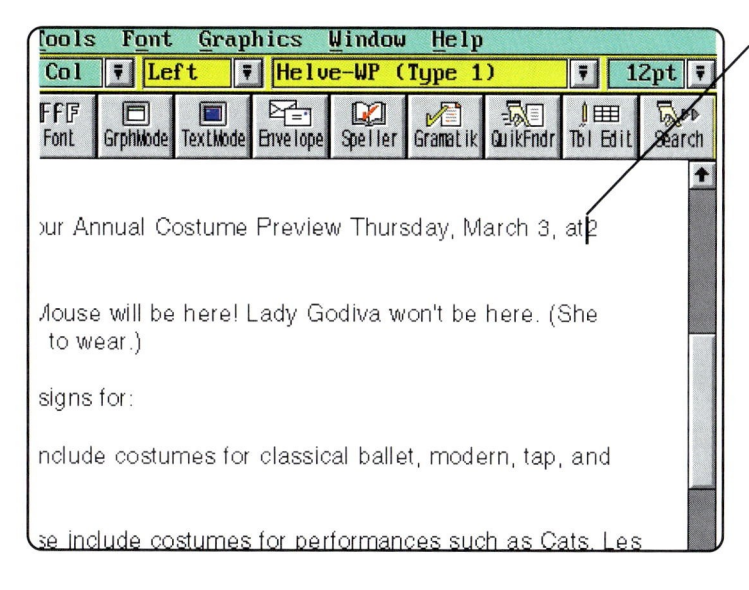

CHAPTER 6: EDITING A DOCUMENT

2. Press the **Backspace key** to delete the space between "at" and "2."

You will now insert what WordPerfect calls a Home Space. This is a space that shows on the screen but is interpreted by WordPerfect as being part of the word.

3. Press and release the **Home key**, then **press** the **Spacebar** (Home, Spacebar). This inserts a Home Space in the text.

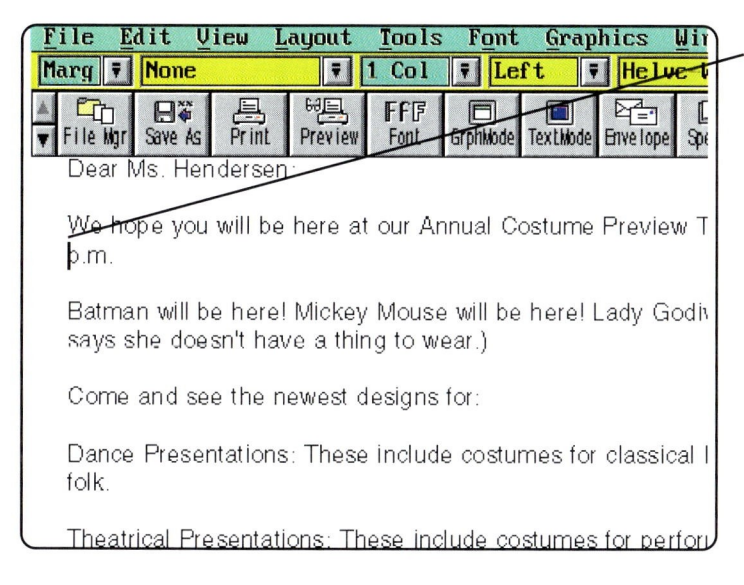

4. Click to the **left of "p.m."** on the second line.

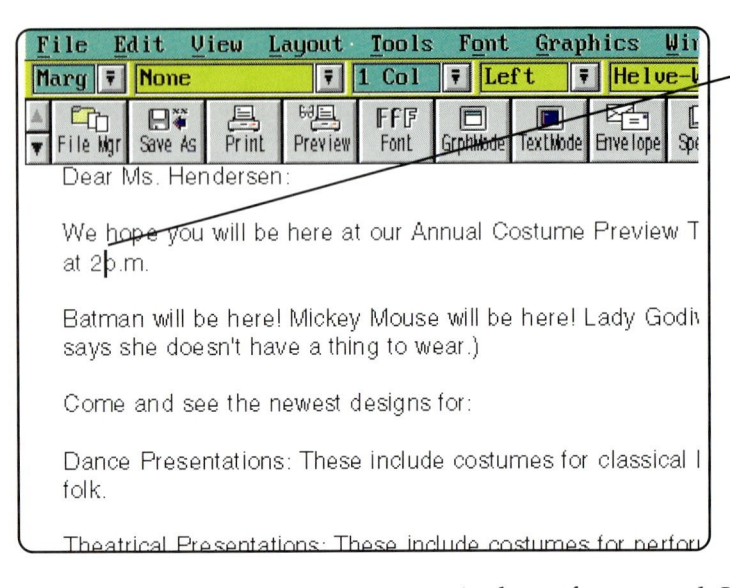

5. Press the **Backspace key**. This will bring "at 2" down to the second line. There will be no space between "2" and "p.m."

6. Press and release the **Home key** then **press** the **Spacebar** (Home, Spacebar) to insert a Home Space between "2" and "p.m."

WordPerfect now considers "at 2 p.m." to be the equivalent of one word. It will stay together and wrap as one word.

Now in this example you will combine "Les" and "Miserables" into one word by deleting the hard space that you inserted with the Spacebar and inserting a Home Space. When "Les Miserables" is one word, WordPerfect will wrap it around to the second line because it is too long to fit on the first line.

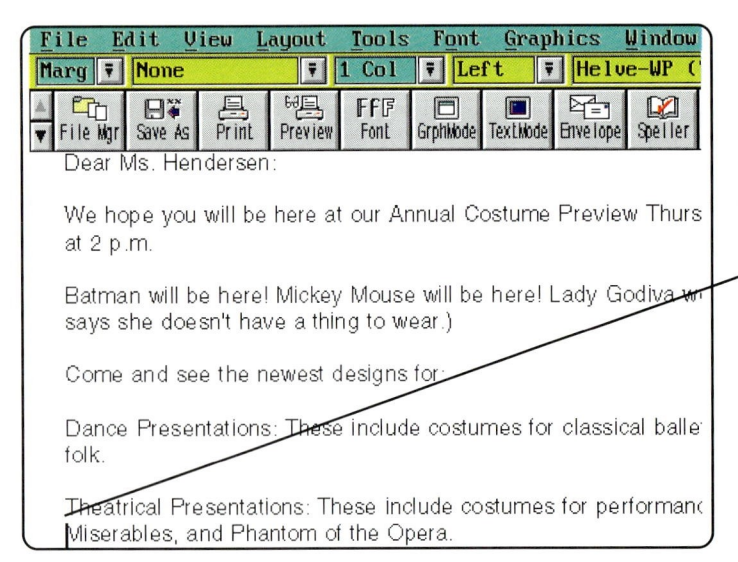

1. Click to the **left of "Miserables"** in the "Theatrical Presentations" paragraph.

CHAPTER 6: EDITING A DOCUMENT

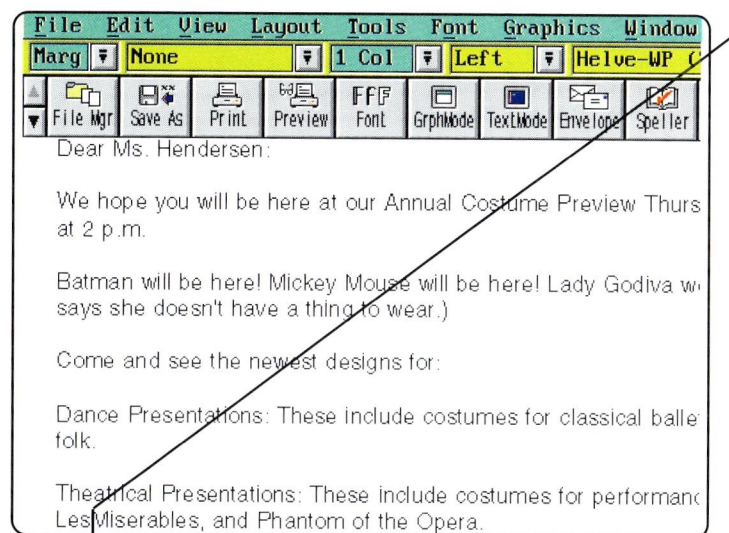

2. Press the **Backspace key**. This will bring "Les" down to the second line with "Miserables." There will be no space between the words.

3. Press the **Home key** then **press** the **Spacebar** (Home, Spacebar). WordPerfect will now consider "Les Miserables" as a single word. It will not be separated by any future text wrapping.

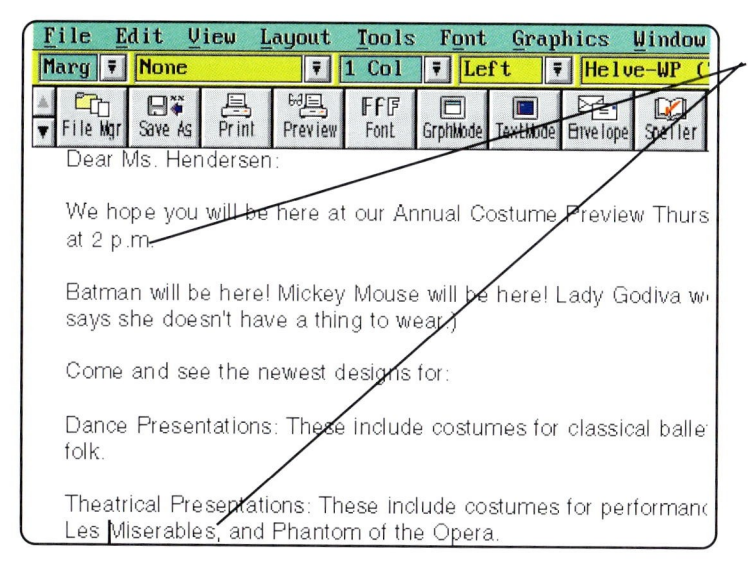

Your screen will look like this.

WORDPERFECT 6 FOR DOS: THE VISUAL LEARNING GUIDE

Inserting a Hard Return

In this example, you will not use the Home Space. Instead you will use a hard return to change the spacing in the very last line of the letter.

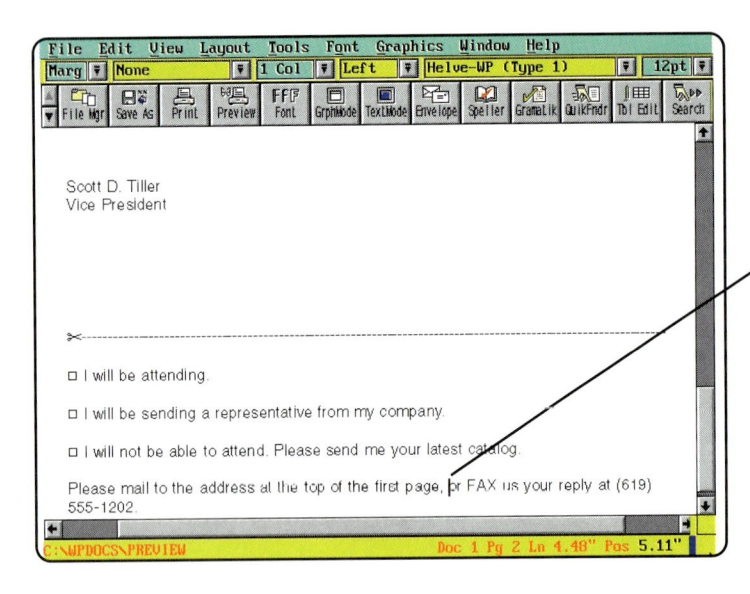

1. Press the **Home key twice** then **press** the **↓ key** (Home, Home, ↓). This will take you to the end of the document.

2. Click to the **left of "or"** in the last line of the letter.

3. Press Enter. This will move the cursor and the following text to the next line. These will now be two separate paragraphs.

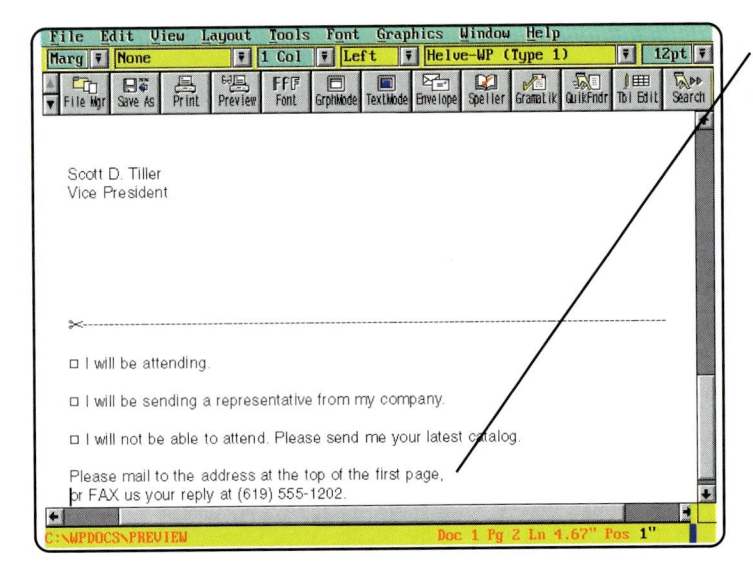

Your screen will look like this.

CHAPTER 6: EDITING A DOCUMENT

USING THE REPLACE COMMAND

In this example you will replace "sen" at the end of "Hendersen" with "son." You can replace each "sen" individually or you can use the Replace command to find and replace each occurrence automatically. You will start at the top of the file since the Replace command begins at the cursor and goes only to the end of the file.

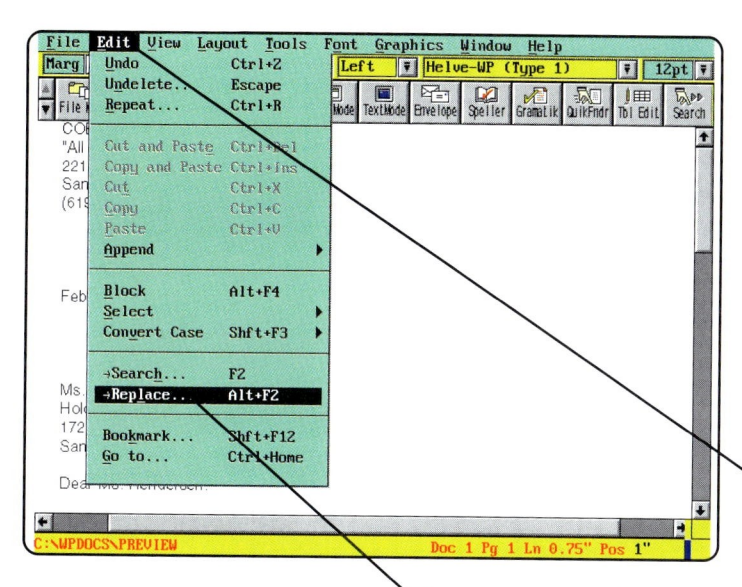

1. Press the **Home key twice**, then **press** the **↑ key** (Home, Home, ↑) to go to the beginning of your file.

2. Click on **Edit** in the menu bar. A pull-down menu will appear.

3. Click on **Replace**. The Replace dialog box will appear. If you have been following along with these chapters, "latest" will show in the Search For text box.

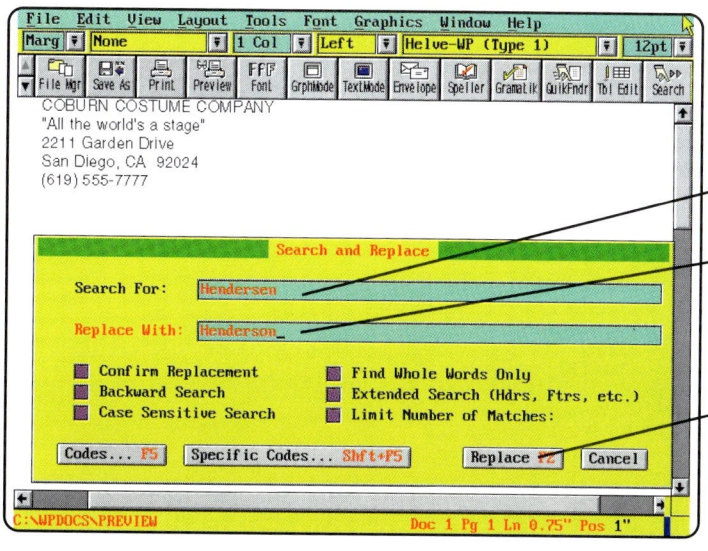

4. Type Hendersen.

5. Click on the **Replace With text box** and **type Henderson**.

6. Click on **Replace**. The Search and Replace Complete dialog box will appear.

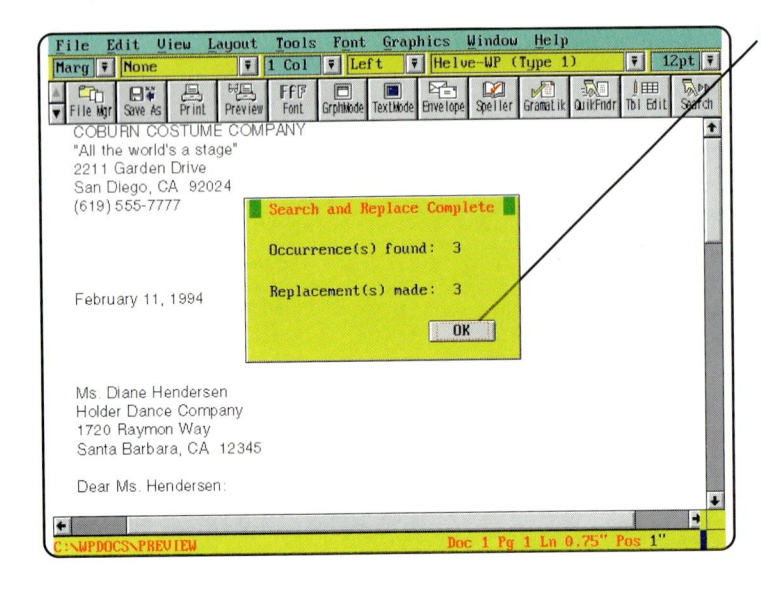

WORDPERFECT 6 FOR DOS: THE VISUAL LEARNING GUIDE

7. Click on **OK**.

The letter will show on your screen with the changes made. The cursor will be flashing at the bottom of your screen after the last occurrence of "Henderson."

A NOTE ABOUT SCROLLING

When you click on the **up arrow** or the **down arrow** on the scroll bar, it moves the cursor up or down one line at a time from wherever it is located.

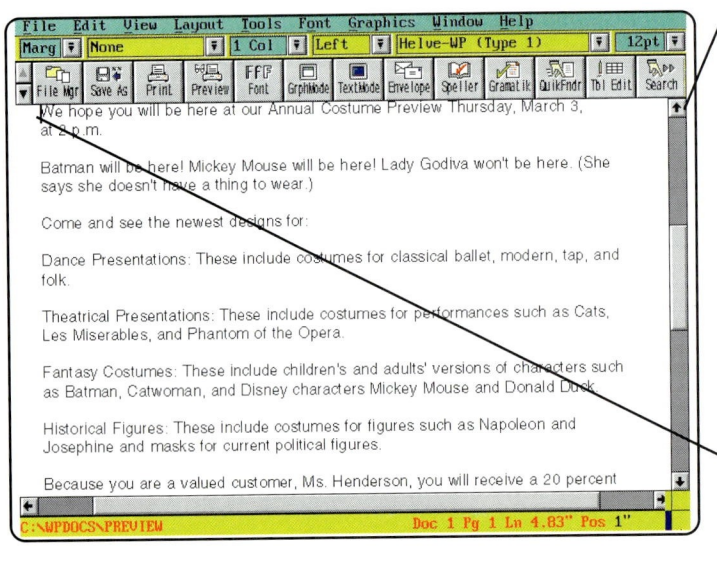

1. Click twice on the **up arrow** and watch the cursor move up two lines. At this rate, it will take an awful lot of clicks to move the cursor to the top of the screen. It's much faster to *place* the cursor at the top (or bottom) of the screen and then use the scroll arrow to move the screen up (or down).

2. Click to the **left of the first word** on your screen to place the cursor.

3. Click on the **up arrow** on the scroll bar until you can see the salutation and the first few paragraphs of the letter.

CHAPTER 6: EDITING A DOCUMENT

DRAG-AND-DROP MOVING

WordPerfect 6 has a wonderful new feature that lets you move text with your mouse. In this example you will move the first sentence.

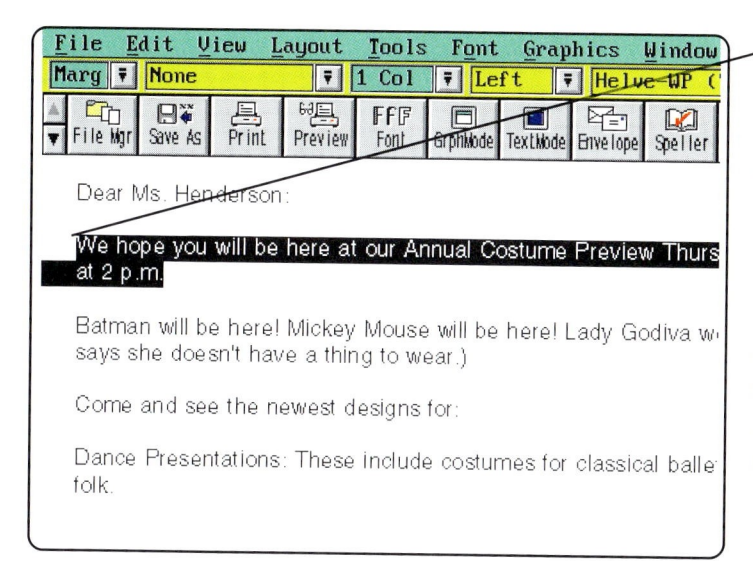

1. Click to the **left of "We hope."**

2. Press and hold the mouse button as you **drag** the highlight bar to the **end of the sentence**. (If the highlight extends too far, simply continue to press and hold the mouse as you drag the highlight bar backwards.)

3. Place the mouse pointer **anywhere** on the highlighted text.

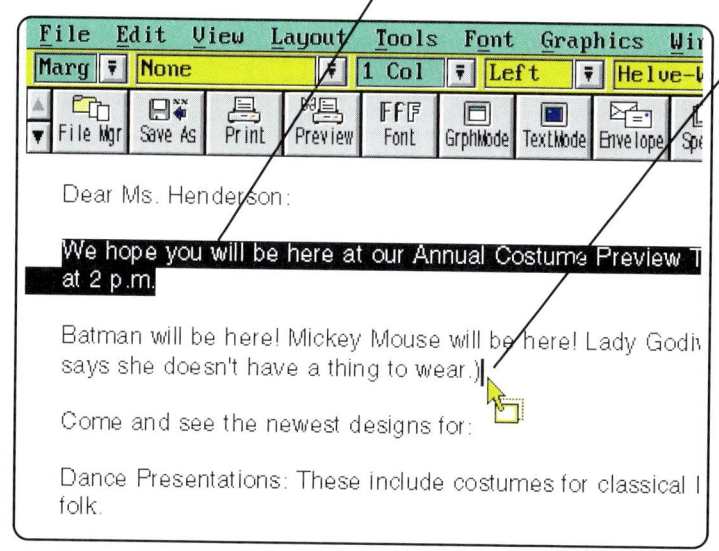

4. Press and hold the mouse button and **drag** the pointer down to the **end of the next paragraph**. You will see two squares being dragged by the arrow.

5. Release the mouse button. The highlighted paragraph will move to that spot.

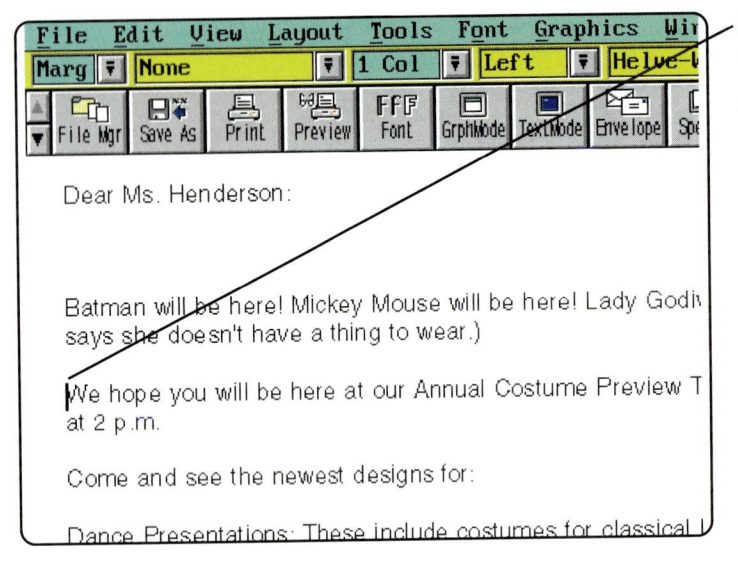

WORDPERFECT 6 FOR DOS: THE VISUAL LEARNING GUIDE

6. **Press Enter twice** to move the "We hope" sentence to a new paragraph.

Notice there are now extra lines at the beginning of the letter.

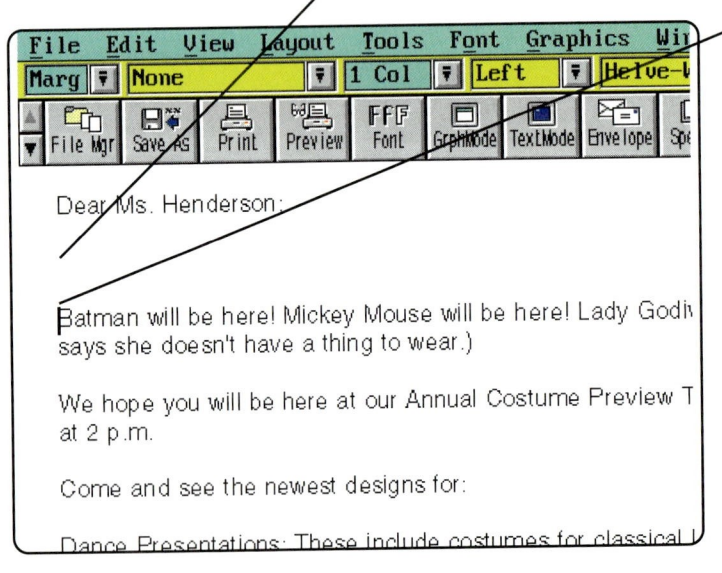

7. **Click** at the **beginning of the "Batman" sentence** to set the cursor in place.

8. **Press Backspace twice**. The sentence will be moved up two lines.

CHAPTER 6: EDITING A DOCUMENT

INSERTING A PAGE BREAK

WordPerfect does not necessarily insert an automatic page break in a place that makes sense within the context of the document. Fortunately, it's easy to change the position of the page break.

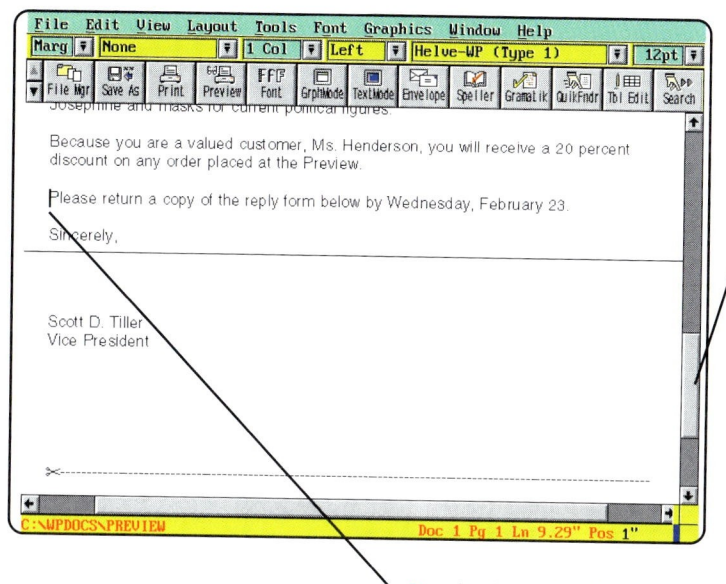

1. Click on and hold the **scroll button** and **drag** it approximately **three-fourths of the way down the scroll bar** so that it looks like the one in this example. You will be able to see the automatic page break.

2. Click to the **left of the "Please return" sentence**.

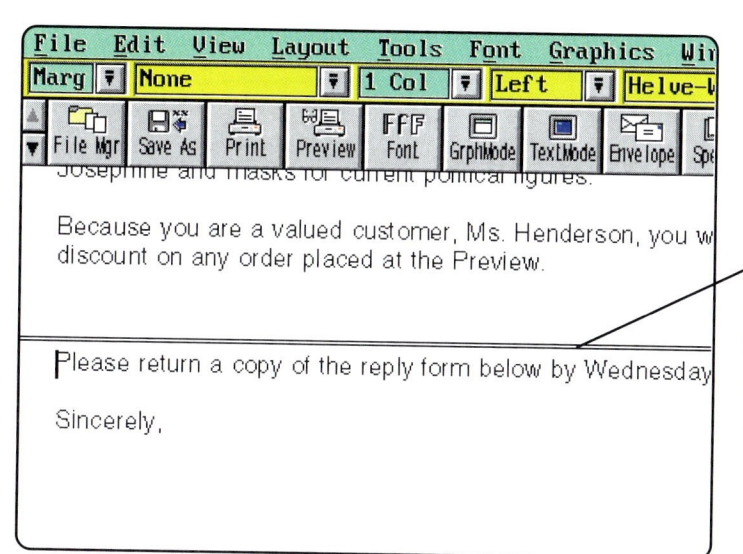

3. Press and hold the **Ctrl key** as you **press Enter** (Ctrl + Enter). A page break will be inserted into the text at the cursor.

A double line will appear showing the position of the inserted page break. The single line that indicated the automatic page break will disappear.

WORDPERFECT 6 FOR DOS: THE VISUAL LEARNING GUIDE

DELETING A PAGE BREAK

It's very easy to delete a page break that you have inserted into the document.

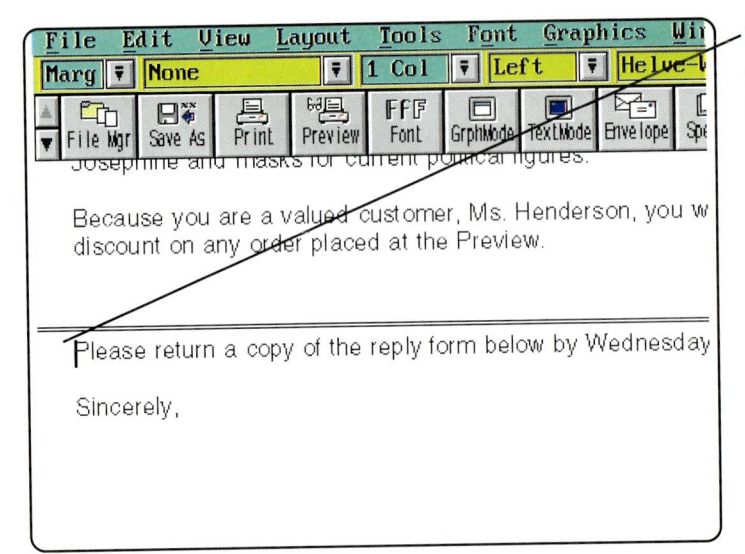

1. Click to the **left of the first line below the page break** if your cursor is not already there.

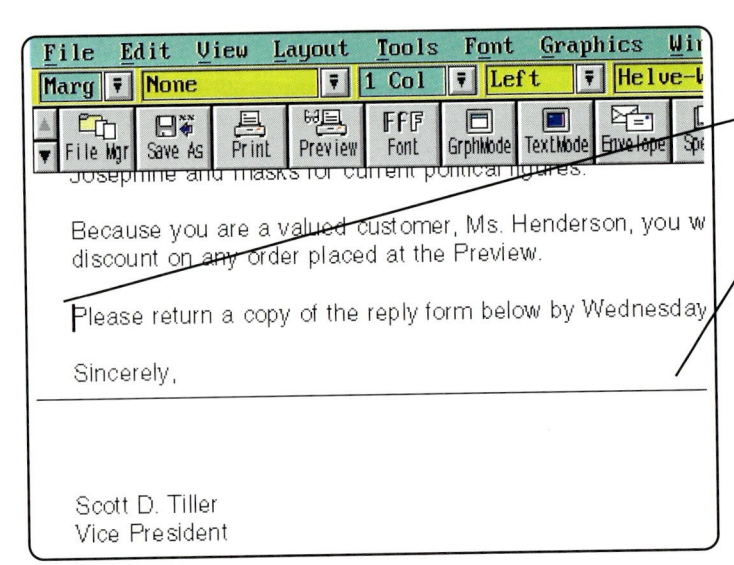

2. Press the **Backspace key**.

The text will be moved up one line and the page break will disappear.

The single line indicating the automatic page break will reappear.

3. Press and hold the **Ctrl key** and **press Enter** (Ctrl + Enter) to insert the page break again.

CHAPTER 6: EDITING A DOCUMENT

DRAG-AND-DROP COPYING

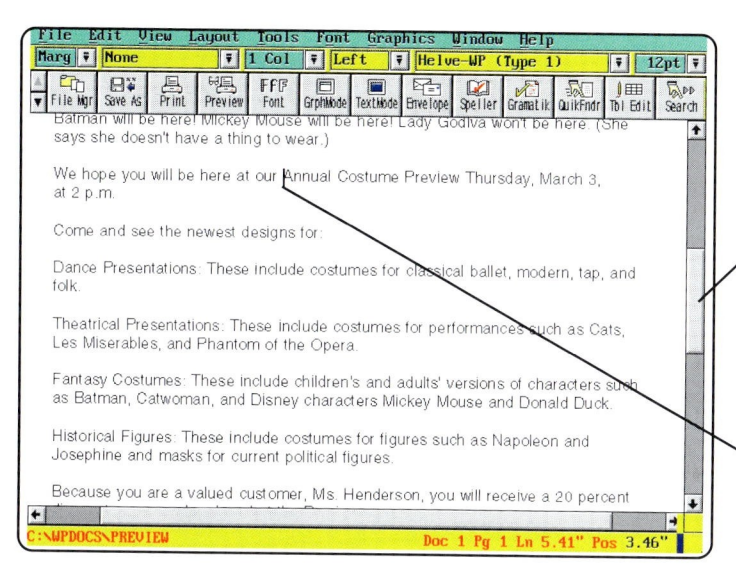

In this example you will copy the phrase "Annual Costume Preview Thursday, March 3" from page 1 to page 2.

1. Click on and hold the **scroll button** and **drag** it up to the **middle of the scroll bar**.

2. Click to the **left of** "**Annual**" in the "We hope" sentence.

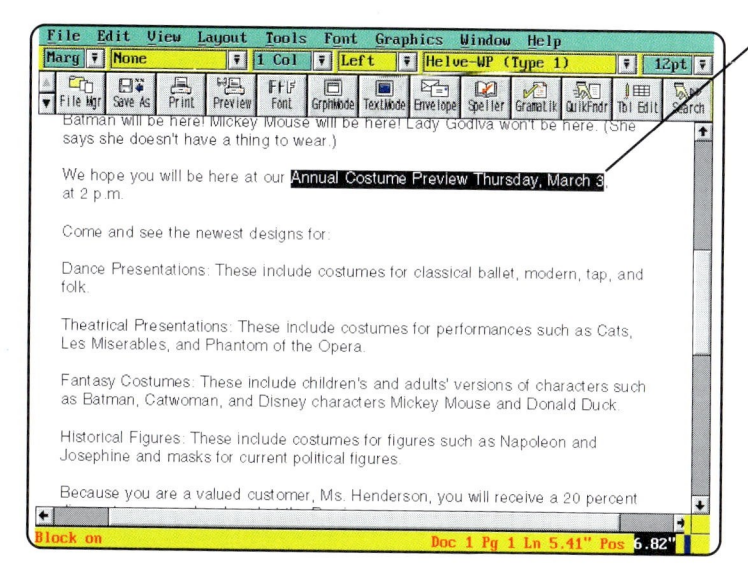

3. Press and hold the mouse button as you **drag** the highlight bar **across** to "**March 3.**" Do not highlight the comma after the "3."

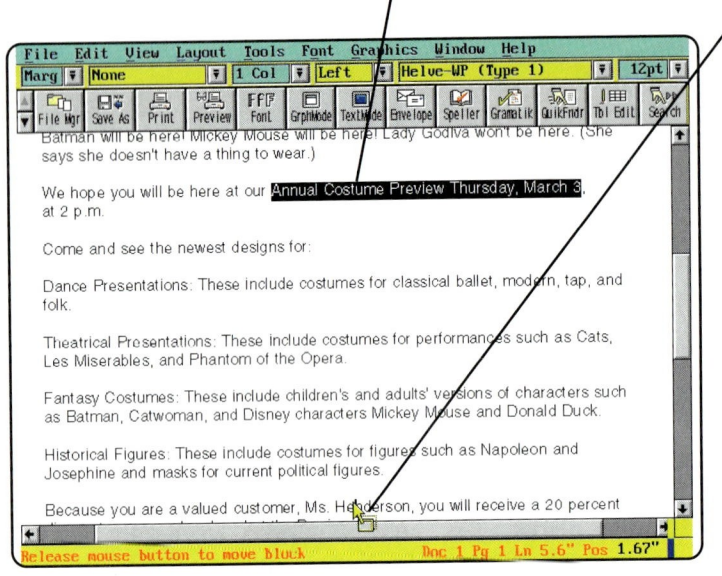

WORDPERFECT 6 FOR DOS: THE VISUAL LEARNING GUIDE

4. Place the mouse **anywhere** on the highlighted text.

5. Press and hold the mouse button as you **drag** the cursor **down the page**. You will see the mouse arrow dragging two squares.

6. Continue to press and hold the mouse button as you **drag** the arrow down **into the bottom of your screen**. Suddenly your screen will start to scroll up. Continue to drag the arrow down until you can see the end of the letter.

7. Place the **cursor and mouse pointer** on the blank line **after the scissors**.

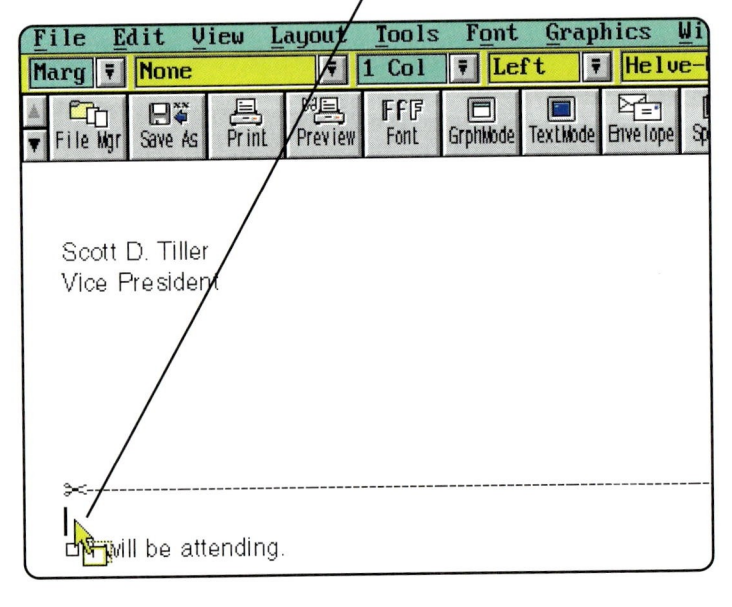

8. Press and hold the **Ctrl key**. Then **release** the mouse button. (Pressing the Ctrl key copies the highlighted text to the cursor spot instead of simply moving it as you did in drag-and-drop moving earlier in the chapter.)

CHAPTER 6: EDITING A DOCUMENT

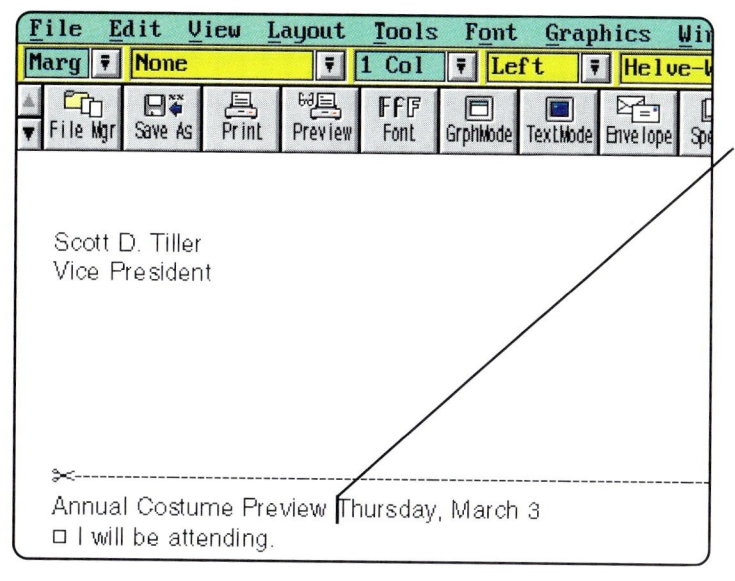

Your screen will look like the example to the left.

9. Click to the **left of "Thursday"** to place the cursor.

10. Press Enter to move the cursor and the following text to the next line.

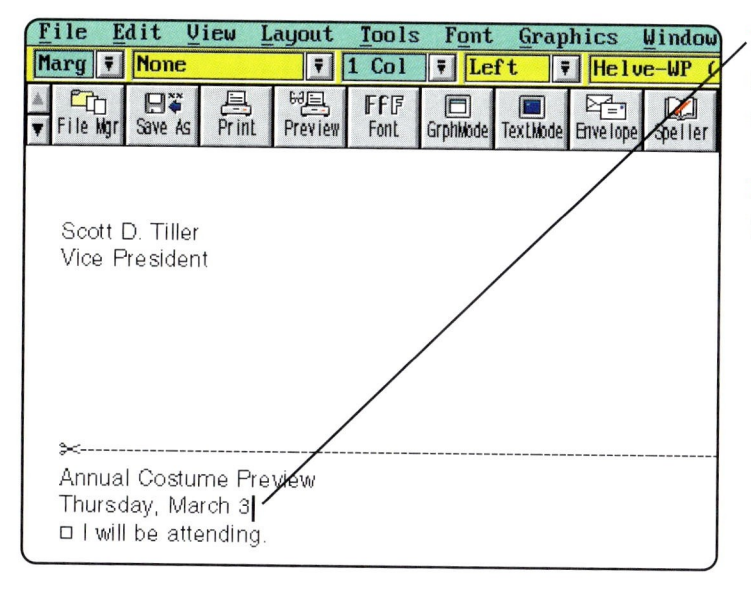

11. Click to the **right of the number "3"** to place the cursor.

12. Press Enter twice to insert two blank lines.

COPYING AND PASTING TEXT

In this three-part example you will use the Copy and Paste functions on the Edit menu to copy the name and address on the first page and place it on the return form on the second page.

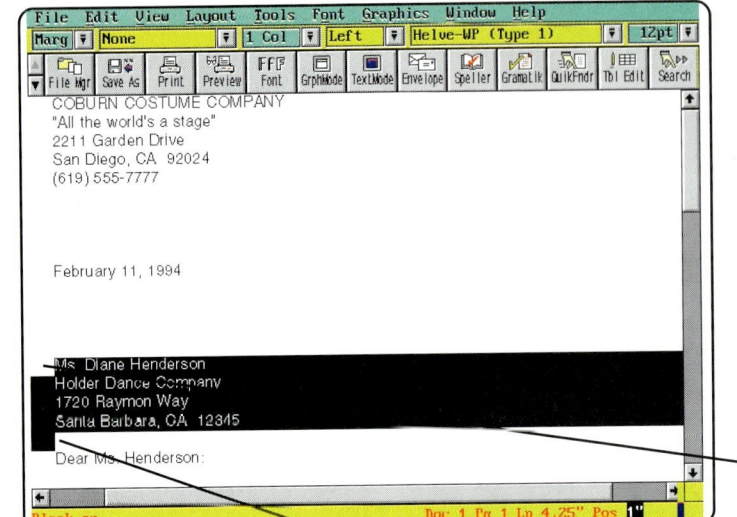

Copying the Text

1. Press Home twice then **press** the ↑ **key** (Home, Home, ↑) to go to the top of the file.

2. Click to the **left of "Ms. Diane Henderson."**

3. Press and hold the mouse button as you **drag** the highlight bar down to the blank line **after the address**.

4. Click on **Edit** in the menu bar. A pull-down menu will appear.

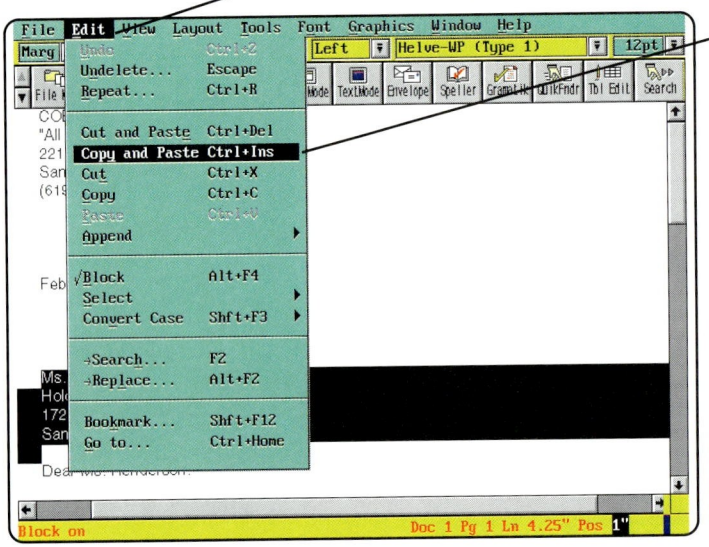

5. Click on **Copy and Paste**. The pull-down menu will disappear and the highlighting will disappear from the text. The highlighted text has been copied to a *buffer*, a temporary storage area in your computer's memory.

CHAPTER 6: EDITING A DOCUMENT

Using the Go To Command

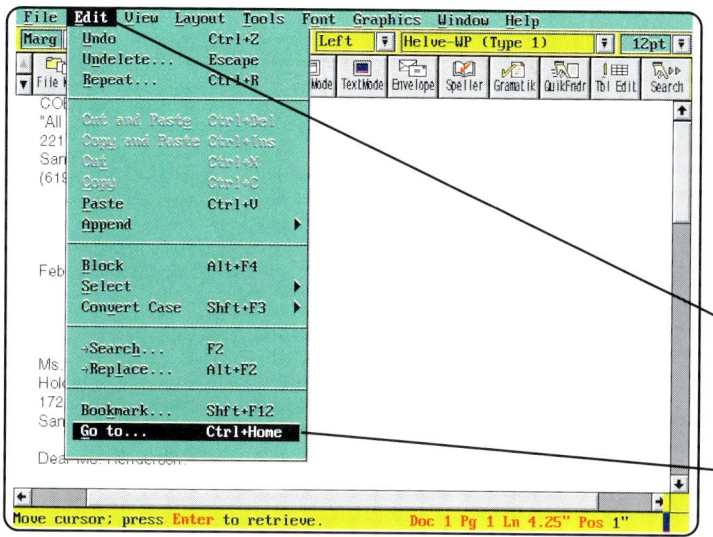

Using the Go To command is a quick way to move around in multipage documents. In this example you will use it to go to the top of page 2 where you will paste the copied text.

1. Click on **Edit** in the menu bar. A pull-down menu will appear.

2. Click on **Go To**. The Go To dialog box will appear.

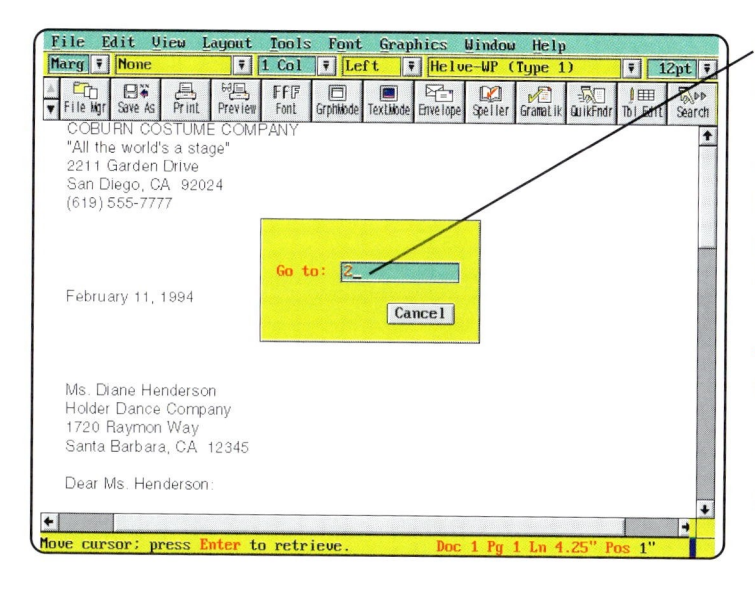

3. Type the number **2**. (Although there is no cursor flashing in the box, don't click on the box or the dialog box will disappear. Every program is entitled to its little idiosyncrasies . . .)

4. Press Enter. (There is no OK button here.)

Your cursor will go to the top of page 2.

Pasting the Text

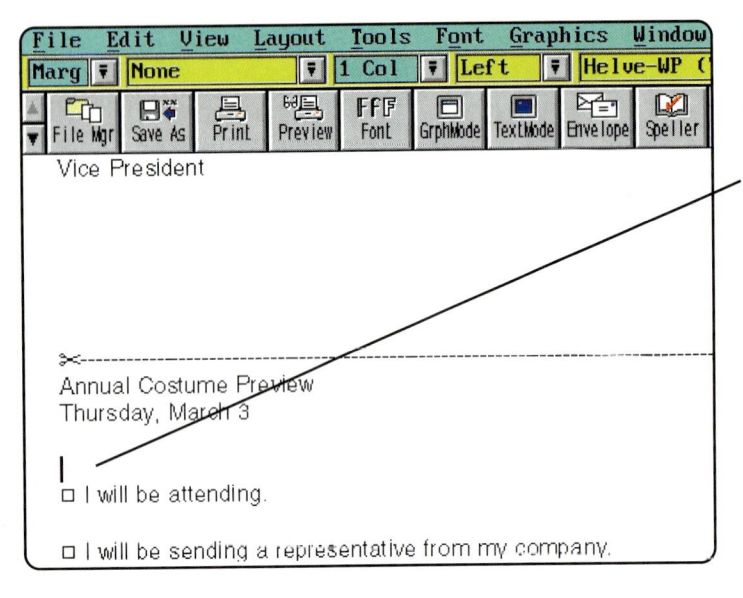

1. Click on and hold the **scroll button** and **drag** it to the **bottom of the scroll bar**.

2. Click on the blank line **above "I will be attending."**

3. Press Enter. The text you copied will be pasted into the document at the cursor.

You can also click on Copy in the Edit pull-down menu to copy text. Then click on Paste in the pull-down menu when you want to paste the text. However, WordPerfect provides the Copy and Paste shortcut combination.

4. Save your work. **Press and hold Ctrl** as you **press** the **F12 key** (Ctrl + F12). Some keyboards label it the SF12 key.

You will use this edited letter in Part II, "Formatting a Document."

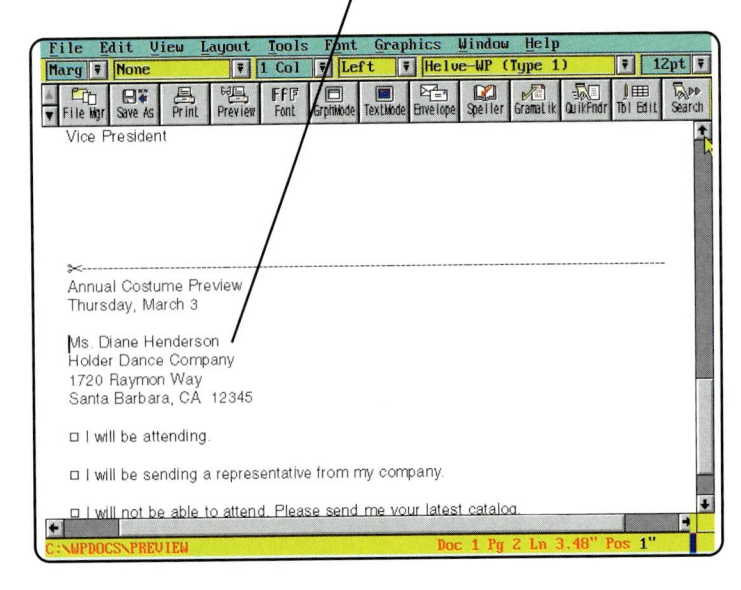

File Manager

Part II Formatting a Document

Chapter 7: Customizing Text	Page 72
Chapter 8: Setting Tabs	Page 88
Chapter 9: Adding a Header and a Page Number	Page 106

Customizing Text

You will love how easy it is to customize the look of your text in WordPerfect 6. With just a few clicks of your mouse button you can center text, change the type size, or make type bold or underlined. You can also create a bulleted list. In addition, you can add special borders around sections of your text, then add shading inside the border to create an exciting visual effect. In this chapter you will do the following:

- ❖ Change type size
- ❖ Make text bold and underlined
- ❖ Center text
- ❖ Add a border around text and add shading inside the border
- ❖ Create a bulleted list

CHANGING TYPE SIZE

In this section you will increase the size of the type in the first line of the letter you created in Part I. If you don't already have PREVIEW open, open it now.

1. Press the **Home key twice** and then **press** the **↑ key** (Home, Home, ↑) to go to the top of the file if you are not already there.

2. Click in the left margin beside "COBURN COSTUME COMPANY."

3. Press and hold the mouse button as you **drag** the highlight bar **across** "**COBURN COSTUME COMPANY.**"

4. Release the mouse button.

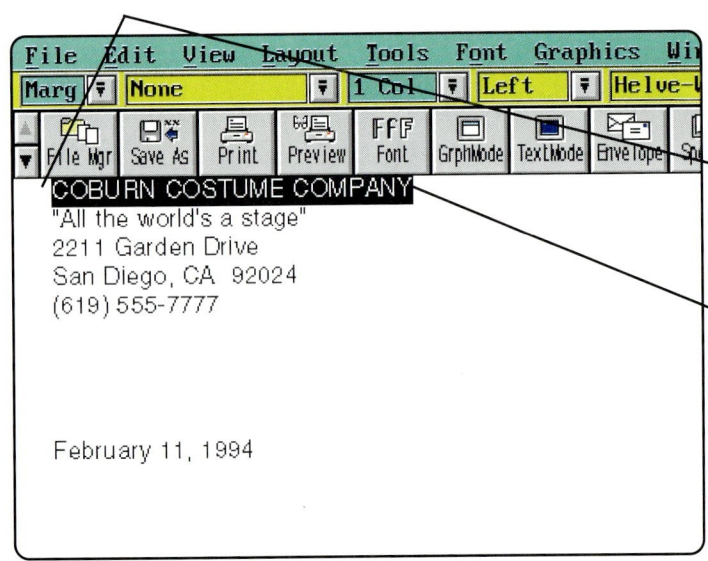

CHAPTER 7: CUSTOMIZING TEXT

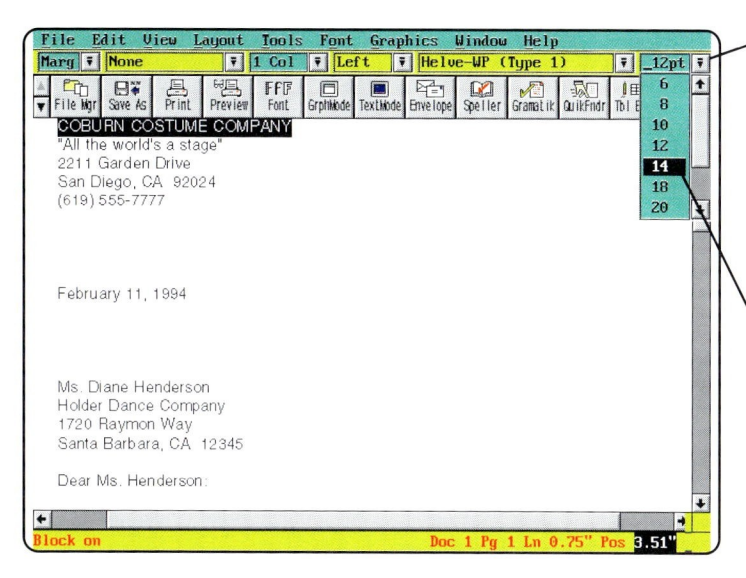

5. Click on the **down arrow** to the **right of 12pt** in the ribbon. A Please Wait message will flash and a drop-down list of point sizes will appear.

6. Click twice on **14**. The drop-down list will disappear and "COBURN COSTUME COMPANY" will change from a 12-point size to a 14-point size.

MAKING TEXT BOLD

In this section you will make the type, "COBURN COSTUME COMPANY," boldface. You must first highlight the text you want to change.

1. Click in the left margin beside **"COBURN COSTUME COMPANY."**

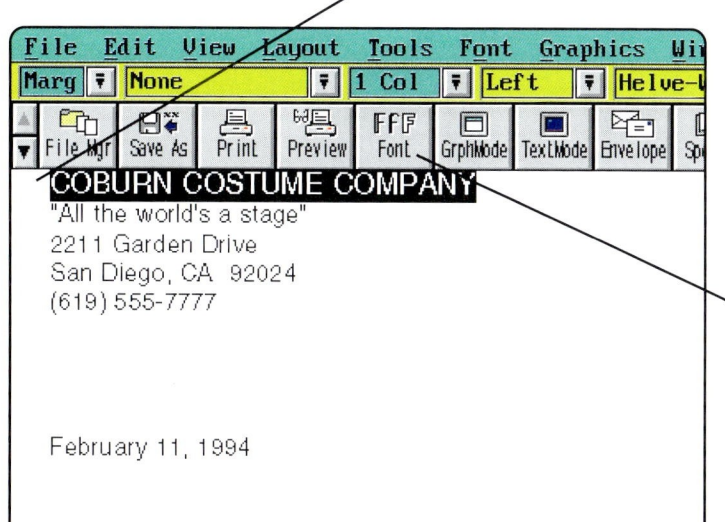

2. Press and hold the mouse button as you **drag** the highlight bar **across "COBURN COSTUME COMPANY."**

3. Click on the **Font button** in the button bar. The Font dialog box will appear.

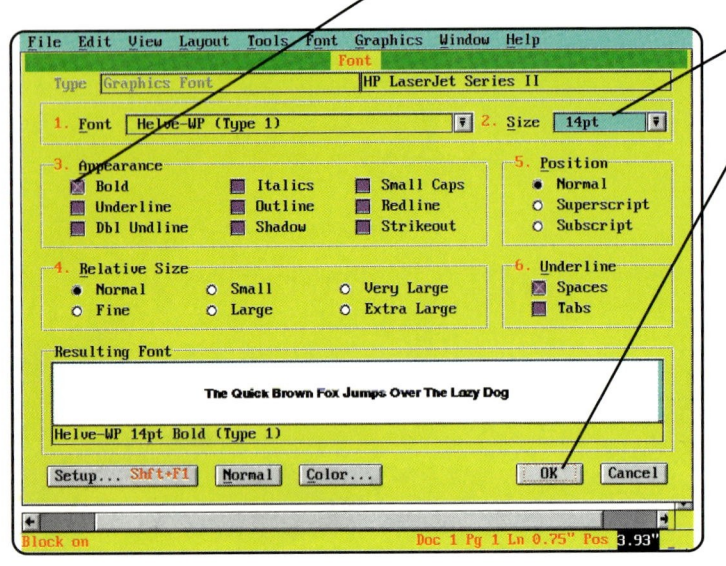

WORDPERFECT 6 FOR DOS: THE VISUAL LEARNING GUIDE

4. Click on **Bold**.

Notice you can change point size in this dialog box too.

5. Click on **OK**. The Font dialog box will disappear and "COBURN COSTUME COMPANY" will appear in bold type.

UNDERLINING TEXT

In this section you will underline text.

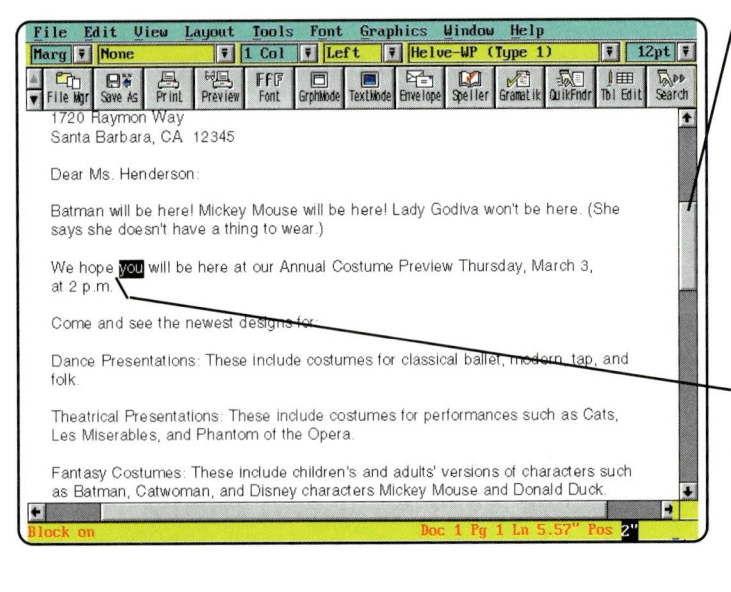

1. Click and drag the scroll button **one-third down the scroll bar**. It will look like the one in this example. (If you scrolled too far up or down, click and drag the scroll button until you can see the same text as in the example to the left.)

2. Click to the **left of "you."**

3. Press and hold the mouse button as you **drag** the highlight bar **across "you."**

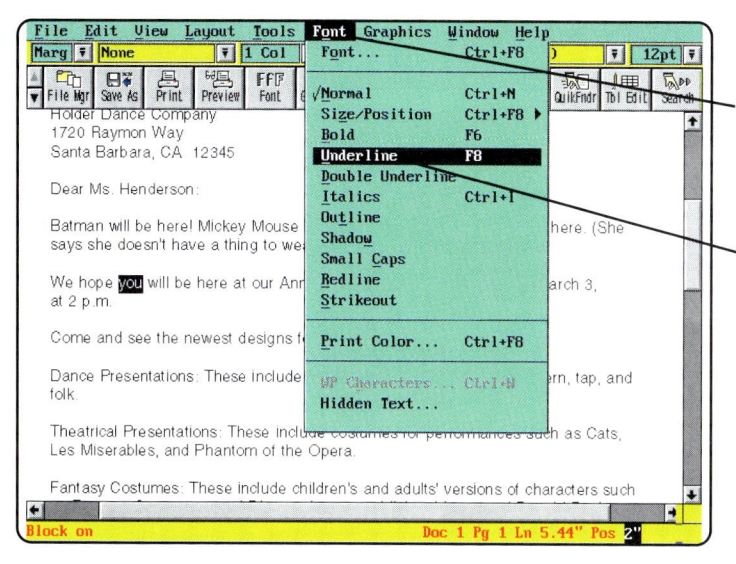

CHAPTER 7: CUSTOMIZING TEXT

4. Click on **Font** in the menu bar. A pull-down menu will appear.

5. Click on **Underline**. The pull-down menu will disappear and the word "you" will be underlined.

CENTERING TEXT

In this section you will center text using two different methods. Both methods require you to highlight the lines you want to center and then apply a command, so that you can center all lines at the same time.

Using the Ribbon

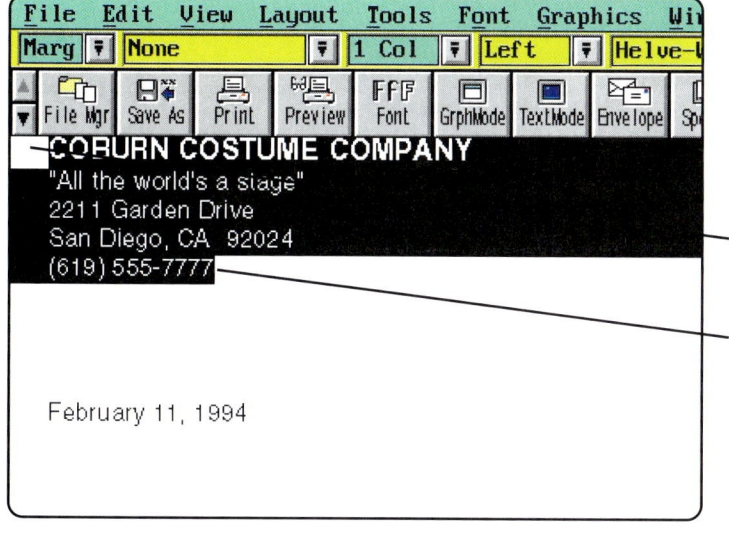

1. Press the **Home key twice** then **press** ↑ (Home, Home, ↑) This will take you to the beginning of PREVIEW.

2. Click to the **left of** "COBURN."

3. Press and hold the mouse button and **drag** the highlight bar to the **end of** "(619) 555-7777."

4. Release the mouse button.

WORDPERFECT 6 FOR DOS: THE VISUAL LEARNING GUIDE

5. **Click** on the **down arrow beside Left** in the ribbon. A pull-down list will appear.

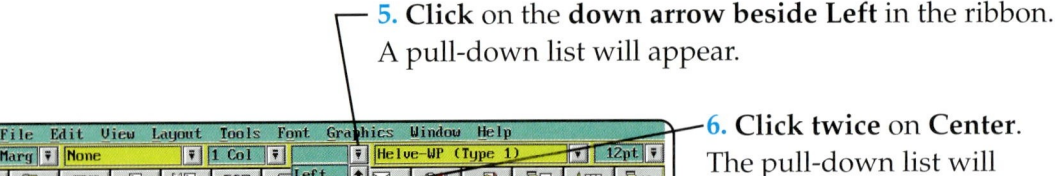

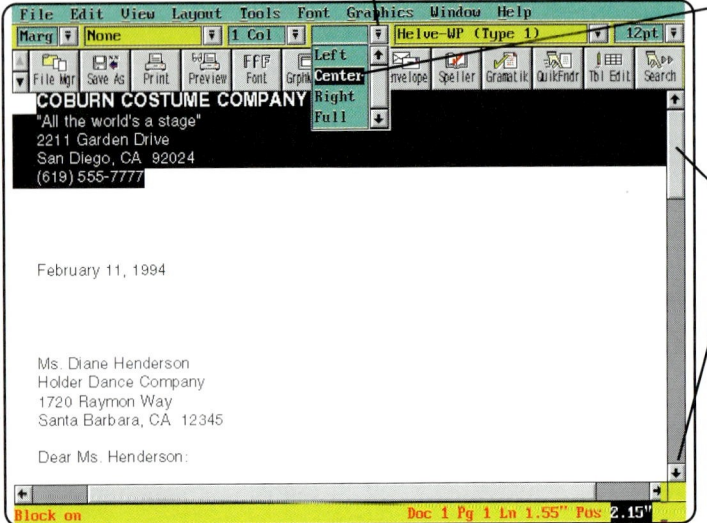

6. **Click twice** on **Center**. The pull-down list will disappear and the five lines of text will be centered.

7. **Click** on the **scroll button** in the scroll bar.

8. **Press and hold** the mouse button and **drag** the **scroll button** to the **bottom of the scroll bar**. Your document screen will show the end of your file.

9. **Click** to the **left of "Annual Costume Preview."**

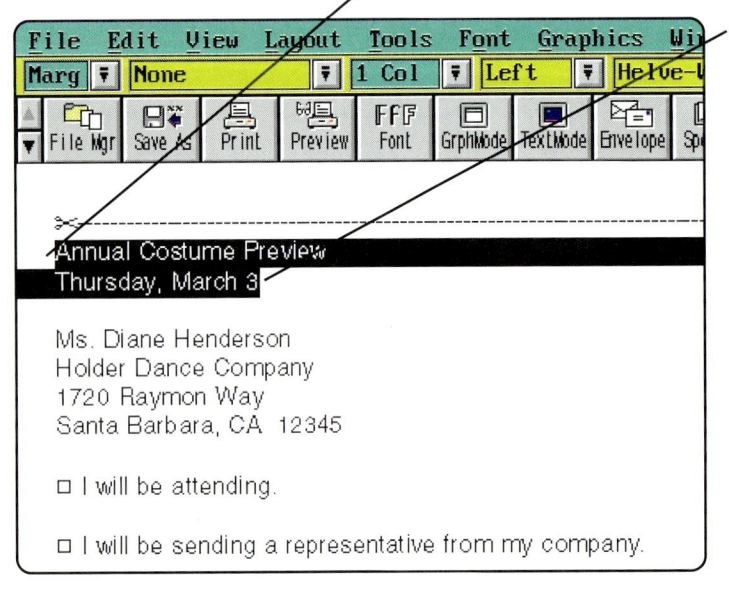

10. **Press and hold** the mouse button and **drag** the cursor to the **end of "March 3."**

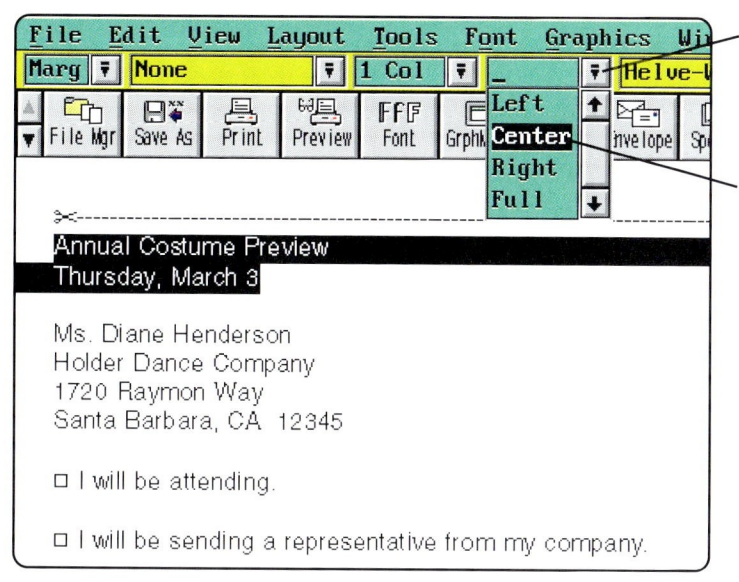

CHAPTER 7: CUSTOMIZING TEXT

11. Click on the **down arrow beside Left** in the ribbon. A pull-down list will appear.

12. Click twice on **Center**. The pull-down list will disappear and the two lines of text will be centered.

Using the Layout Menu

1. Click to the **left of "Please mail"** at the bottom of the letter.

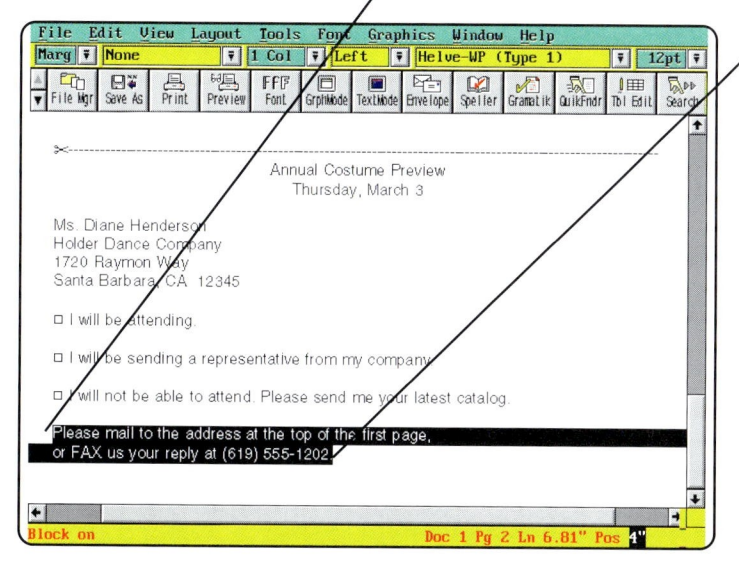

2. Press and hold the mouse button and **drag** the highlight bar to the **end of "(619) 555-1202."**

WORDPERFECT 6 FOR DOS: THE VISUAL LEARNING GUIDE

3. **Click** on **Layout** in the menu bar. A pull-down menu will appear.

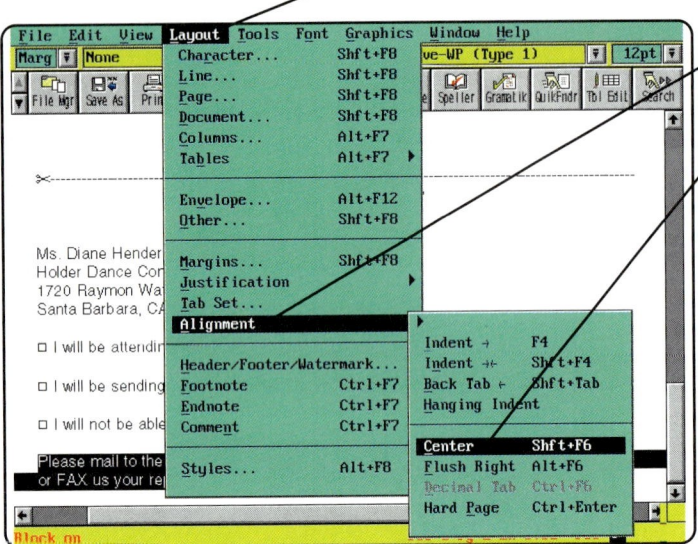

4. **Click** on **Alignment**. A second menu will appear.

5. **Click** on **Center**. The menus will disappear and your document screen will appear with the previously highlighted text centered.

UNDOING TEXT ALIGNMENT

In this example you will change text that is center aligned to make it left aligned. Then you will undo the change.

1. **Click** to the **left of "Please mail"** at the bottom of the letter.

2. **Press and hold** the mouse button and **drag** the highlight bar to the **end of "(619) 555-1202."**

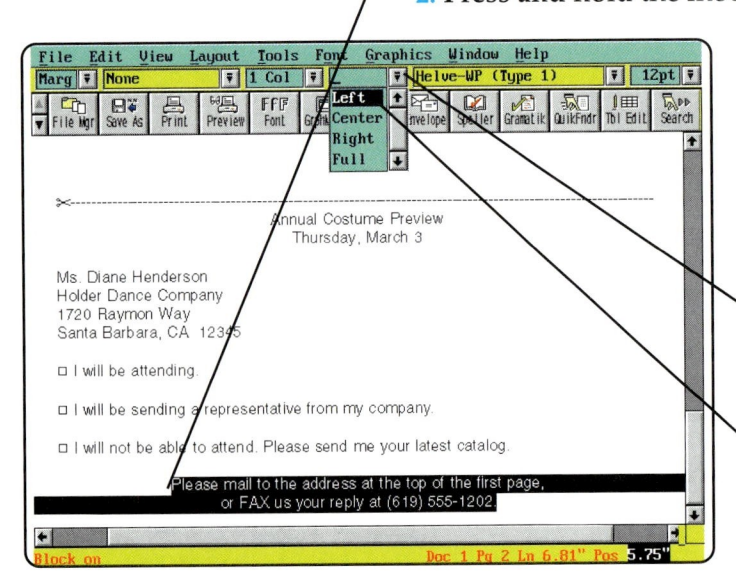

Notice that the alignment box in the ribbon says Center to show the alignment of the highlighted text.

3. **Click** on the **down arrow** beside Center in the ribbon. A pull-down list will appear.

4. **Click twice** on **Left**. The pull-down list will disappear and the two lines of text will be left aligned.

CHAPTER 7: CUSTOMIZING TEXT

In the PREVIEW example, we want the text centered instead of left aligned, so you need to undo your last move.

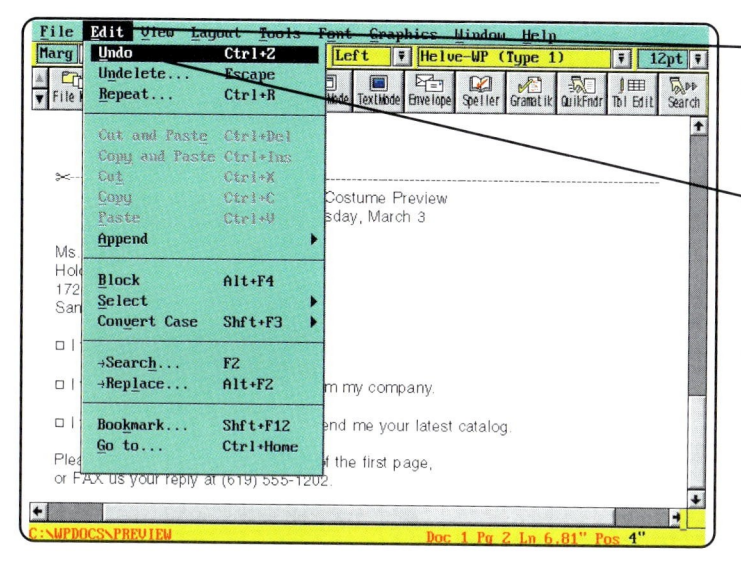

5. Click on **Edit** in the menu bar. A pull-down menu will appear.

6. Click on **Undo**. The pull-down menu will disappear and the document screen will appear with the text centered as it was in the previous section.

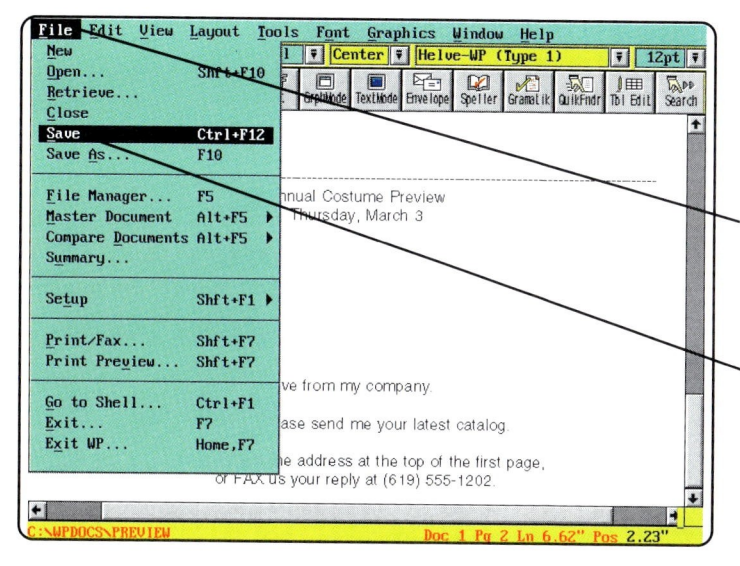

Now would be a good time to save your changes. You should get into the habit of saving while you work.

7. Click on **File** in the menu bar. A pull-down menu will appear.

8. Click on **Save**. The changes will be saved and you will be returned to the document screen.

WORDPERFECT 6 FOR DOS: THE VISUAL LEARNING GUIDE

ADDING A BORDER AND SHADING

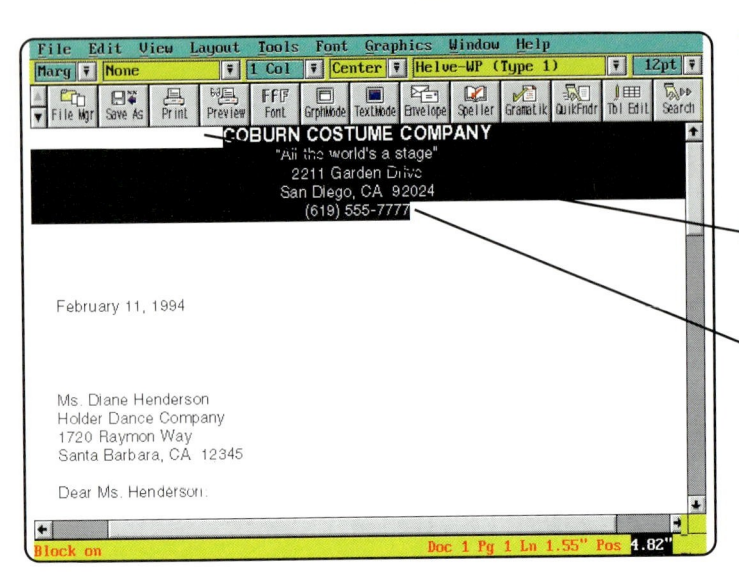

1. Press the **Home key twice**, then **press** ↑ (Home, Home, ↑) to go to the top of the file.

2. Click to the **left of** "**COBURN.**"

3. Press and hold the mouse button and **drag** the highlight bar to the **end of** "**(619) 555-7777.**"

4. Click on **Graphics** in the menu bar. A pull-down menu will appear.

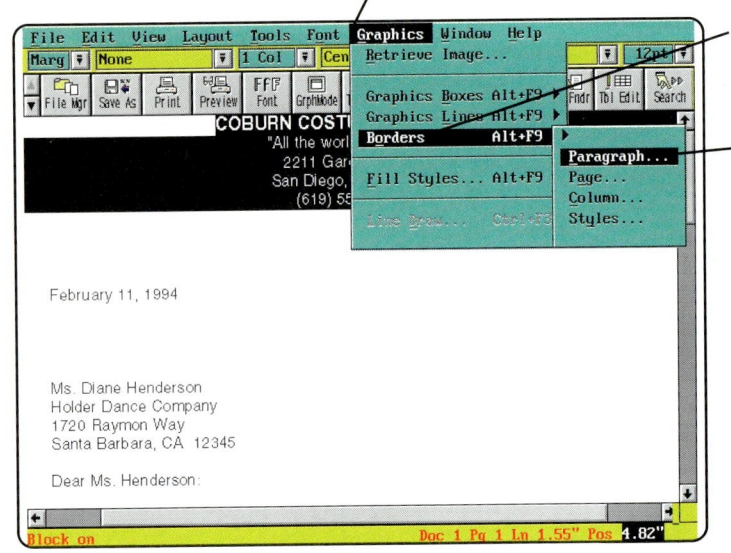

5. Click on **Borders**. A second menu will appear.

6. Click on **Paragraph**. The Create Paragraph Border dialog box will appear.

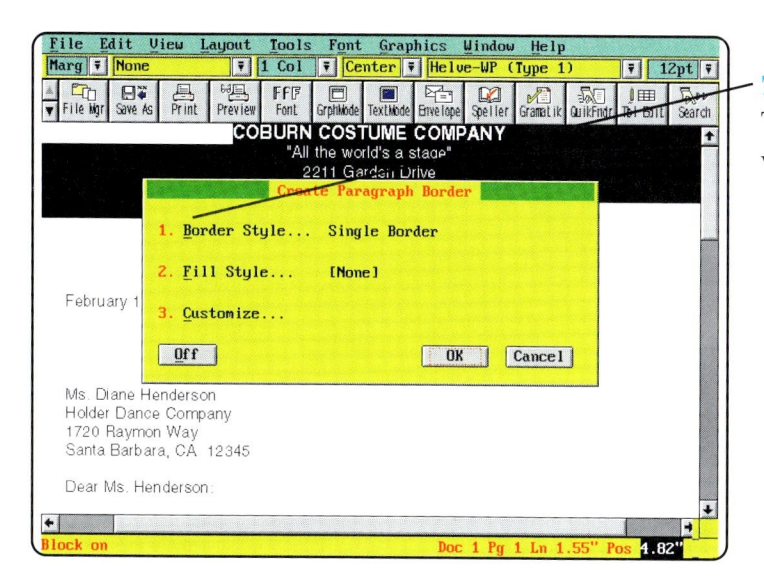

CHAPTER 7: CUSTOMIZING TEXT

7. Click on **Border Style**. The Border Styles dialog box will appear.

8. Click twice on **Double Border**. (Or click once on Double Border, then click on Select in the right-hand list.) The Border Styles dialog box will disappear and the Create Paragraph Border dialog box will appear again.

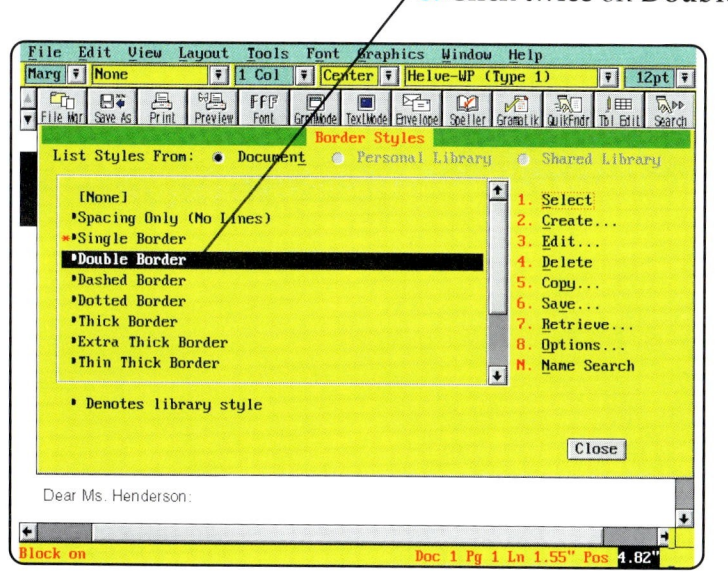

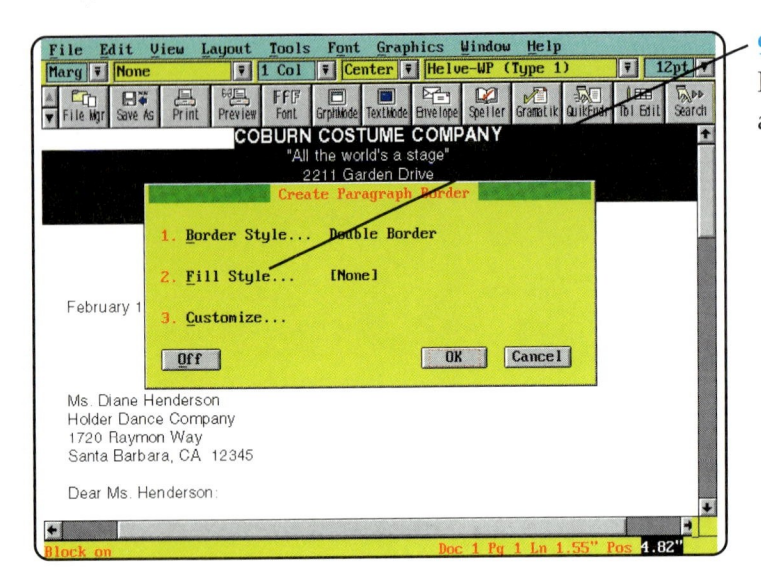

WORDPERFECT 6 FOR DOS: THE VISUAL LEARNING GUIDE

9. Click on **Fill Style**. The Fill Styles dialog box will appear.

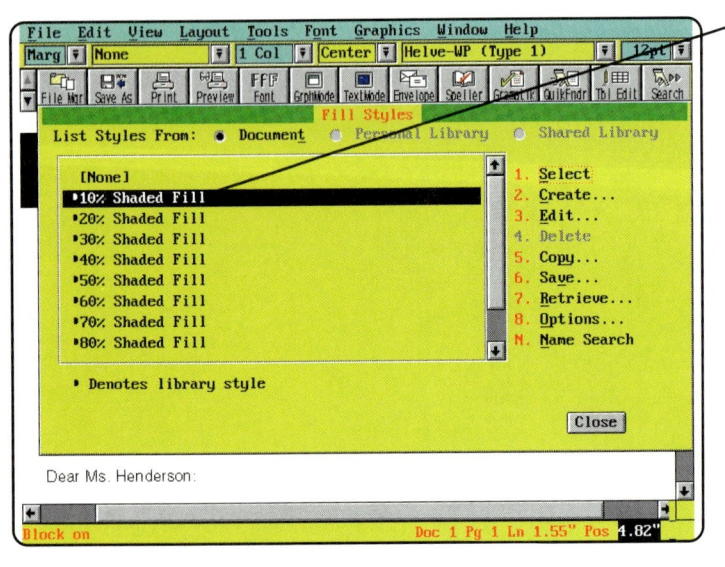

10. Click twice on **10% Shaded Fill**. The Fill Styles dialog box will disappear and the Create Paragraph Border dialog box will appear.

CHAPTER 7: CUSTOMIZING TEXT

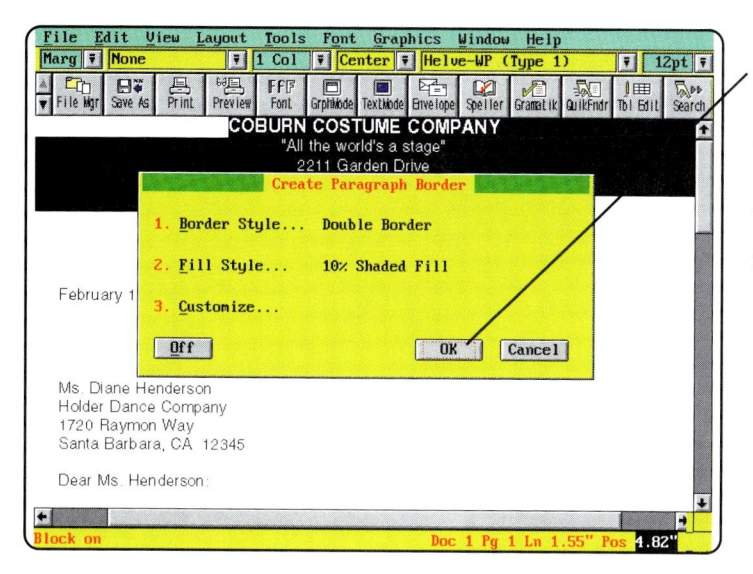

11. Click on **OK**. Your document screen will appear with the five lines of text surrounded by a double border and shaded in. Pretty neat!

DELETING BORDERS AND SHADING

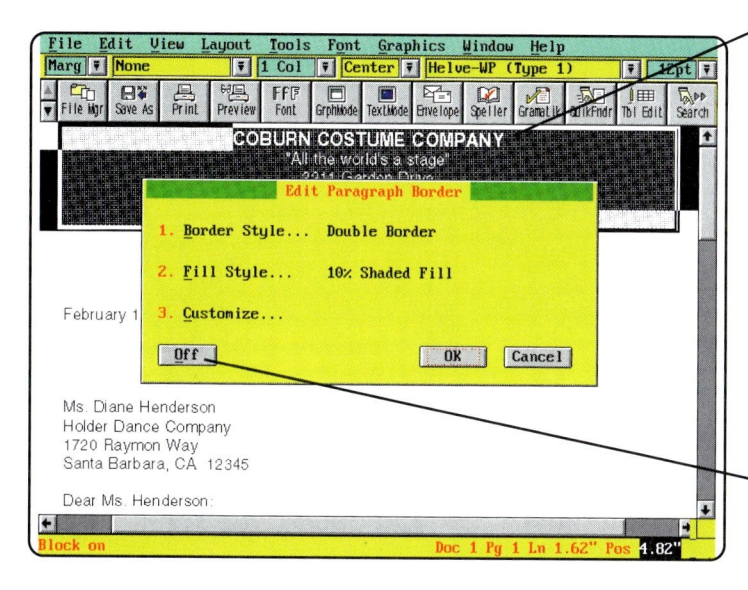

1. Highlight the **five lines** of text **in the shaded border**.

2. Repeat steps 4 through 6 of the previous section to return to the Create Paragraph Border dialog box. Notice that the Create Paragraph Border dialog box is now named **Edit Paragraph Border**.

3. Click on **Off**. The document screen will appear and the text will appear without the border and shading.

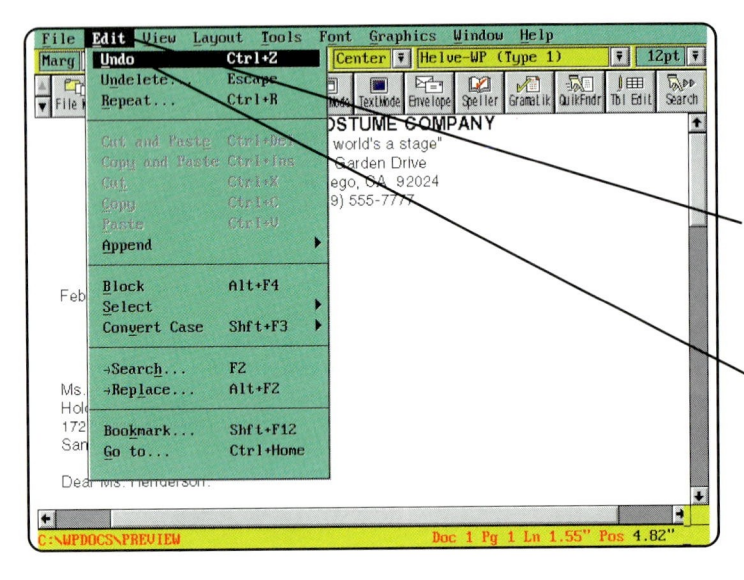

WORDPERFECT 6 FOR DOS: THE VISUAL LEARNING GUIDE

Since you went to the effort to create a shaded border for the company name, you surely don't want to delete it.

4. Click on **Edit** in the menu bar. A pull-down menu will appear.

5. Click on **Undo**. The document screen will appear with the border and shading you created in the previous section.

CREATING A BULLETED LIST

In this section you will create a bulleted list using the four paragraphs describing the costumes carried by the Coburn Costume Company.

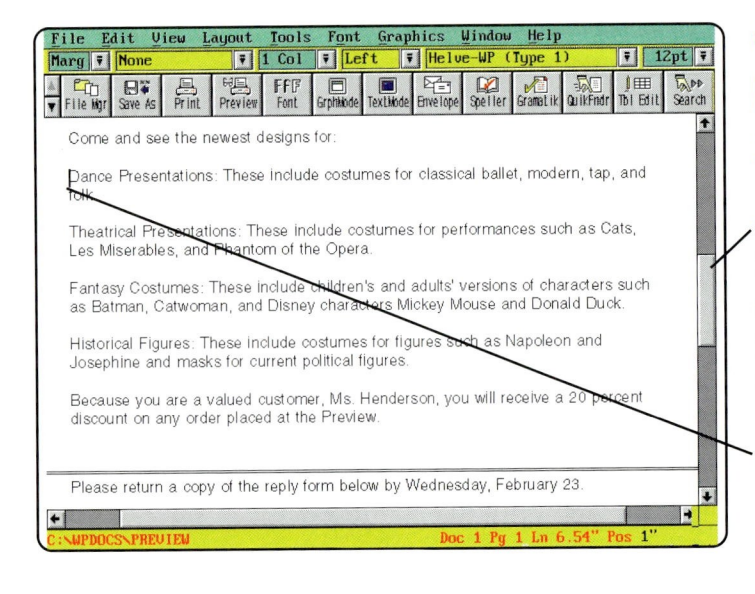

Creating a New Bullet Style

1. Drag the **scroll button halfway down** the scroll bar so you can see the paragraphs that describe the newest costume designs.

2. Click to the **left of "Dance Presentations."**

CHAPTER 7: CUSTOMIZING TEXT

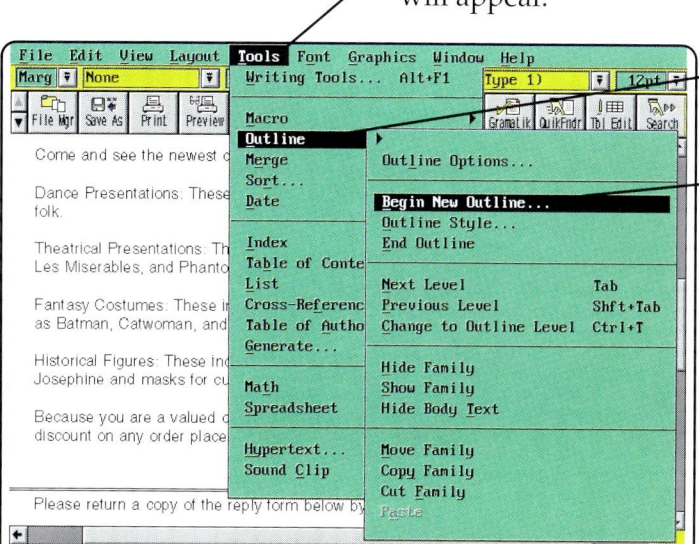

3. Click on **Tools** in the menu bar. A pull-down menu will appear.

4. Click on **Outline**. A second menu will appear.

5. Click on **Begin New Outline**. The Outline Style List dialog box will appear.

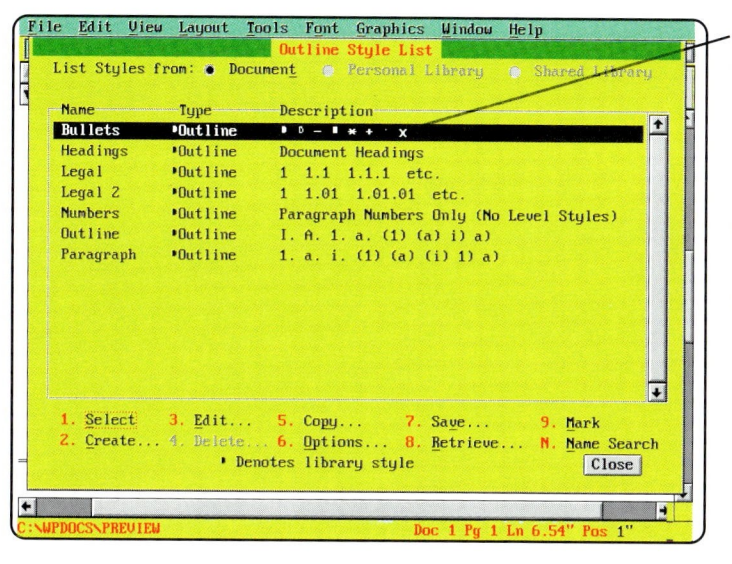

6. Click twice on **Bullets**. The document screen will appear. The "Dance Presentations" paragraph will be indented with a bullet at the left margin. There's a little too much space between the bullet and the paragraph. You will fix that in Chapter 8, "Setting Tabs."

Applying the Bullet Style to Other Paragraphs

1. **Click** to the **left of "Theatrical Presentations."**

2. **Click** on **Tools** in the menu bar. A pull-down menu will appear.

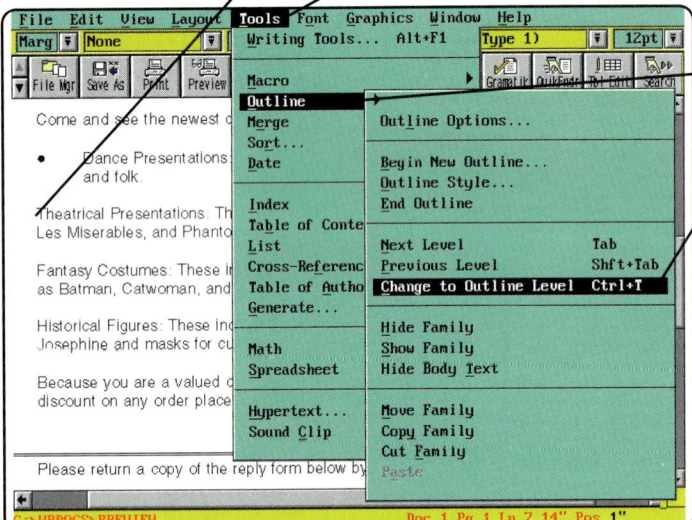

3. **Click** on **Outline**. A second menu will appear.

4. **Click** on **Change to Outline Level**. The document screen will appear with the paragraph bulleted and indented just like the previous one.

5. **Repeat steps 1 through 4** for the **next two paragraphs**.

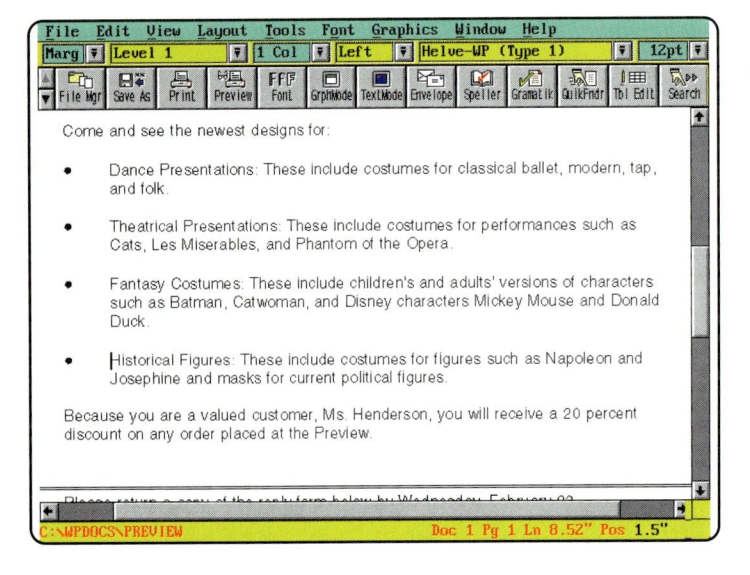

Your finished bulleted list will look like this.

CHAPTER 7: CUSTOMIZING TEXT

DELETING A BULLET

1. Click to the **left of "Historical Figures"** if your cursor is not already there.

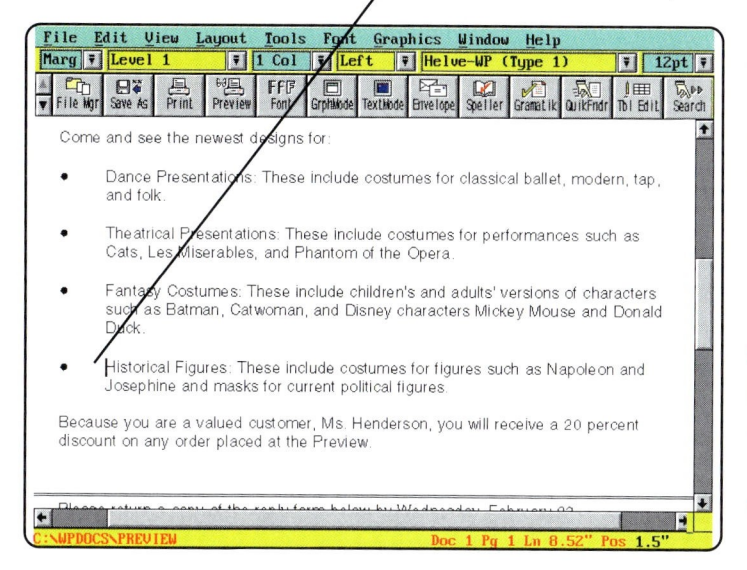

2. Press the **Backspace key**. The bullet will be deleted and the paragraph will be aligned at the left margin.

Use the Undo feature to restore the bullet.

3. Click on **Edit** in the menu bar. A pull-down menu will appear.

4. Click on **Undo**. The bullet will be restored.

SAVING YOUR WORK

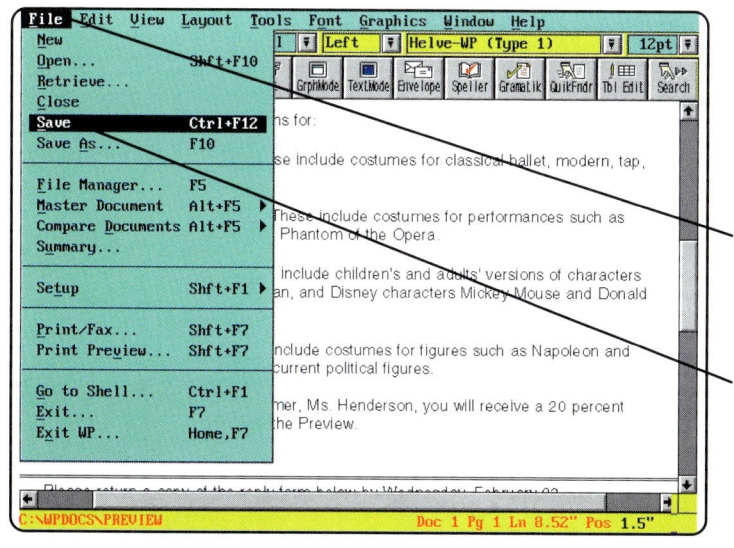

You definitely need to save after all this work. Press and hold the Ctrl key and press F12 (Ctrl + F12) to save. Or, do the following:

1. Click on **File** in the menu bar. A pull-down menu will appear.

2. Click on **Save**.

Setting Tabs

WordPerfect 6 has tabs pre-set every half inch. To insert a tab, simply press the Tab key. You can also set your own tabs. When you set a tab, it is set from that point on for the rest of the document until you reset the tabs. You can reset tabs as many times as you like within a document. In this chapter you will set and apply the following kinds of tabs:

* The *left-aligned tab* that aligns words or numbers on the first character: Josh
  Jessica
* A *leader* (line) that ends at a *right-aligned tab*:   Josh _____
  Jessica___
* A *right-aligned tab* that aligns words or numbers on the last character: Josh
  Jessica
* A *center-aligned tab* that center words or numbers: Josh
  Jessica
* A *decimal tab* that aligns numbers on the decimal point: 13.95
  105.00

SETTING A LEFT-ALIGNED TAB WITH THE MOUSE

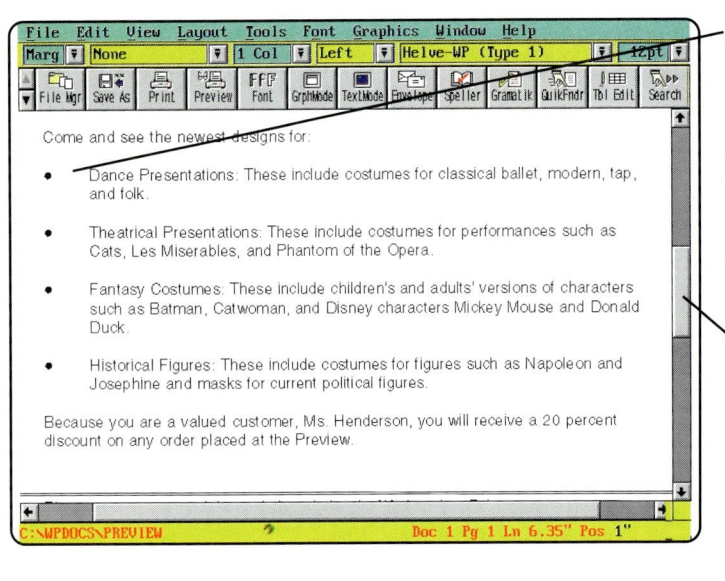

In this example you will set a tab that closes up some of the extra space between the bullets and the paragraphs in the bulleted list you created in the PREVIEW document in Chapter 7.

1. Click and drag the **scroll button** to the **middle of the scroll bar** so you can see the four bulleted paragraphs.

CHAPTER 8: SETTING TABS

Resetting Tabs for a Bulleted List

In a bulleted list, the paragraph is indented a tab width (the pre-set half inch) to the right of the bullet. You can, however, change the space between the bullet and the paragraph by simply resetting the tab.

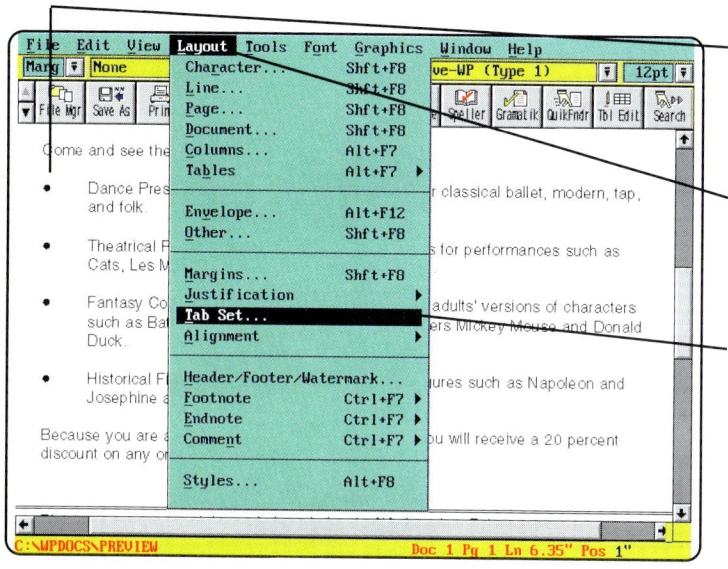

1. Click on the blank line **above the first bulleted paragraph**.

2. Click on **Layout** in the menu bar. A pull-down menu will appear.

3. Click on **Tab Set**. The Tab Set dialog box will appear.

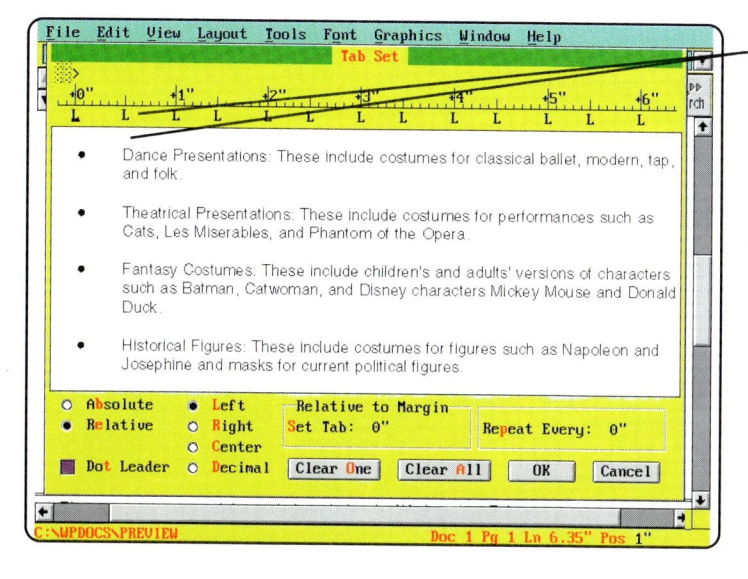

Notice the "L"s in the ruler. These are *left-aligned tabs*, which means that each line of text in the indented paragraph aligns on the first letter of the first word as you see in this example.

Notice also that the letter is shown in relation to the tabs. In this example the bulleted paragraphs line up with the first tab at .5 inch.

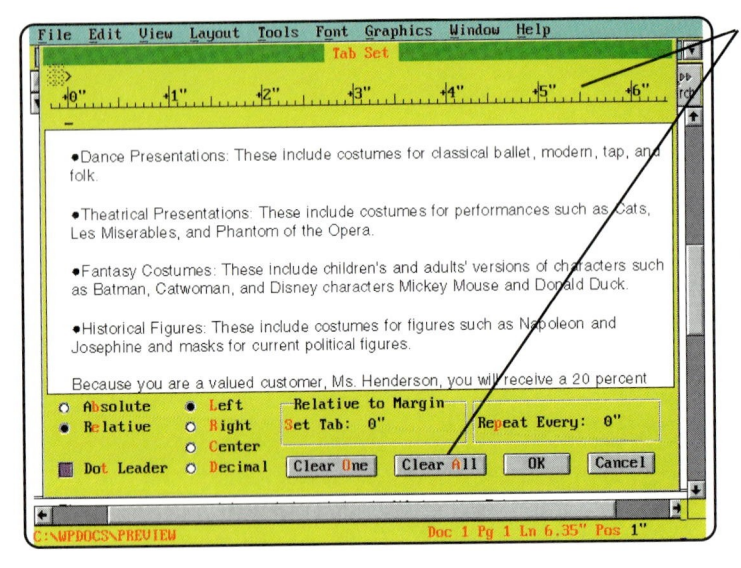

WORDPERFECT 6 FOR DOS: THE VISUAL LEARNING GUIDE

4. Click on **Clear All** to clear all pre-set tabs. All the "L"s will disappear from the ruler.

Notice that the space between the bullet and each paragraph has disappeared.

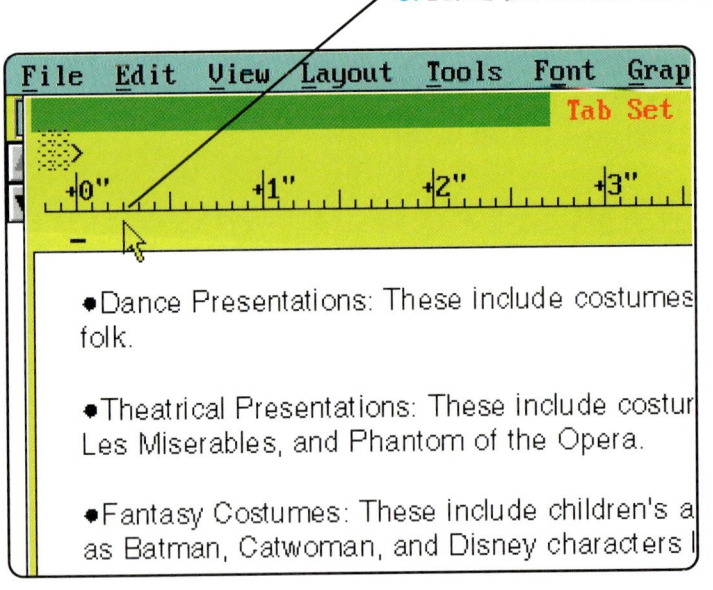

5. Place the mouse arrow in the ruler line at the **.25-inch mark** and **click** to set it in place. You will see a small underline mark appear at the .25-inch mark in the ruler.

CHAPTER 8: SETTING TABS

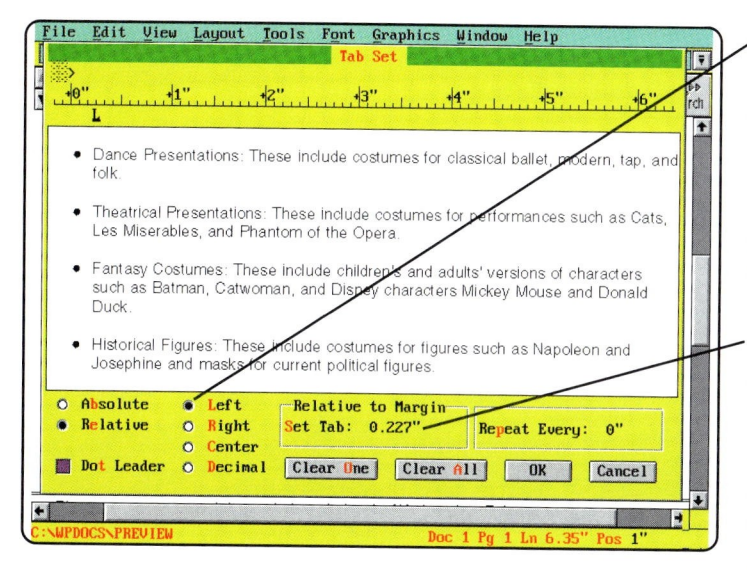

6. Click on **Left**. An "L" will appear in the ruler line at .25 inch.

Notice that the bulleted paragraphs have been realigned at the new tab.

Notice also that the actual tab setting is shown here. When you set a tab in the ruler, the measurement may not be precise. In most cases, however, it really doesn't matter whether a tab is exactly at .25 inch or .227 inch. You will learn how to create an exact tab setting later in this chapter in "Setting Tabs with the Set Tab Command."

This tab will apply throughout the rest of the document until you delete or reset it.

Notice that Relative is pre-selected (already has a dot in the circle). *Relative* means the tab is set in relation to the left margin. If you change the margin, the tab will stay the same distance from the left margin (in this case, .227 inch). An *absolute* tab, on the other hand, is measured from the edge of the paper. If you change the margin, the distance from the edge of the paper to the tab does not change.

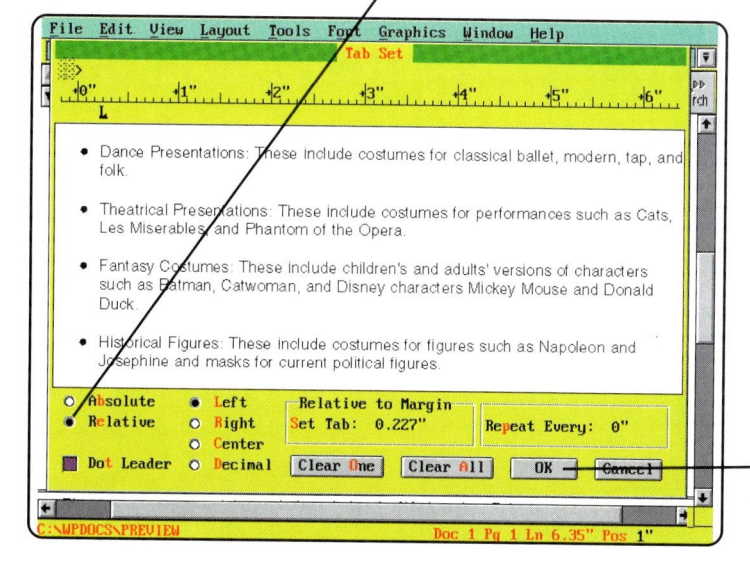

7. Click on **OK**. You will be returned to the document.

USING A PRE-SET TAB

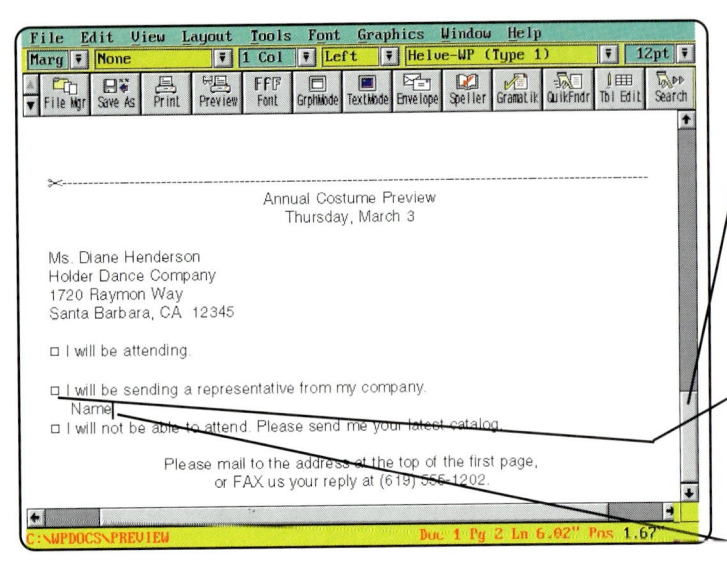

In this example you will use the left-aligned tab you set in the last example.

1. Click and hold the **scroll button** and **drag** it to the **bottom of the scroll bar**. This will take you to the end of the letter.

2. Click on the blank line **above "I will not be able to attend."**

3. Press Tab and **type Name**.

INSERTING A RIGHT-ALIGNED TAB

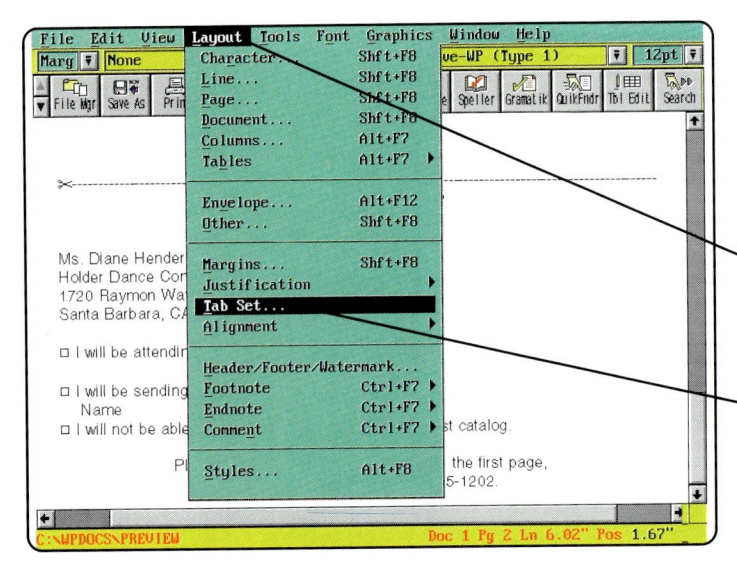

In this section you will insert a solid line (or leader) after "Name." You will use a right-aligned tab to ensure that it ends at a specific spot.

1. Click on **Layout** in the menu bar. A pull-down menu will appear.

2. Click on **Tab Set**. The Tab Set dialog box will appear.

CHAPTER 8: SETTING TABS

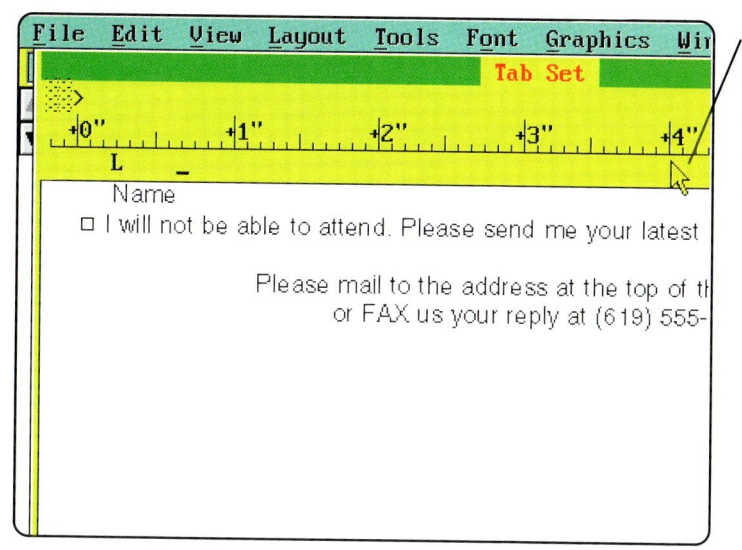

3. Place the mouse pointer in the ruler at the **4-inch mark** and **click** to set it in place. A small horizontal bar will appear at the 4-inch mark.

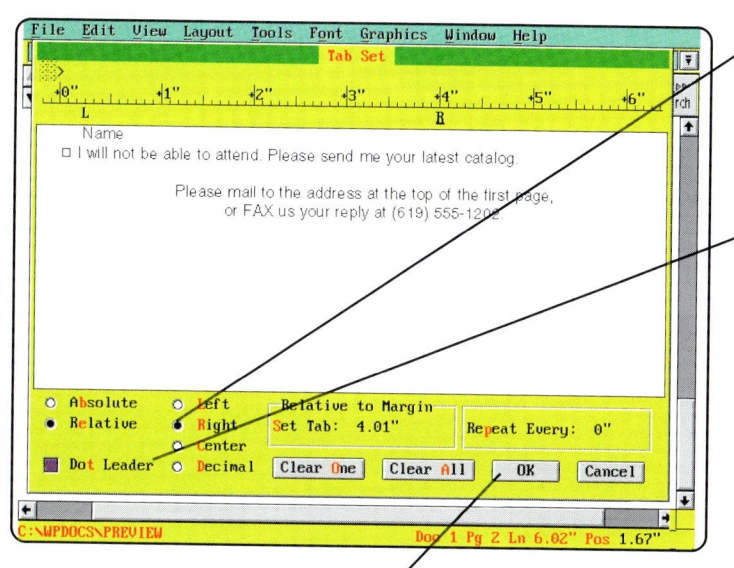

4. Click on **Right** to insert a dot in the circle. The letter "R" will appear in the ruler line at the 4-inch mark.

If you wanted a dotted-line leader (like you often see in a Table of Contents) you would click on Dot Leader while the "R" in the ruler is still underlined. Since you are going to make a solid line for this example, there are a few more steps.

5. Click on **OK**. You will be returned to the document.

WORDPERFECT 6 FOR DOS: THE VISUAL LEARNING GUIDE

Making a Solid-Line Leader

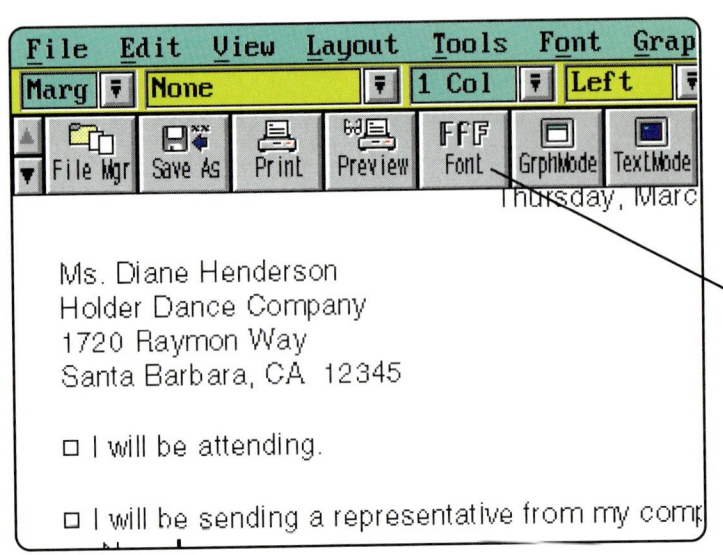

You create a solid-line leader by telling WordPerfect to underline the spaces created when you tab. First you have to turn on the Underline function.

1. **Click** on the **Font button** in the button bar. The Font dialog box will appear.

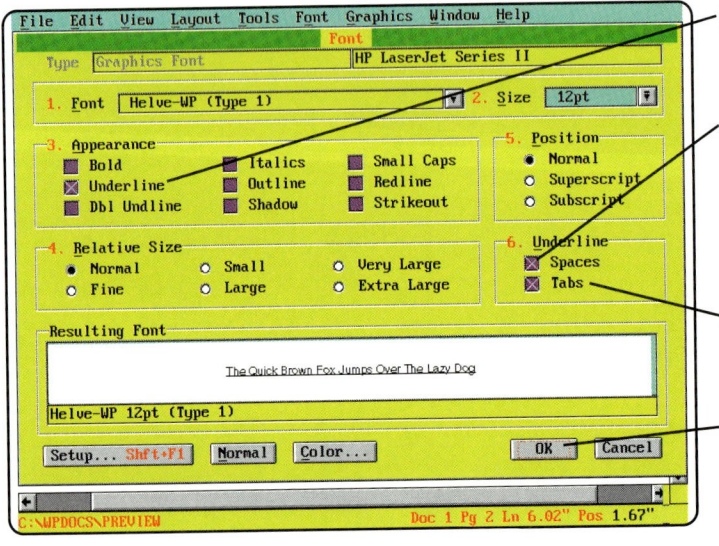

2. **Click** on **Underline** to insert an ✕ in the box.

Notice that Spaces already has an ✕ in the box. WordPerfect is set up so you can underline spaces.

3. **Click** on **Tabs** to insert an ✕ in the box.

4. **Click** on **OK**. You will be returned to the document.

CHAPTER 8: SETTING TABS

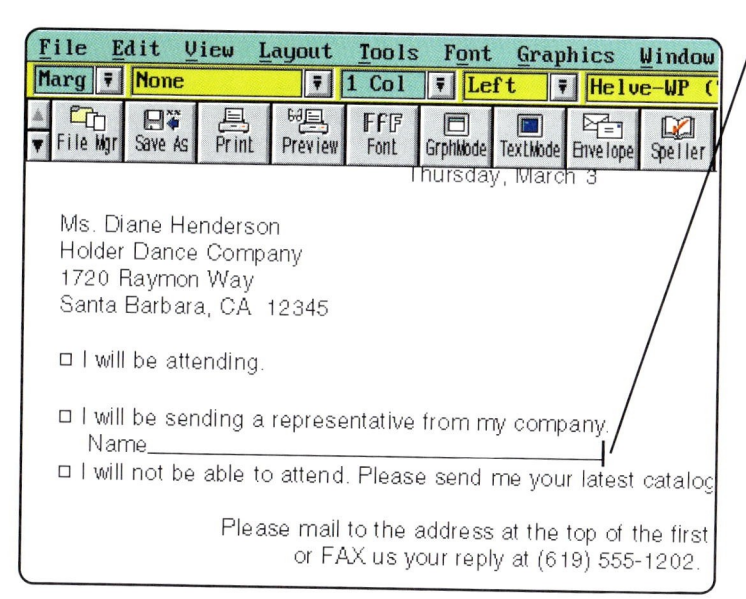

5. Press Tab. A solid line will appear in your text.

Now you have to turn *off* the Underline function or it will apply to the next tab you will set, which is a left-aligned tab.

6. Click on the **Font button** in the button bar. The Font dialog box will appear.

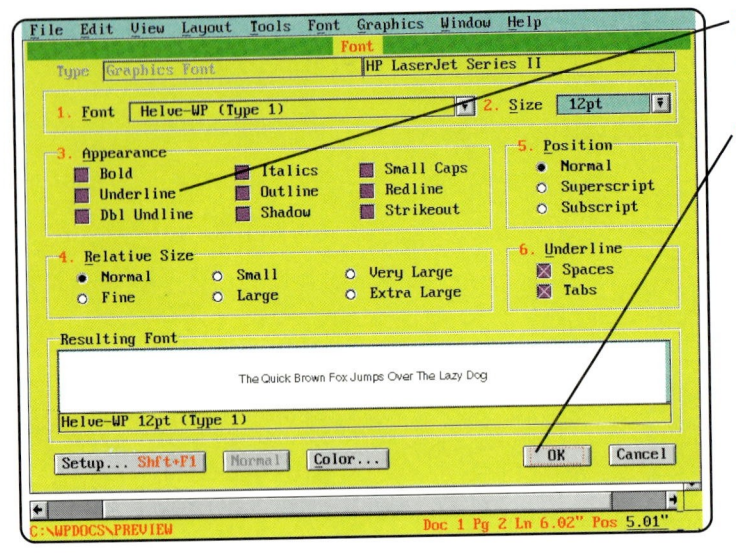

WORDPERFECT 6 FOR DOS: THE VISUAL LEARNING GUIDE

7. **Click** on **Underline** to *remove* the × from the box.

8. **Click** on **OK**. You will be returned to the document.

SETTING A TAB WITH THE SET TAB COMMAND

If you need to set a tab at a precise position, use the Set Tab command instead of the mouse and ruler. In this example you will set a second tab at precisely .5 inch.

1. **Press Enter** to insert a blank line after the "Name" line and move the cursor.

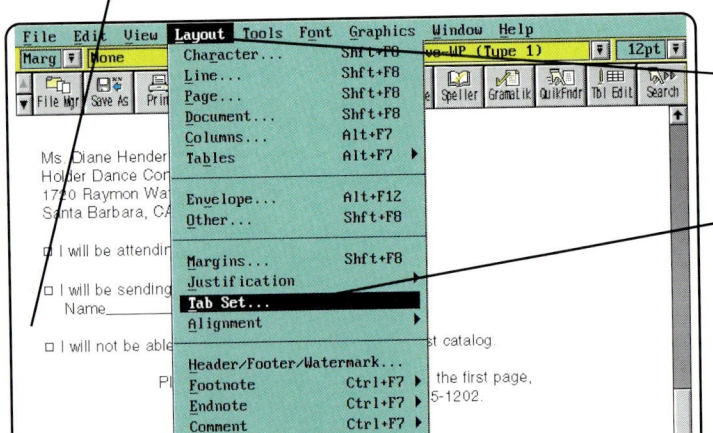

2. **Click** on **Layout** in the menu bar. A pull-down menu will appear.

3. **Click** on **Tab Set**. The Tab Set dialog box will appear.

CHAPTER 8: SETTING TABS

4. **Click** on **Set Tab**. 1" will appear in the Set Tab box. It will be highlighted.

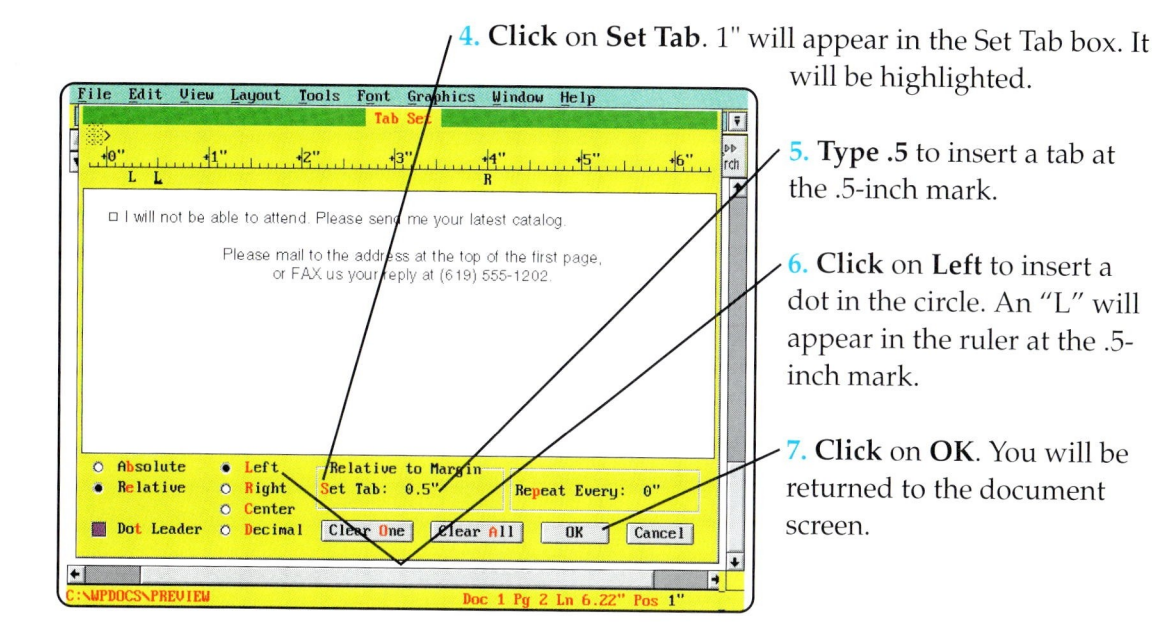

5. **Type .5** to insert a tab at the .5-inch mark.

6. **Click** on **Left** to insert a dot in the circle. An "L" will appear in the ruler at the .5-inch mark.

7. **Click** on **OK**. You will be returned to the document screen.

8. **Press** the **Tab key twice**. This will move you to the tab you just set at the .5-inch mark.

9. **Type Title**.

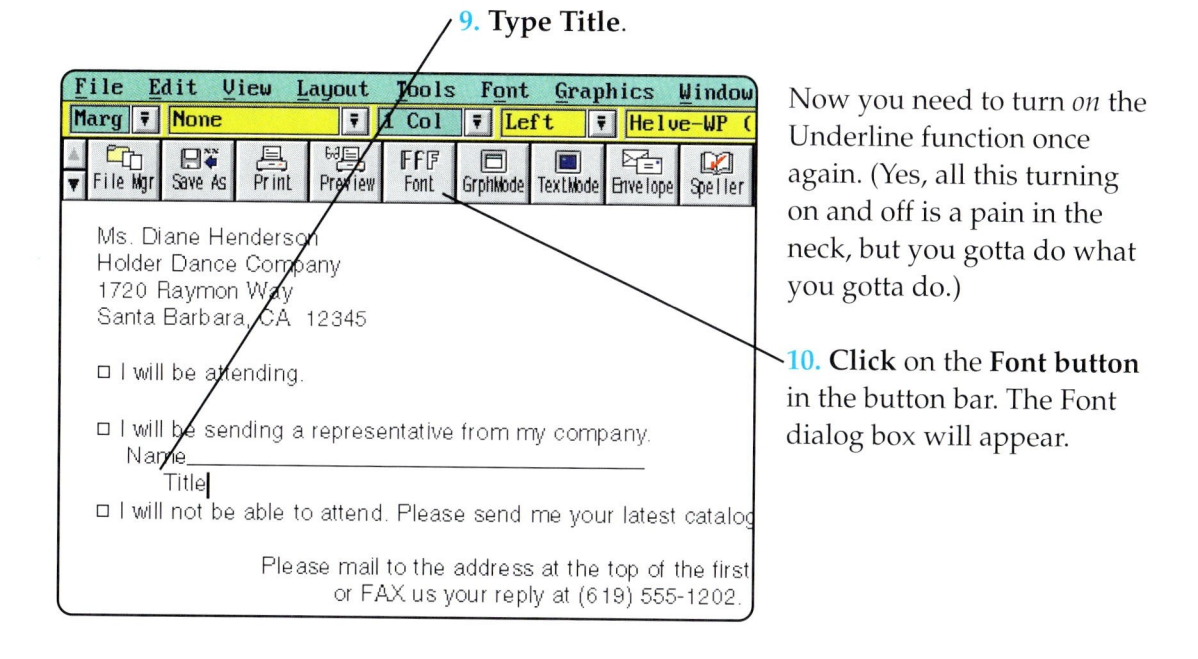

Now you need to turn *on* the Underline function once again. (Yes, all this turning on and off is a pain in the neck, but you gotta do what you gotta do.)

10. **Click** on the **Font button** in the button bar. The Font dialog box will appear.

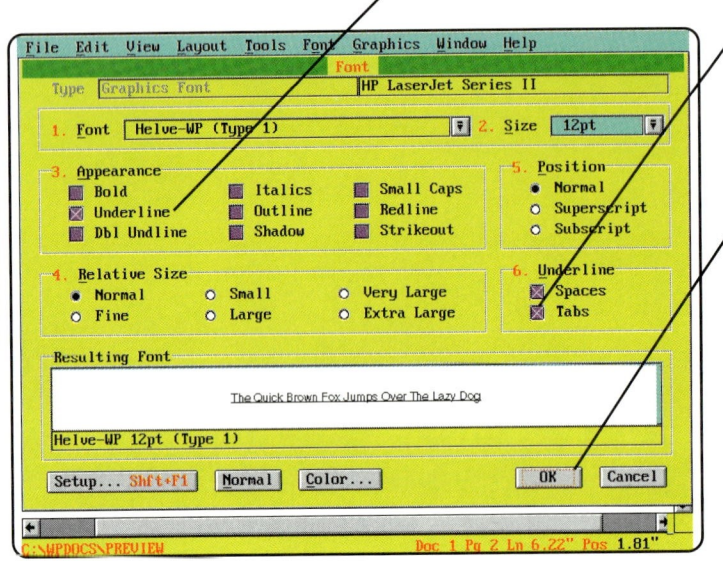

WORDPERFECT 6 FOR DOS: THE VISUAL LEARNING GUIDE

11. **Click** on **Underline** to insert an × in the box.

(There is already an × in the Tabs box from the last time you turned this function on in the previous section.)

12. **Click** on **OK**. You will be returned to the document screen.

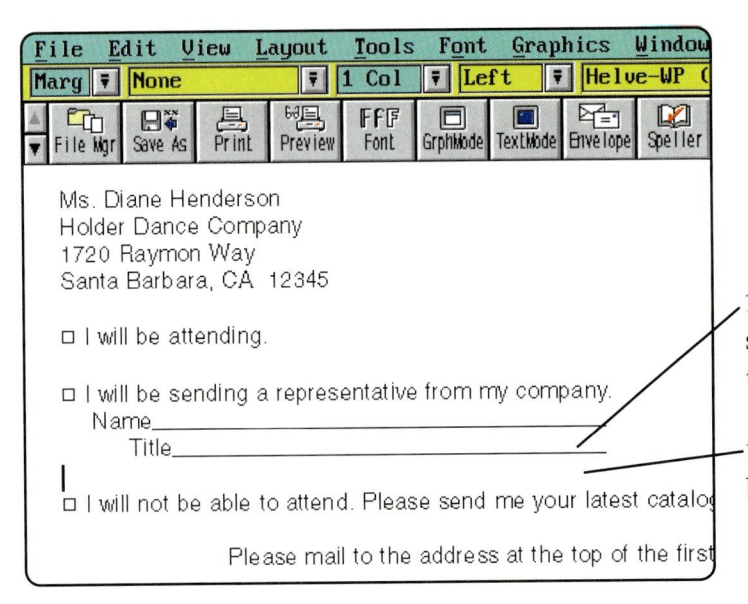

13. **Press** the **Tab key**. A solid line will appear in the text.

14. **Press Enter** to insert a blank line in the text.

CHAPTER 8: SETTING TABS

DELETING A TAB

In this example you will delete the tab you set at .5 inch.

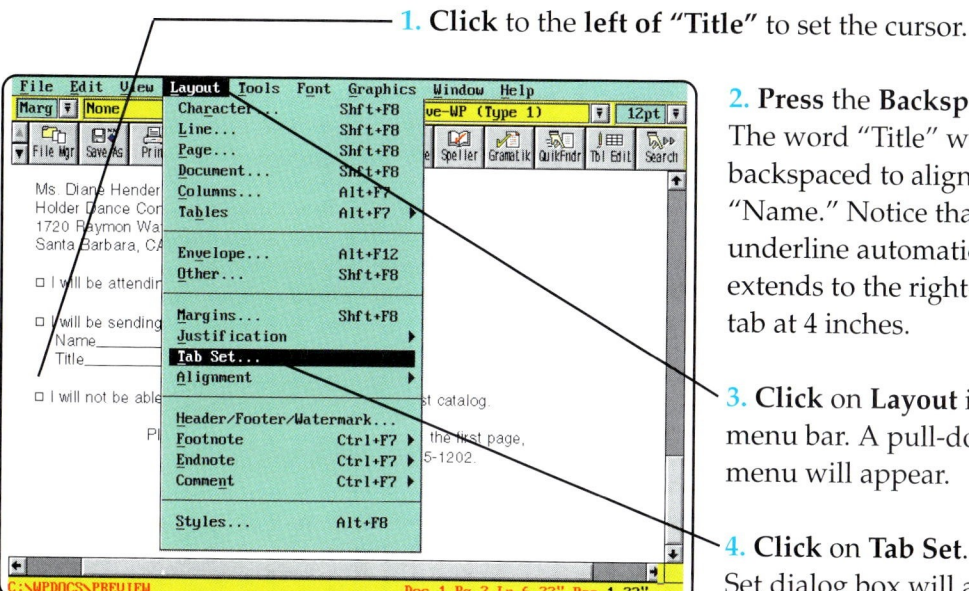

1. **Click** to the **left of "Title"** to set the cursor.

2. **Press** the **Backspace key**. The word "Title" will be backspaced to align under "Name." Notice that the underline automatically extends to the right-aligned tab at 4 inches.

3. **Click** on **Layout** in the menu bar. A pull-down menu will appear.

4. **Click** on **Tab Set**. The Tab Set dialog box will appear.

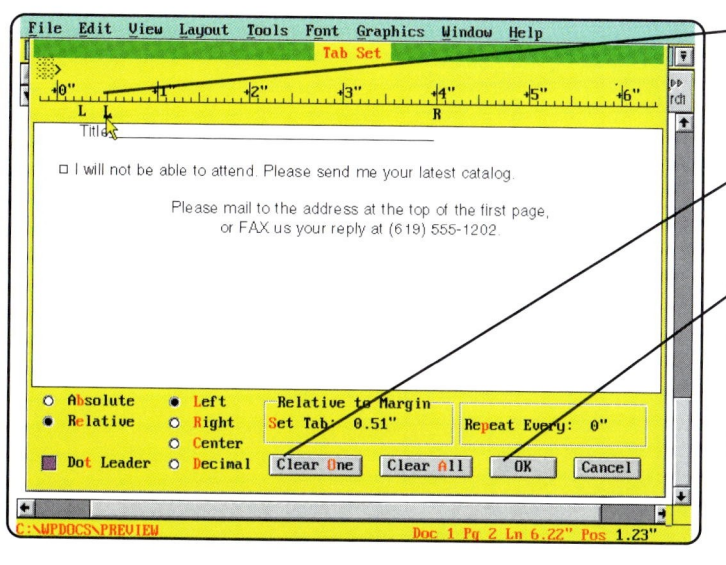

5. **Click** on the **"L" at .5 inch**. A small bar will appear under the "L."

6. **Click** on **Clear One**. The "L" will disappear.

7. **Click** on **OK**. You will be returned to the document screen.

8. **Press and hold Ctrl** then **press** the **F12 key** (Ctrl + F12) to save your work.

OPENING A NEW DOCUMENT

In the remaining sections of the chapter, you'll review setting left-aligned and right-aligned tabs. You will also learn how to set a center-aligned tab and a decimal tab. Since the tabs will not be used in the PREVIEW letter, you will open a new document. You don't need to close PREVIEW in order to open a new document though. WordPerfect allows up to nine documents to be open at a time.

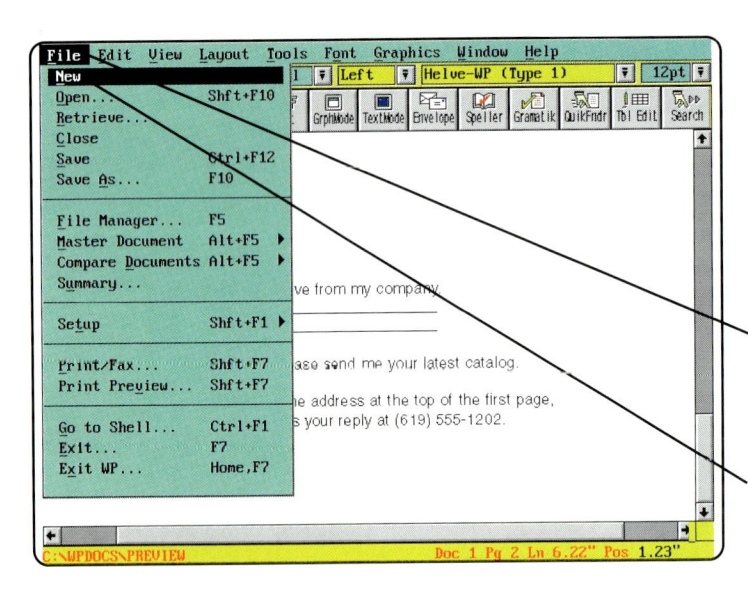

1. Click on **File** in the menu bar. A pull-down menu will appear.

2. Click on **New**. A new document screen will appear.

SETTING A RIGHT-ALIGNED TAB

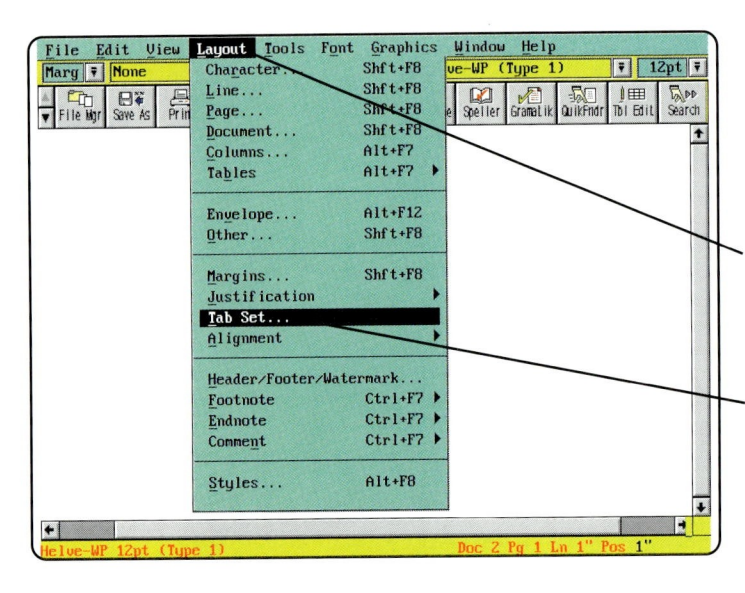

1. Click on **Layout** in the menu bar. A pull-down menu will appear.

2. Click on **Tab Set**. The Tab Set dialog box will appear.

CHAPTER 8: SETTING TABS

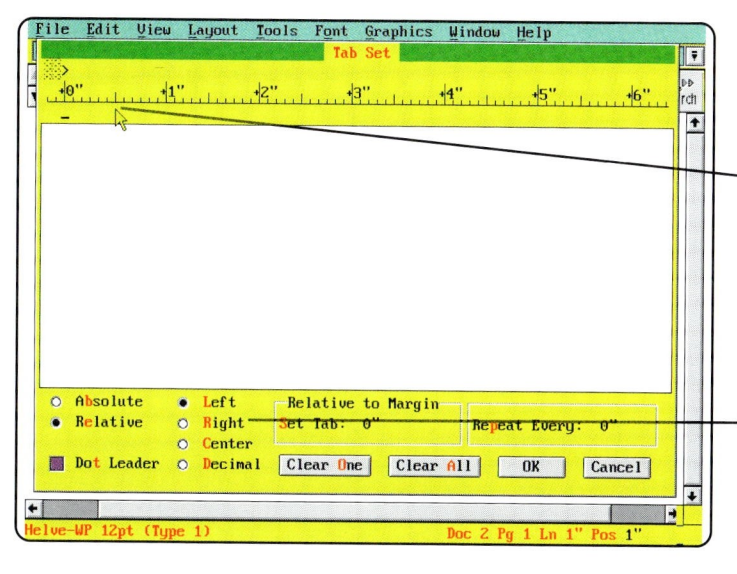

3. **Click** on **Clear All** at the bottom of your screen to clear all pre-set tabs.

4. **Place** the mouse pointer in the ruler at the **.5-inch mark** and **click** to set it in place. A small horizontal bar will appear under the .5-inch mark.

5. **Click** on **Right** to insert a dot in the circle. An "R" will appear in the ruler at the .5-inch mark.

SETTING A CENTER-ALIGNED TAB

You can set different kinds of tabs within the same dialog box.

1. **Place** the mouse pointer in the ruler at the **2-inch mark** and **click** to set it in place. A small horizontal bar will appear under the 2-inch mark.

2. **Click** on **Center** to insert a dot in the circle. The letter "C" will appear in the ruler at the 2-inch mark.

SETTING DECIMAL TABS

In this section you will set two decimal tabs. You should be in the Tab Set dialog box.

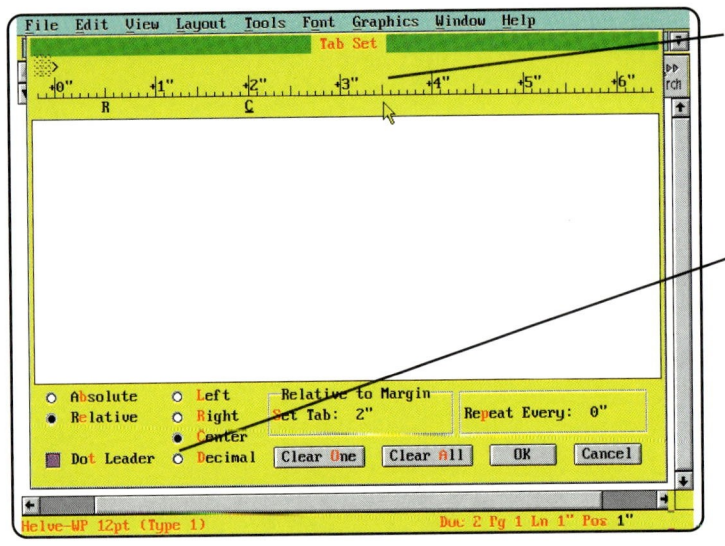

1. **Place** the mouse pointer in the ruler at the **3.5-inch mark**. **Click** to set it in place. A small horizontal line will appear at that spot.

2. **Click** on **Decimal** to insert a dot in the circle. The letter "D" will appear at the 3.5-inch mark in the ruler.

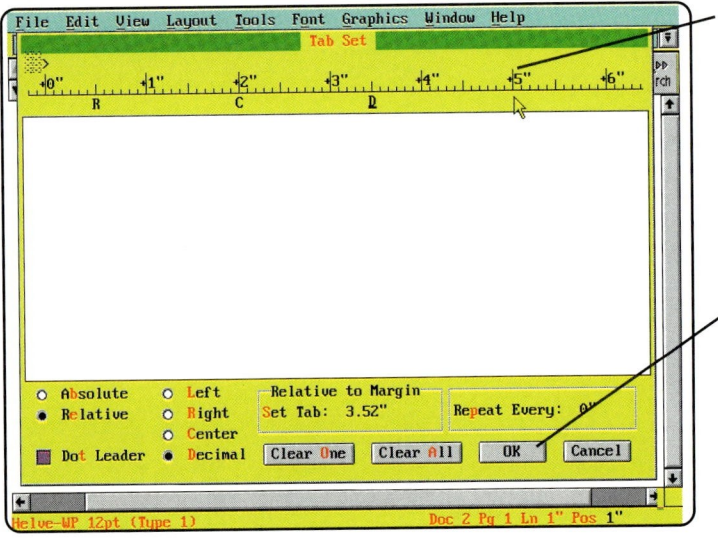

3. **Repeat steps 1 and 2 above** to set a decimal tab at the **5-inch mark**. (You need to click on Decimal at the bottom of your screen even though there is already a dot in the circle.)

4. **Click** on **OK**. You will be returned to the document screen.

CHAPTER 8: SETTING TABS

APPLYING TABS

In this section you will apply the tabs you set in the previous sections. Notice how each text entry aligns on the tabs you set.

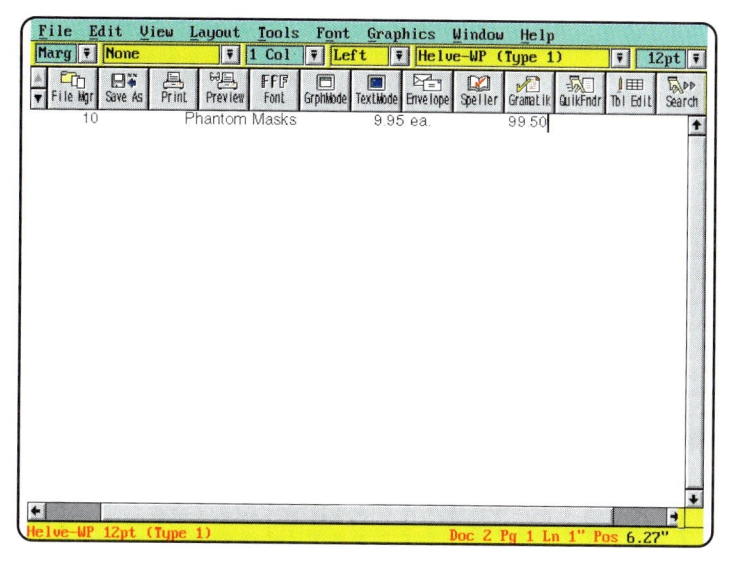

1. Press Tab and **type 10**.

2. Press Tab and **type Phantom Masks**. Notice that the text moves backwards as you type.

3. Press Tab and **type 9.95 ea**.

4. Press Tab and **type 99.50**.

5. Press Enter to move to the next line.

6. Press Tab and **type 5**. Notice the "5" is right-aligned under "10."

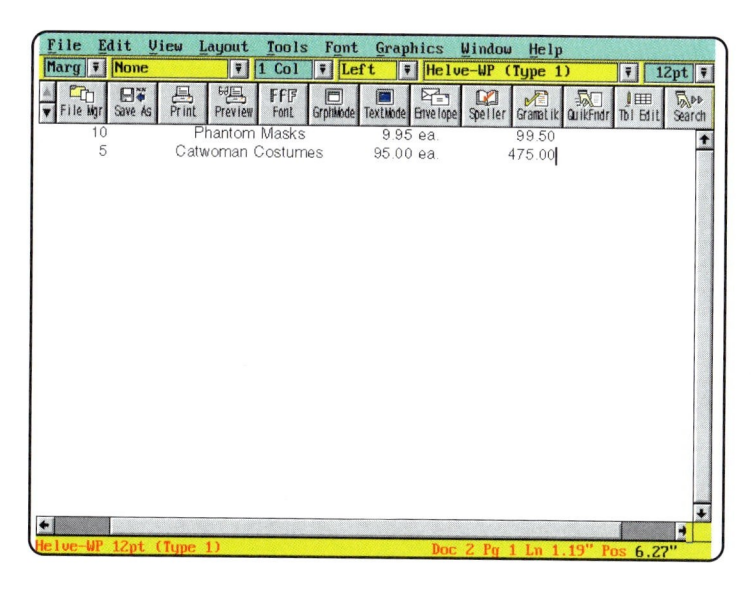

7. Press Tab and **type Catwoman Costumes**. Notice that it is centered under the entry above it.

8. Press Tab and **type 95.00 ea**. Notice that the decimal points are lined up.

9. Press Tab and **type 475.00**. Again, notice the decimal points are aligned.

SWITCHING BETWEEN OPEN DOCUMENTS

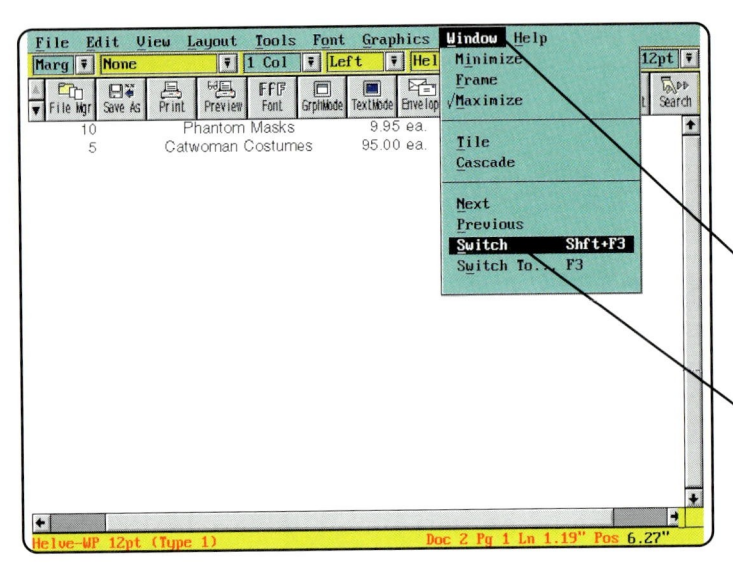

In this section you will switch back and forth between the un-named file on your screen and PREVIEW.

1. Click on **Window** in the menu bar. A pull-down menu will appear.

2. Click on **Switch**. The PREVIEW file will appear on your screen.

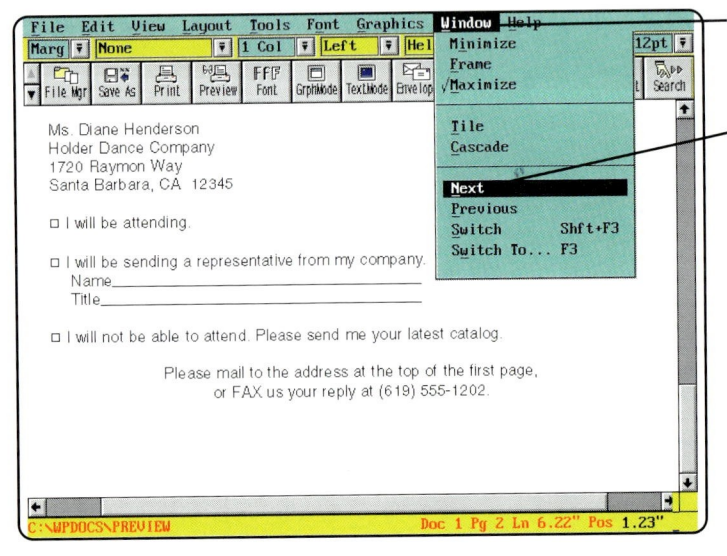

3. Click on **Window**. A pull-down menu will appear.

4. Click on **Next** to go back to the tab document.

Next, Previous, Switch, and Switch To will all take you back and forth between documents. Try playing with the various choices before you go on to the next section.

CHAPTER 8: SETTING TABS

CLOSING WITHOUT SAVING

Since the previous tab example was meant only as practice in setting different types of tabs and will not be used later in the book, you don't need to save the document.

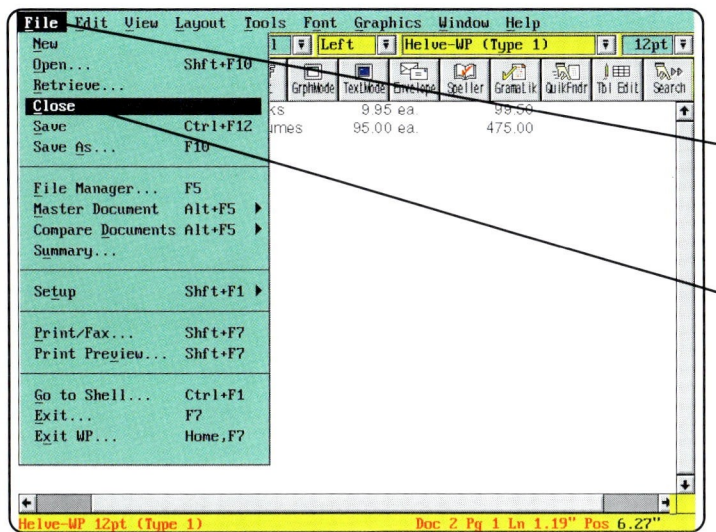

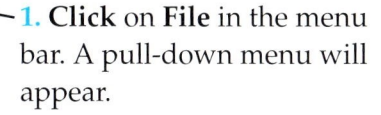

1. Click on **File** in the menu bar. A pull-down menu will appear.

2. Click on **Close**. A dialog box will appear.

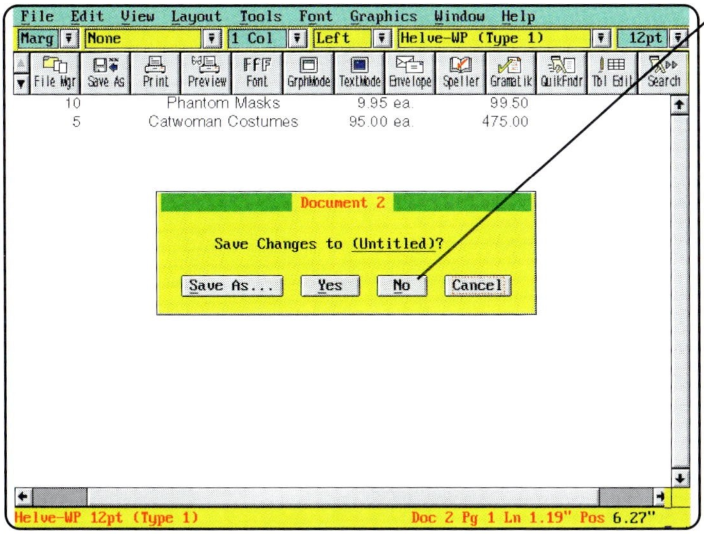

3. Click on **No**. The file will close without being saved. Since you never saved this document to begin with, it will simply disappear.

Closing without saving is a handy trick to remember if you have made changes to your document that you don't like. Closing without saving will cause a previously saved document to revert to what it was the last time you saved it.

Adding a Header and a Page Number

A *header* or *footer* is information that is printed at the top or bottom of each page, respectively. For example, in this book the page number and book title is a header on every left page and the chapter number and title and page number is a header on every right page. In this chapter you will do the following:

❖ Change the margin on page 2 of the PREVIEW sample document
❖ Insert a header on page 2
❖ Insert a page number on page 2
❖ View the header and page number in Page Mode and Print Preview

CHANGING THE MARGIN

In WordPerfect you can change margins as many times as you want within a document. Each time you make a change, the new margin applies in the document until you change it again. In this example you will change the top margin on the second page to make space for a header. First, you must go to the top of the page on which you want to make the change.

1. Click on **Edit**. A pull-down menu will appear.

2. Click on **Go to**. The Go to dialog box will appear.

CHAPTER 9: ADDING A HEADER AND A PAGE NUMBER

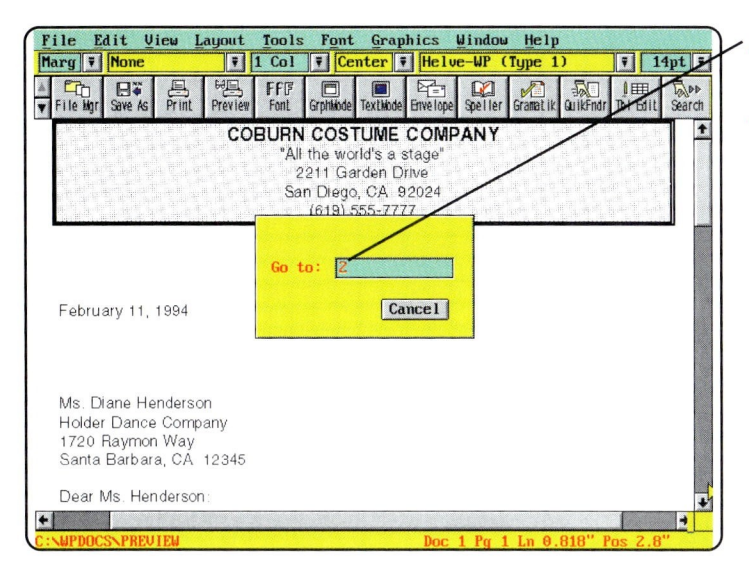

3. **Type 2**.

4. **Press Enter**. The cursor will go to the first line on page 2.

5. **Click** on **Layout** in the menu bar. A pull-down menu will appear.

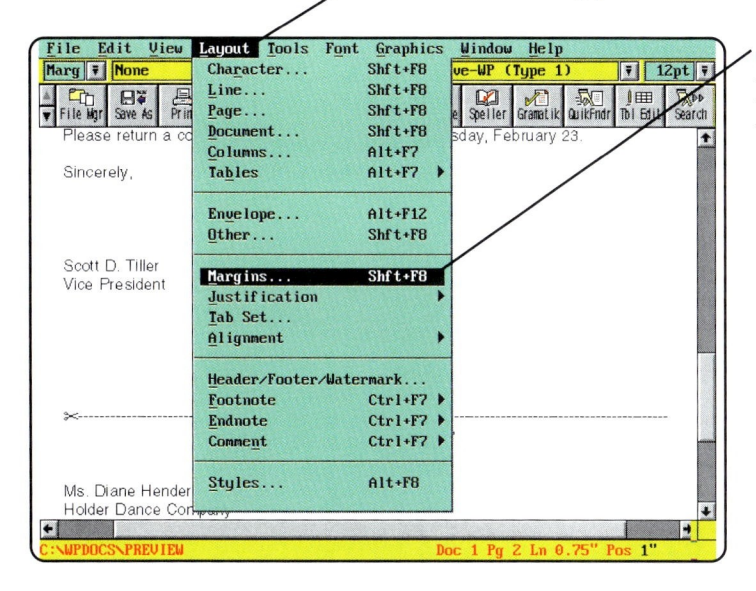

6. **Click** on **Margins**. The Margin Format dialog box will appear.

WORDPERFECT 6 FOR DOS: THE VISUAL LEARNING GUIDE

7. **Click** on **Top Margin**. The value .75" will be highlighted.

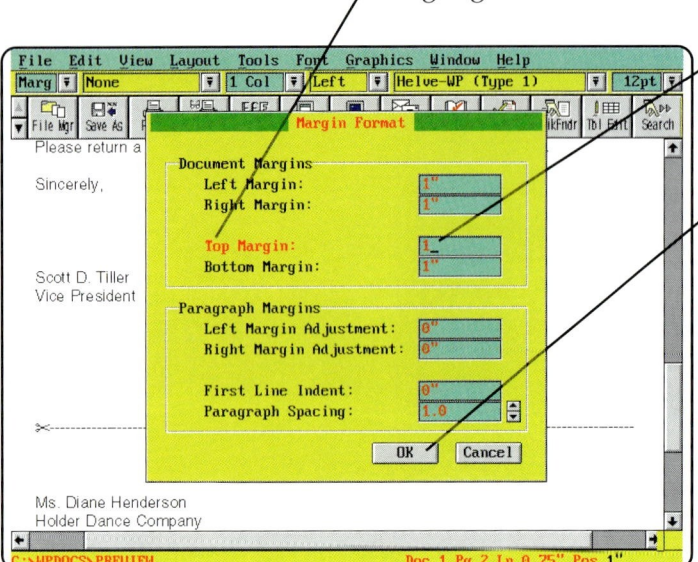

8. **Type 1**. It will replace the 0.75" that you inserted in Chapter 1.

9. **Click** on **OK**. The document screen will appear with the second page now having a 1-inch top margin.

ADDING A HEADER

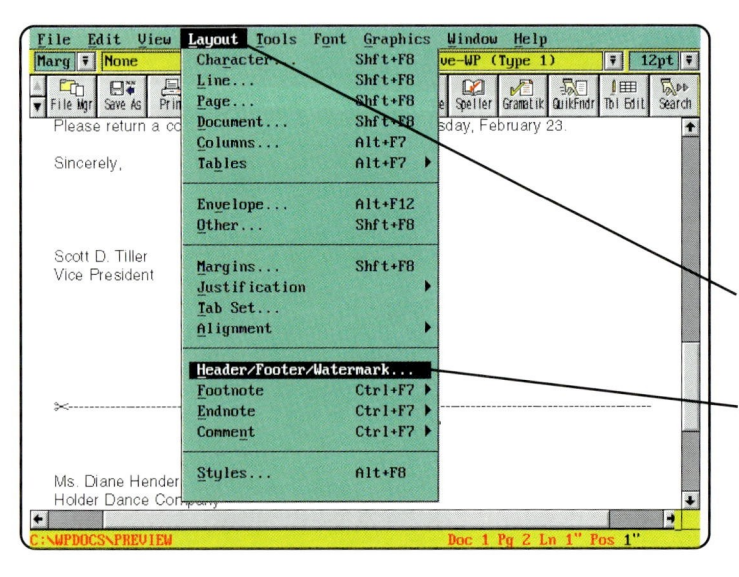

In this section you will create a header for page 2 using the words "Ms. Diane Henderson" and the date. Your cursor should be at the top of page 2.

1. **Click** on **Layout**. A pull-down menu will appear.

2. **Click** on **Header/Footer/Watermark**. The Header/Footer/Watermark dialog box will appear.

CHAPTER 9: ADDING A HEADER AND A PAGE NUMBER

Changing the Space Between the Header and the Text

In this example you will increase the space between the header and the document text from .167" to .5".

1. Click on **Space Below Header**. The number 0.167" will be highlighted.

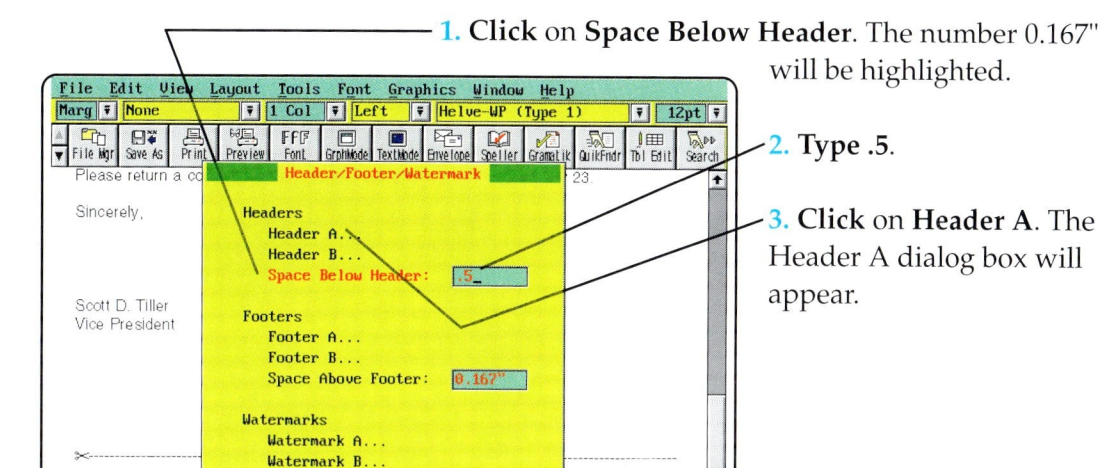

2. Type .5.

3. Click on **Header A**. The Header A dialog box will appear.

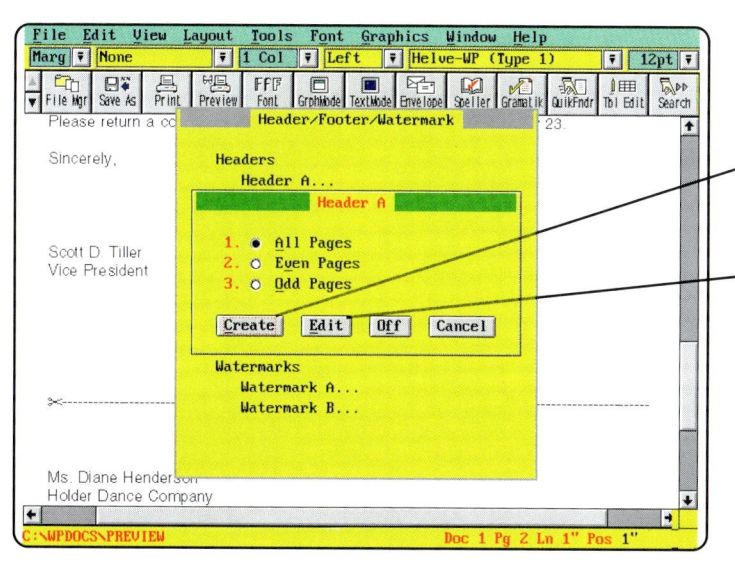

Creating the Header

1. Click on **Create**. A blank screen will appear.

Notice that you can edit an existing header by clicking on Edit.

WORDPERFECT 6 FOR DOS: THE VISUAL LEARNING GUIDE

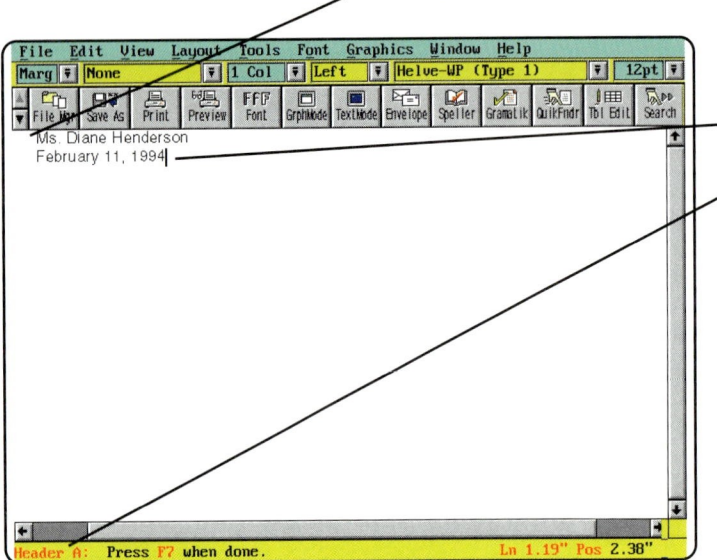

2. **Type Ms. Diane Henderson**.

3. **Press** the **Enter key**.

4. **Type February 11, 1994**.

Notice the status line shows this is a screen for Header A.

5. **Click** on **File** in the menu bar. A pull-down menu will appear.

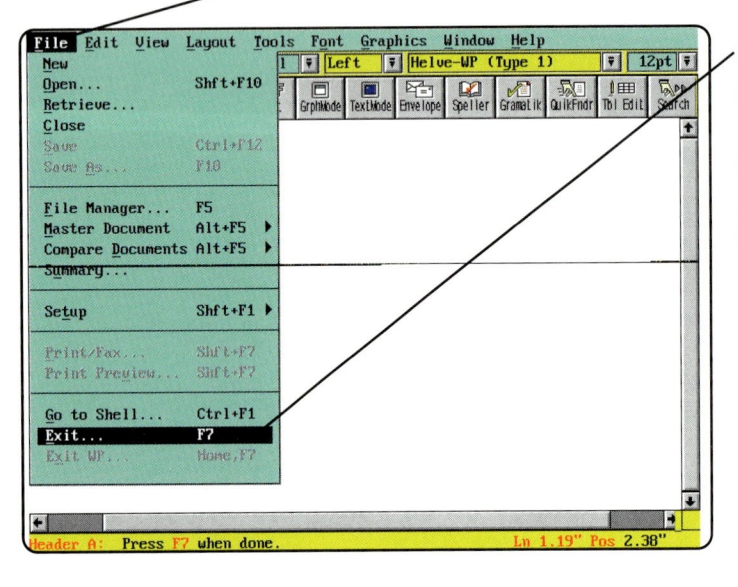

6. **Click** on **Exit**. (You could press F7 after step 4 instead of doing steps 5 and 6.) The document screen will appear. You cannot see a header on your screen in this view. You will be able to view it later in this chapter.

CHAPTER 9: ADDING A HEADER AND A PAGE NUMBER

INSERTING A PAGE NUMBER

In order to insert a page number, the cursor must be on the page where you want the page numbering to begin.

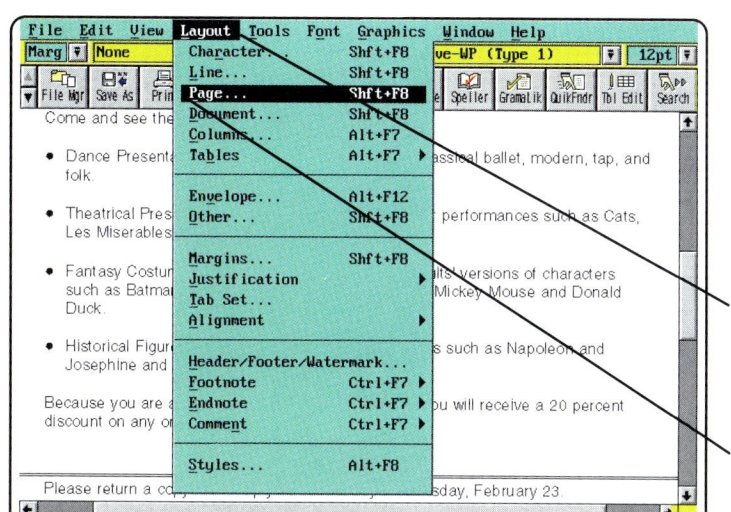

1. Click at the **top of page 2** if your cursor is not already there.

2. Click on **Layout** in the menu bar. A pull-down menu will appear.

3. Click on **Page**. The Page Format dialog box will appear.

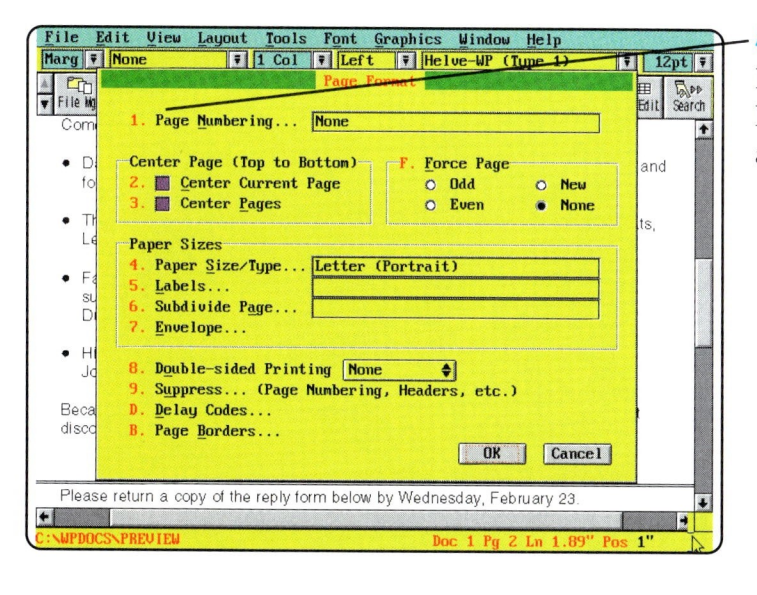

4. Click on **Page Numbering**. The Page Numbering dialog box will appear.

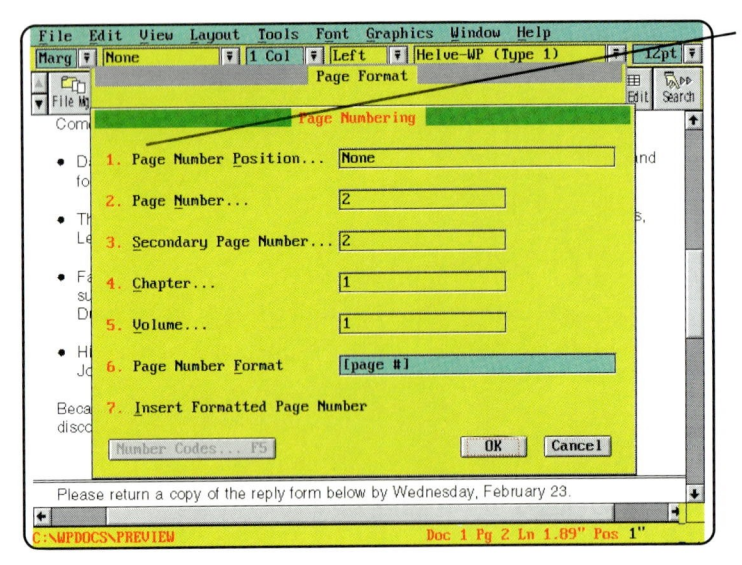

WORDPERFECT 6 FOR DOS: THE VISUAL LEARNING GUIDE

5. Click on **Page Number Position**. The Page Number Position dialog box will appear.

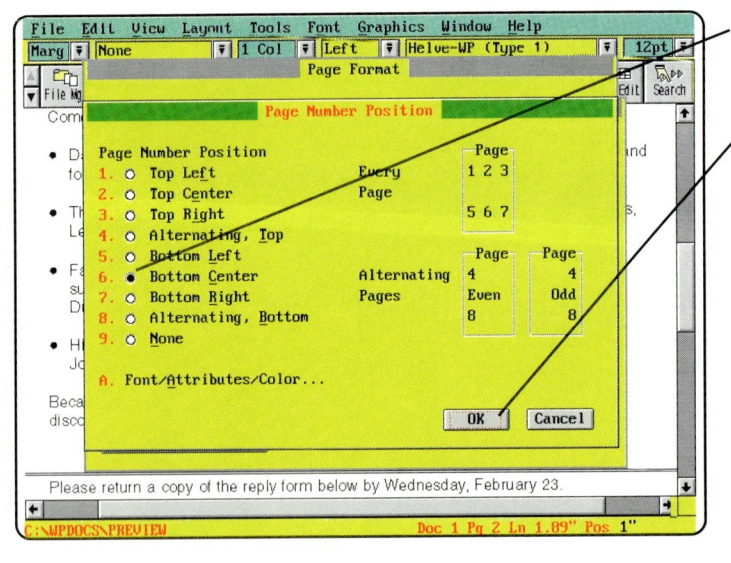

6. Click on **Bottom Center** to insert a dot in the circle.

7. Click on **OK**. You will be returned to the Page Numbering dialog box.

CHAPTER 9: ADDING A HEADER AND A PAGE NUMBER

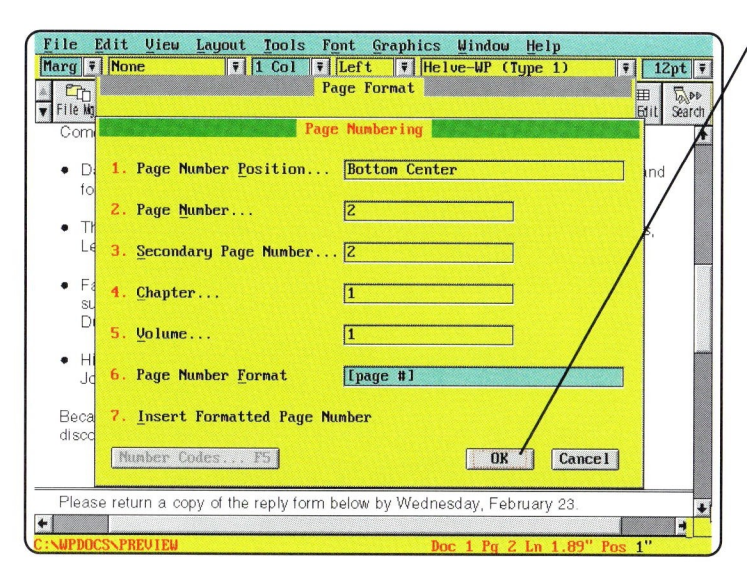

8. Click on **OK**. The Page Format dialog box will reappear.

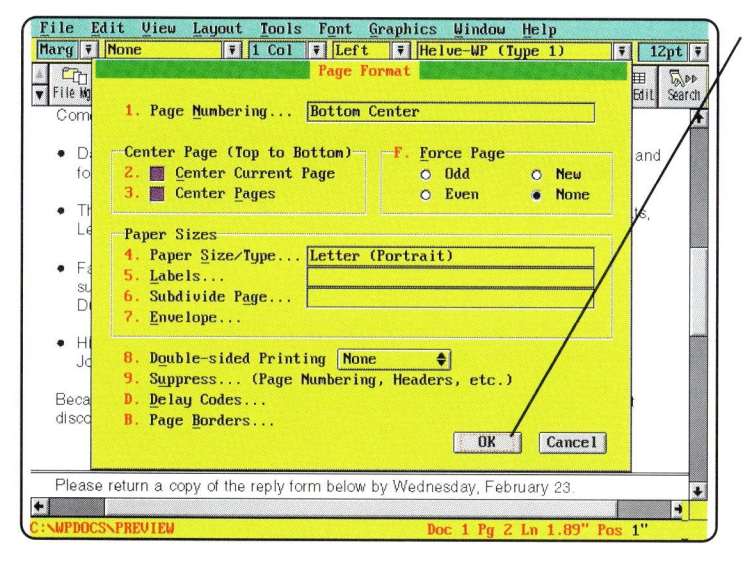

9. Click on **OK**. The document screen will appear. The page number will not be visible in this view.

You will learn how to view the header and page number in the next section.

VIEWING THE HEADER AND PAGE NUMBER

Since you cannot see the header or page number in the normal view, you must go to either the Page Mode view or Print Preview.

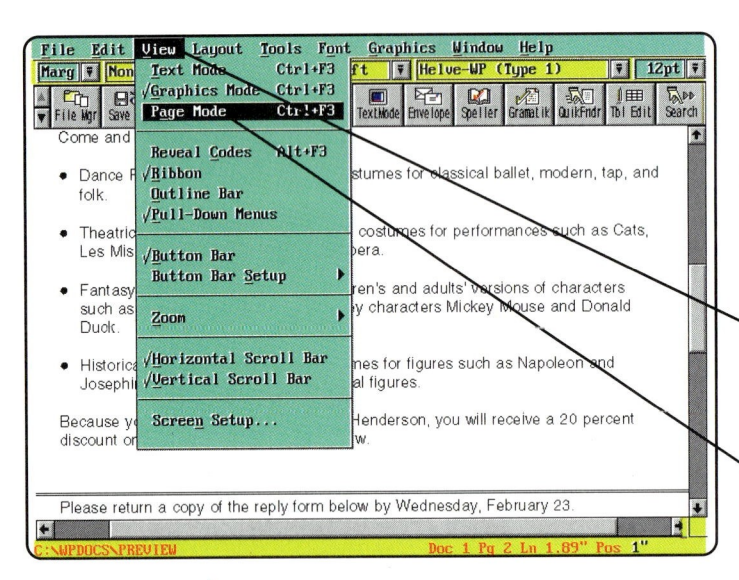

Using Page Mode

1. Click at the **top of page 2** if your cursor is not already there.

2. Click on **View** in the menu bar. A pull-down menu will appear.

3. Click on **Page Mode**. The screen will change to the Page Mode view.

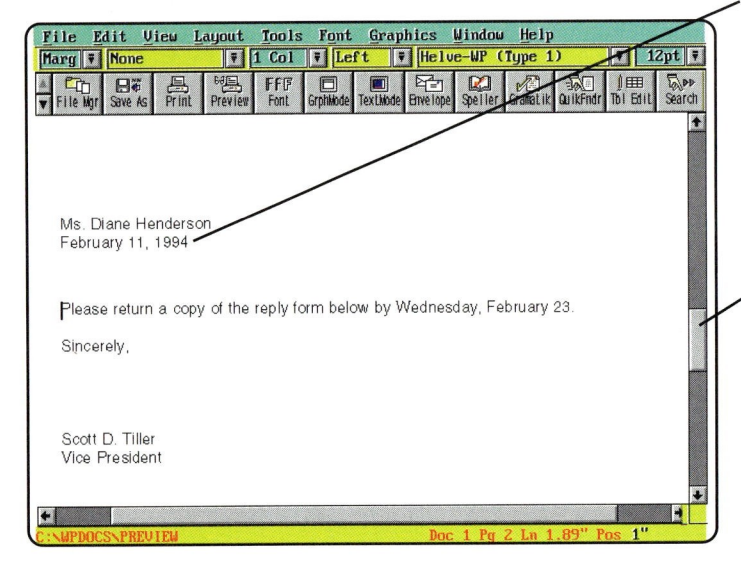

Notice you can now see the header. (You cannot edit or delete the header in this mode. You must go back to the Header/Footer/Watermark dialog box to edit or delete.)

4. Click on and hold the **scroll button** and **drag** it to the **bottom of the scroll bar**. This will take you to the bottom of the file so you can see the page number, as shown on the next page.

CHAPTER 9: ADDING A HEADER AND A PAGE NUMBER

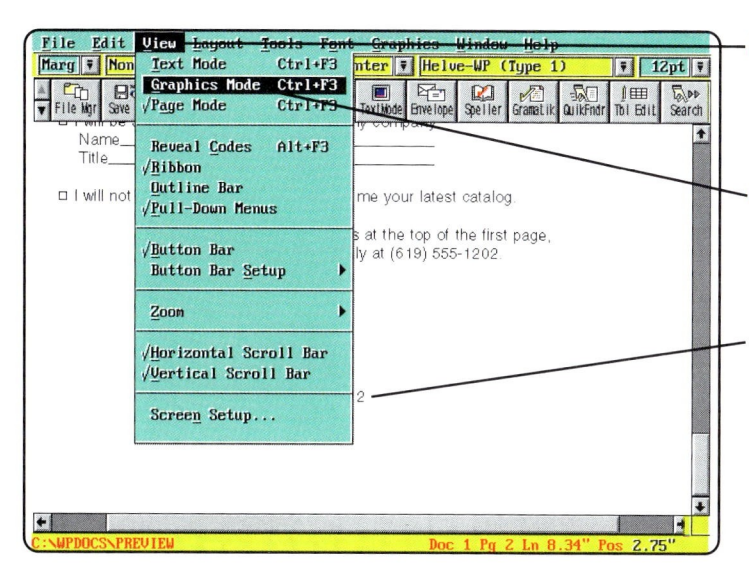

5. Click on **View** in the menu bar. A pull-down menu will appear.

6. Click on **Graphics Mode** to return to the Graphics mode.

Notice the page number at the bottom of your screen.

Using Print Preview

You can also view the header and page number in Print Preview.

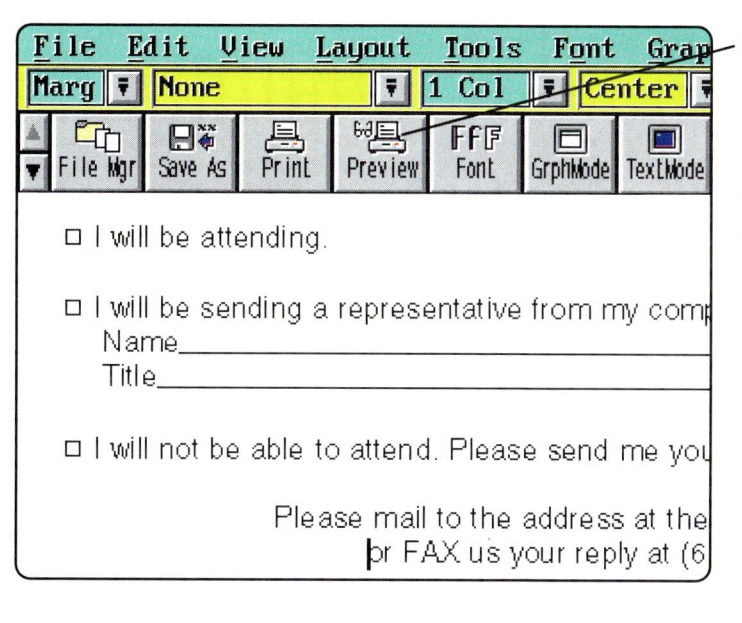

1. Click on the **Preview button** in the button bar. Your screen will change to the Preview mode. Refer to Chapter 3, "Previewing and Printing a Document," if you need help with the Preview screen.

File Manager

Part III Mailing Lists, Form Letters, and Envelopes

Chapter 10: Printing an Envelope	Page 118
Chapter 11: Creating a Mailing List	Page 133
Chapter 12: Editing a Mailing List	Page 142
Chapter 13: Setting Up a Form Letter for Merge Printing	Page 151
Chapter 14: Printing a Form Letter	Page 164
Chapter 15: Printing Envelopes for a Mailing List	Page 169
Chapter 16: Converting a Mailing List Created in Another Program	Page 189

Printing an Envelope

Unlike old-fashioned DOS-based word-processing programs, WordPerfect 6 has an Envelope button to make it easy for you to set up and print an envelope. In this chapter you will do the following:

❖ Use the Envelope button to print a standard business envelope that has a preprinted return address on it on a HP LaserJet Series II or III printer and on a dot-matrix printer
❖ Customize the envelope text
❖ Print a letter with an attached envelope

USING THE ENVELOPE BUTTON TO PRINT

In this section you will print a standard business envelope with a preprinted return address using the manual feed feature of your printer.

(**Note:** You will learn how to print multiple envelopes using an envelope tray in Chapter 15 in the section entitled, "Setting Up WordPerfect to Use an Envelope Tray.") After you complete the steps below, refer to the directions for either HP LaserJet Series II or III printers (and printers that emulate them) or dot-matrix printers.

1. **Open** the **PREVIEW** file if it is not already on your screen.

2. **Click** on the **Envelope button** in the button bar. The Envelope dialog box will appear.

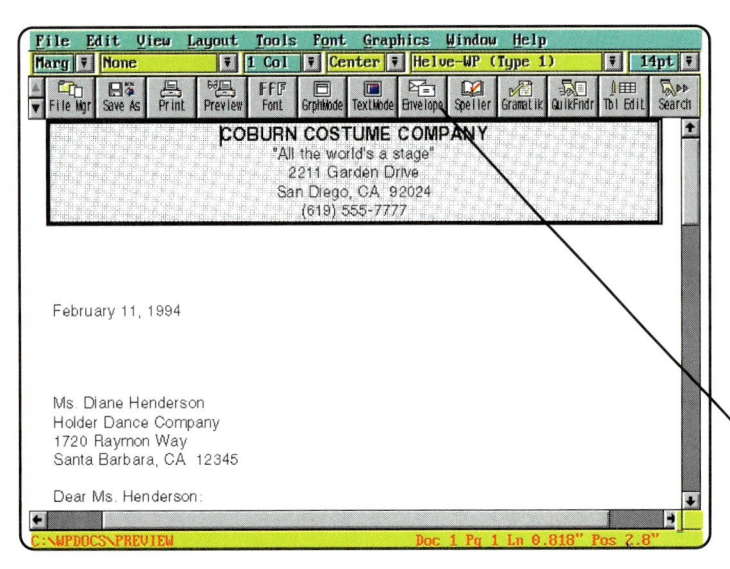

Printing with a HP LaserJet II or III Series Printer

Notice that WordPerfect automatically filled in the Mailing Address box. At this rate, it won't be long before WordPerfect will put a stamp on the envelope for you!

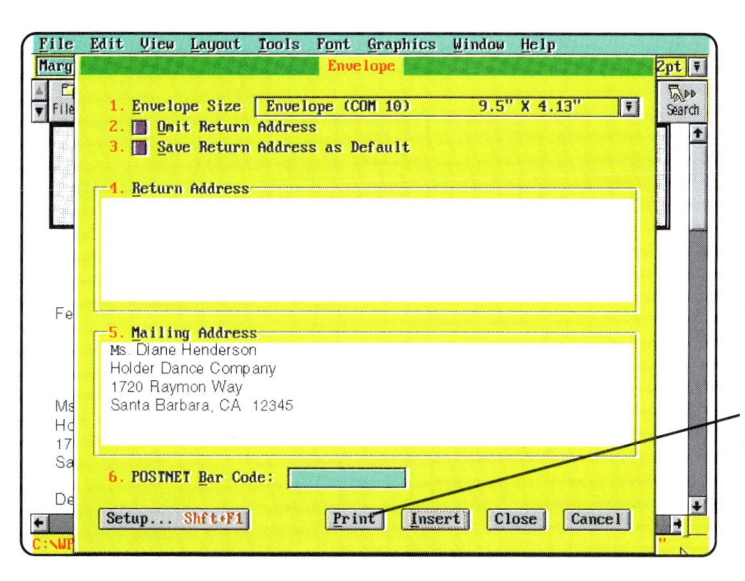

1. **Place** a **single envelope** in the **manual feed slot** on your printer's paper tray. Since each brand of printer operates slightly differently, see your printer's manual for the exact placement of the envelope as you feed it into the printer.

2. **Click** on **Print**. A message box will appear. Check your printer's manual to see if you have to press a Form Feed or other similar button.

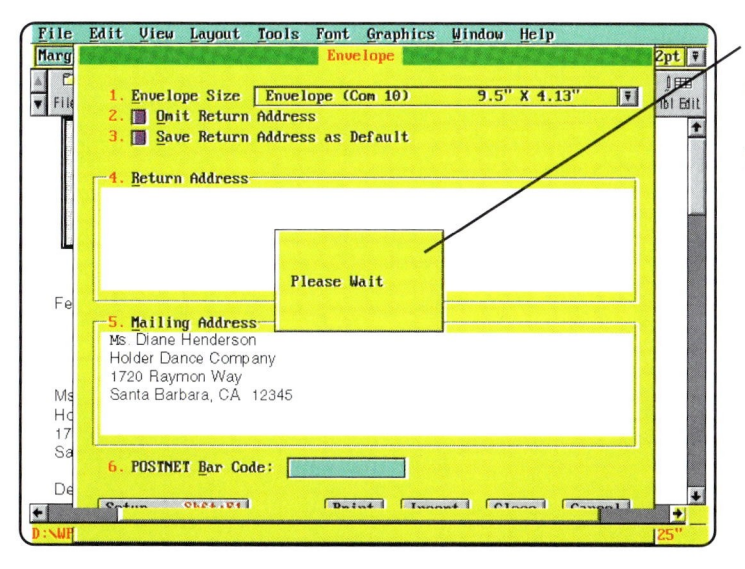

A Please Wait message box will briefly appear on your screen before your envelope begins to print.

Printing with a Dot-Matrix Printer

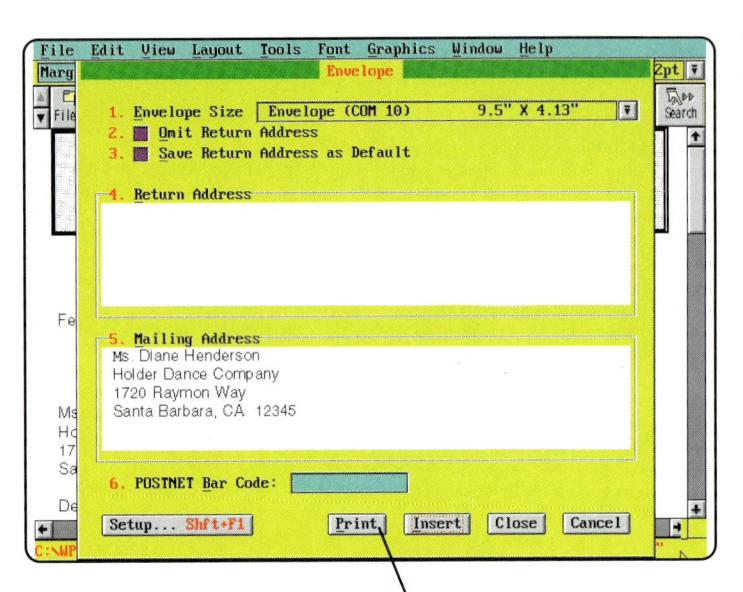

1. Remove the **tractor feed paper** from your printer and **insert** an **envelope**. If you want the return address to be printed further down on the envelope, adjust the envelope's position manually before printing. Your printer may allow you to feed an envelope without removing the tractor feed paper. Check your printer's manual for help.

2. Click on **Print**. A message box will appear.

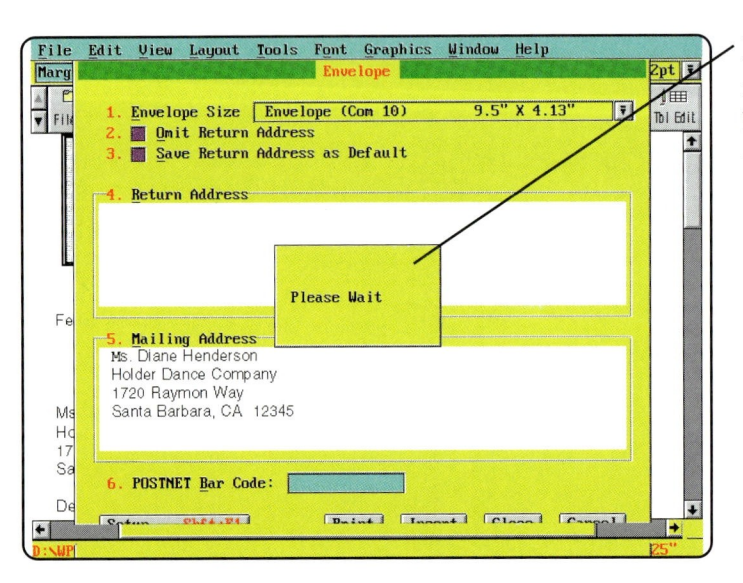

Notice a Please Wait message will briefly appear before the envelope begins to print.

CHAPTER 10: PRINTING AN ENVELOPE

PRINTING THE RETURN ADDRESS

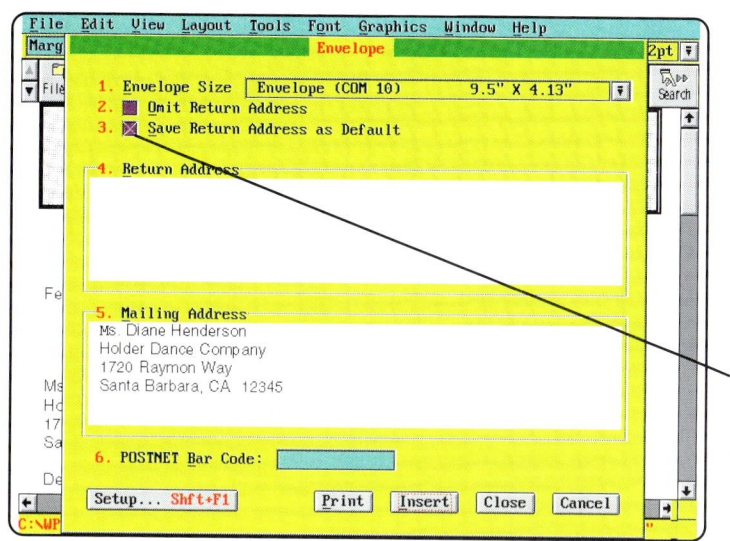

Place a single envelope in your printer's paper tray or tractor feed. See the previous sections if you need help.

1. Click on the **Envelope button** in the button bar. The Envelope dialog box will appear.

2. Click on **Save Return Address as Default** to insert an × in the box. This means the return address will be permanently attached to your letter.

3. Click on the left corner of the **Return Address box** to set the insertion point.

4. Type the first line of the return address, **COBURN COSTUME COMPANY,** and press **Enter**.

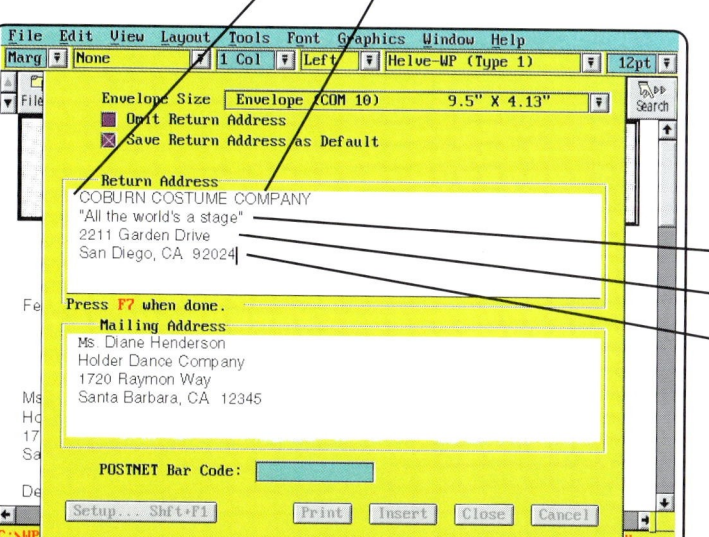

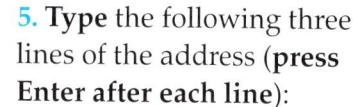

5. Type the following three lines of the address (**press Enter after each line**):

"All the world's a stage"
2211 Garden Drive
San Diego, CA 92024

6. Press the **F7 key**. The buttons at the bottom of the dialog box will become active.

WORDPERFECT 6 FOR DOS: THE VISUAL LEARNING GUIDE

Notice that the buttons at the bottom of the dialog box are now active.

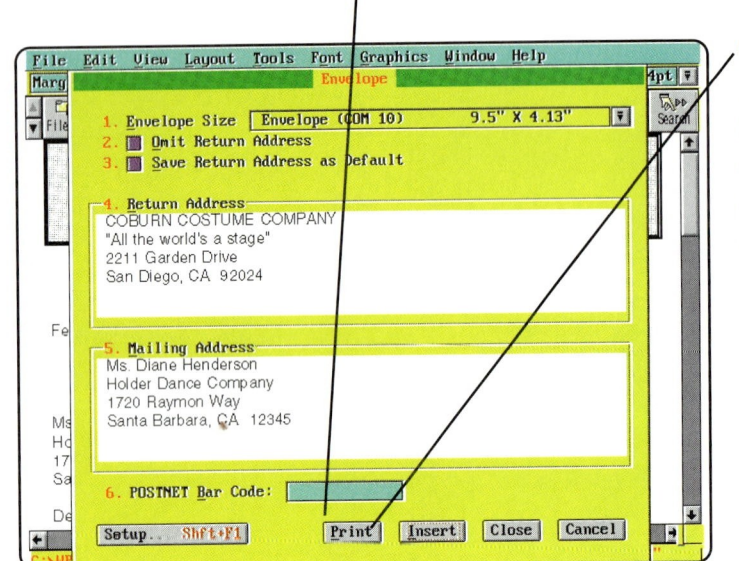

7. Click on **Print**. You will see a Please Wait message box. Check your printer's manual to see if you need to press a Form Feed or other similar button.

Omitting and Restoring the Standard Return Address

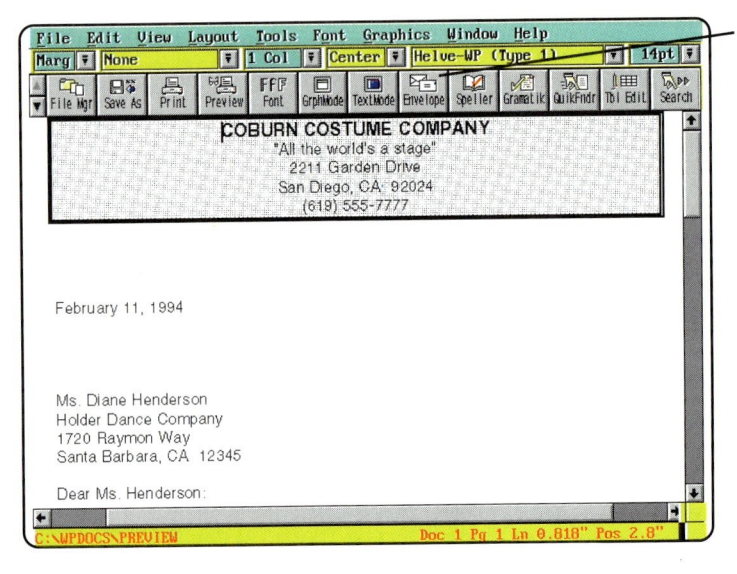

1. Click on the **Envelope button** in the button bar. The Envelope dialog box will appear.

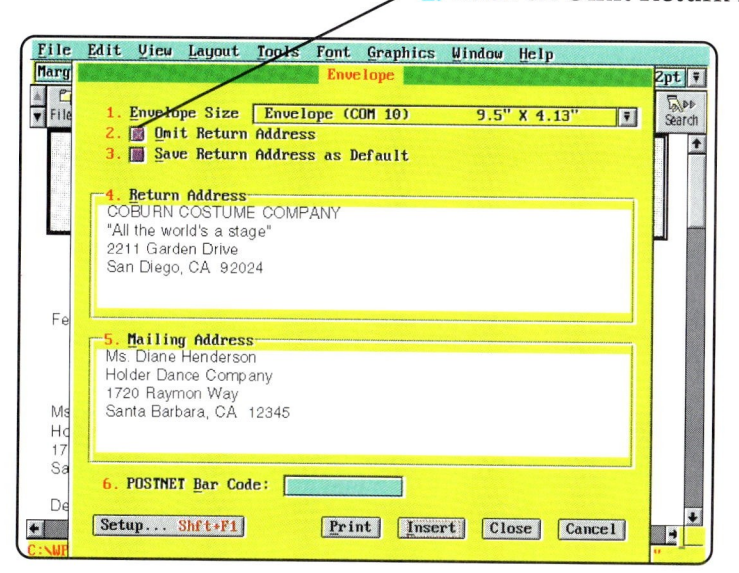

CHAPTER 10: PRINTING AN ENVELOPE

2. Click on **Omit Return Address** to insert an ✕ in the box if you don't want to print the return address. The address will remain on your screen, but it will not print.

3. Click on **Omit Return Address** again to *remove* the ✕ and restore the address. Go to step 2 in the next section to learn how to customize the return address.

CUSTOMIZING THE ENVELOPE TEXT

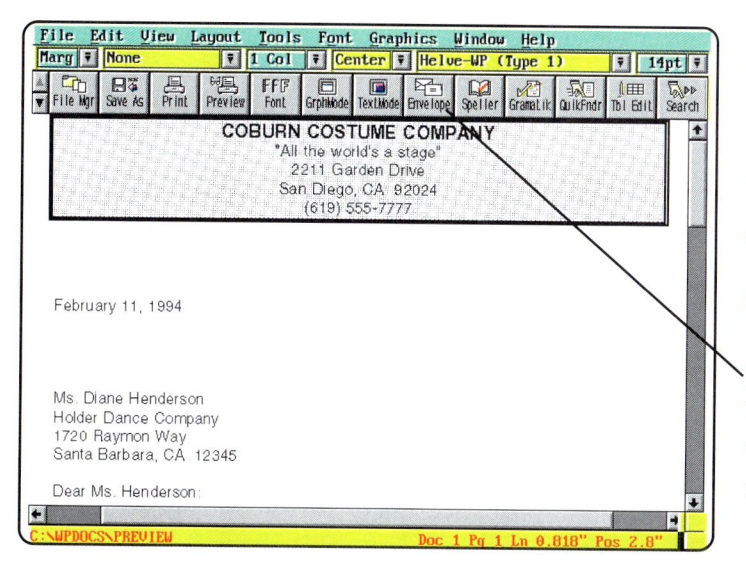

It's easy to make formatting changes to the return address.

Changing the Font and Point Size

1. Click on the **Envelope button** in the button bar if the Envelope dialog box is not already open.

2. **Click** to the **left of "COBURN"** in the Return Address box to set the cursor.

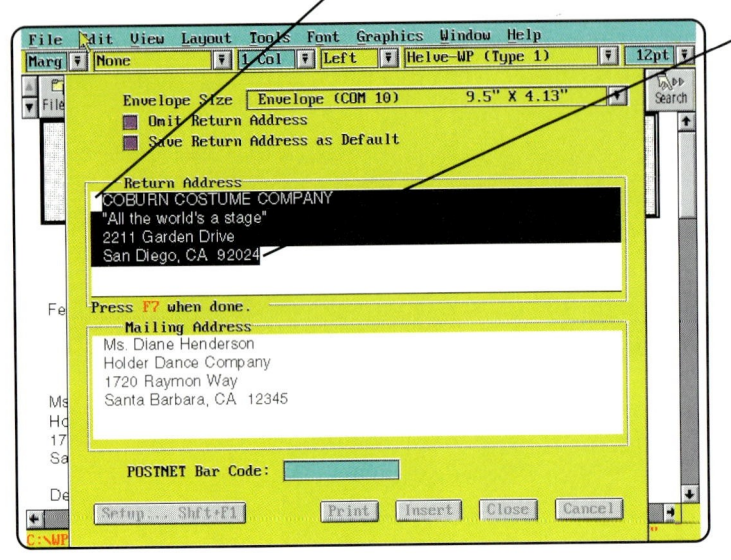

3. **Press and hold** the mouse button as you **drag** the cursor to **highlight the return address**. **Release** the mouse button.

4. **Click** on **Font** in the menu bar. A pull-down menu will appear.

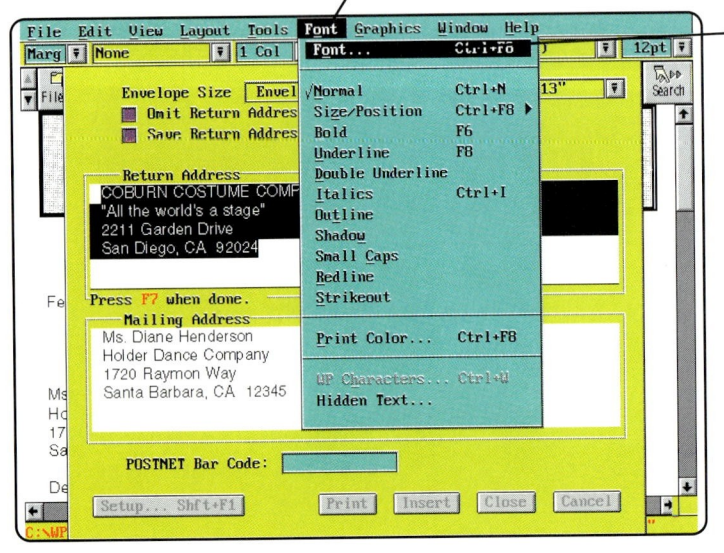

5. **Click** on **Font**. The Font dialog box will appear.

CHAPTER 10: PRINTING AN ENVELOPE

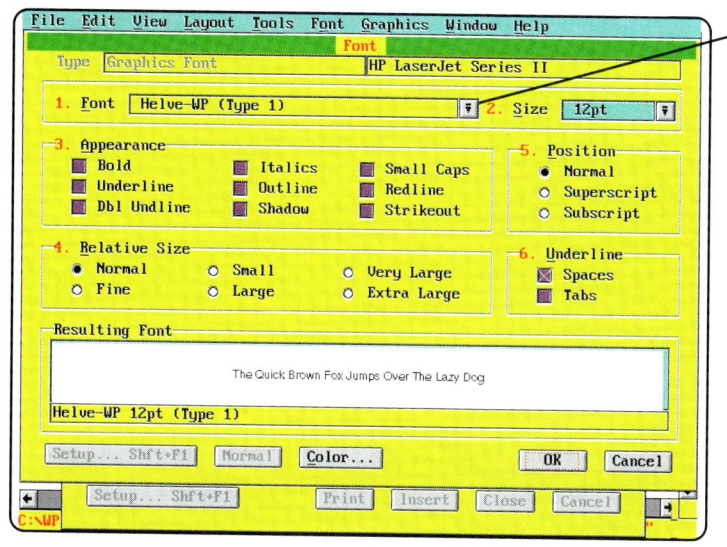

6. Click on the **down arrow** to the **right of the Font box**. A drop-down list of fonts will appear.

"Helve-WP (Type 1)" (Helvetica) will be highlighted as it is the setting for the current document.

7. Click on the **up arrow** on the scroll bar to scroll up the list of available fonts until you see Dutch 801 Bold (Speedo). (Your list of fonts may be different from the one shown here.)

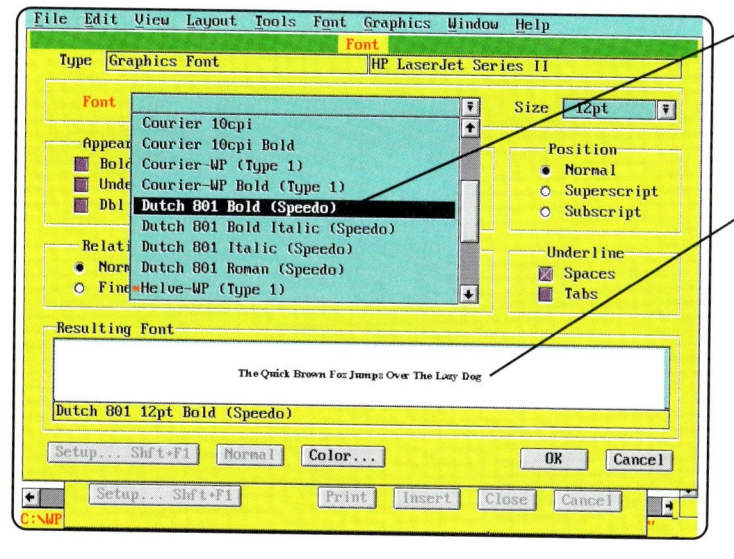

8. Click twice on **Dutch 801 Bold (Speedo)** or any other font you choose. The drop-down list will disappear.

Notice that an example of the Dutch Bold font will appear in the Resulting Font box.

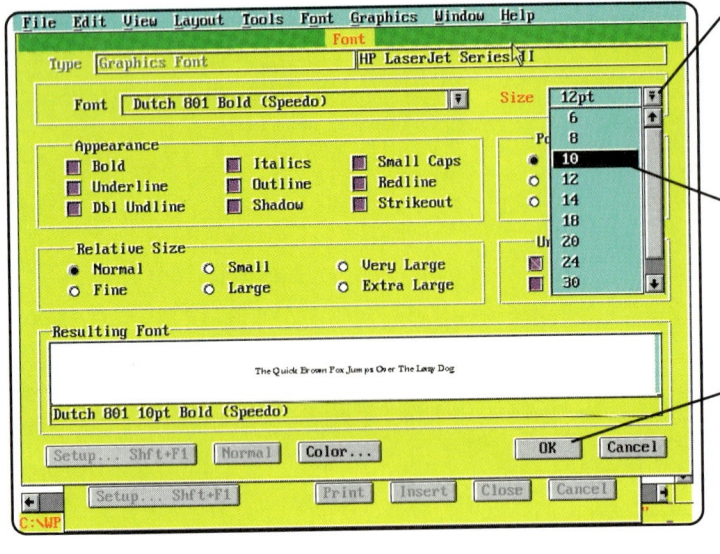

WORDPERFECT 6 FOR DOS: THE VISUAL LEARNING GUIDE

9. Click on the **down arrow** to the **right of the Size (point) box**. A drop-down list of point sizes will appear.

10. Click twice on **10**. The drop-down list will disappear and the number "10" will appear in the Size box.

11. Click on **OK**. The Envelope dialog box will appear. The return address will change to 10-point Dutch Bold type.

Making the First Line of the Address Bold

1. Click to the **left of "COBURN"** to set the cursor.

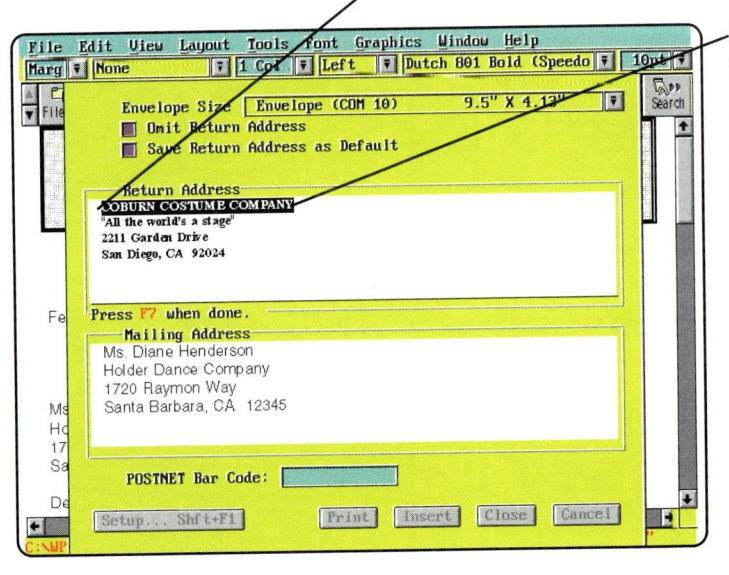

2. Press and hold the mouse button as you **drag** the cursor to **highlight** the **company name**. **Release** the mouse button.

CHAPTER 10: PRINTING AN ENVELOPE

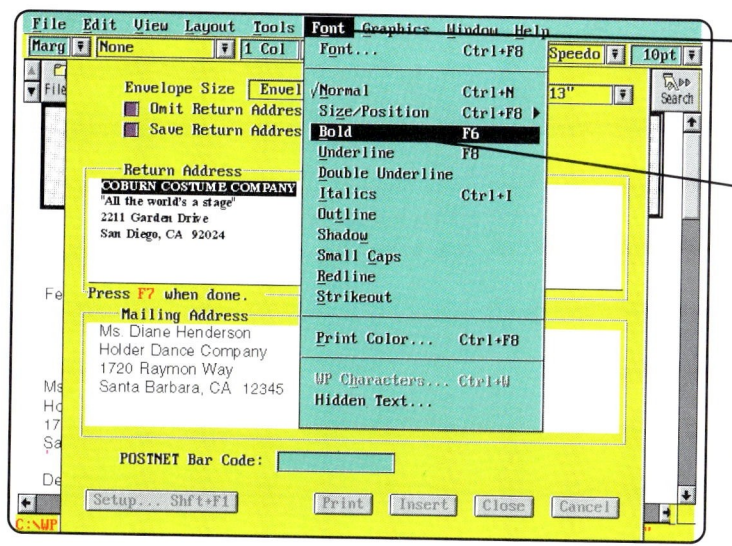

3. Click on **Font** in the menu bar. A pull-down menu will appear.

4. Click on **Bold**. The pull-down menu will disappear and the company name will be in boldface type.

You can use these same steps to change the appearance of the font in the mailing address.

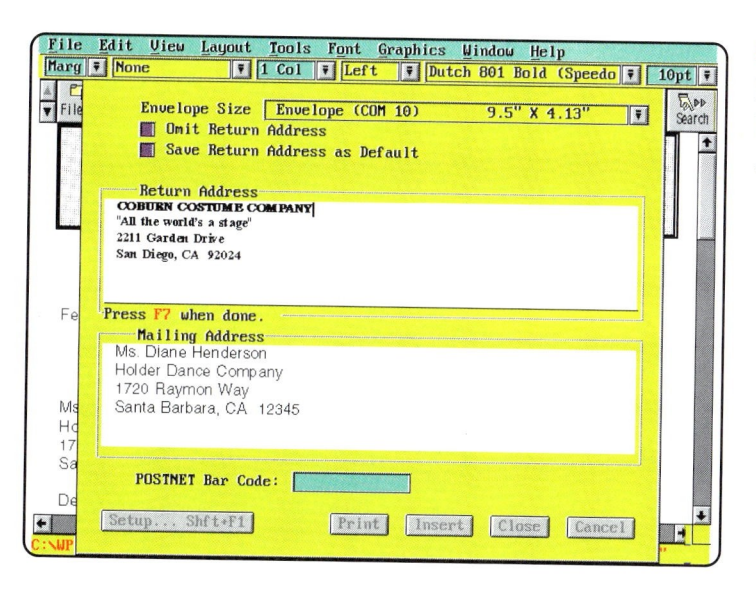

5. Press the **F7 key** on your keyboard to activate the buttons at the bottom of the dialog box.

WORDPERFECT 6 FOR DOS: THE VISUAL LEARNING GUIDE

6. **Click** on **Save Return Address as Default** to permanently save the changes to the return address.

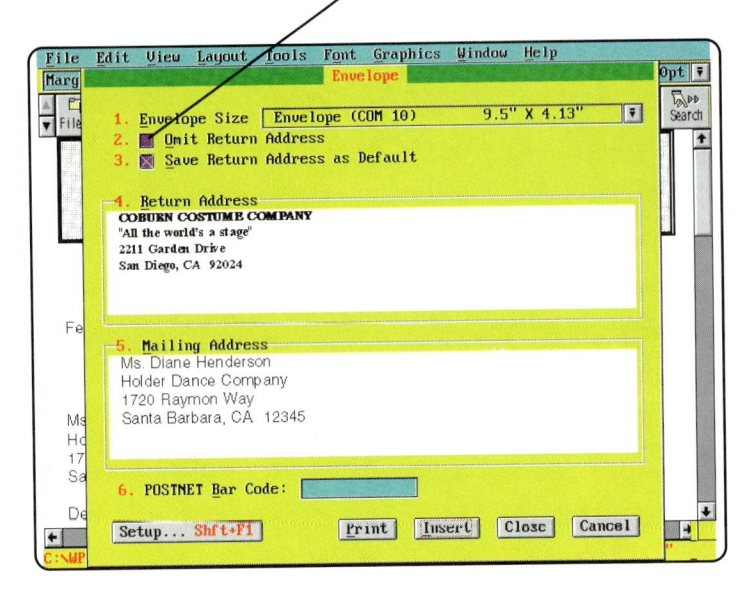

Important Note: Since the return address will show up on all future envelopes, you will need to change the Coburn Costume Company return address to your own when you are through with the examples in this book. Simply highlight and delete the Coburn Costume Company address. Type in your own address. Press F7. Then click on Save Return Address as Default.

PRINTING A LETTER WITH AN ATTACHED ENVELOPE

When you attach an envelope to a WordPerfect document, the envelope becomes the last page of the letter, or page 3 in this case. When you print, the letter will be printed first, and then the envelope.

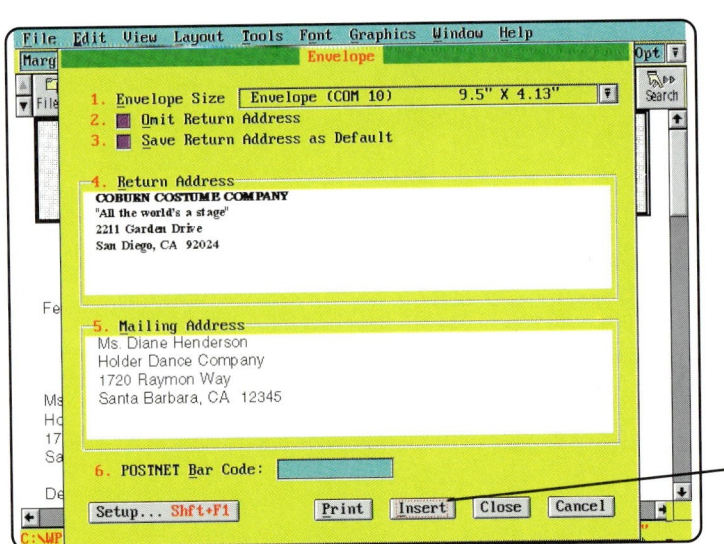

Attaching an Envelope to a Letter

1. **Click** on **Insert** to attach the letter.

CHAPTER 10: PRINTING AN ENVELOPE

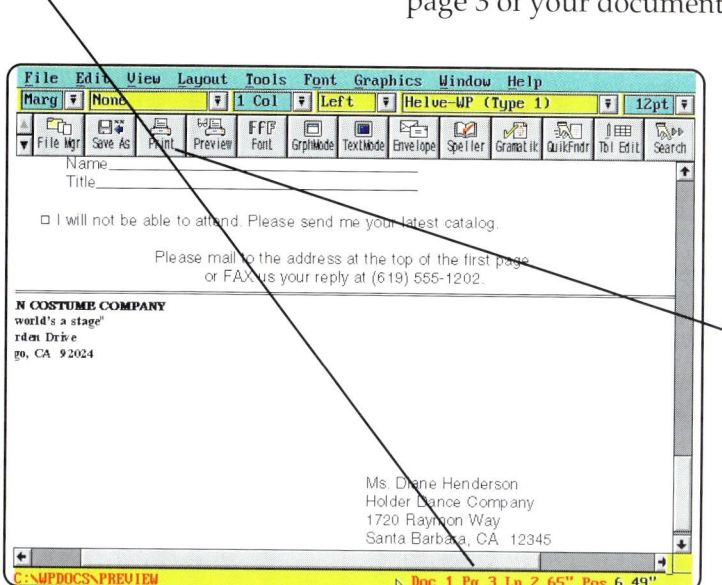

Notice that the newly attached envelope will appear as page 3 of your document.

Printing a Letter with an Attached Envelope

1. Click on the **Print button** in the button bar. The Print dialog box will appear.

Notice that in the Print box the circle next to Full Document has a dot in it. If it does not, click on Full Document to insert a dot in the circle.

2. Click on **Print**. WordPerfect will print both the envelope and the letter. (Check your printer's manual to see if you need to press Form Feed or any other special buttons.)

WORDPERFECT 6 FOR DOS: THE VISUAL LEARNING GUIDE

PRINTING AN ATTACHED ENVELOPE WITHOUT A LETTER

1. **Click** on the **Print button** in the button bar. The Print dialog box will appear.

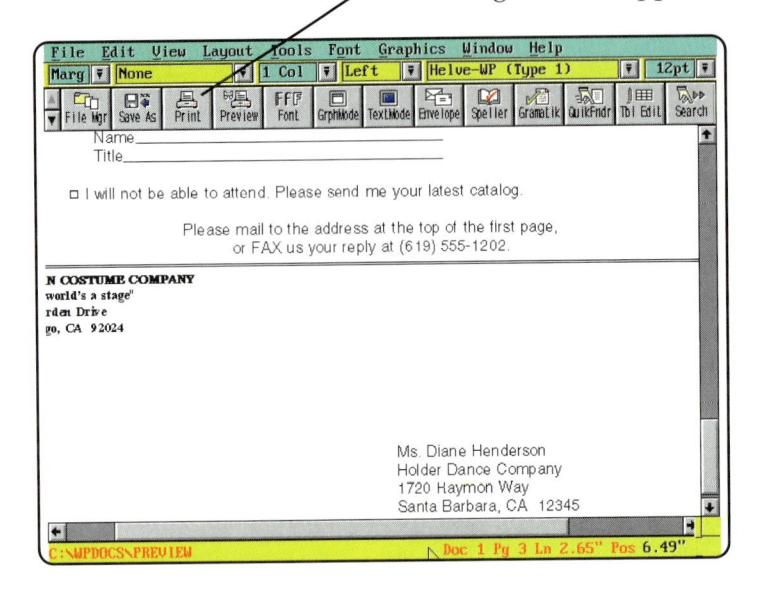

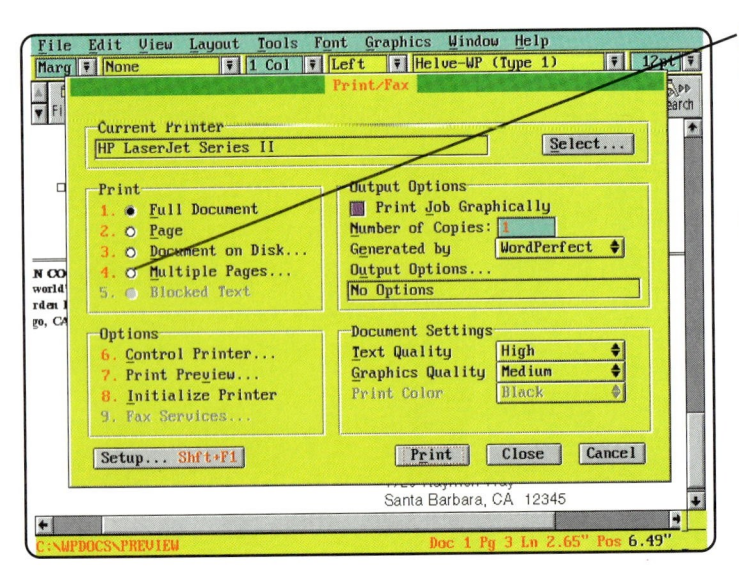

2. **Click** on **Multiple Pages** in the Print box. The Print Multiple Pages dialog box will appear with "(all)" in the Page/Label Range text box.

CHAPTER 10: PRINTING AN ENVELOPE

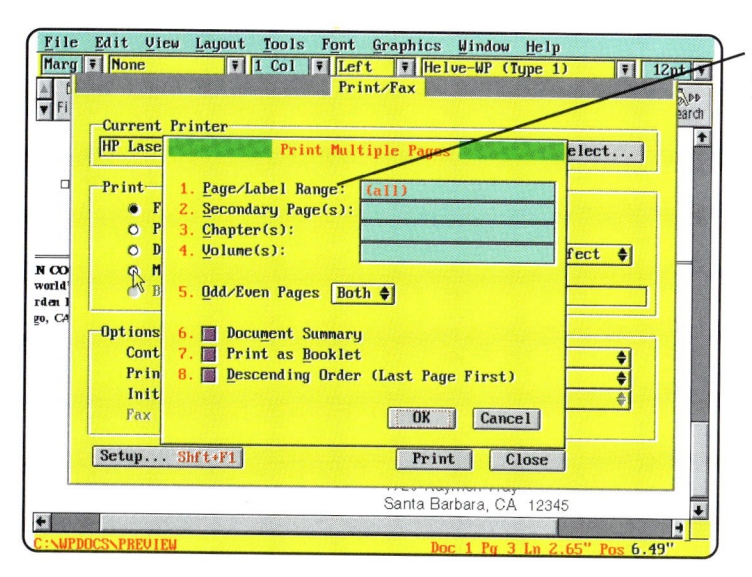

3. **Click** on **Page/Label Range** to highlight "(all)."

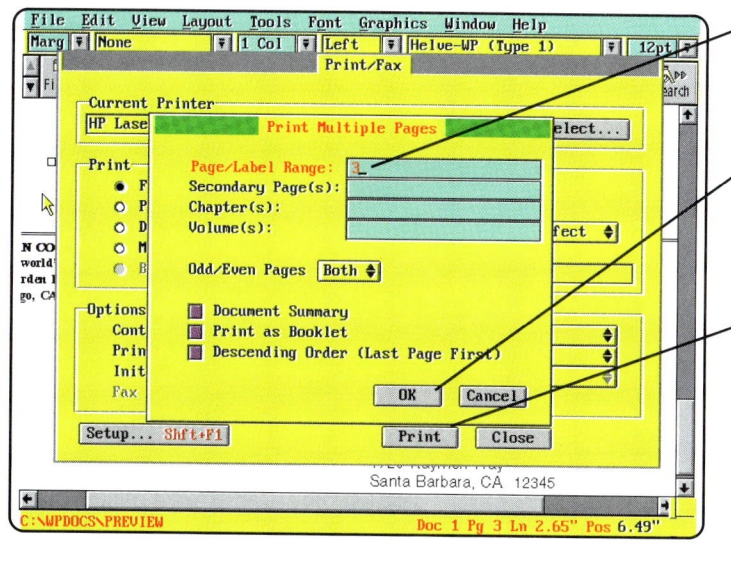

4. **Type** the number **3**, which is the page number for the attached envelope.

5. **Click** on **OK**. The Print Multiple Pages dialog box will disappear.

6. **Click** on **Print** in the Print dialog box. The envelope will print. (Again, check your printer's manual for the exact steps.)

WORDPERFECT 6 FOR DOS: THE VISUAL LEARNING GUIDE

PRINTING A LETTER WITHOUT AN ATTACHED ENVELOPE

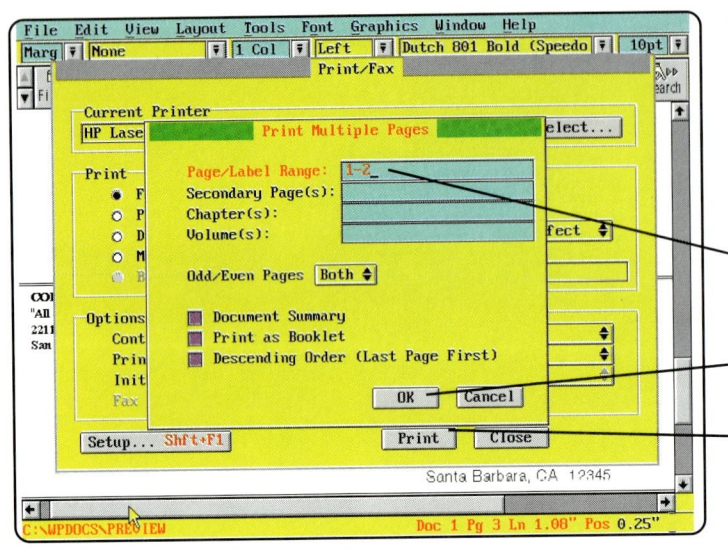

1. **Repeat steps 1 through 3** in the previous section entitled "Printing an Attached Envelope Without a Letter."

2. **Type** the range **1-2** in the Page/Label Range text box.

3. **Click** on **OK**.

4. **Click** on **Print**. The two-page letter will print. The envelope will not print.

CLOSING A LETTER WITHOUT SAVING AN ATTACHED ENVELOPE

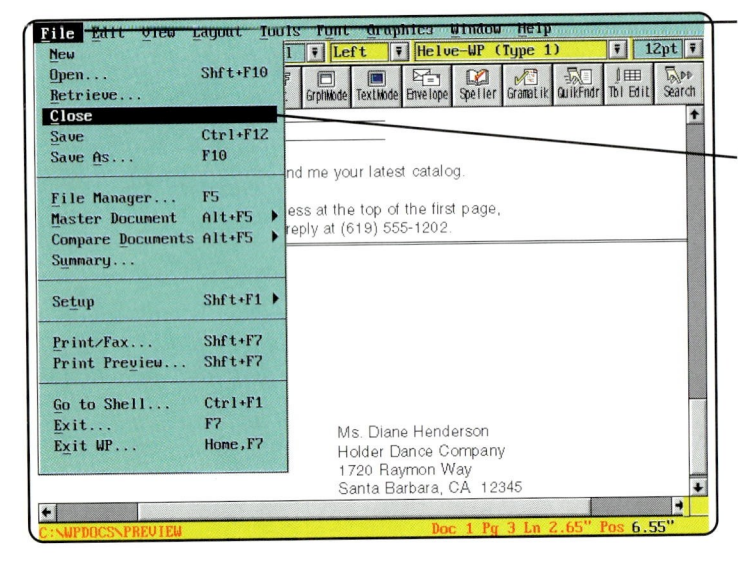

1. **Click** on **File** in the menu bar. A pull-down menu will appear.

2. **Click** on **Close**. The Save message box will appear and ask if you want to save changes to your document.

3. **Click** on **No**.

The letter will close and the envelope will not be attached when you reopen the letter in later chapters.

Creating a Mailing List

With the WordPerfect 6 Merge feature, you can send the same letter to different people and have the individual's name, address, salutation, and other information personalized on each letter without having to retype each letter. After you've written the letter, you begin the merge process by creating a mailing list, as shown in this chapter. Then you edit the mailing list (Chapter 12), attach, code, and print the letters (Chapters 13 and 14). Finally you print personalized envelopes (Chapter 15).

Even if you have a mailing list already created in another word-processing program, such as WordStar, work through Chapters 11, 12, 13, and 14 first to learn how WordPerfect's Merge feature works. Then go to Chapter 16, "Converting a Mailing List Created in Another Program," to convert your mailing list to WordPerfect. In this chapter you will do the following:

❖ Create a data entry table
❖ Create a mailing list

SETTING UP A DATA TABLE

To create a mailing list, you must first enter the information for your mailing list into a *data entry table*.

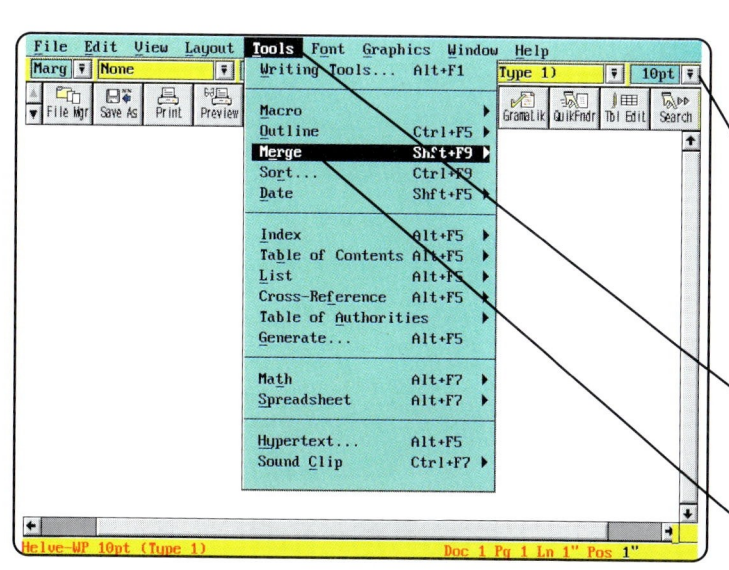

1. Open a **new document file** if one is not already on your screen.

2. Click on the **Point Size box** and **change the point size** of the text to **10pt**.

Opening a Data Table

1. Click on **Tools** in the menu bar. A pull-down menu will appear.

2. Click on **Merge**. A second menu will appear.

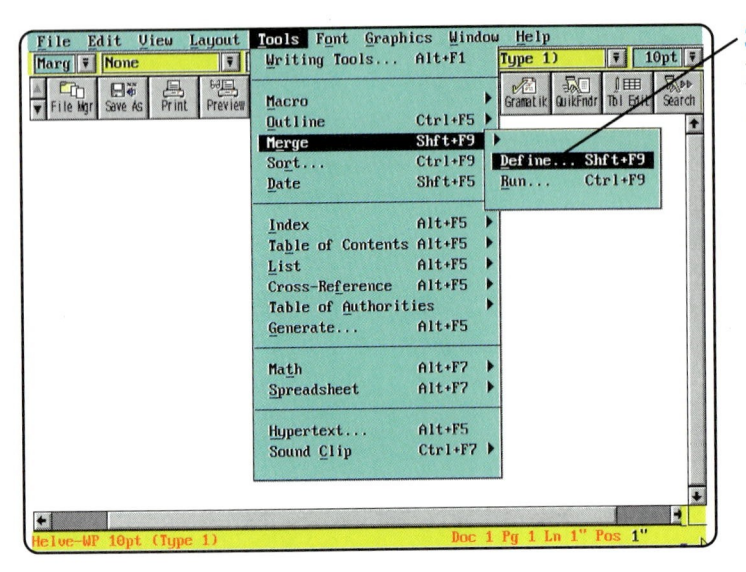

WORDPERFECT 6 FOR DOS: THE VISUAL LEARNING GUIDE

3. Click on **Define**. The Merge Codes dialog box will appear.

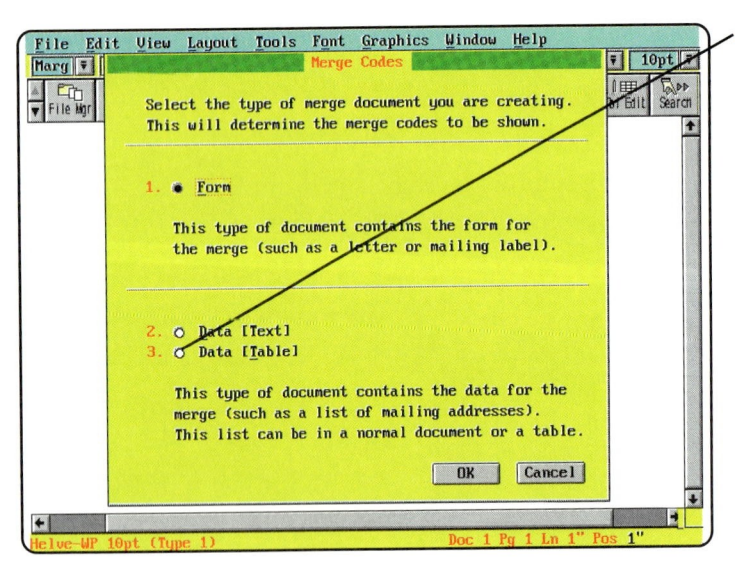

4. Click on **Data (Table)** to insert a dot in the circle. The Merge Codes (Table Data File) dialog box will appear.

CHAPTER 11: CREATING A MAILING LIST

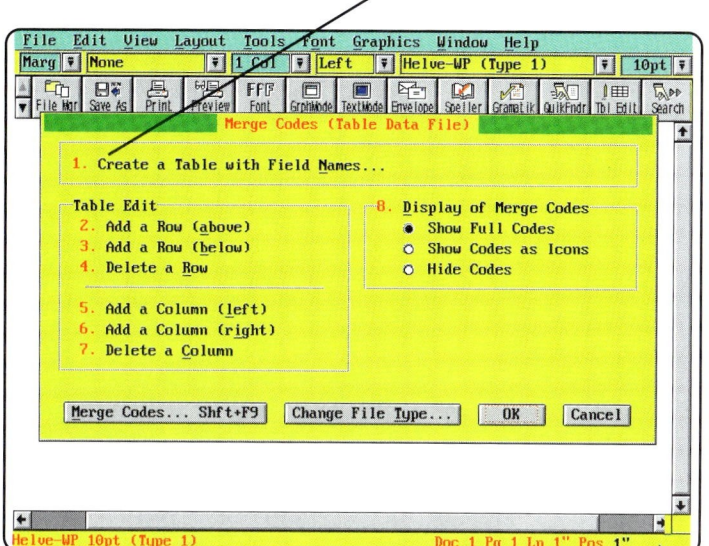

5. Click on **Create a Table with Field Names**. The Field Names dialog box will appear. The cursor will be flashing in the Field Name text box.

Entering Field Names

1. Type the word **LAST** in the Field Name text box and **press Enter**. You don't have to type the word in all capitals. You can type it any way you want. The word "LAST" will appear in the Field Name List box. The cursor will be flashing in the Field Name text box, just waiting for the next entry.

Warning: Do not click on OK, or you will end up creating a one-column mailing list of last names only! If this happens, start over again.

2. Type the word **FIRST** in the Field Name text box and **press Enter**.

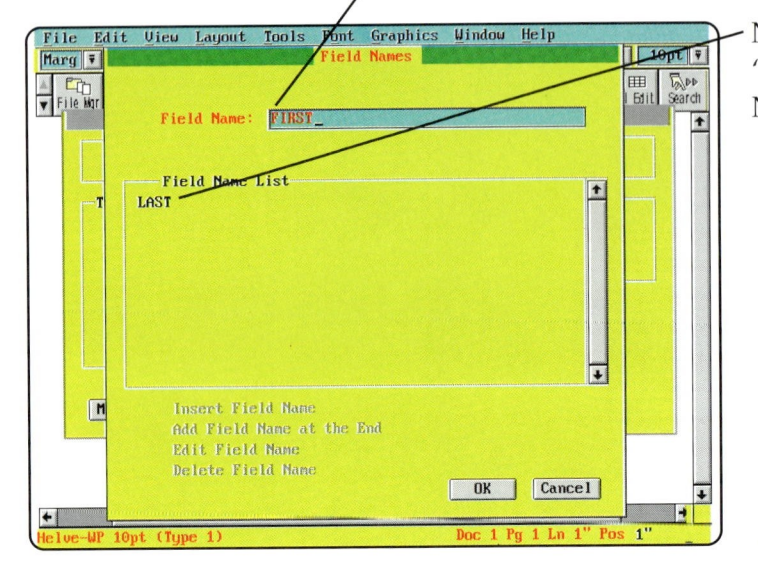

Notice that the word "LAST" appears in the Field Name List box.

3. Repeat step 1 to enter the following words (field names) in the Field Name List box:

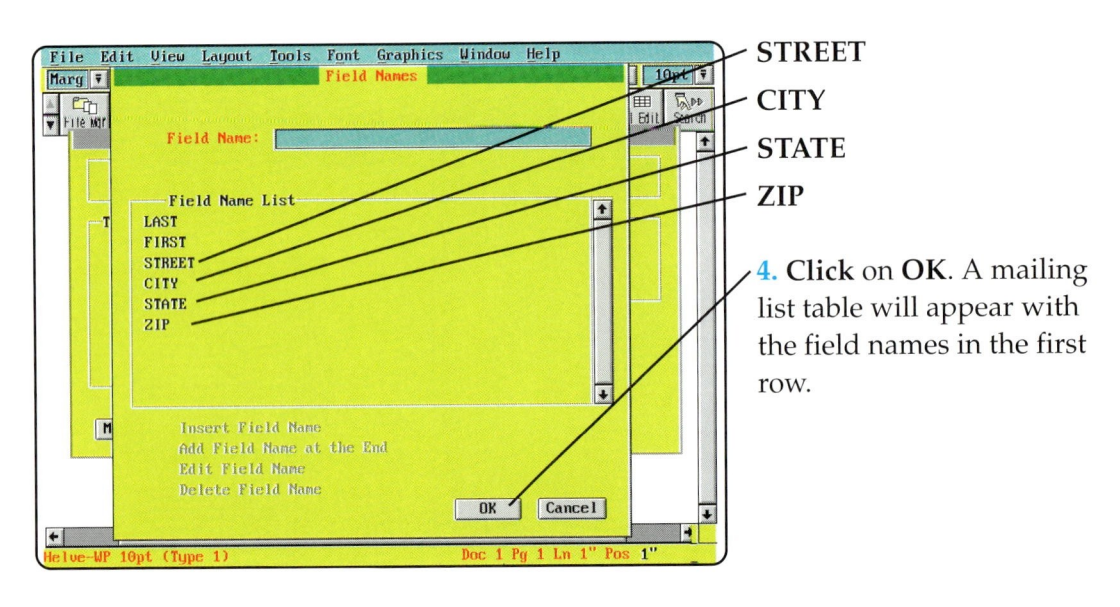

- STREET
- CITY
- STATE
- ZIP

4. Click on **OK**. A mailing list table will appear with the field names in the first row.

CHAPTER 11: CREATING A MAILING LIST

CREATING A MAILING LIST

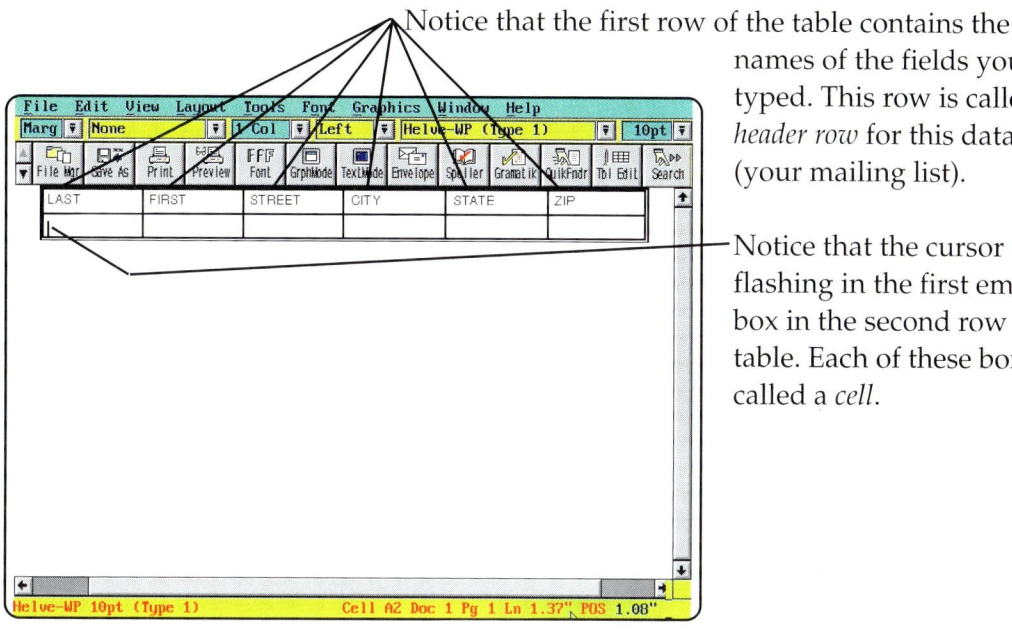

Notice that the first row of the table contains the names of the fields you just typed. This row is called the *header row* for this data file (your mailing list).

Notice that the cursor is flashing in the first empty box in the second row of the table. Each of these boxes is called a *cell*.

1. **Type Chambers** under the cell labeled "LAST."

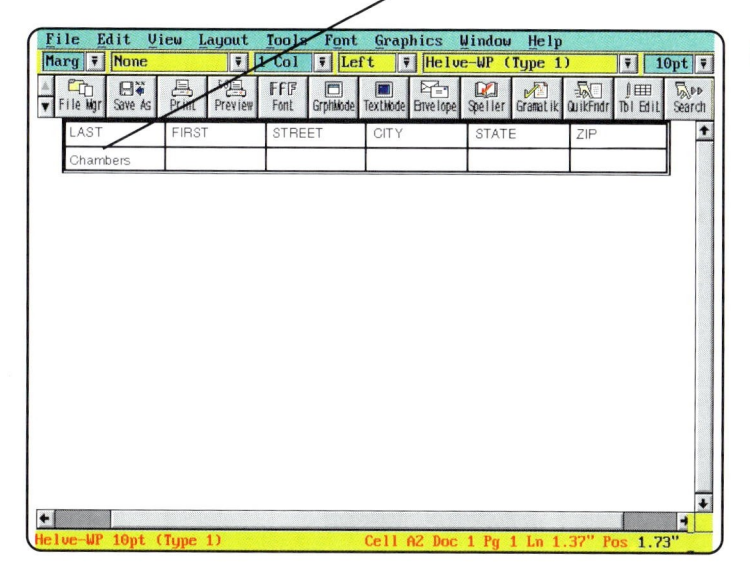

2. **Press Tab**. The cursor will move to the next cell.

WORDPERFECT 6 FOR DOS: THE VISUAL LEARNING GUIDE

3. **Type Jane** in the cell under "FIRST."

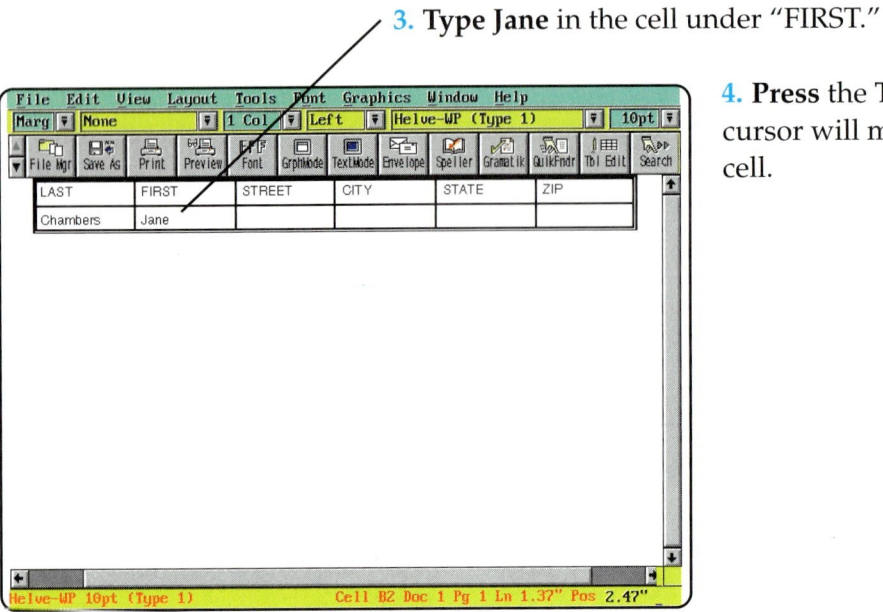

4. **Press** the **Tab key**. The cursor will move to the next cell.

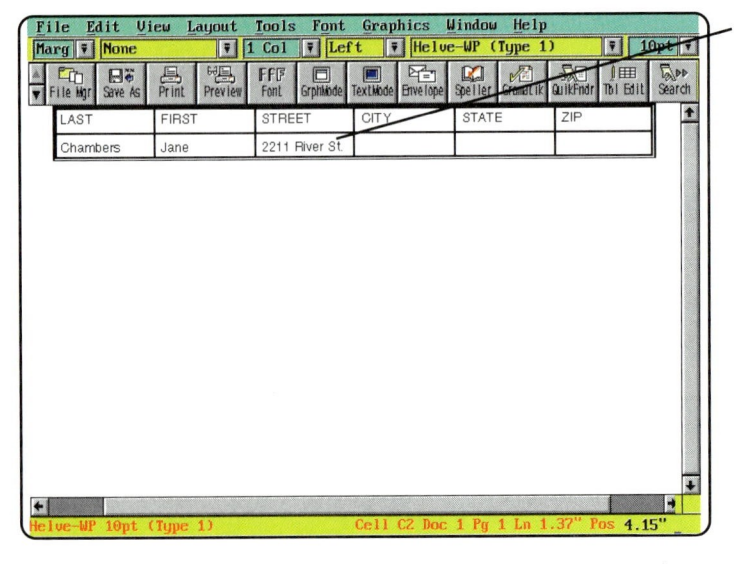

5. **Type 2211 River St.**

6. **Press** the **Tab key**. The cursor will move to the next cell.

CHAPTER 11: CREATING A MAILING LIST

7. Type the following information in the next three cells. **Press Tab** to move to each new cell:

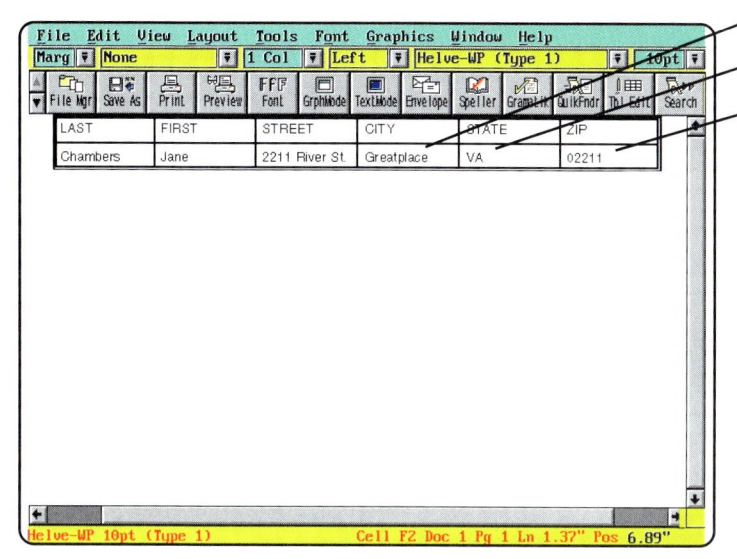

- Greatplace
- VA
- 02211

When you press Tab after the last entry in the row (the ZIP cell), WordPerfect automatically creates a new empty row in the table. The cursor will be flashing in the first cell of the new, empty row. (If you press Enter, WordPerfect adds an extra line to the current row. Simply press the Backspace key and the extra line will be deleted.)

8. Type Avery in the cell under "LAST."

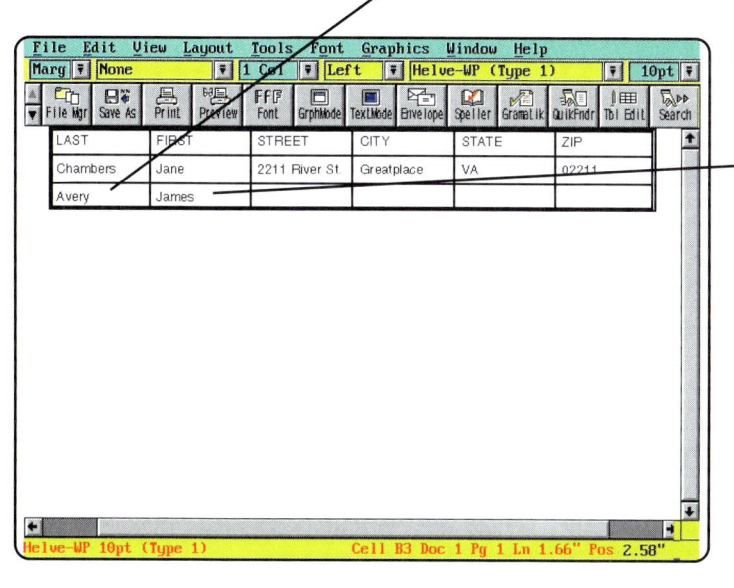

9. Press Tab. The cursor will move to the next cell.

10. Type James in the cell under "FIRST."

11. Press Tab. The cursor will move to the next cell.

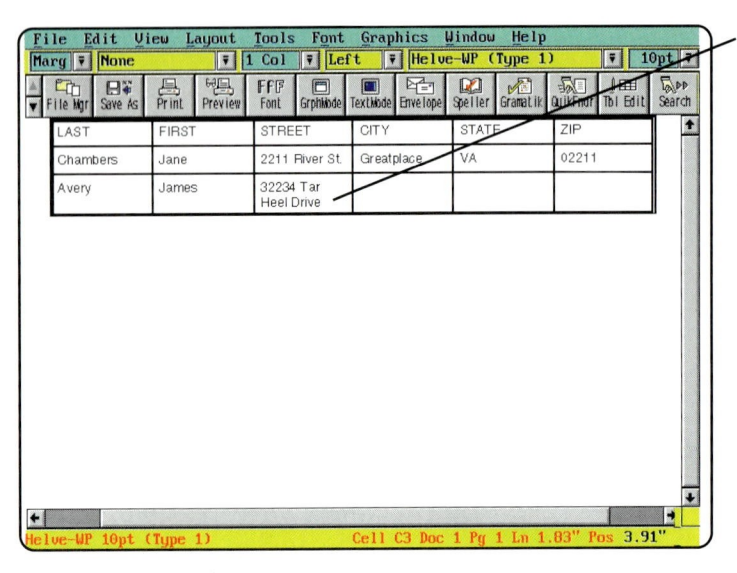

12. Type 32234 Tar Heel Drive in the cell under "STREET."

13. Press the **Tab key**. The cursor will move to the next cell.

14. Type the following address information into the next three cells. **Press** the **Tab Key** to go to each new cell:

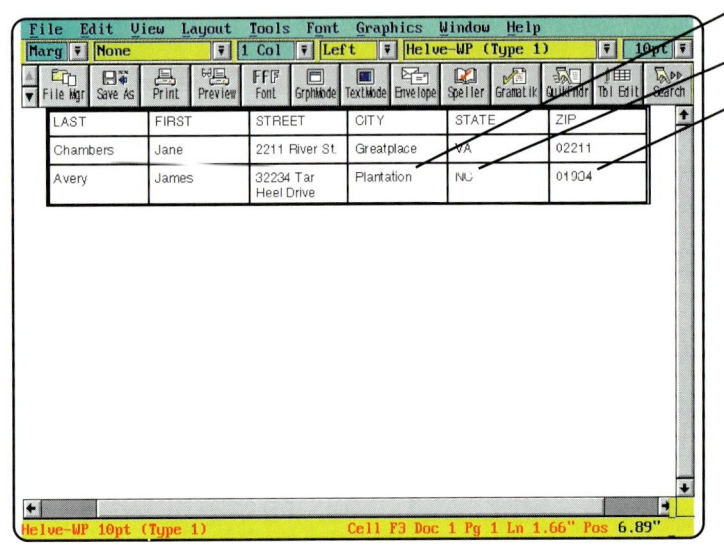

Plantation
NC
01934

You will enter only these two names now. When you are making your own mailing list, you can enter as many names as you like. If you do not have information to enter into a particular cell, just press the Tab key to leave that cell empty. Do not use the Spacebar to put spaces in an empty cell, or WordPerfect will enter the spaces into your document when you print.

CHAPTER 11: CREATING A MAILING LIST

SAVING THE MAILING LIST

1. Click on **File** in the menu bar. A pull-down menu will appear.

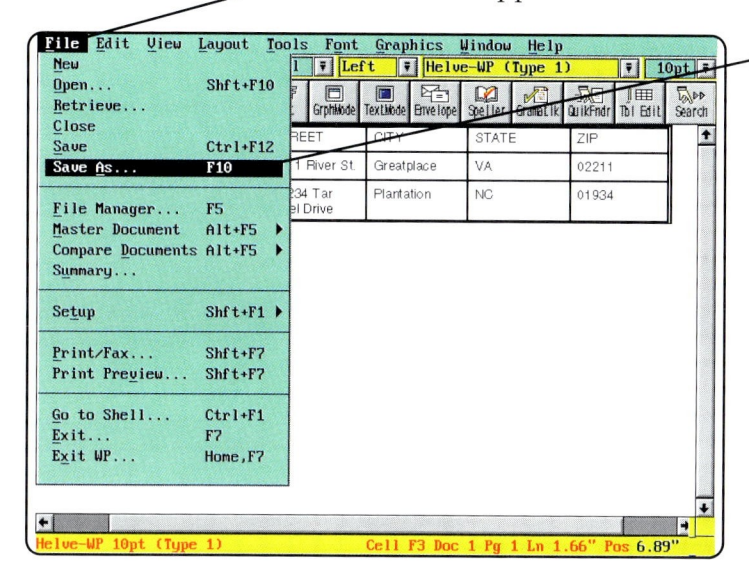

2. Click on **Save As**. The Save Document dialog box will appear.

3. Type c:\wpdocs\mylist.

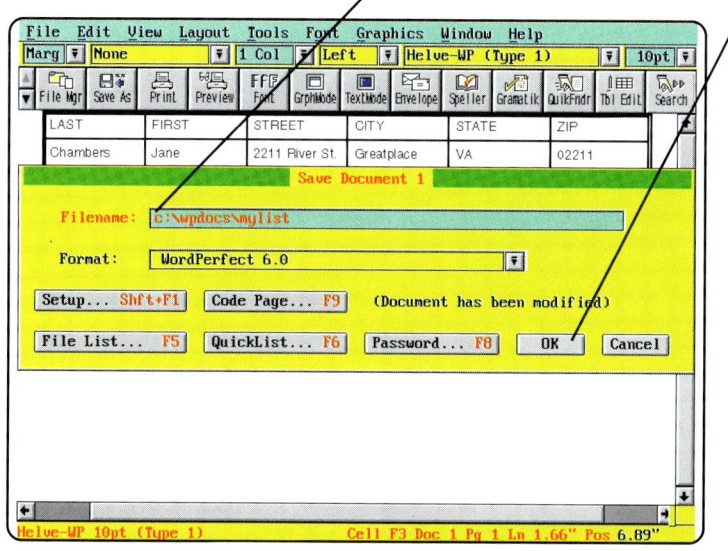

4. Click on **OK**. Your MYLIST mailing list is now saved. The table you created will appear. If you plan to follow along with the next chapter, do not exit the file.

Congratulations! You have created a mailing list without memorizing a single keystroke.

Editing a Mailing List

Suppose you created and saved a mailing list, as you did in Chapter 11, and then discovered that you didn't include fields for the company name and the person's title, for example. In WordPerfect 6 it is easy to make additions to your mailing list. First you will add the new fields to the list and then adjust the size of the cells to make room for the newly added fields. After that, it is a simple task to add more data in the mailing list table. In this chapter you will do the following:

- ❖ Add two new fields to a mailing list
- ❖ Adjust column widths of a mailing list table
- ❖ Enter more data in a mailing list table

ADDING FIELDS TO THE MAILING LIST

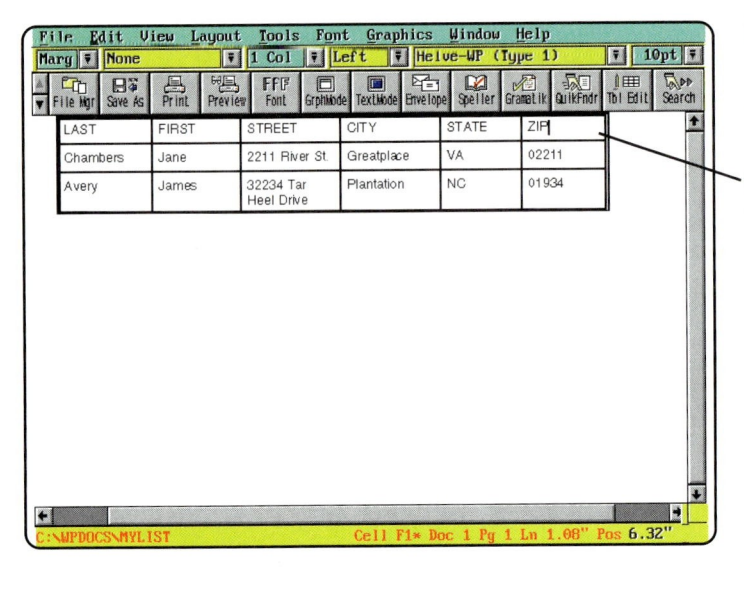

1. Open the **MYLIST** file that you created in Chapter 11 if it is not already open.

2. Click in the **ZIP cell** to set the cursor.

CHAPTER 12: EDITING A MAILING LIST

3. **Click** on **Tools** in the menu bar. A pull-down menu will appear.

4. **Click** on **Merge**. A second menu will appear.

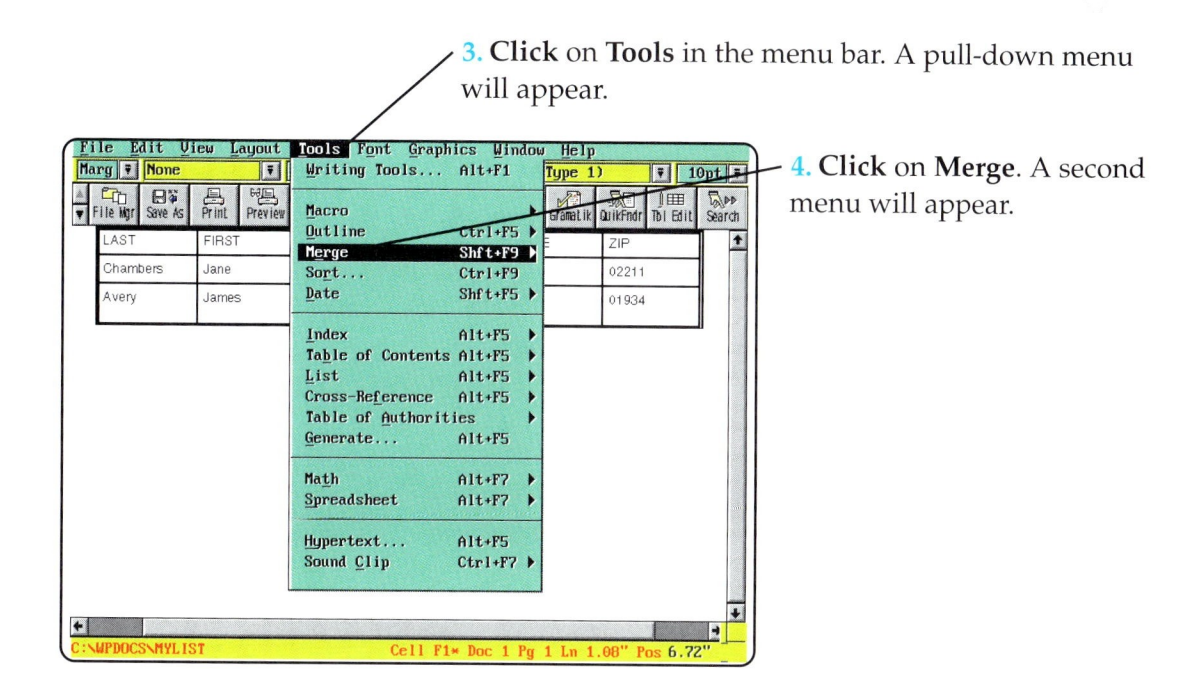

5. **Click** on **Define**. The Merge Codes (Table Data File) dialog box will appear.

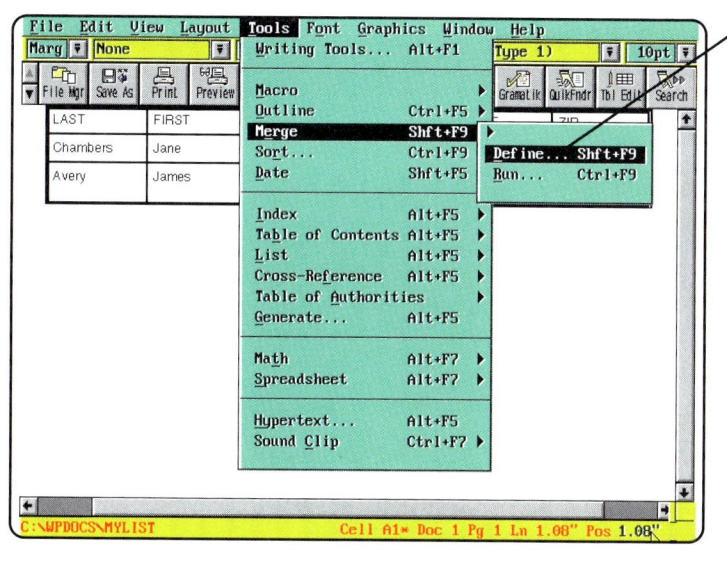

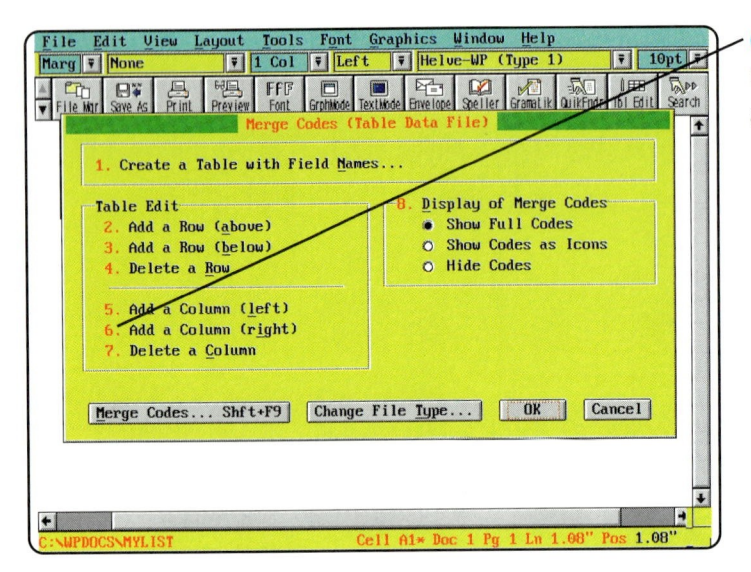

WORDPERFECT 6 FOR DOS: THE VISUAL LEARNING GUIDE

6. Click on **Add a Column (right)**. A new column will appear in the table.

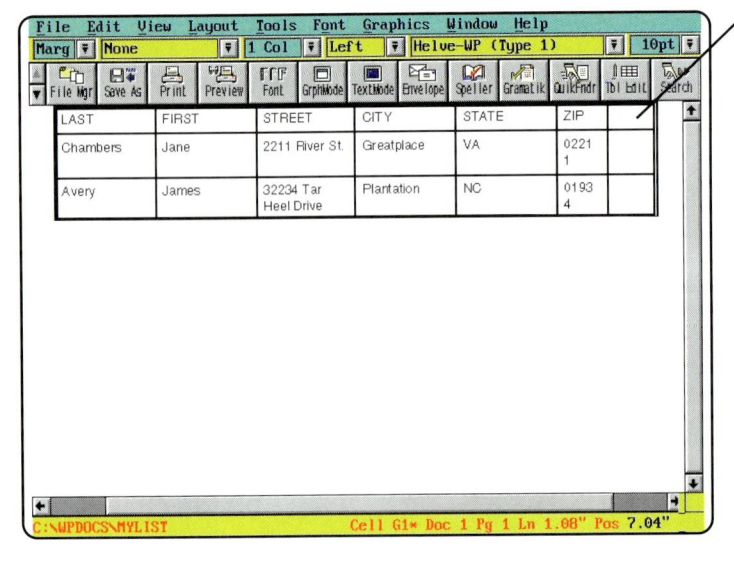

Notice the new column appears to the right of the ZIP field column.

CHAPTER 12: EDITING A MAILING LIST

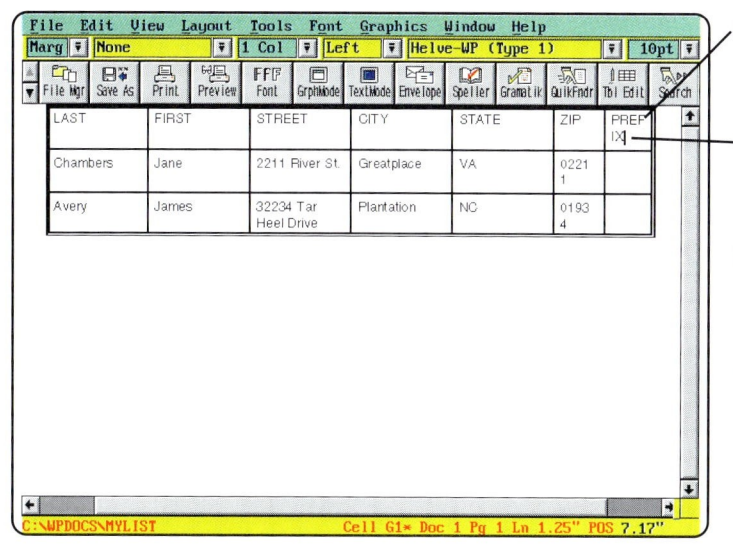

7. **Type PREFIX** in the field name cell.

Note: Leave the cursor flashing in this cell.

8. **Repeat steps 3 through 6** to **add a second column** to the right of the PREFIX column.

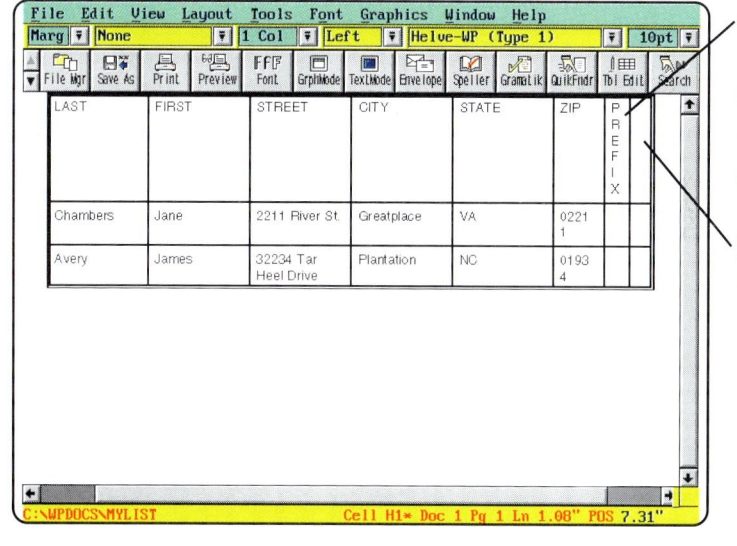

Notice that the columns are squashed and weird looking. In the next section you can make the columns more uniform.

9. **Type COMPANY** in the new field name cell.

WORDPERFECT 6 FOR DOS: THE VISUAL LEARNING GUIDE

Adjusting the Column Width

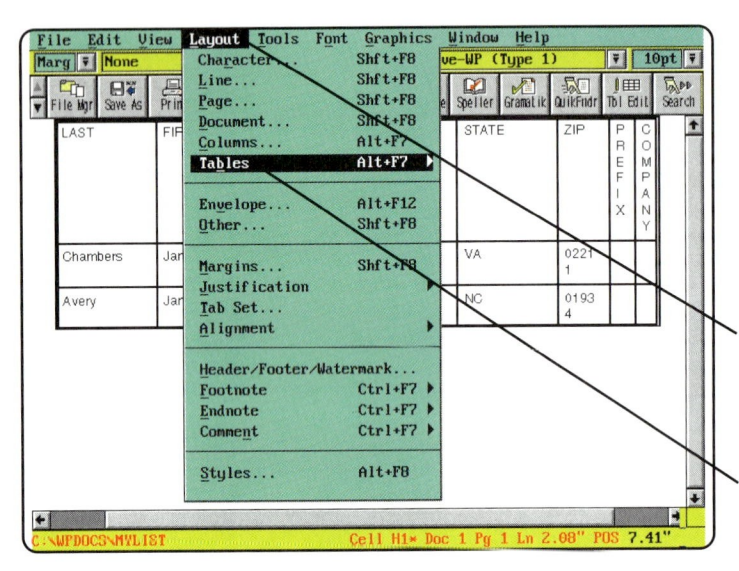

If you don't like a table with uneven column widths, follow the steps below. If you don't care, go to the next section entitled, "Entering More Data in a Mailing List Data Table."

1. Click on **Layout** in the menu bar. A pull-down menu will appear.

2. Click on **Tables**. A second menu will appear.

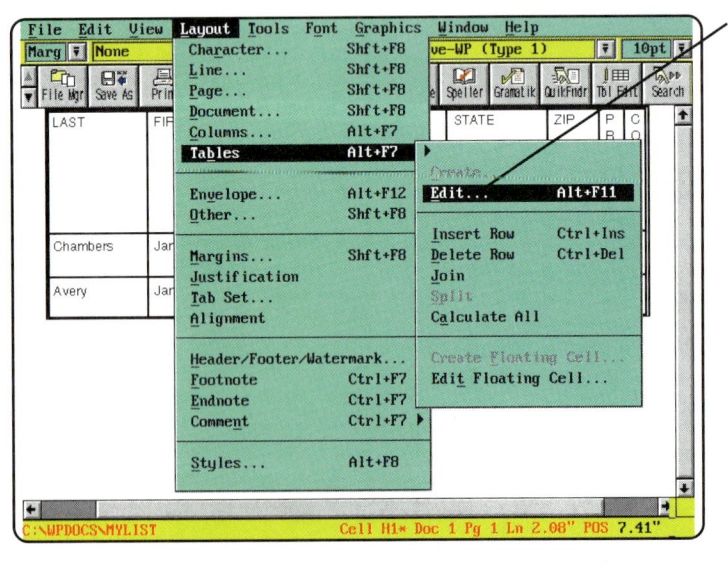

3. Click on **Edit**. The mailing list table will appear again, but this time it's in Table Edit mode. It will look very strange. Don't panic. You did nothing wrong.

CHAPTER 12: EDITING A MAILING LIST

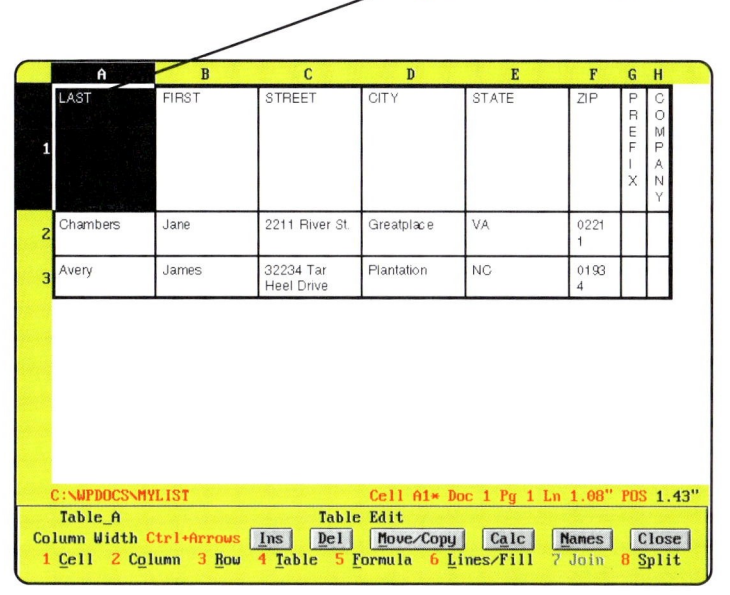

4. Click on **column A** to set the cursor.

5. Press and hold the **Ctrl key** as you **press** the ← **key**. The cell will shrink in small increments each time you press the ← key. **Release** the key when the cell has reached the size you want. If you make the cell too small, press and hold the Ctrl key as you press the → key to make it larger.

6. Press the **Tab key**. Column B will become highlighted.

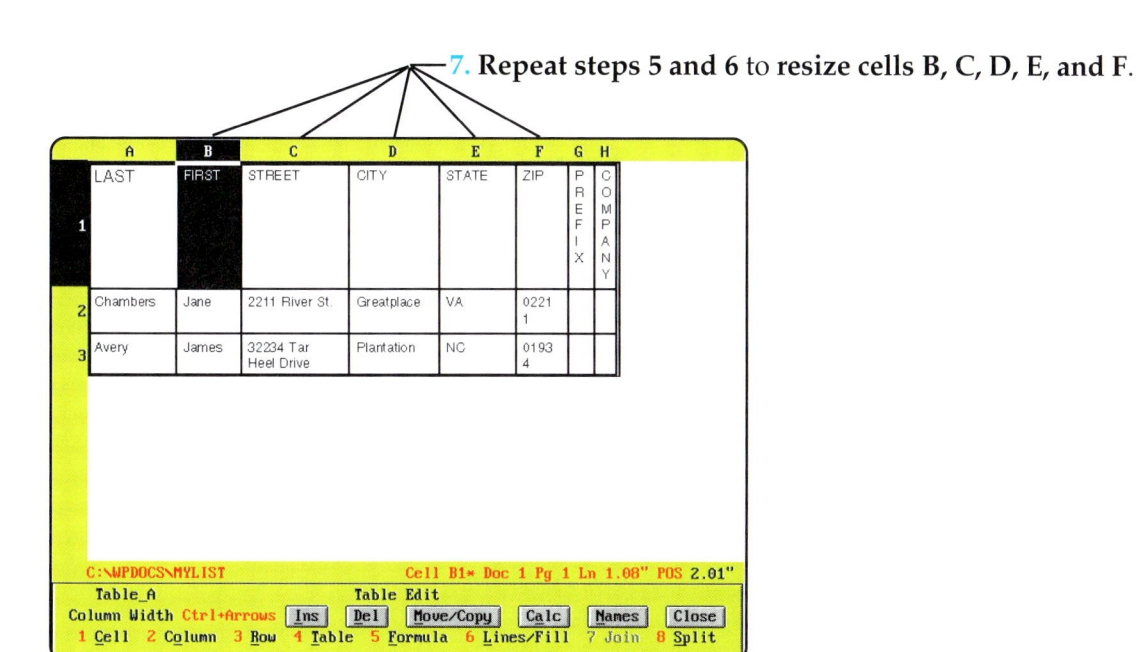

7. Repeat steps 5 and 6 to **resize cells B, C, D, E, and F**.

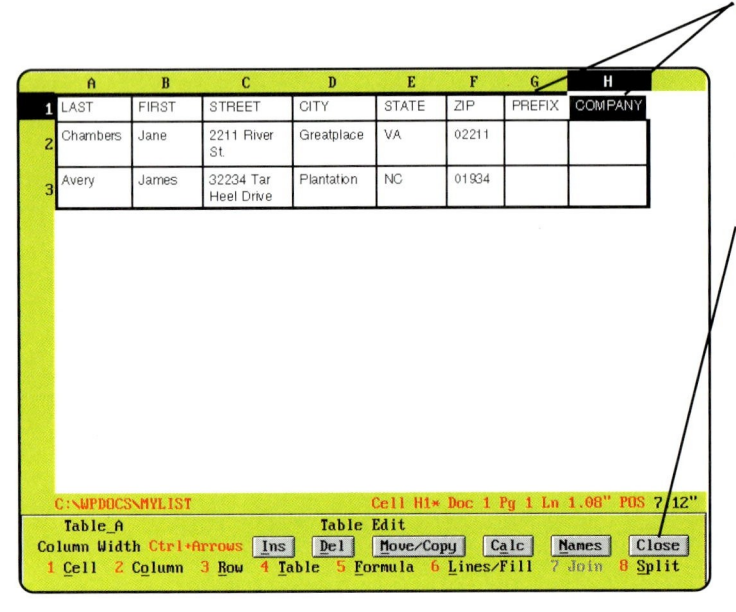

WORDPERFECT 6 FOR DOS: THE VISUAL LEARNING GUIDE

8. **Repeat steps 5 and 6** to resize (make larger) **cells G and H**. Use the → rather than ← to enlarge these cells.

9. **Click** on **Close**. The resized mailing list table will appear. Lookin' good!

ENTERING MORE DATA IN A MAILING LIST DATA TABLE

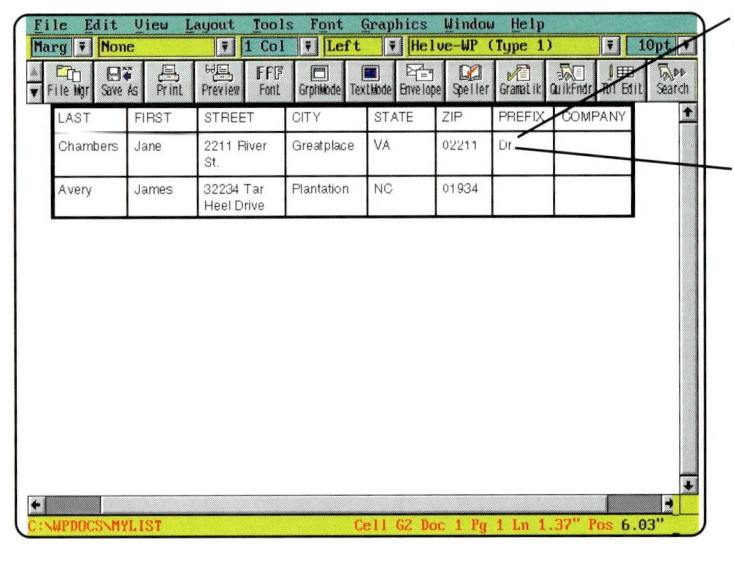

1. **Click** on the **empty cell below "PREFIX"** to set the cursor.

2. **Type Dr.** and **press** the **Tab key**. The cursor will move to the COMPANY cell.

CHAPTER 12: EDITING A MAILING LIST

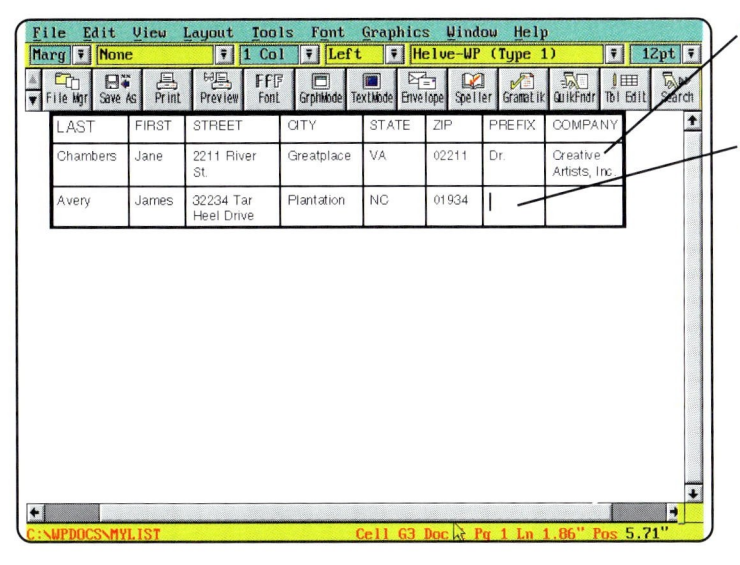

3. Type Creative Artists, Inc. *Do not press the Tab key.*

4. Click on the **empty PREFIX cell** to set the cursor.

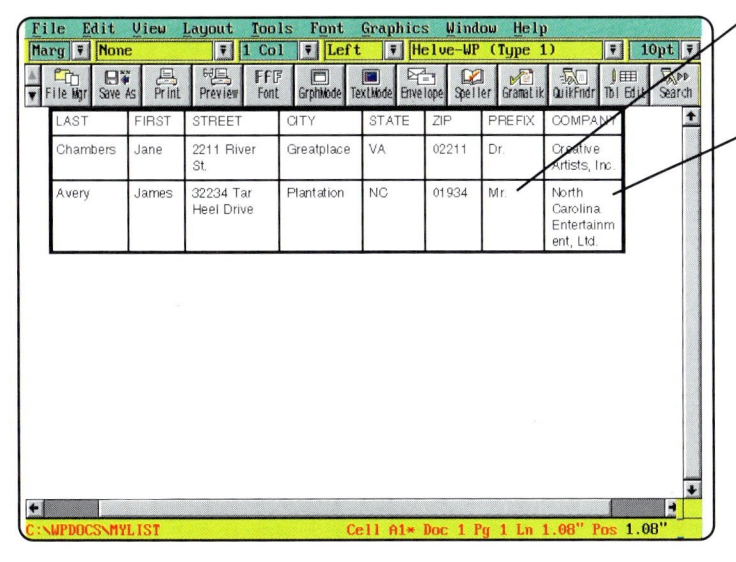

5. Type Mr. in the PREFIX cell and **press Tab**.

6. Type North Carolina Entertainment, Ltd. in the company cell.

Even though words may divide in strange places in the data table, they will print correctly in your document.

SAVING THE EDITED MAILING LIST

1. Click on **File** in the menu bar. A pull-down menu will appear.

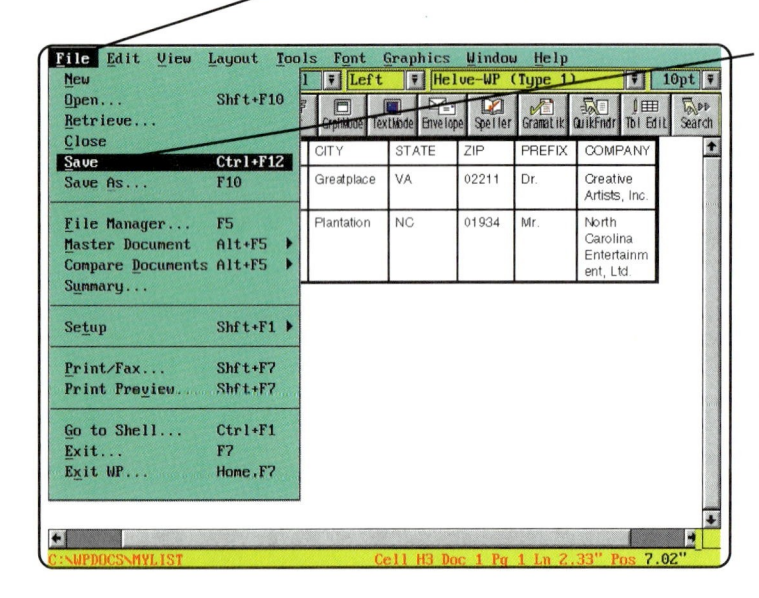

2. Click on **Save**. Your mailing list is now updated.

In the next chapter you will set up the PREVIEW letter as a form letter, ready for printing with this mailing list. If you plan to follow along with the next two chapters, you can leave this file open and go to the next chapter.

Setting Up a Form Letter for Merge Printing

In Chapter 12 you completed your mailing list by adding new fields and data. You are now ready to code the letter to match the mailing list so that it will print personalized letters correctly. In this chapter you will do the following:

❖ Code a form letter

OPENING A LIST OF FIELD NAMES

1. **Open** the **PREVIEW** document that you created in Chapters 1–9.

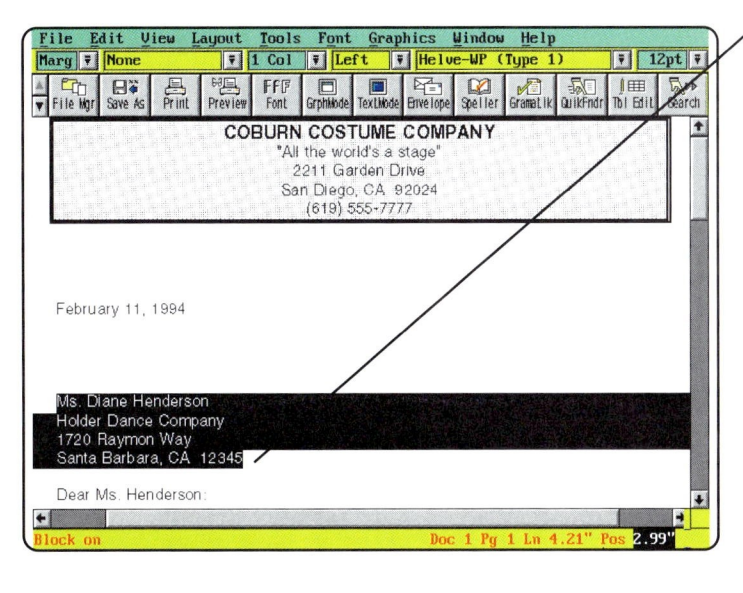

2. **Click** to the **right of the zip code** in the mailing address to set the cursor.

3. **Press and hold** the mouse button as you **drag** it up to **highlight the entire address**. **Release** the mouse button.

4. **Press** the **Backspace key** to delete the address. The cursor will be flashing in front of the space where the word "Ms." was located.

WORDPERFECT 6 FOR DOS: THE VISUAL LEARNING GUIDE

5. **Click** on **Tools** in the menu bar. A pull-down menu will appear.

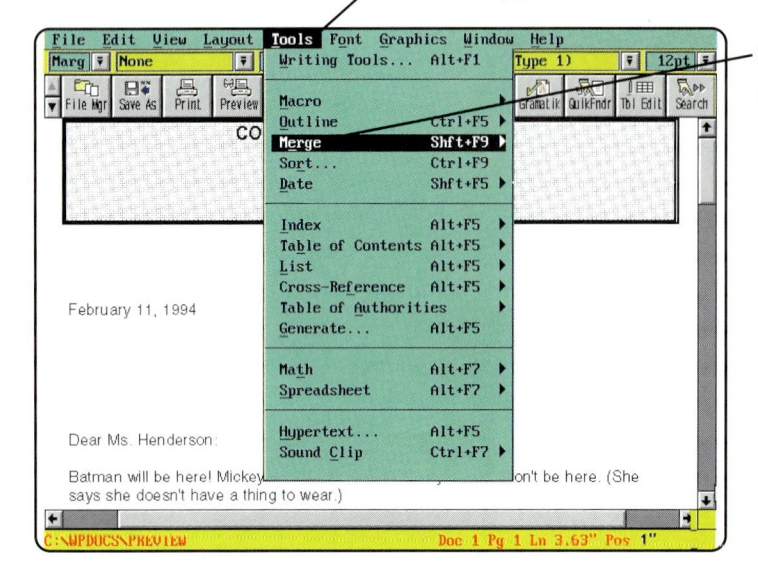

6. **Click** on **Merge**. A second menu will appear.

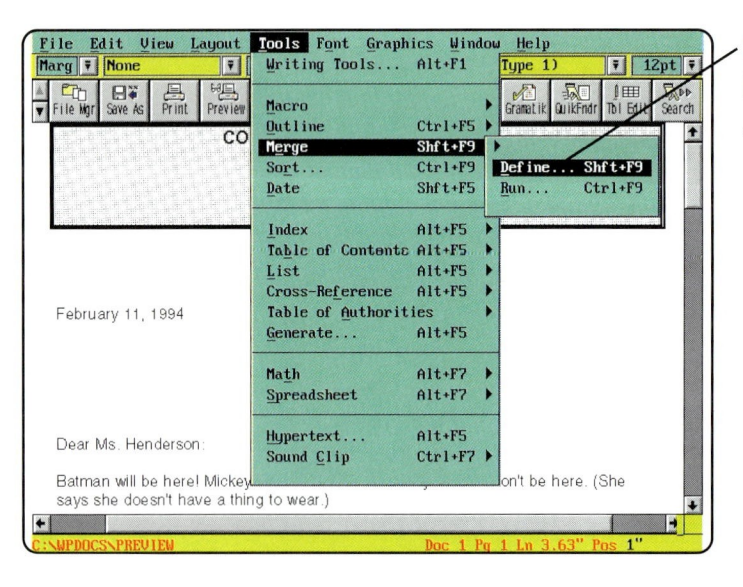

7. **Click** on **Define**. The Merge Codes dialog box will appear.

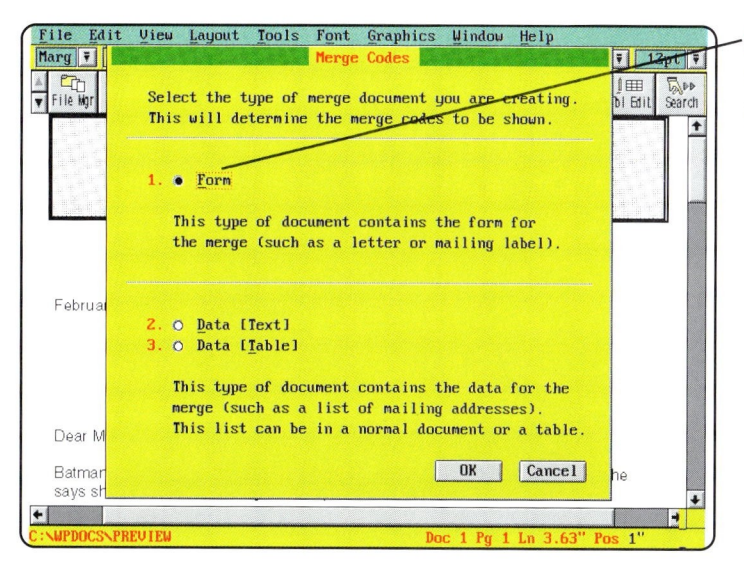

CHAPTER 13: SETTING UP A FORM LETTER FOR MERGE PRINTING

8. Click on **Form**. The Merge Codes (Form File) dialog box will appear.

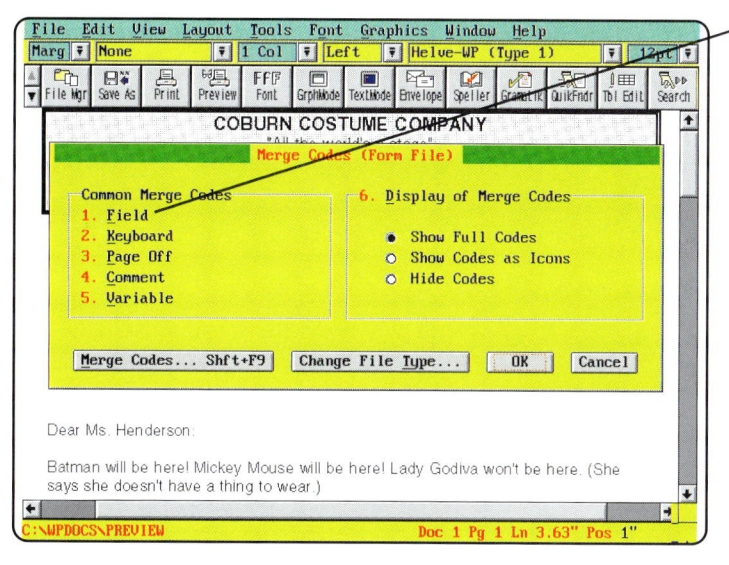

9. Click on **Field** in the Common Merge Codes box. The Parameter Entry dialog box will appear.

WORDPERFECT 6 FOR DOS: THE VISUAL LEARNING GUIDE

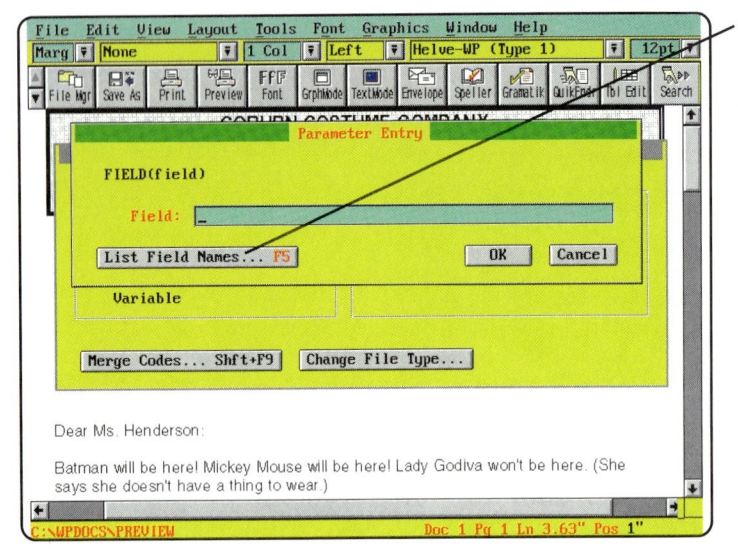

10. Click on **List Field Names**. The Select Data File for Field Names dialog box will appear. The cursor will be flashing in the Data File Name text box.

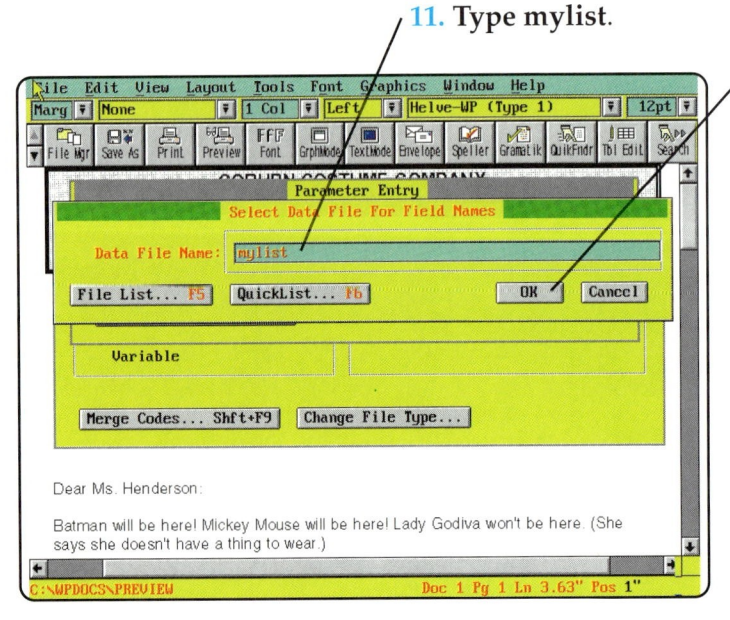

11. Type mylist.

12. Click on **OK**. The list of field names you created in Chapters 11 and 12 will appear.

CHAPTER 13: SETTING UP A FORM LETTER FOR MERGE PRINTING

INSERTING MERGE FIELDS INTO A FORM LETTER

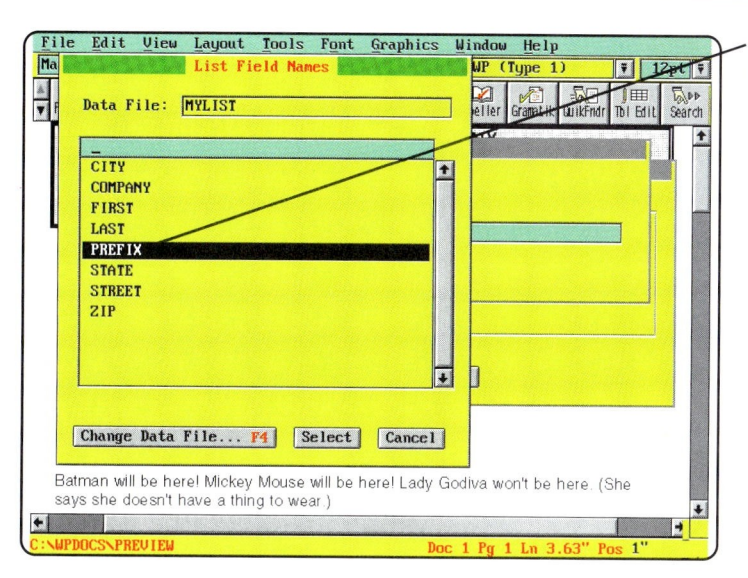

1. Click twice on **PREFIX**. The Parameter Entry dialog box will appear. "PREFIX" will appear in the Field text box.

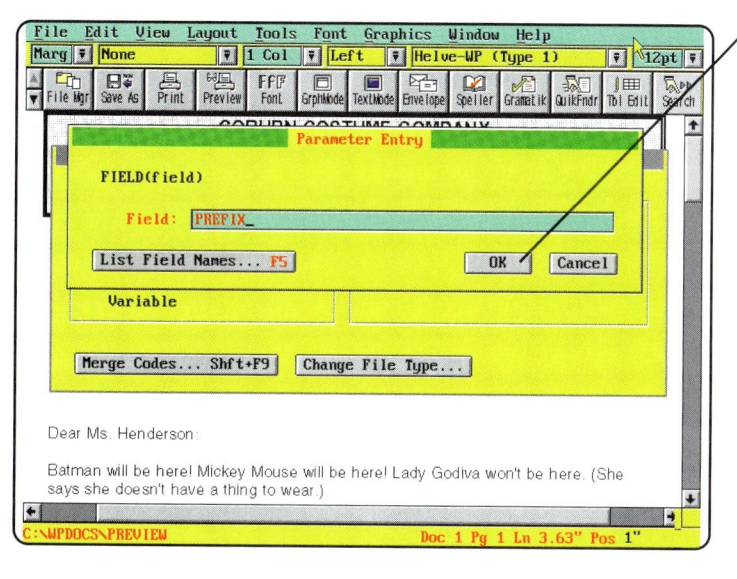

2. Click on **OK**. The PREVIEW document will appear. "FIELD(PREFIX)" will appear on the first line of the address. The cursor will be flashing after "FIELD(PREFIX)" on the address line.

3. Press the **Spacebar once** to insert a space after the PREFIX field.

WORDPERFECT 6 FOR DOS: THE VISUAL LEARNING GUIDE

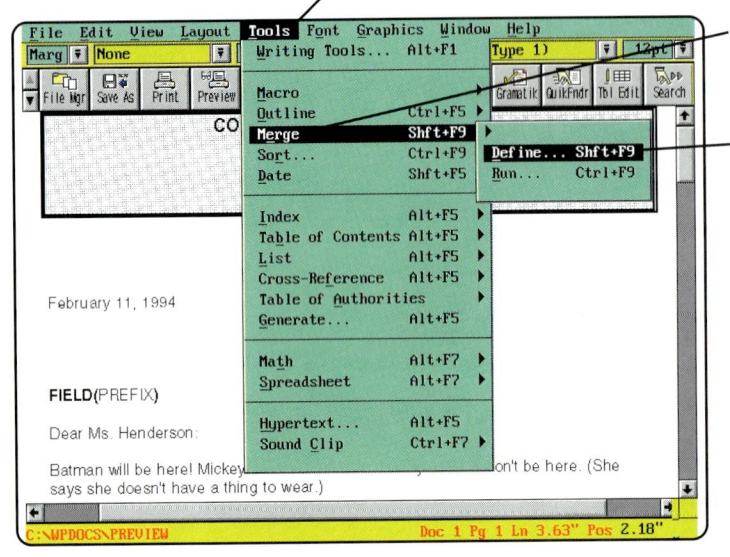

4. Click on **Tools** in the menu bar. A pull-down menu will appear.

5. Click on **Merge**. A second menu will appear.

6. Click on **Define**. The Merge Codes (Form File) dialog box will appear.

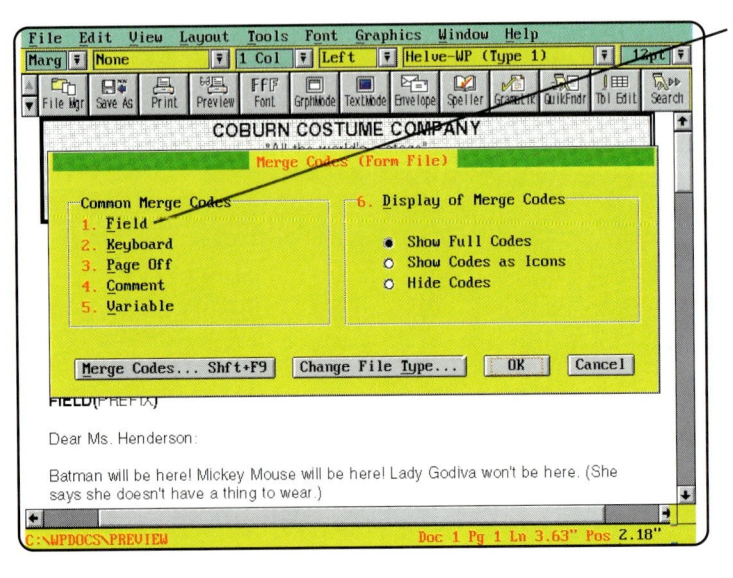

7. Click on **Field** in the Common Merge Codes box. The Parameter Entry dialog box will appear.

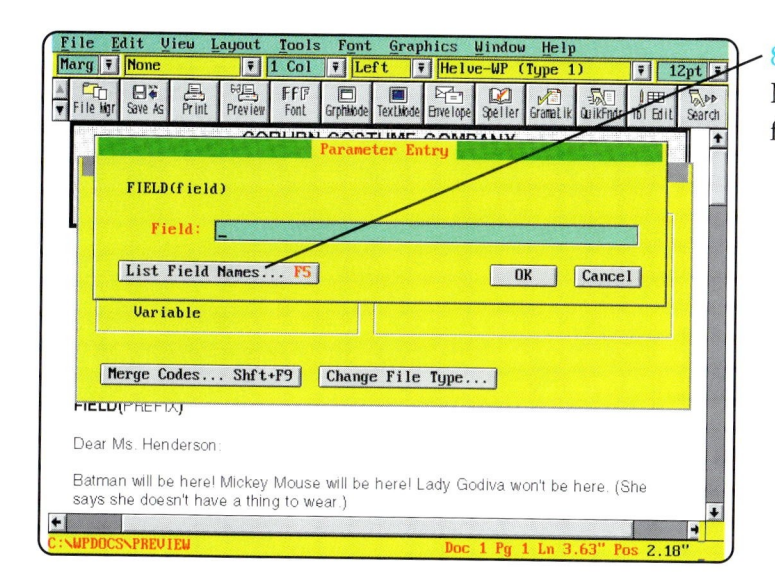

CHAPTER 13: SETTING UP A FORM LETTER FOR MERGE PRINTING

8. Click on **List Field Names**. A drop-down list of field names will appear.

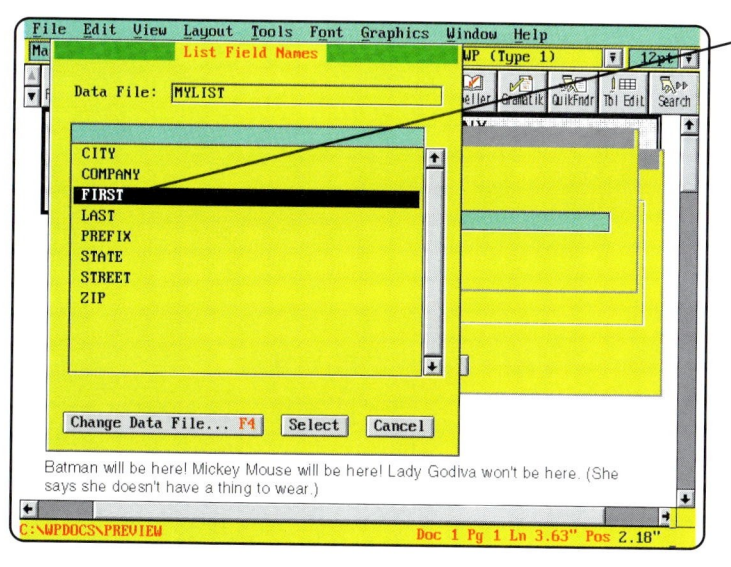

9. Click twice on **FIRST**. The Parameter Entry dialog box will appear. "FIRST" will appear in the Field text box.

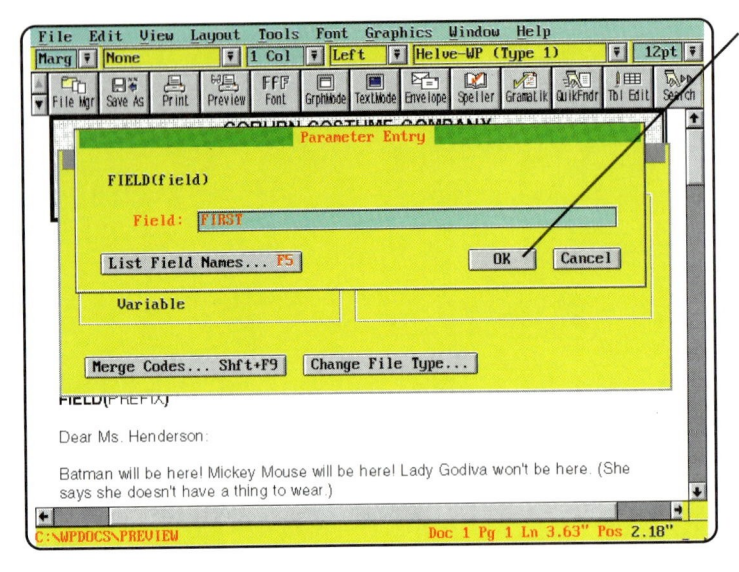

10. Click on **OK**. The PREVIEW document will appear. "FIELD(FIRST)" will appear after "FIELD(PREFIX)" on the first line of the address.

11. Press the **Spacebar** to insert a space after the FIRST field.

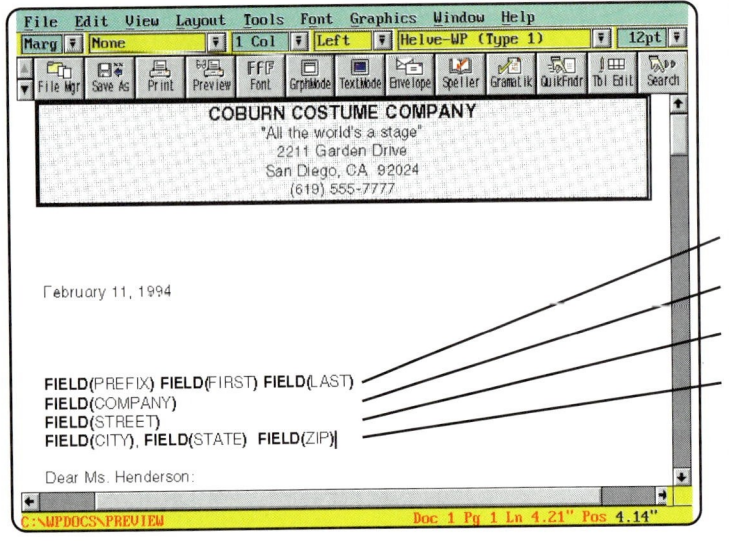

12. Repeat steps 4 through 10 in this section to enter the following words (field names) in the mailing address area of the letter:

- **LAST**
- **COMPANY**
- **STREET**
- **CITY, STATE ZIP**

Press the Enter key at the end of each line. Insert a comma and a space after "FIELD(CITY)." Put two spaces between the STATE and ZIP fields.

If you goof and put a merge field in the wrong place, highlight it and delete it. Then repeat steps 4 through 10 to replace it with the correct merge field.

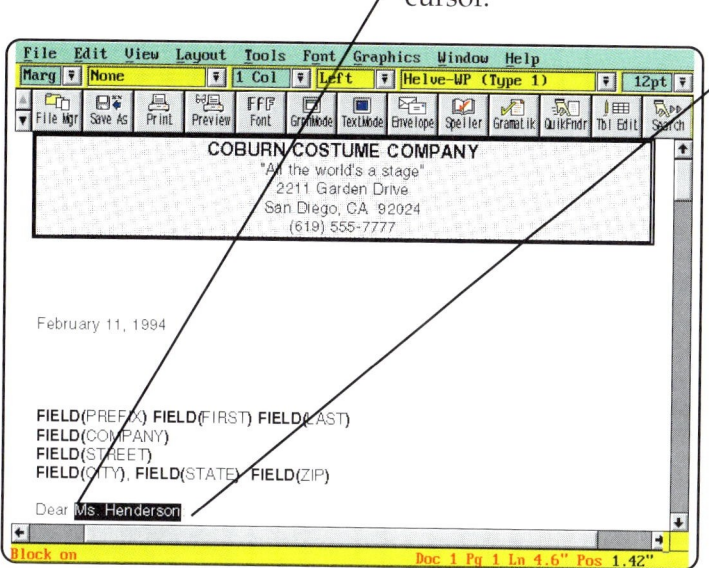

CHAPTER 13: SETTING UP A FORM LETTER FOR MERGE PRINTING

13. Click to the **left of "Ms. Henderson"** to set the cursor.

14. Press and hold the mouse button as you **drag the highlight bar over the name and prefix. Release** the mouse button. Be careful not to highlight the colon.

15. Press the **Backspace key** to delete the prefix and name.

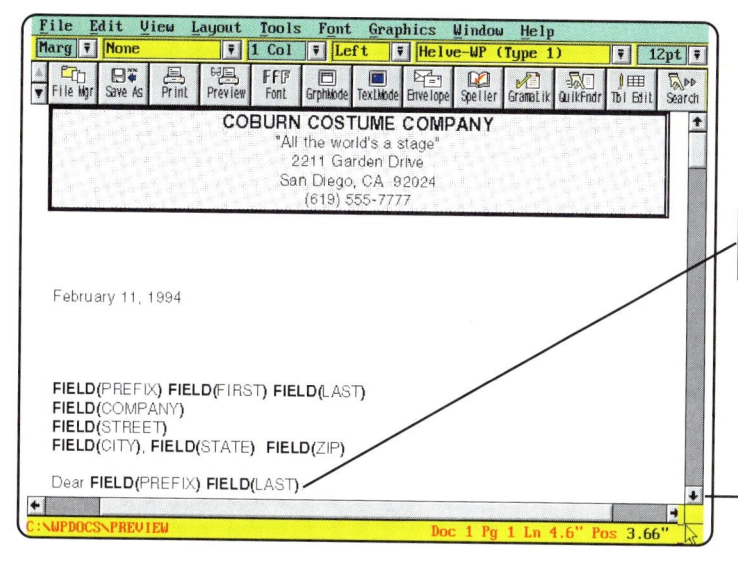

16. Repeat steps 4 through 10 in this section to add the following two fields to the salutation:

PREFIX

LAST

Remember to press the Spacebar between the PREFIX and the LAST fields.

17. Click repeatedly on the **down arrow** until you can see the double line indicating the page break.

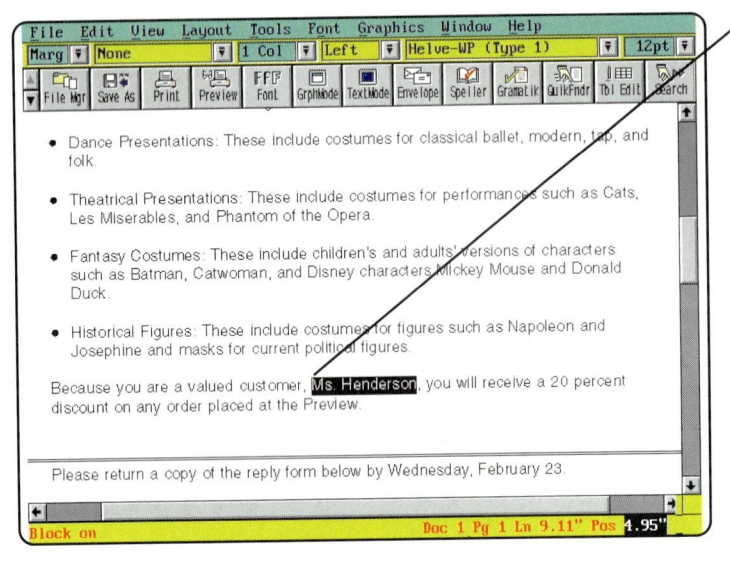

WORDPERFECT 6 FOR DOS: THE VISUAL LEARNING GUIDE

18. Click to the **left of "Ms. Henderson"** to set the cursor.

19. Press and hold the mouse button as you **drag** it **across the name and prefix**. **Release** the mouse button.

20. Press the **Backspace key** to delete the prefix and name.

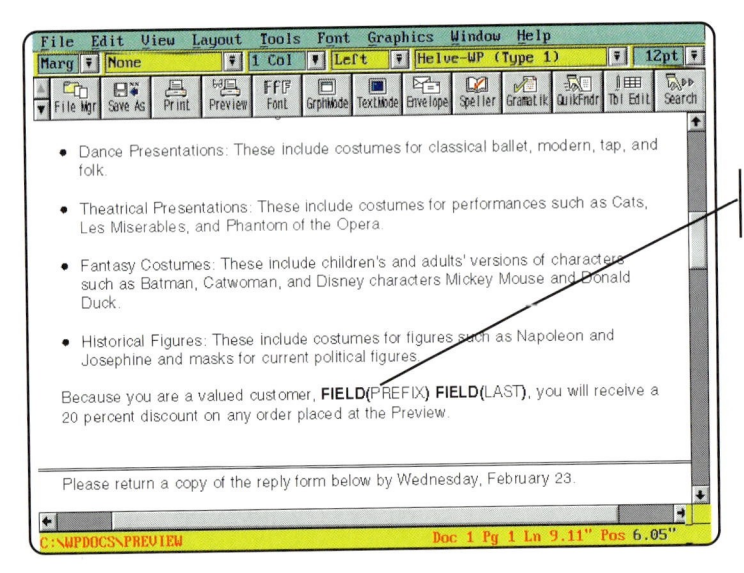

21. Repeat steps 4 through 10 in this section to insert the following two fields:

PREFIX
LAST

CHAPTER 13: SETTING UP A FORM LETTER FOR MERGE PRINTING

COPYING AND PASTING MERGE FIELDS

You can use the Copy and Paste feature to copy the merge fields from the mailing address on page 1 to page 2.

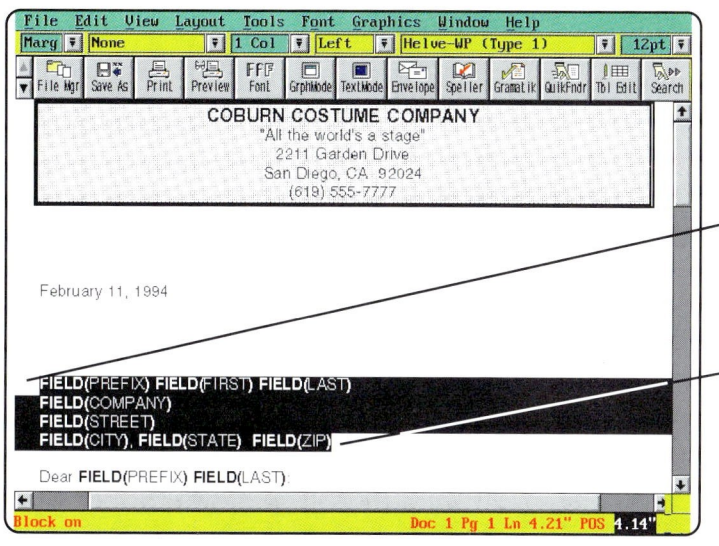

1. Press the **Home key twice** then **press** ↑ (Home, Home, ↑) to go to the top of the file.

2. Click to the **left of the first line** in the mailing address.

3. Press and hold the mouse button and **drag** the highlight bar **over the four lines of the address**.

4. Click on **Edit** in the menu bar. A pull-down menu will appear.

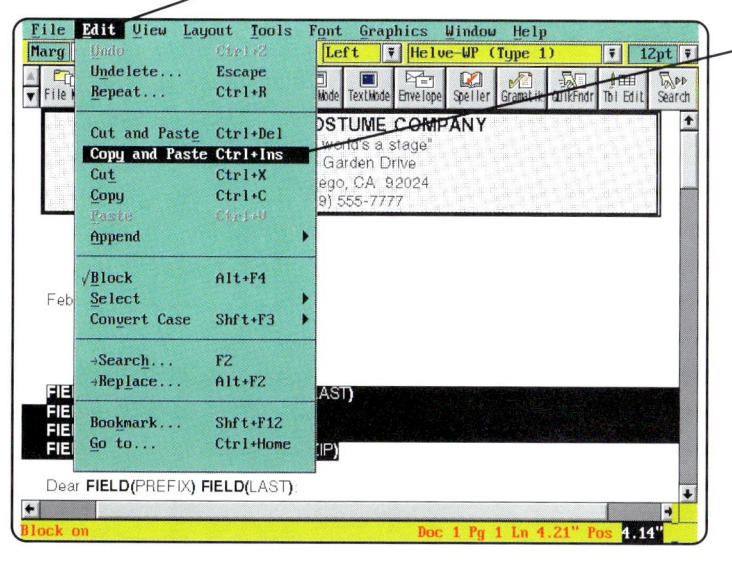

5. Click on **Copy and Paste**. The highlight will disappear from the mailing address lines. These lines are now copied to the buffer, a temporary storage area in your computer's memory.

WORDPERFECT 6 FOR DOS: THE VISUAL LEARNING GUIDE

6. **Press** the **Home key twice** then **press** ↓ (Home, Home, ↓) to go to the end of the file.

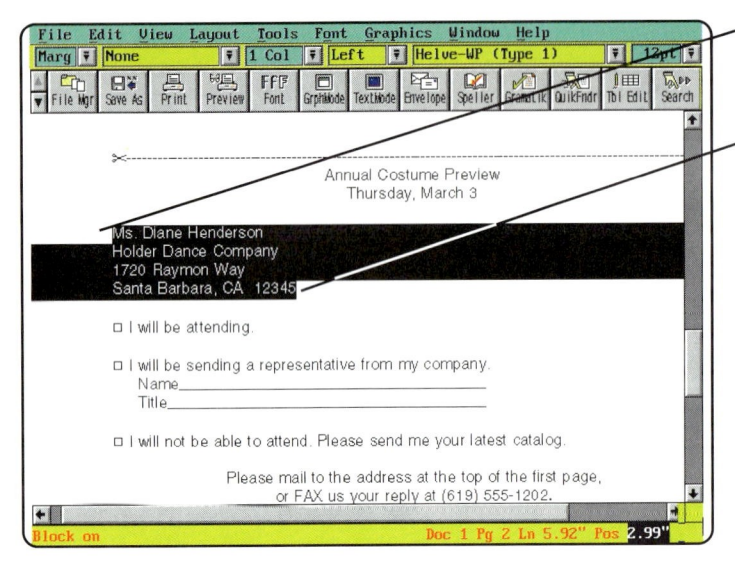

7. **Click** to the **left of "Ms. Diane Henderson."**

8. **Press and hold** the mouse button and **drag** the highlight bar **over the four lines of the address**.

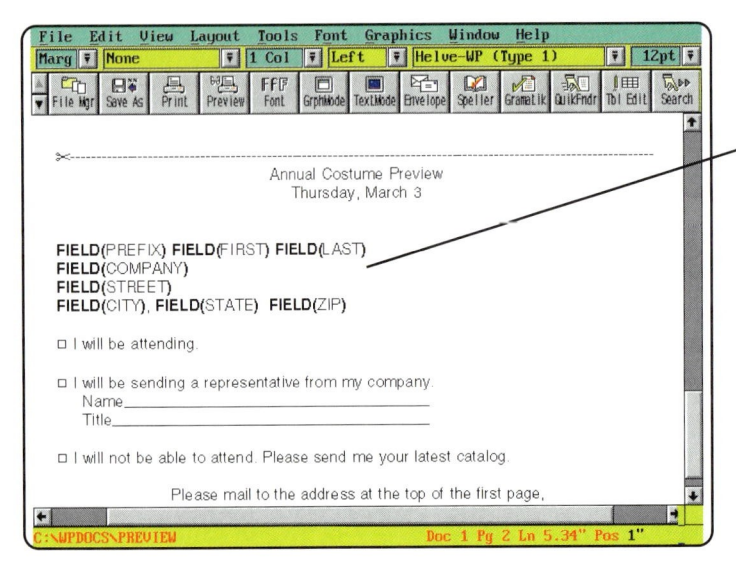

9. **Press** the **Backspace key** to erase the lines.

10. **Press** the **Enter key** to paste the copied merge fields into the text.

11. **Open** the **Header/Footer/Watermark dialog box**. Refer to "Adding a Header" in Chapter 9 for directions on creating and editing a header.

12. **Repeat steps 2 through 10** above to **replace "Ms. Diane Henderson"** in the header with the PREFIX, FIRST, and LAST merge fields.

SAVING THE FORM LETTER WITH THE SAVE AS COMMAND

If you use the Save command to save changes to the PREVIEW file, you will replace the original letter with the coded letter. You can keep the original PREVIEW letter unchanged if you use the Save As command. This command allows you to give a new name to the changed version and keep the original letter intact.

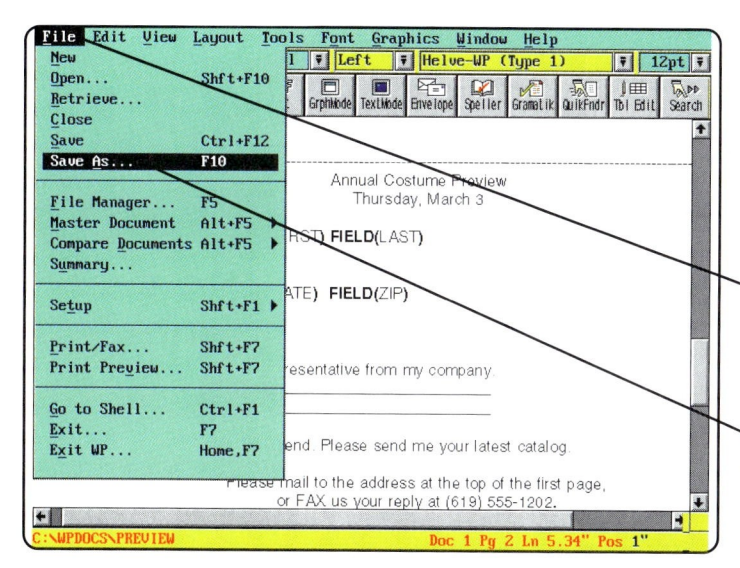

1. Click on **File** in the menu bar. A pull-down menu will appear.

2. Click on **Save As**. The Save Document dialog box will appear.

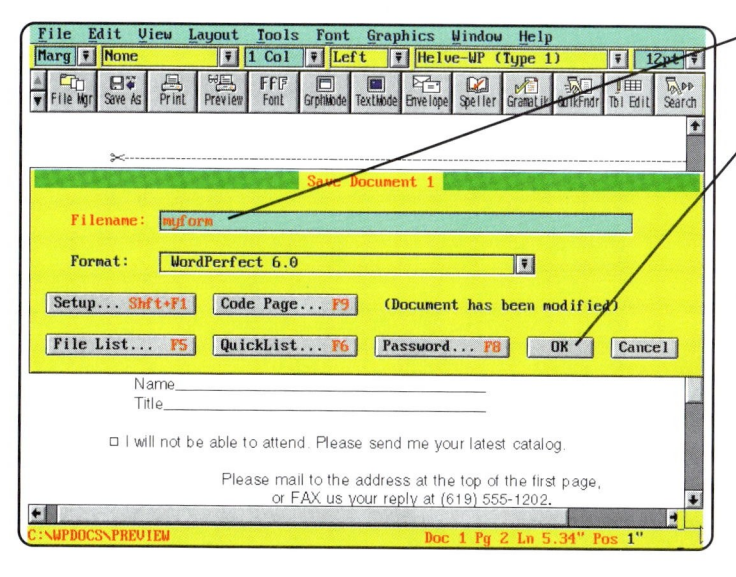

3. Type myform in the Filename text box.

4. Click on **OK**.

You are now ready to merge print the form letter with the mailing list you created in Chapters 11 and 12.

Printing a Form Letter

Now that you have finished coding the form letter in Chapter 13, you are ready to print it by merging the coded letter with the data file (the mailing list). WordPerfect 6 will print as many personalized copies of the form letter as there are names on the mailing list. In this chapter you will do the following:

❖ Print two personalized copies of a form letter using a mailing list

SETTING UP TO PRINT A FORM LETTER

You can begin the merge printing process without having any files open on your screen. However, if you have been following along with the previous chapters in this Part, you have the MYFORM document on your screen.

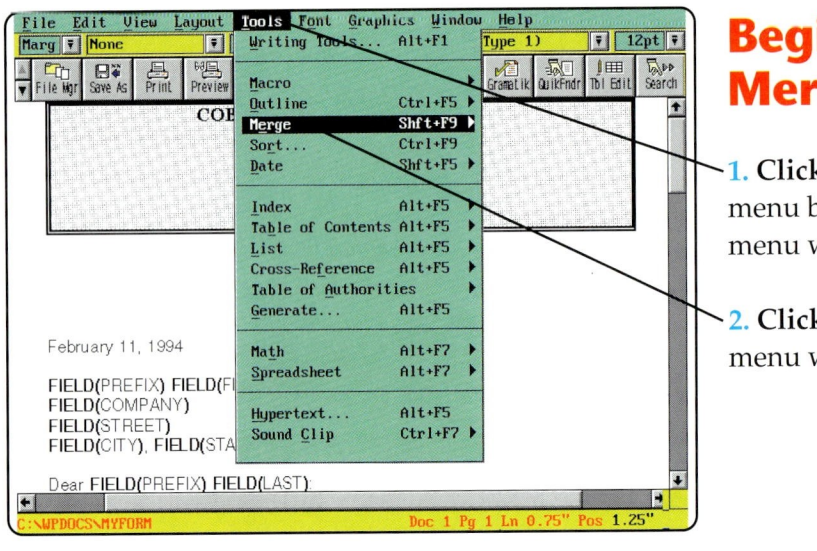

Beginning the Merge Process

1. Click on **Tools** in the menu bar. A pull-down menu will appear.

2. Click on **Merge**. A second menu will appear.

CHAPTER 14: PRINTING A FORM LETTER

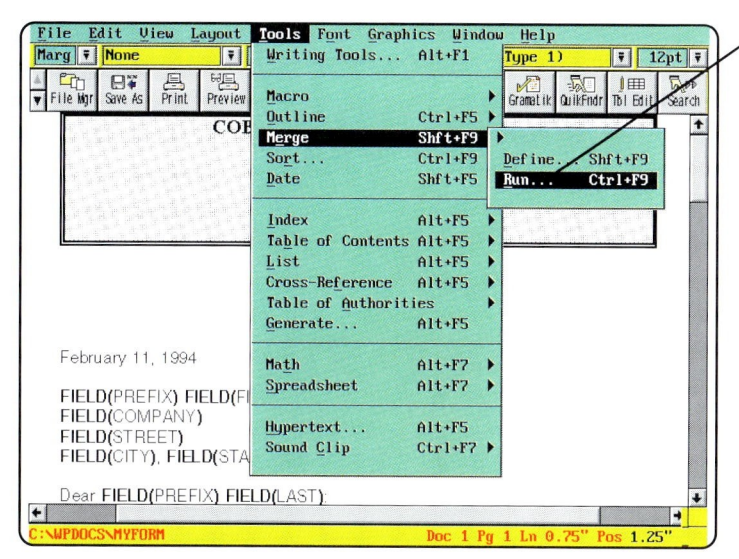

3. Click on **Run**. The Run Merge dialog box will appear.

Selecting the Form File and Data File to Merge Print

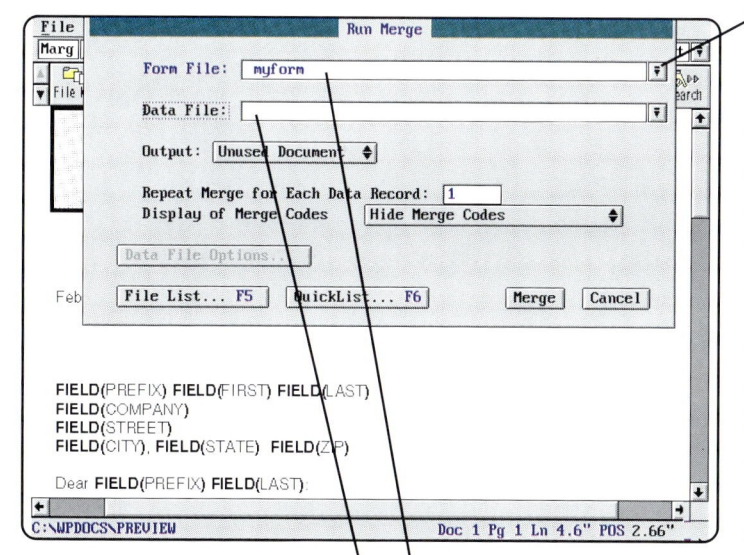

1. Click on the **down arrow** to the **right of the Form File text box**. A drop-down list of files will appear. In this case MYFORM will be the only file listed unless you have other files in this directory.

Note: WordPerfect remembers the last four form letters you used. The most recently used one will appear if you have merge printed before.

2. Click twice on **C:\WPDOCS\MYFORM**. It will appear in the Form File text box. If you have used a mailing list previously, the name of the last data file used will appear in the Data File text box automatically.

3. Type mylist in the Data File text box. You are now ready to merge print.

PRINTING THE LETTER

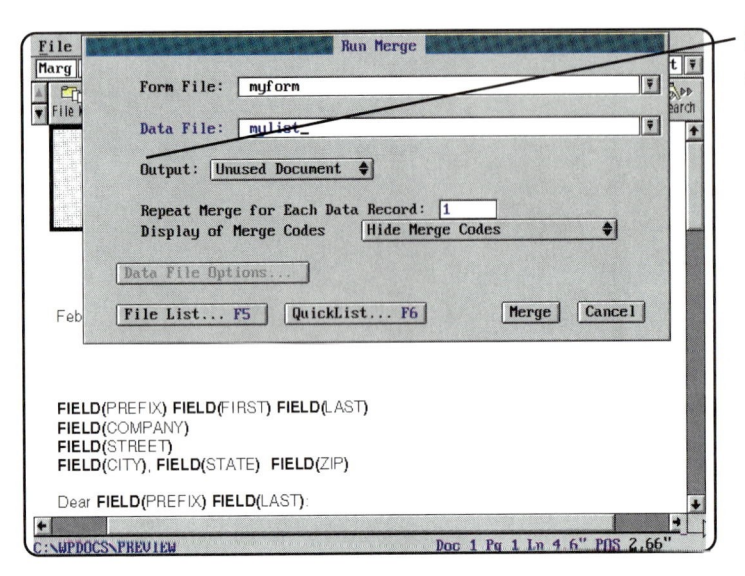

1. Click on **Output**. A drop-down list will appear.

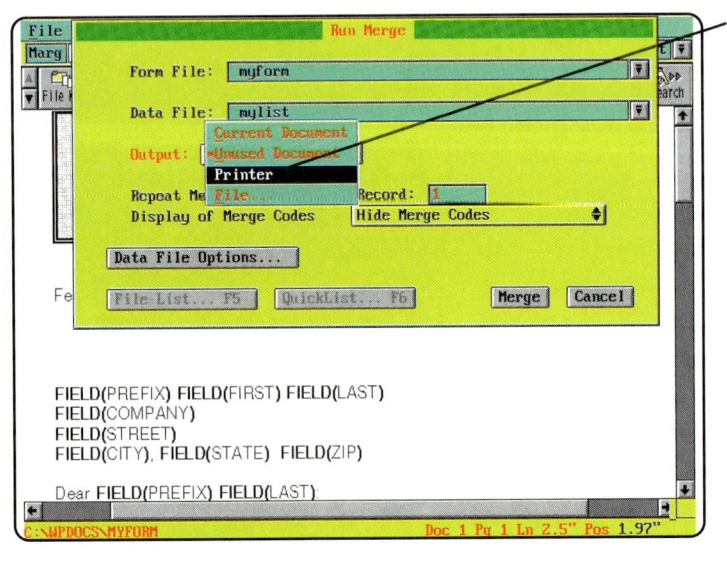

2. Click on **Printer**. The word "Printer" will appear in the Output box.

CHAPTER 14: PRINTING A FORM LETTER

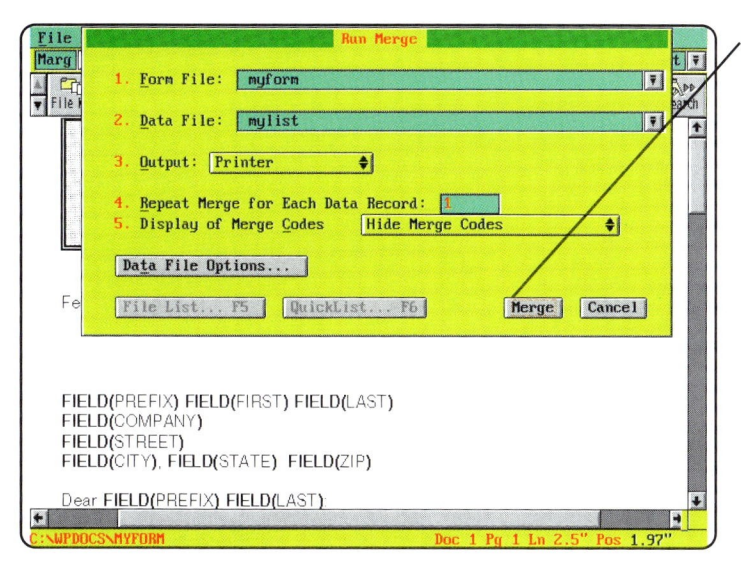

3. Click on **Merge**. WordPerfect will print two personalized copies of the letter.

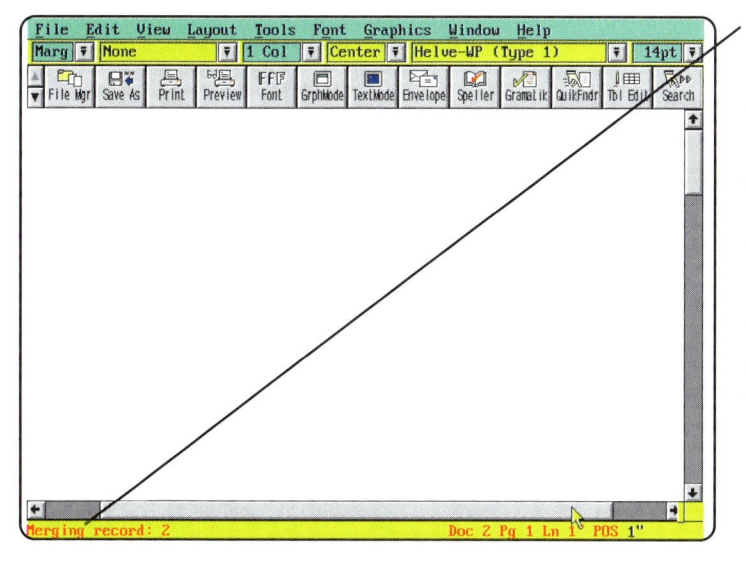

Note that WordPerfect lets you know its status here as it merges the mailing list with the form letter as it prints.

In Chapter 15, "Printing Envelopes for a Mailing List," you will print envelopes for this form letter.

CLOSING THE FILE

1. Click on **File** in the menu bar. A pull-down menu will appear.

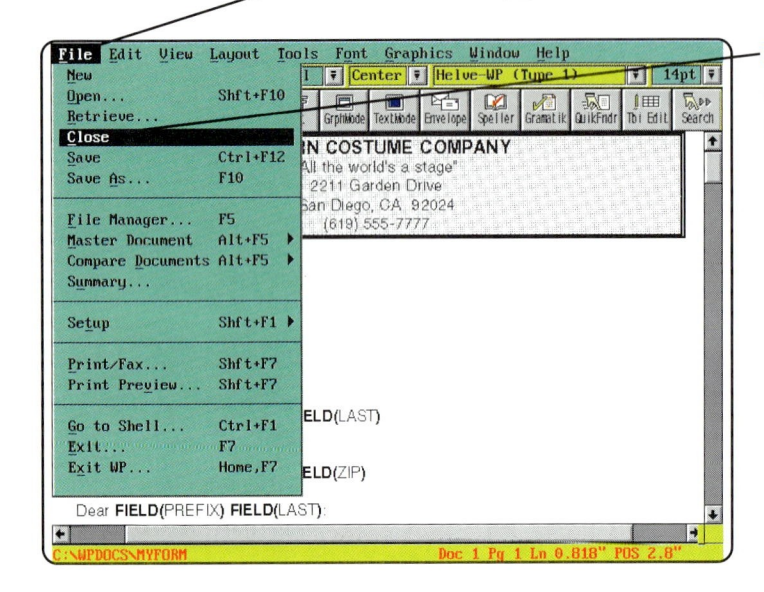

2. Click on **Close**. A new document window will appear.

Printing Envelopes for a Mailing List

Once you have created a mailing list (Chapter 11), you can print the entire list of envelopes or just a selected envelope. We recommend that you use an envelope feeder for a laser printer or tractor feed envelopes for a dot-matrix printer if you want to print envelopes for a mailing list or else you will have to insert envelopes into your printer manually. In this chapter you will do the following:

- ❖ Create an envelope file to be used to print a mailing list
- ❖ Print envelopes from the mailing list
- ❖ Set up WordPerfect to print with an envelope tray
- ❖ Print a selected envelope from a mailing list

CREATING AN ENVELOPE TO PRINT A MAILING LIST

1. Open a **new document**. If you need help opening a document, see the section in Chapter 8 entitled "Opening a New Document."

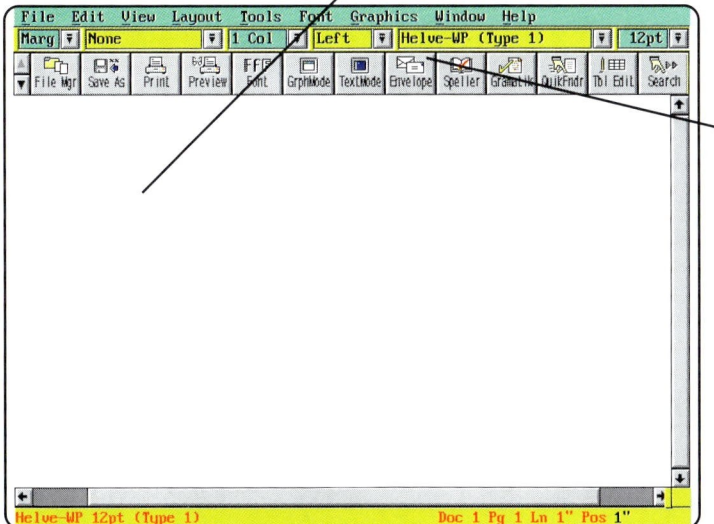

2. Click on the **Envelope button** in the button bar. The Envelope dialog box will appear.

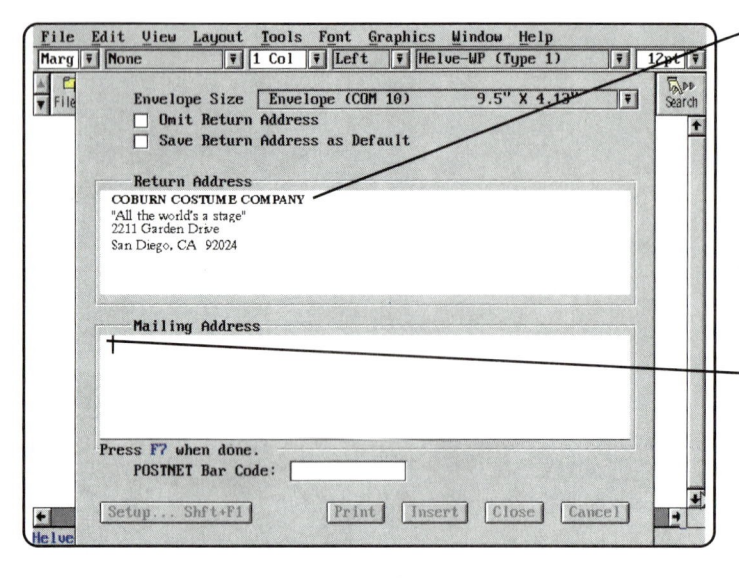

WORDPERFECT 6 FOR DOS: THE VISUAL LEARNING GUIDE

If you clicked on the Save Return Address as Default option in Chapter 10, you will notice that the return address of the MYFORM sample form letter is already entered in the Return Address box.

3. Click on the **left corner of the Mailing Address box** to set the cursor.

Entering Merge Fields for the Mailing Address

1. Click on **Tools** in the menu bar. A pull-down menu will appear.

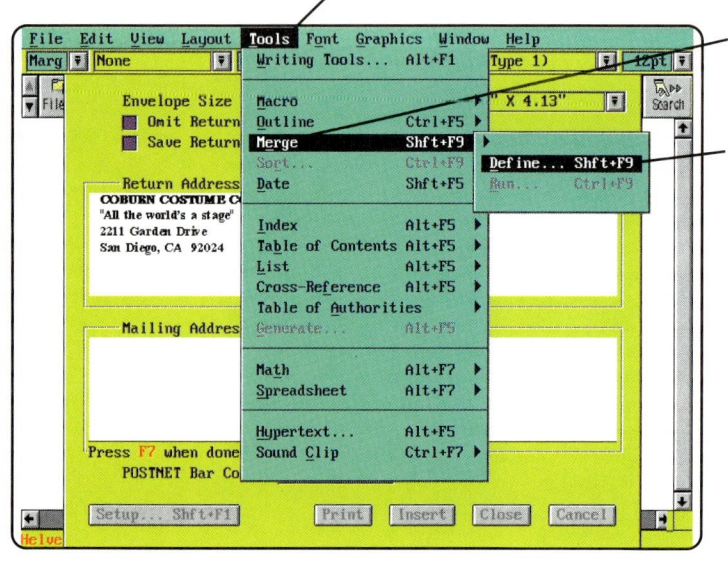

2. Click on **Merge**. A second menu will appear.

3. Click on **Define**. The Merge Codes dialog box will appear.

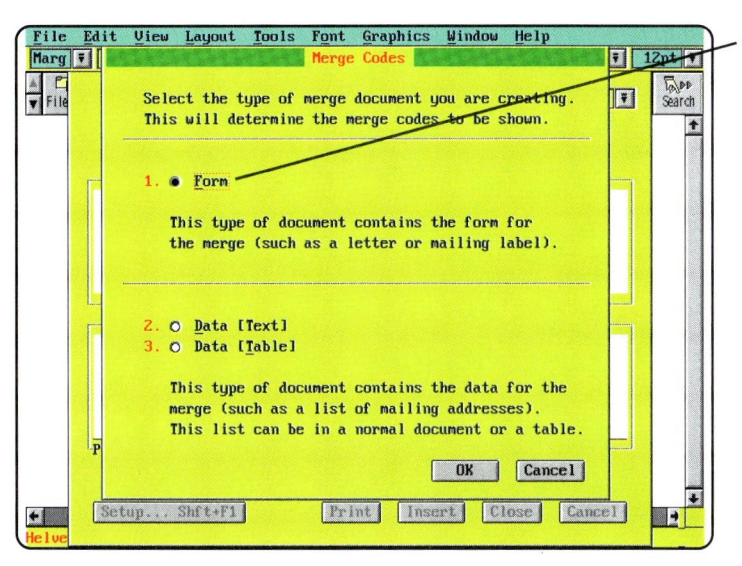

CHAPTER 15: PRINTING ENVELOPES FOR A MAILING LIST

4. Click on **Form**. The Merge Codes (Form File) dialog box will appear.

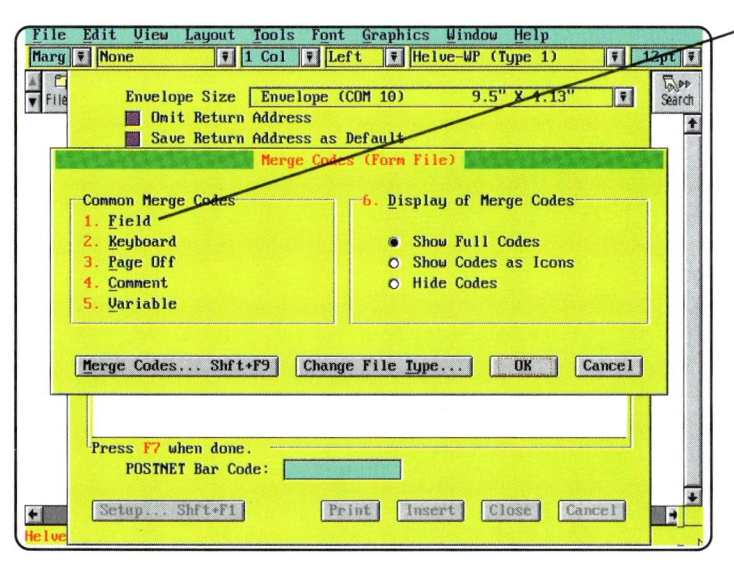

5. Click on **Field** in the Common Merge Codes box. The Parameter Entry dialog box will appear.

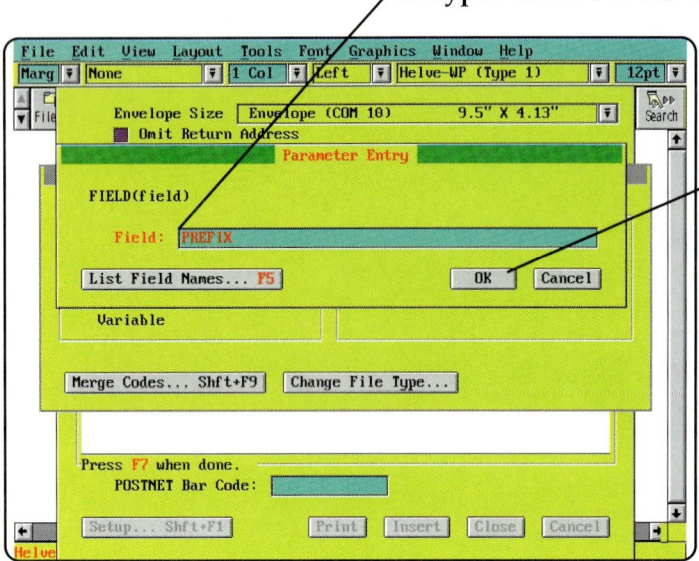

WORDPERFECT 6 FOR DOS: THE VISUAL LEARNING GUIDE

6. Type PREFIX in the Field text box. (The examples in this book are in capital letters, but you can type them any way you want.

7. Click on **OK**. The Envelope dialog box will appear. "FIELD(PREFIX)" will appear in the Mailing Address text box.

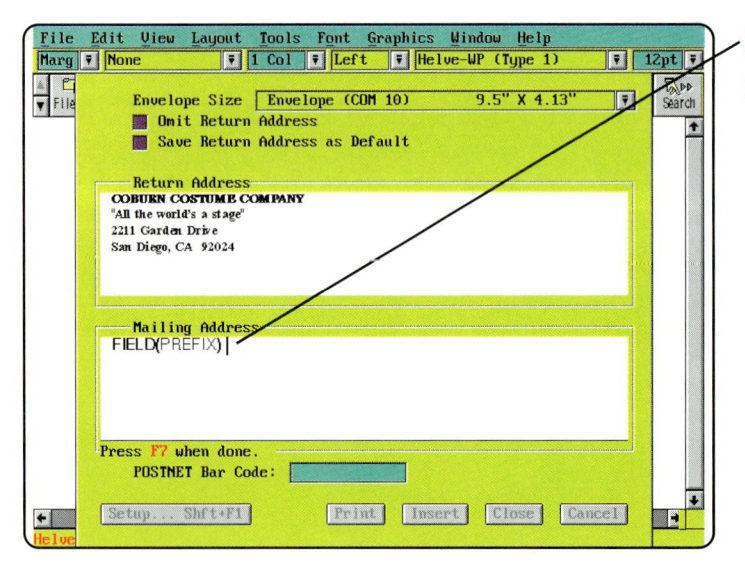

8. Press the **Spacebar** to place a space after "FIELD(PREFIX)."

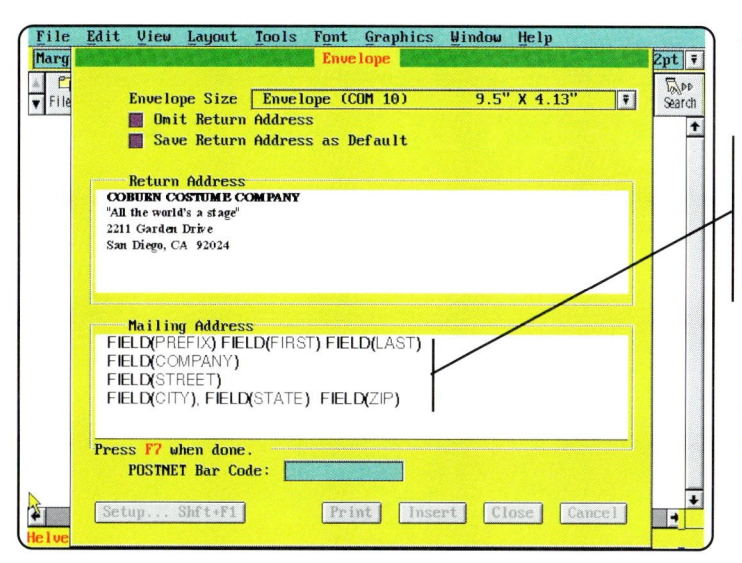

CHAPTER 15: PRINTING ENVELOPES FOR A MAILING LIST

9. Repeat steps 1 through 7 to enter the following fields:

FIRST LAST

COMPANY

STREET

CITY, STATE ZIP

Don't forget to put a comma and a space after the CITY field and two spaces between the STATE and ZIP fields.

10. Press the **F7 key**. The buttons at the bottom of the dialog box will become active.

Inserting the Mail Merge Envelope in the Document

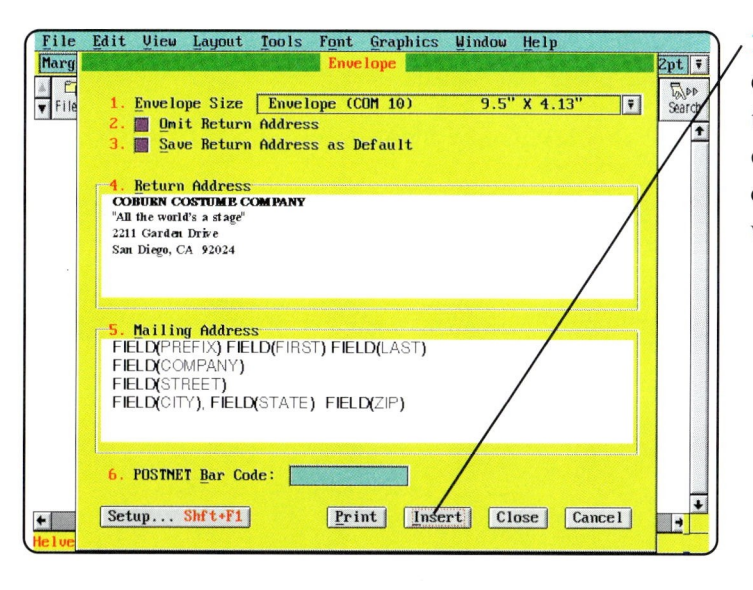

1. Click on **Insert**. The envelope text will appear in the document. Since the document file does not contain a letter, the envelope will be page 1 of the file.

SAVING THE ENVELOPE

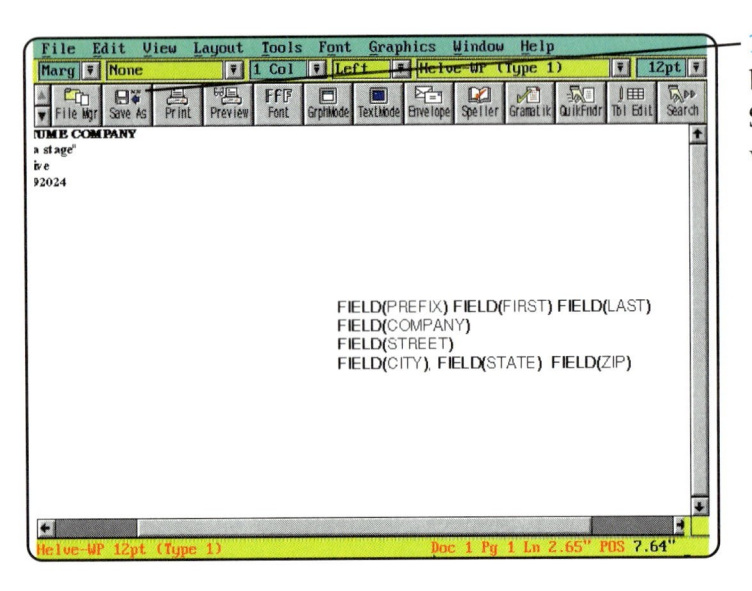

1. Click on the **Save As button** in the button bar. The Save Document dialog box will appear.

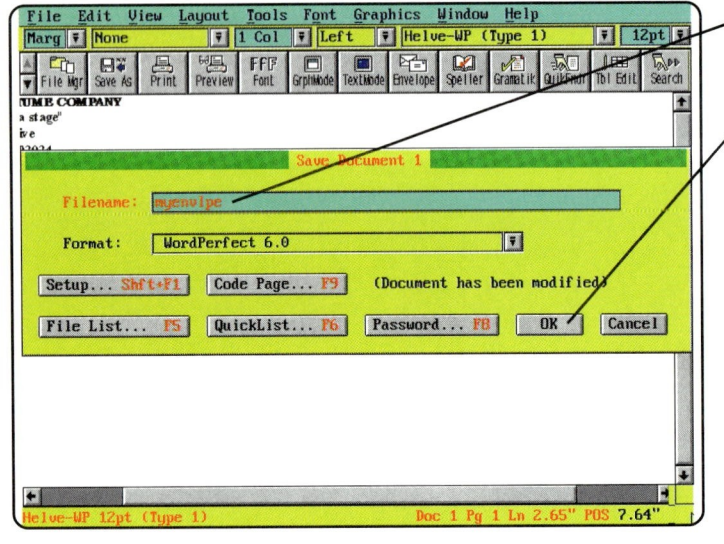

2. Type myenvlpe in the Filename text box.

3. Click on **OK**. The document window will appear.

CHAPTER 15: PRINTING ENVELOPES FOR A MAILING LIST

PRINTING ENVELOPES FOR A MAILING LIST

1. Load an envelope in your HP LaserJet Series II or III manual feed slot or your dot-matrix printer. (See Chapter 10, the section entitled "Printing with a LaserJet II or III Series Printer" or "Printing with a Dot-Matrix Printer" if you need help.)

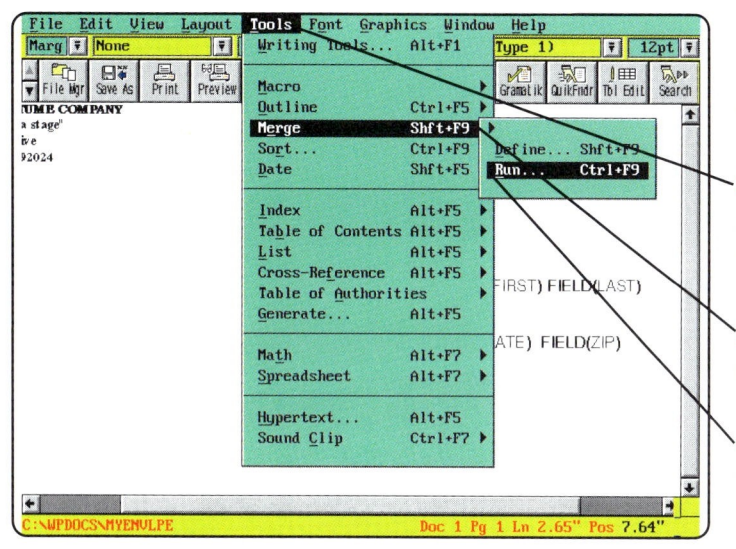

2. Click on **Tools** in the menu bar. A pull-down menu will appear.

3. Click on **Merge**. A second menu will appear.

4. Click on **Run**. The Run Merge dialog box will appear.

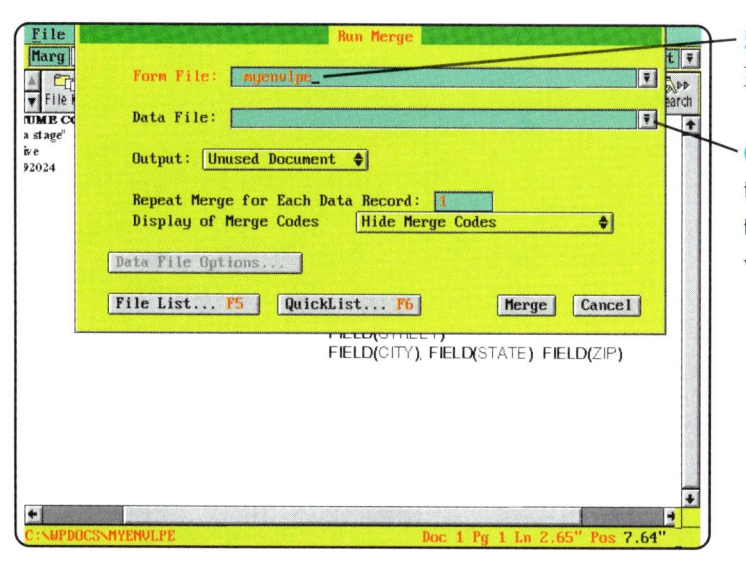

5. Type myenvlpe in the Form File text box.

6. Click on the **down arrow** to the **right of the Data File text box**. A drop-down list will appear.

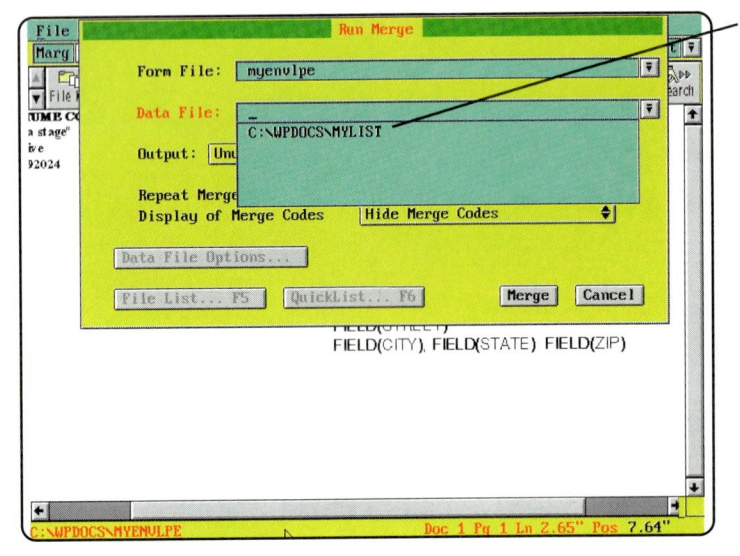

7. Click twice on **C:\WPDOCS\MYLIST**. It will appear in the Data File text box. (If by some quirk of fate the list does not appear, **type c:\wpdocs\mylist** in the Data File text box.)

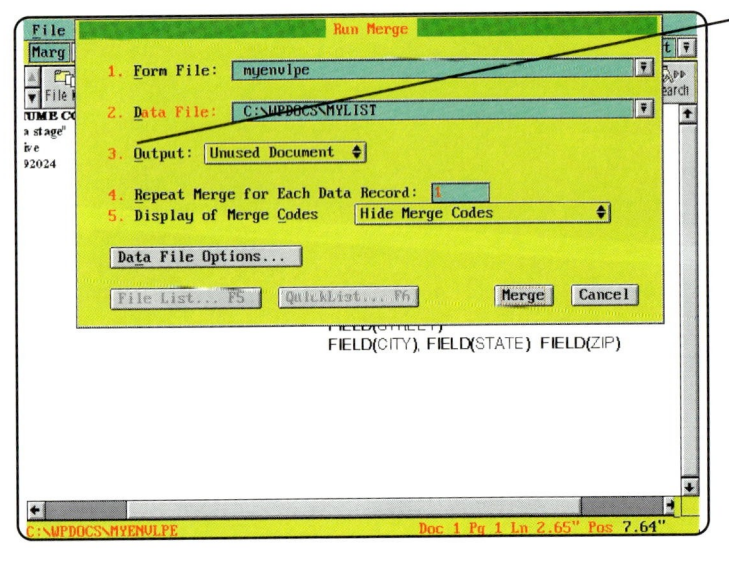

8. Click on **Output**. A pop-up list will appear.

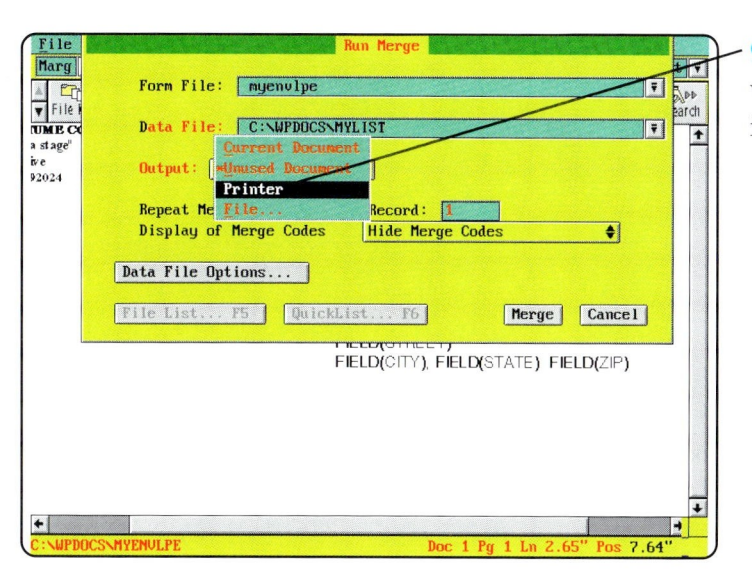

CHAPTER 15: PRINTING ENVELOPES FOR A MAILING LIST

9. Click on **Printer**. The word "Printer" will appear in the Output text box.

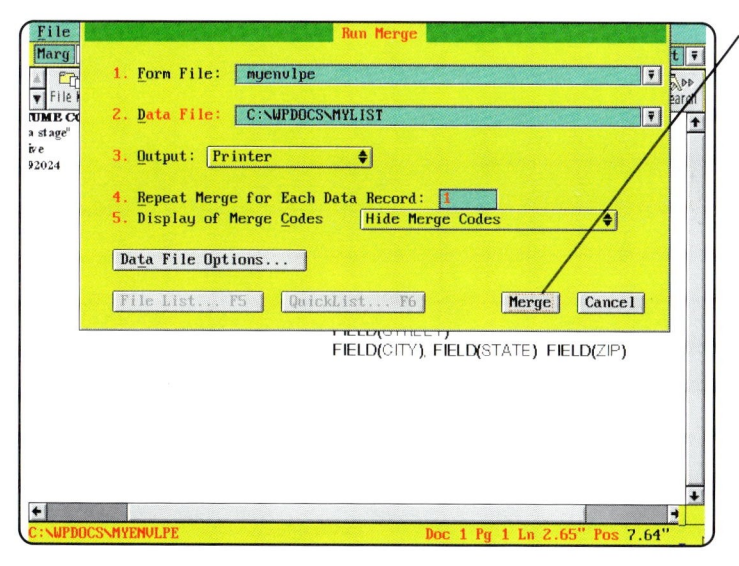

10. Click on **Merge**. The document dialog box will appear. A Please Wait message box may flash across your screen if you have lots of memory. If not, the message box will linger awhile. If you are using an HP LaserJet II or III or a dot-matrix printer, you will have to manually feed each envelope when the printer requests it.

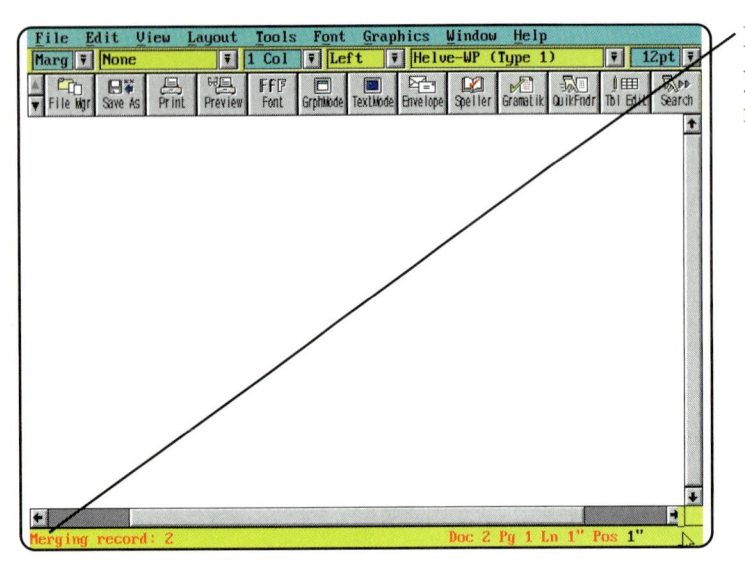

WORDPERFECT 6 FOR DOS: THE VISUAL LEARNING GUIDE

Notice that WordPerfect tells you which records are being merged (sent) to the printer.

SETTING UP WORDPERFECT TO PRINT WITH AN ENVELOPE TRAY

1. Click on **Layout** in the menu bar. A pull-down menu will appear.

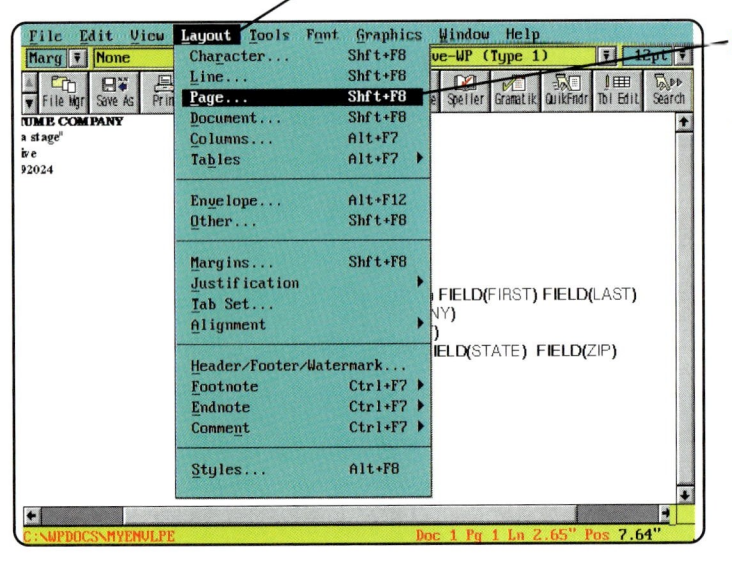

2. Click on **Page**. The Page Format dialog box will appear.

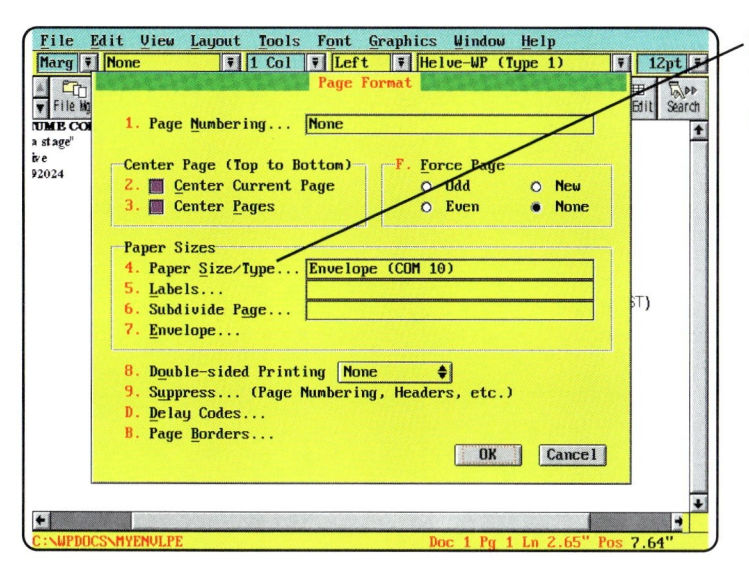

CHAPTER 15: PRINTING ENVELOPES FOR A MAILING LIST

3. Click on **Paper Size/Type**. The Paper Size/Type dialog box will appear.

4. Click on either the **down arrow** or the **up arrow** on the scroll bar to highlight **Envelope (COM 10)**.

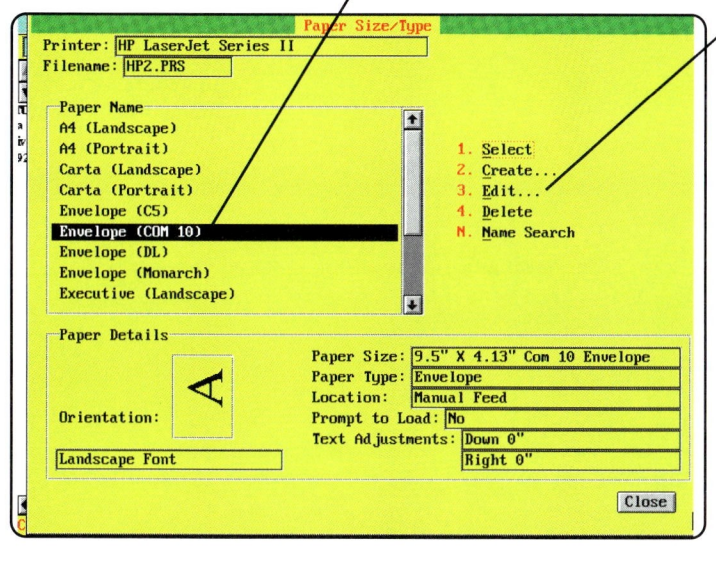

5. Click on **Edit**. The Edit Paper Size/Type dialog box will appear.

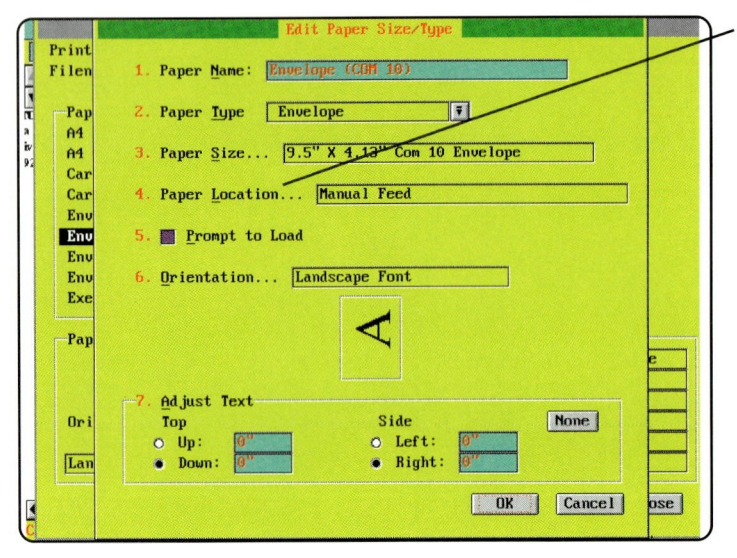

WORDPERFECT 6 FOR DOS: THE VISUAL LEARNING GUIDE

6. Click on **Paper Location**. The Paper Location dialog box will appear.

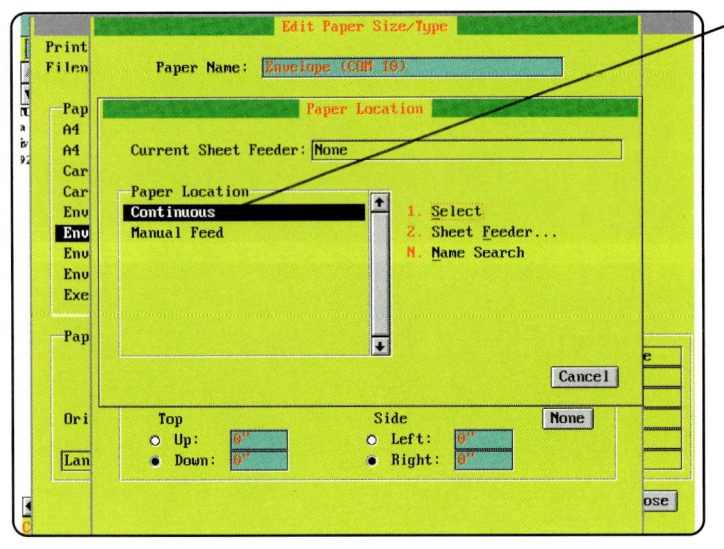

7. Click twice on **Continuous**. The Paper Location dialog box will disappear and you will be returned to the Edit Paper Size/Type dialog box.

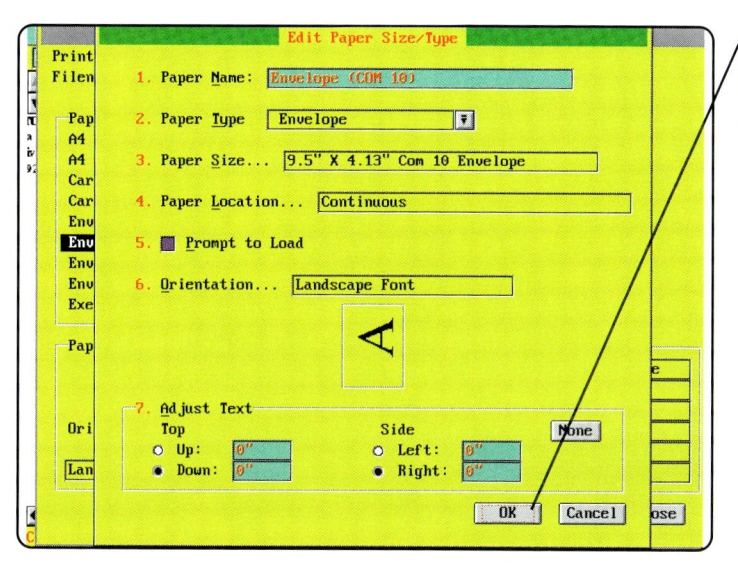

CHAPTER 15: PRINTING ENVELOPES FOR A MAILING LIST

8. Click on **OK**. The Paper Size/Type dialog box will appear.

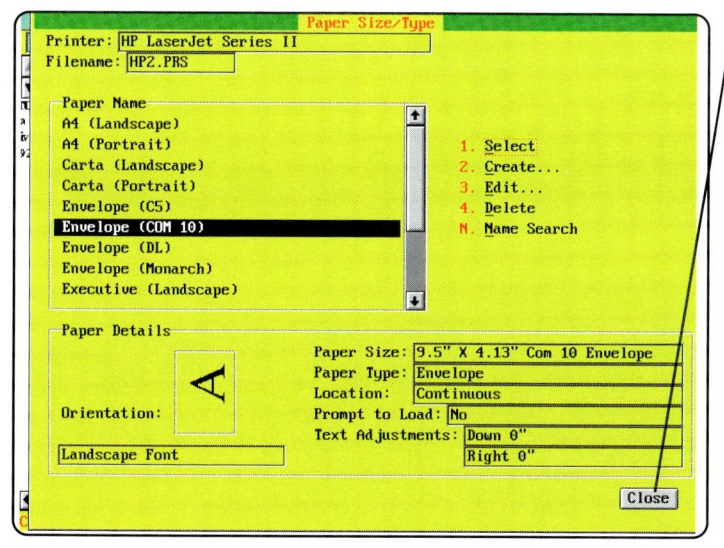

9. Click on **Close**. The Page Format dialog box will reappear.

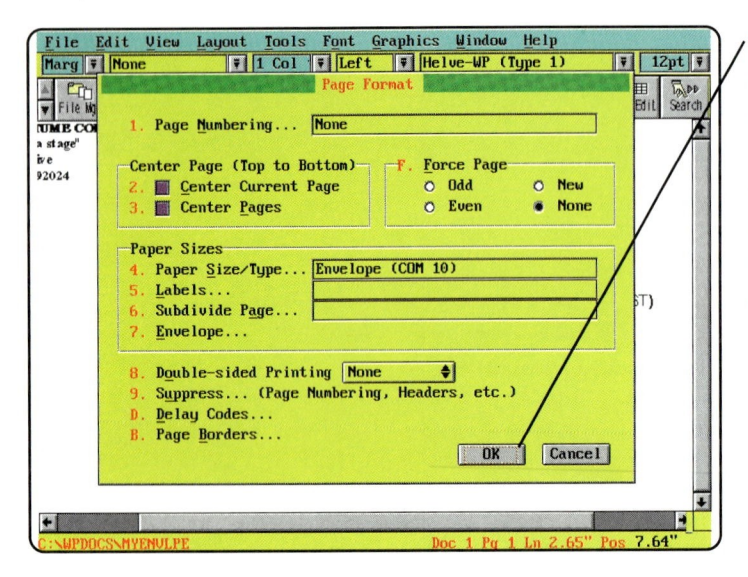

WORDPERFECT 6 FOR DOS: THE VISUAL LEARNING GUIDE

10. **Click** on **OK**. The envelope document will appear. The next time you want to print more than one envelope (merge print) you can insert your envelope tray into your HP LaserJet II or III series printer and WordPerfect will do the rest!

Saving the Envelope Tray Setup

1. **Click** on the **Save As button** in the button bar. The Save Document dialog box will appear.

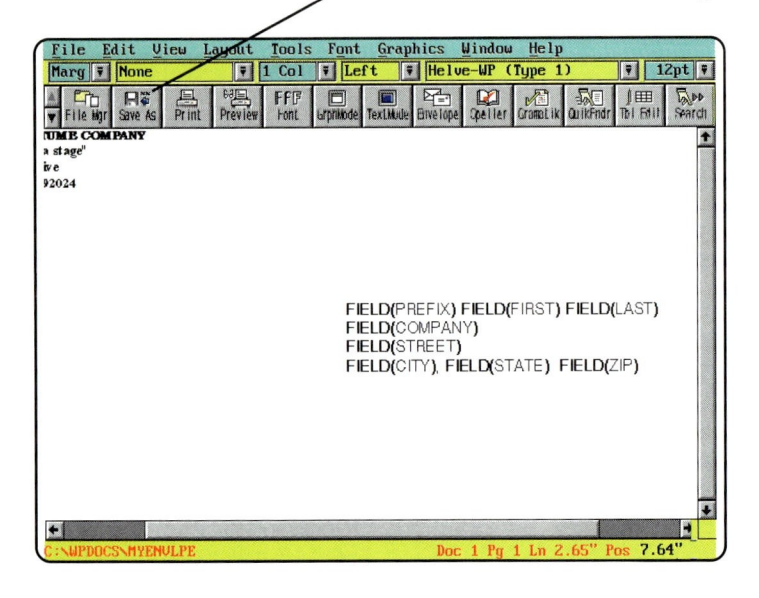

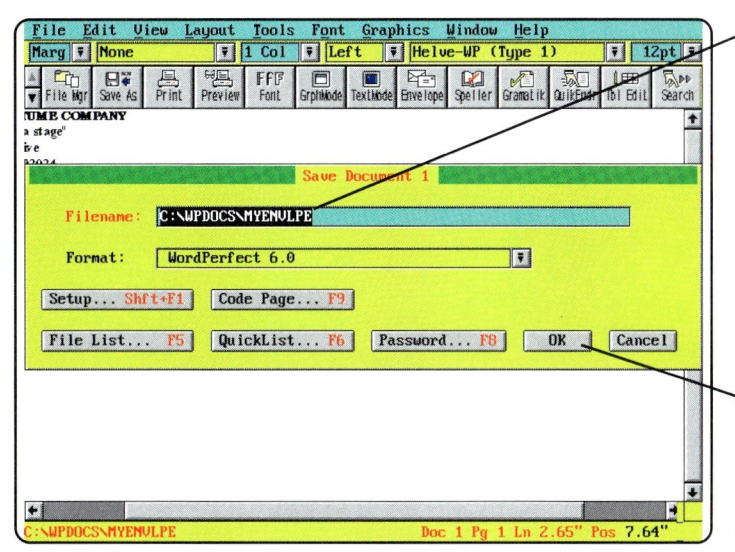

CHAPTER 15: PRINTING ENVELOPES FOR A MAILING LIST

2. Type C:\WPDOCS\ MYENVLPE in the Filename text box if it is not already there. You can type it in lowercase letters, too. However, if it is already there, it will appear in all capital letters, as shown on the screen.

3. Click on **OK**. A Replacement message box will appear.

4. Click on **Yes**.

PRINTING A SPECIFIC ENVELOPE FROM A MAILING LIST

First you must mark a specific envelope (or envelopes) that you would like to selectively print.

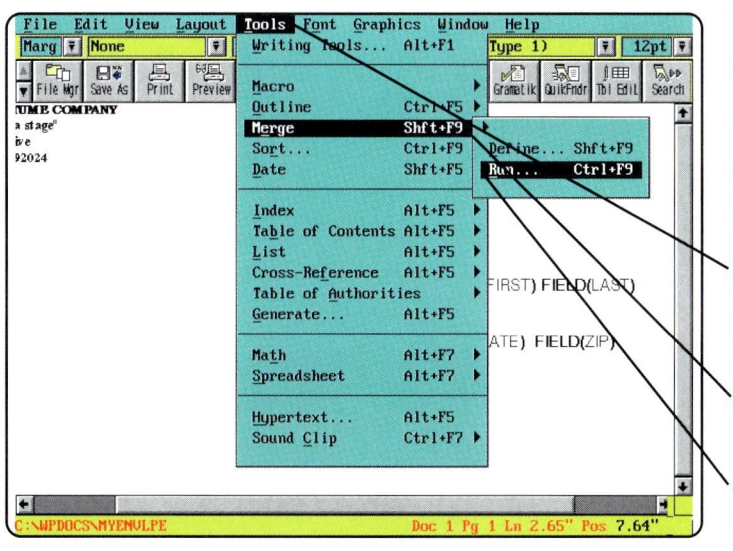

Marking an Envelope to Print

1. Open MYENVLPE if it is not already on your screen.

2. Click on **Tools** in the menu bar. A pull-down menu will appear.

3. Click on **Merge**. A second menu will appear.

4. Click on **Run**. The Run Merge dialog box will appear.

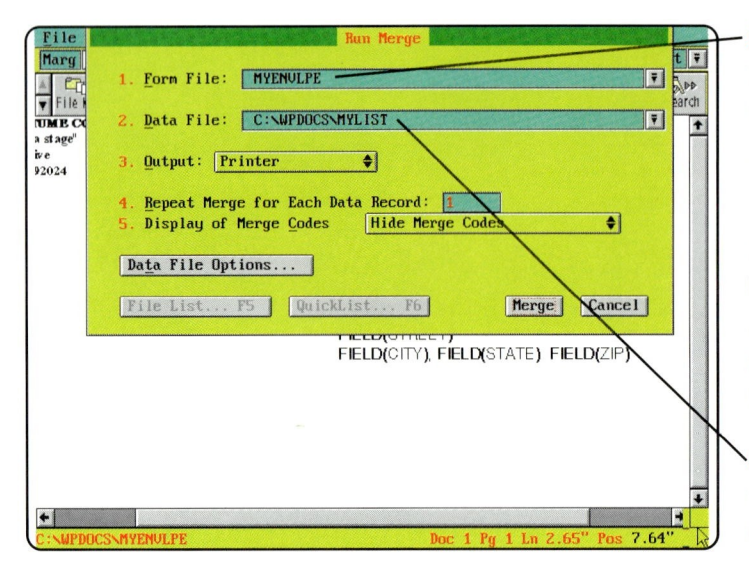

5. Type C:\WPDOCS\ MYENVLPE in the Form File text box if it is not already there.

You can type field names in lower- or uppercase letters because WordPerfect will accept either. In this case, we typed them in all capital letters.

6. Type C:\WPDOCS\ MYLIST in the Data File text box if it is not already there.

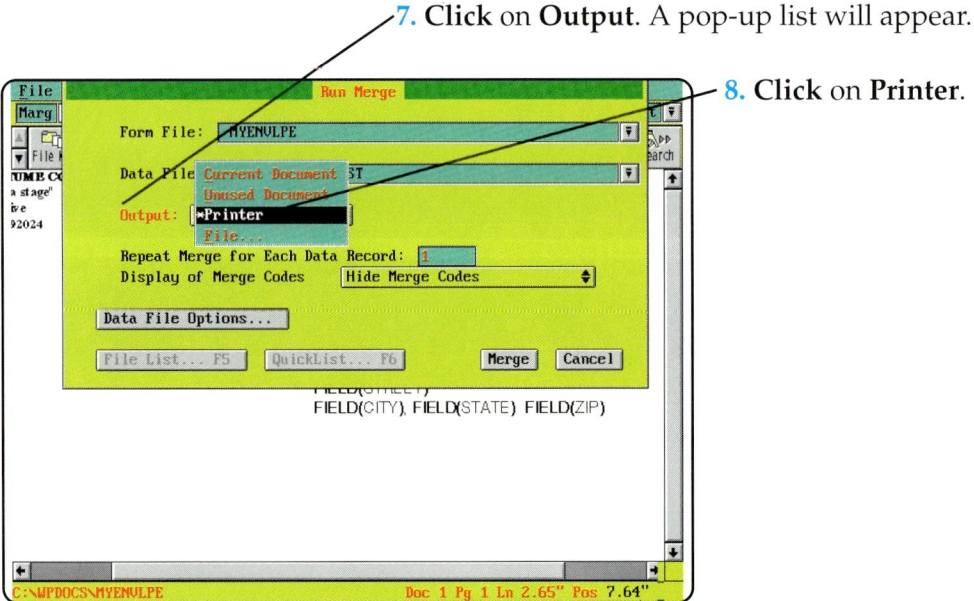

7. Click on **Output**. A pop-up list will appear.

8. Click on **Printer**.

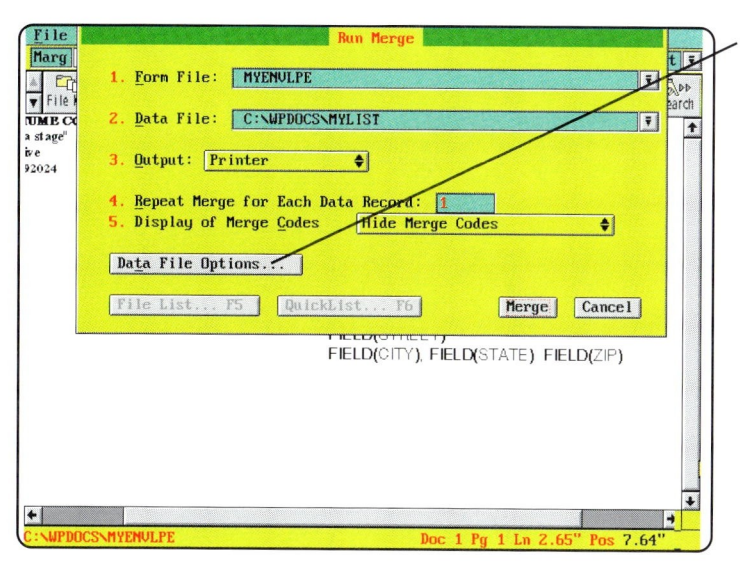

CHAPTER 15: PRINTING ENVELOPES FOR A MAILING LIST

9. Click on **Data File Options**. Another dialog box with the same name, RUN MERGE, will appear. Even though it has the same name, it is a different dialog box.

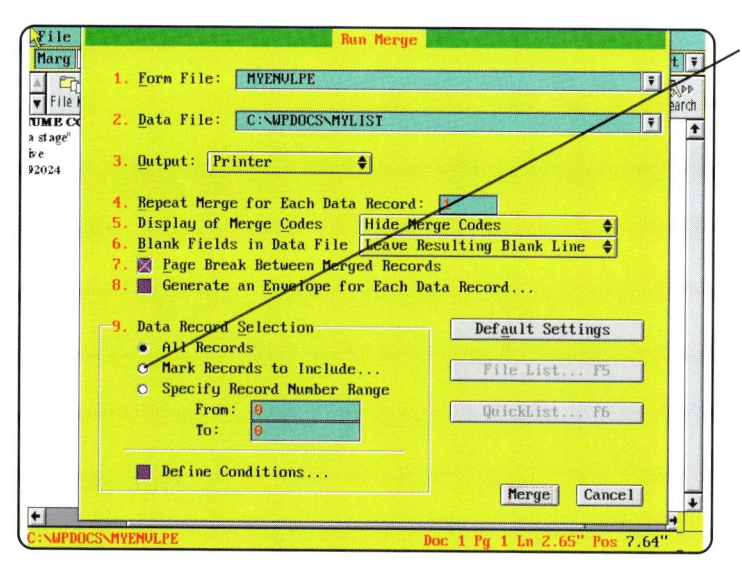

10. Click on **Mark Records to Include**. The List Field Names dialog box will appear.

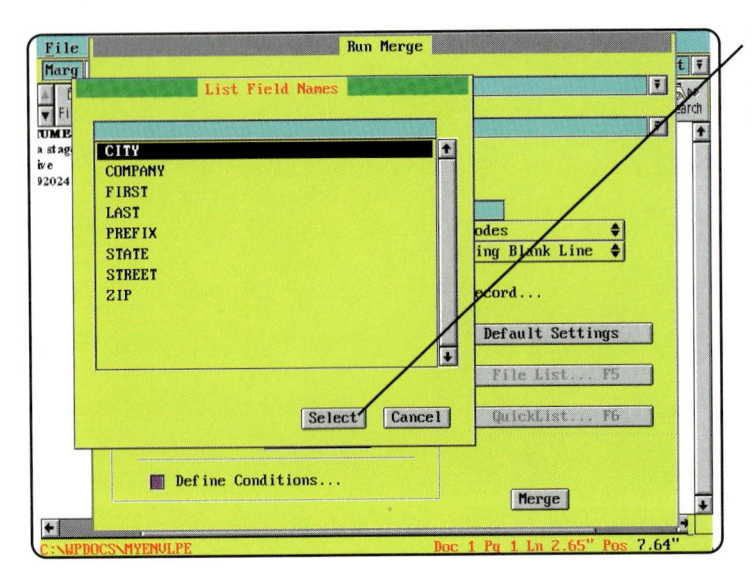

WORDPERFECT 6 FOR DOS: THE VISUAL LEARNING GUIDE

11. Click on **Select**. The Mark Data Records dialog box will appear. (At last!)

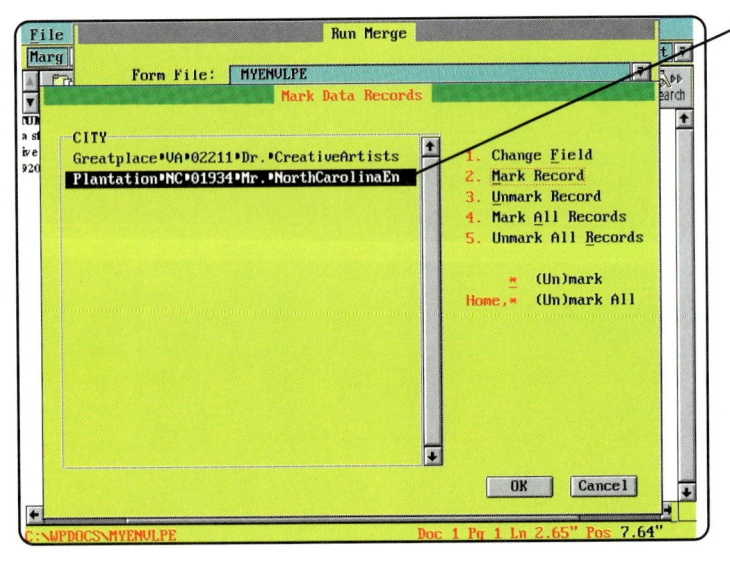

12. Click on the **"Plantation NC" line** to highlight it.

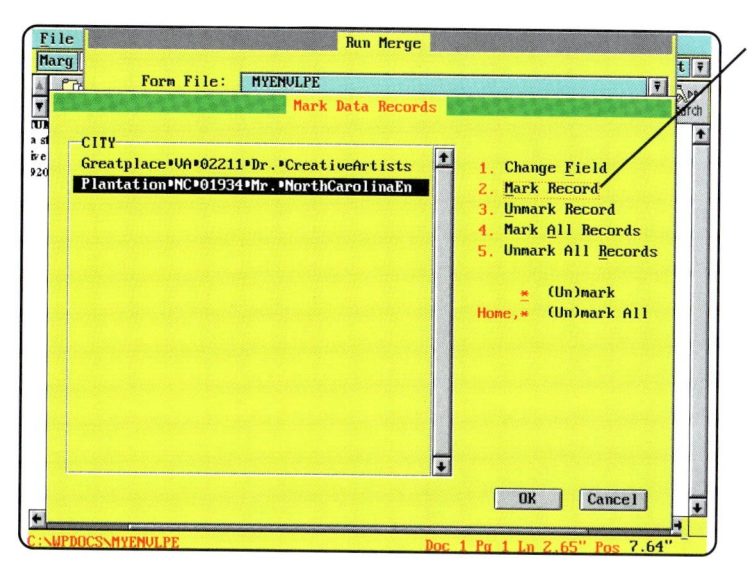

CHAPTER 15: PRINTING ENVELOPES FOR A MAILING LIST

13. Click on **Mark Record**. An asterisk (*) will appear to the left of the Plantation record.

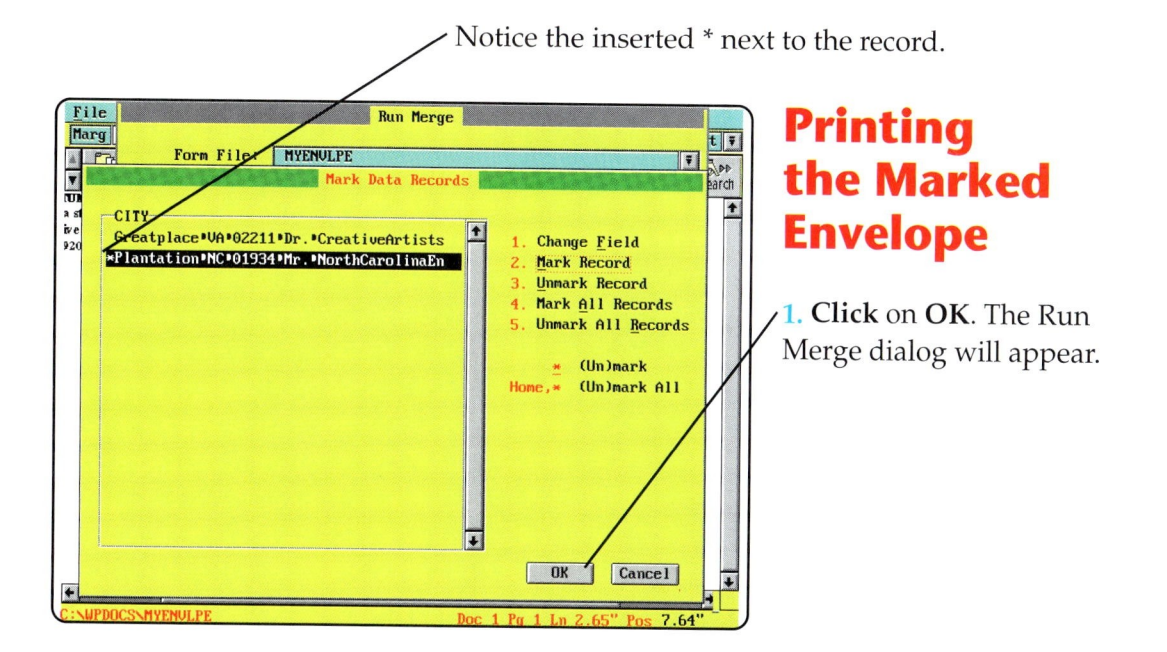

Notice the inserted * next to the record.

Printing the Marked Envelope

1. Click on **OK**. The Run Merge dialog will appear.

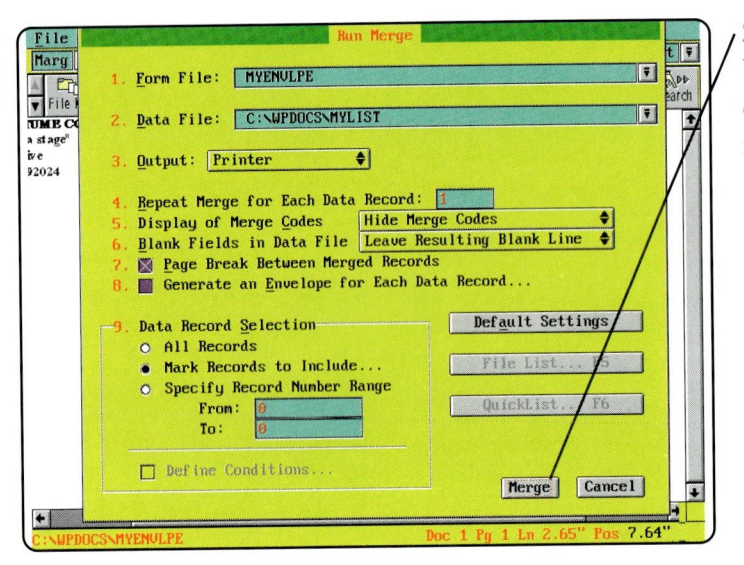

WORDPERFECT 6 FOR DOS: THE VISUAL LEARNING GUIDE

2. Click on **Merge**. WordPerfect will print an envelope(s) only for the record(s) you marked.

CLOSING THE ENVELOPE FILE WITHOUT SAVING

1. Click on **File** in the menu bar. A pull-down menu will appear.

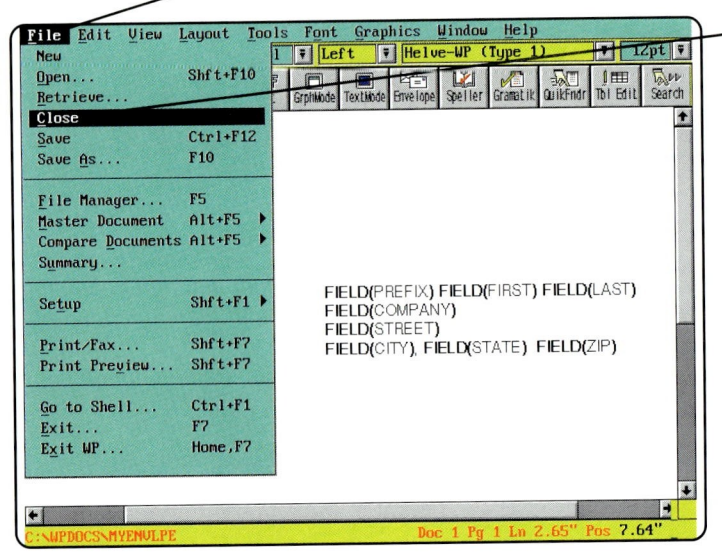

2. Click on **Close**. A Save Changes To dialog box will appear.

3. Click on **No** so that you don't save any changes to the file. A new document window will appear.

Converting a Mailing List Created in Another Program

If you have a mailing list created in another word-processing program, you can easily convert the mailing list into a WordPerfect 6 file. You don't have to create the list all over again. In this chapter you will do the following:

❖ Convert a mailing list from another DOS-based program or from a Windows-based program
❖ Add field names to the converted mailing list
❖ Save the mailing list as a WordPerfect data file

CONVERTING A MAILING LIST

Although this example shows an empty document screen, you can open a new file at any time. WordPerfect allows you to have up to nine files open at the same time.

1. Click on **File** in the menu bar. A pull-down menu will appear.

2. Click on **Open**. The Open Document dialog box will appear.

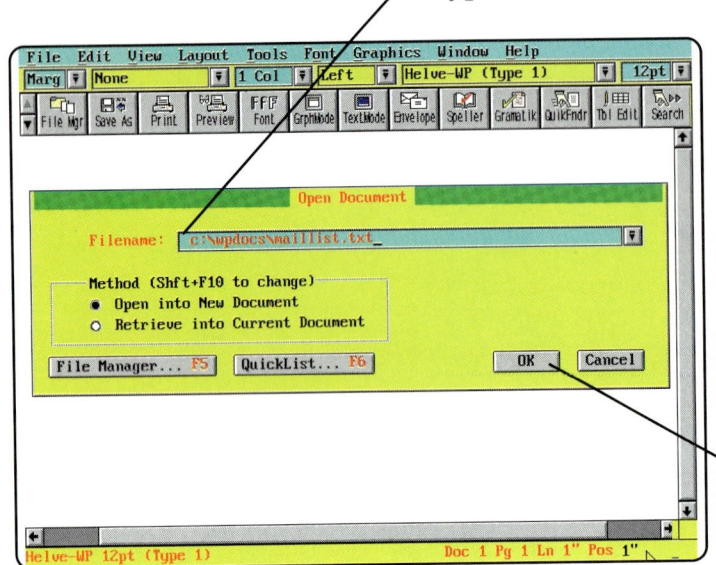

3. **Type** the **name of the mailing list file** you want to convert in the Filename text box (include the directory where it is located if it is not in the WPDOCS directory). If the filename has an extension, such as DOC, be sure to type it also. In this example we are using a mailing list file (called MAILLIST.TXT) in the WPDOCS directory.

4. **Click** on **OK**. The File Format dialog box will appear.

Notice that the file format of the mailing list you are opening is automatically highlighted. In this example the format of the MAILLIST.TXT file is ASCII Text. If your file was created in another word-processing program, it may be in a different format. Go to the next section, "Converting a File from a Specific Program." If your file is in the ASCII Text format, continue with step 5.

5. **Click** on **Select**. The mailing list window will appear.

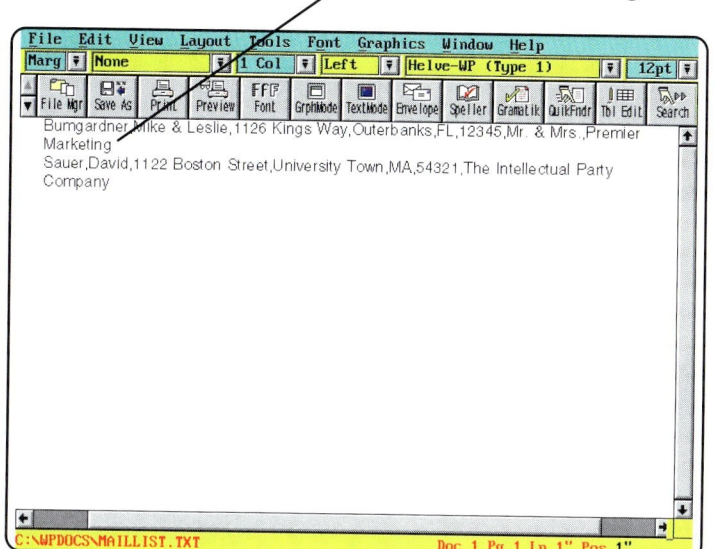

CHAPTER 16: CONVERTING A MAILING LIST

Notice in this example that each person's record in the converted mailing list has part of the company name wrapped around to the next line. It is very difficult to edit a mailing list file in this form. In the next section you will change the view so that each person's record is on one line.

Converting a File from a Specific Program

WordPerfect takes its best guess about which program created your mailing list. When you open the File Format dialog box, the program format that WordPerfect selects will be highlighted. If this is not the program format of the file you want to convert, follow the steps below:

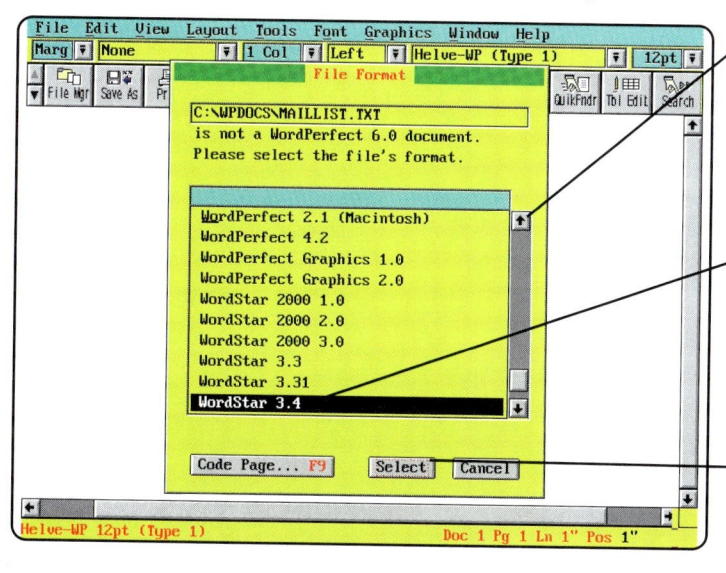

1. **Click** on the **up arrow** or the **down arrow** on the scroll bar to scroll up or down to select the appropriate program name.

2. **Click** on the **name of the word-processing program** in which you created the file. In this example, it is WordStar 3.4.

3. **Click** on **Select**. The mailing list will appear on your screen.

ADDING FIELD NAMES TO A CONVERTED MAILING LIST

It is easier to edit a mailing list if all of the information for each record is on one line. So, before you add field names to the file, you can change the view by making the font size smaller.

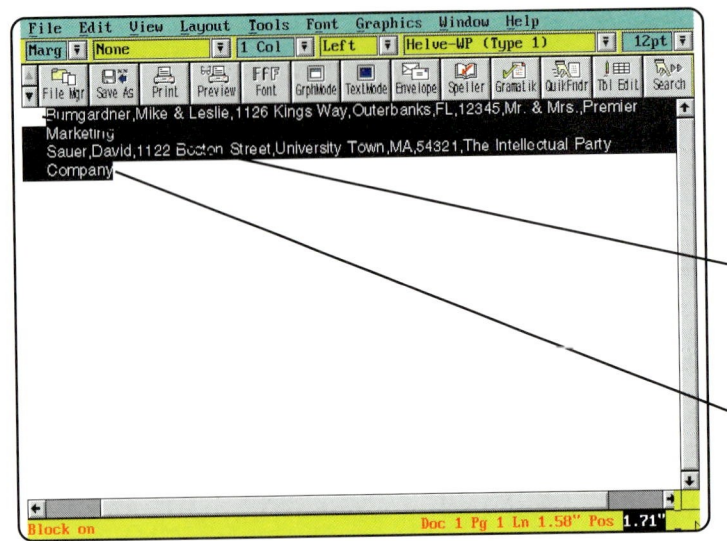

Changing the View

1. Click to the **left of the first letter ("B")** in the first row to set the cursor.

2. Press and hold the mouse button as you **drag** it down to **highlight all of the text**. **Release** the mouse button.

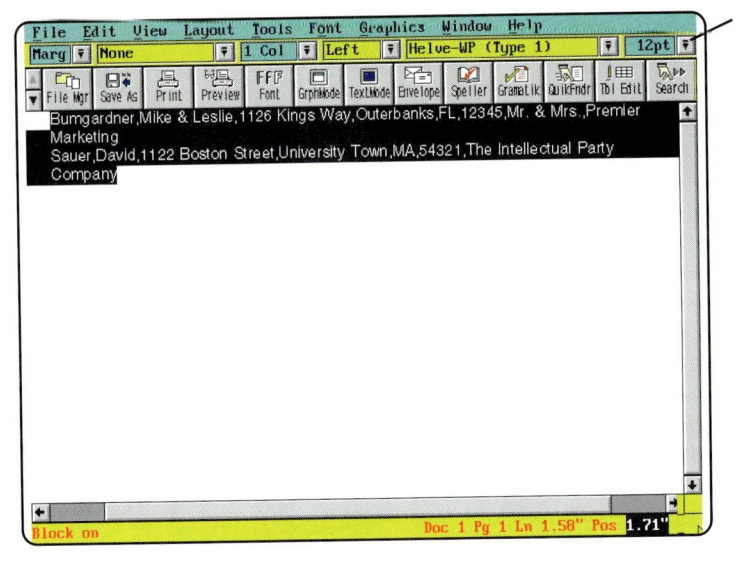

3. Click on the **down arrow** to the **right of 12pt** in the ribbon. A drop-down list of point sizes will appear.

CHAPTER 16: CONVERTING A MAILING LIST

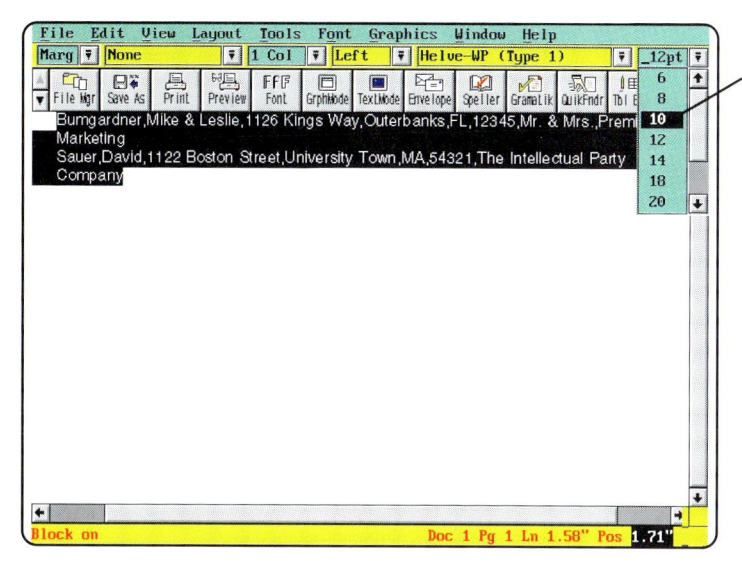

4. Click twice on **10**. The font size will change to 10 point and each record will now appear on one line.

Entering Field Names

1. Click to the **left of the first letter ("B")** on the first line to set the cursor.

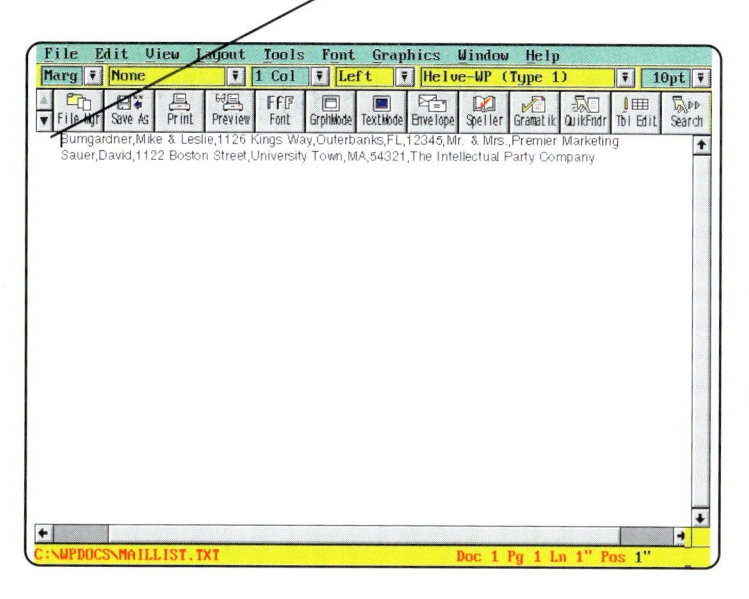

2. Press the **Enter key** on your keyboard. The first line of text will move down one line. There will be an empty line above it.

3. Press the **↑ key** on your keyboard to place the cursor at the beginning of the first row.

WORDPERFECT 6 FOR DOS: THE VISUAL LEARNING GUIDE

4. Type the following words (field names). Put a comma after each word. *But do not put a space after the comma* or this mailing list will not merge print correctly. Do not put a comma after the last field name.

LAST
FIRST
STREET
CITY
STATE
ZIP
PREFIX
COMPANY

You can type field names in lower- or uppercase letters because WordPerfect will accept either. In this case, we typed them in all capital letters.

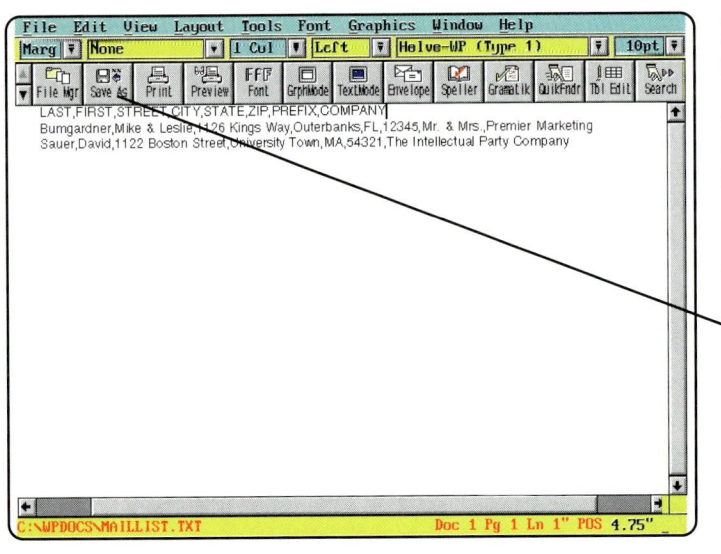

SAVING THE MAILING LIST AS A WORDPERFECT DATA FILE

1. Click on the **Save As button** in the button bar. The Save Document dialog box will appear.

CHAPTER 16: CONVERTING A MAILING LIST

2. Click on **Format**. A drop-down list will appear.

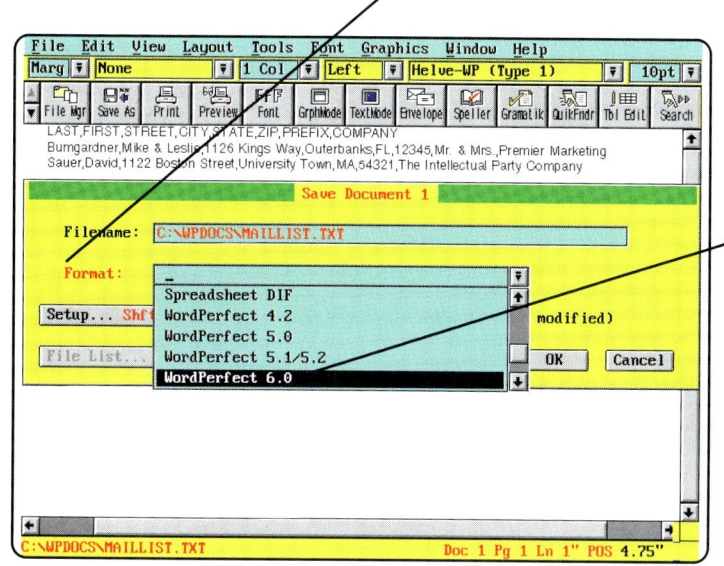

3. Click on the **up arrow** or the **down arrow** on the scroll bar until you **highlight WordPerfect 6.0**.

4. Click twice on **WordPerfect 6.0**. The Save Document dialog box will appear.

Warning: If you want to keep the mailing list file in its original program format (for example, WordStar, ASCII Text, etc.) do not save it with its original name or else the original file will be replaced with the new file.

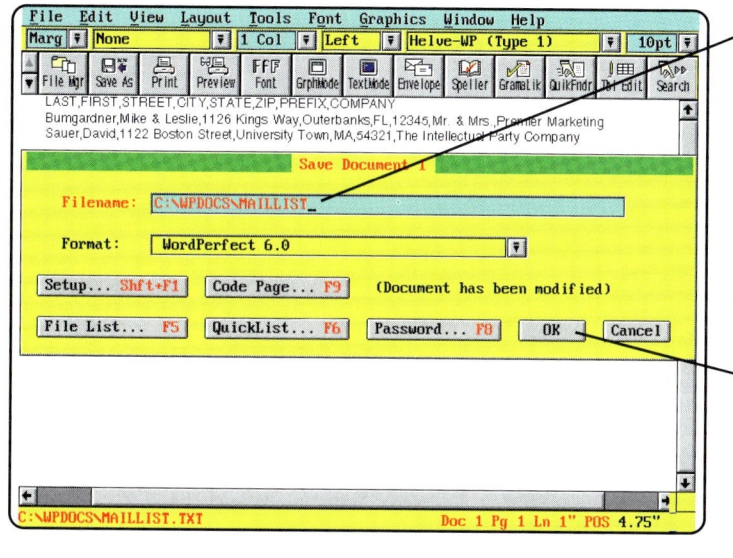

5. Click to the **right of C:\WPDOCS\MAILLIST.TXT**.

6. Press the **Backspace key four times**. The new filename will now be C:\WPDOCS\MAILLIST.

7. Click on **OK**.

File Manager

Part IV   Introducing Tables

Chapter 17: Creating a Table	Page 198
Chapter 18: Editing a Table	Page 205
Chapter 19: Formatting Numbers and Writing Formulas	Page 221

Creating a Table

The Tables feature in WordPerfect 6 makes it easy to organize information into columns and rows. Once the table is created, it operates like a basic spreadsheet. For example, you can join cells in the table to make room for a heading, increase the numbers of lines in a cell for a large entry, and increase or decrease the width of a column. You can even enter a formula into a cell and copy that formula to adjacent cells and sort data within a row or column. In this chapter you will do the following:

- Create a table
- Join cells
- Enter text and numbers

CREATING A TABLE

In this example you will create a table that has four columns and six rows. Although you can insert a table anywhere in an existing document, in this example you will open a new document for the table if you do not already have a blank document on your screen.

1. **Click** on **File** in the menu bar. A pull-down menu will appear.

2. **Click** on **New**. A new document will appear on your screen.

CHAPTER 17: CREATING A TABLE

3. **Type** the sentence **This is our new price list and order form.** Then **press Enter twice**.

4. **Click** on **Layout** in the menu bar. A pull-down menu will appear.

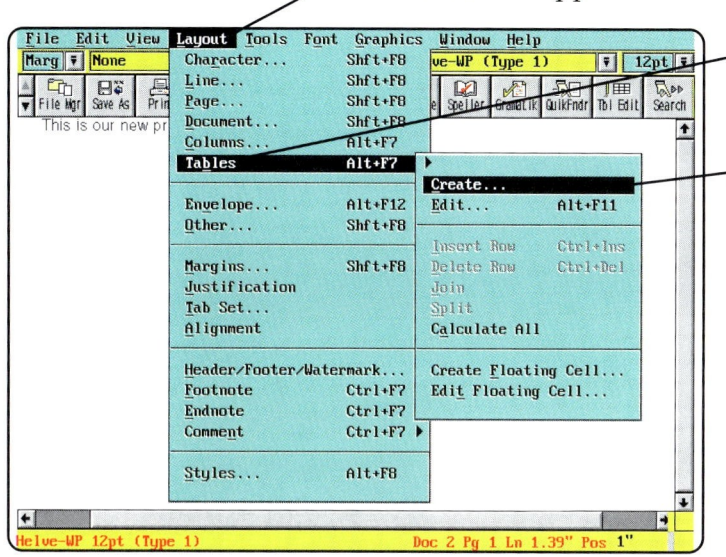

5. **Click** on **Tables**. Another menu will appear.

6. **Click** on **Create**. The Create Table dialog box will appear.

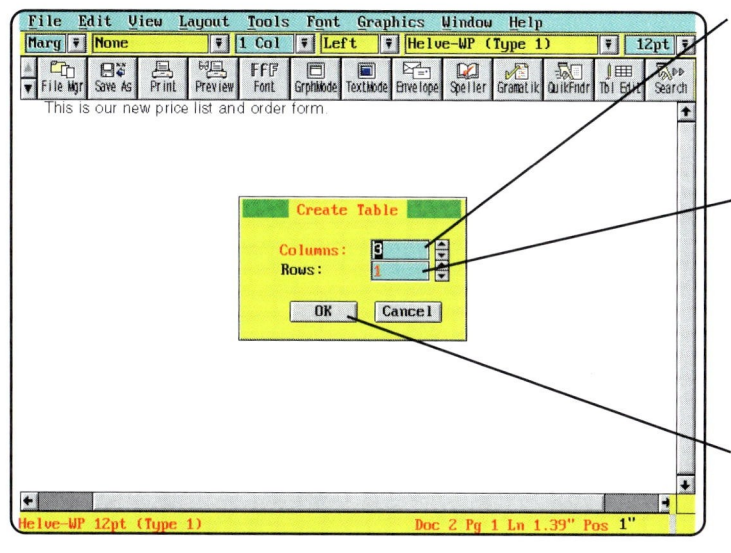

7. **Type 4** to replace the highlighted 3 in the Columns box. This will create four columns in the table.

8. **Click** anywhere **in the Rows box**. The number 1 will be highlighted.

9. **Type 6** to create six rows in the table.

10. **Click** on **OK**. The dialog box will disappear and the Table Edit screen will appear.

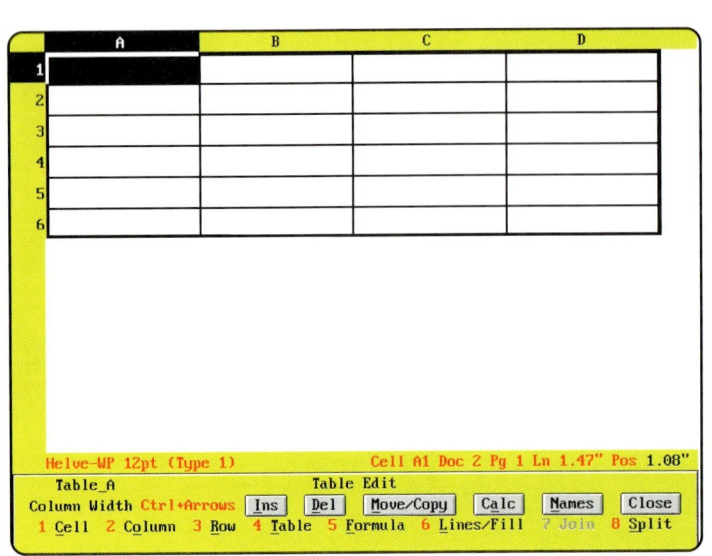

WORDPERFECT 6 FOR DOS: THE VISUAL LEARNING GUIDE

This is how the table first appears on your screen. It is shown in the Table Edit mode. In this mode you can edit the structure of the table itself, but you cannot enter any text or numbers in it.

Notice that the columns of the table are labeled A through D and the rows are labeled 1 through 6.

The intersection of each column and row creates *cells*. The cells are referred to as A1 through D6.

JOINING CELLS

When you join cells you remove the dividing line between them to create a single, larger cell. In this section you will join the cells in the first row to create a single cell for a heading.

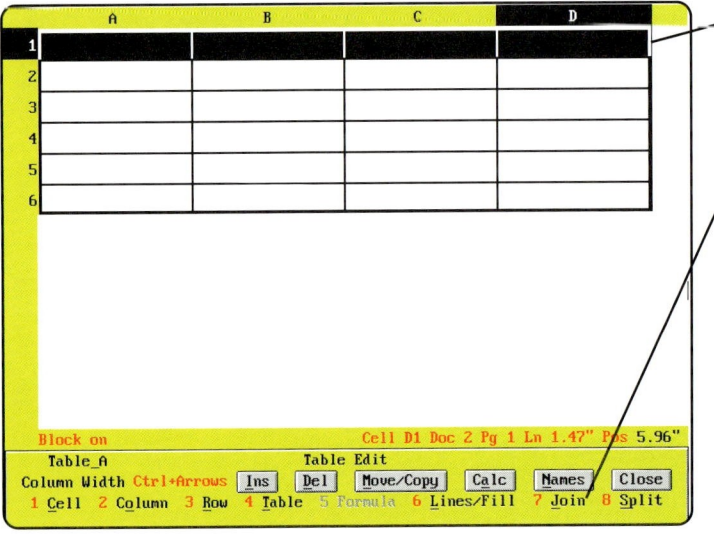

1. **Press and hold** the mouse button and **drag** the highlight bar **across the first row of the table to D1**.

2. **Click** on **Join**. The Join Cells? dialog box will appear.

CHAPTER 17: CREATING A TABLE

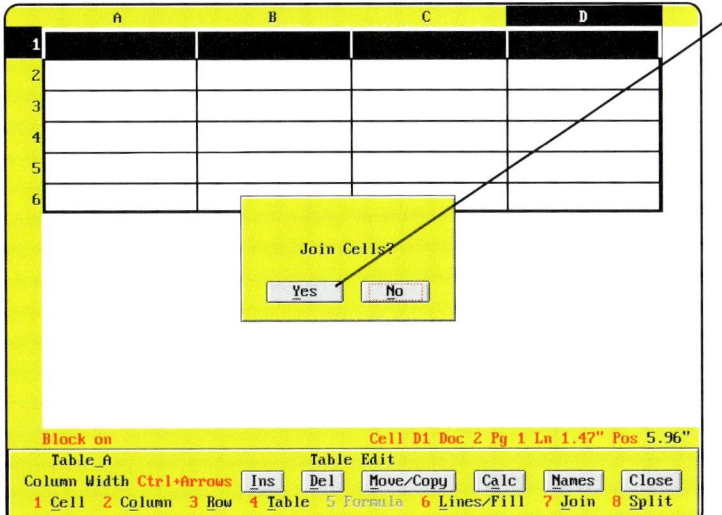

3. Click on **Yes** to join the cells.

This example joined cells in a row. You can follow this same process to join cells in a column.

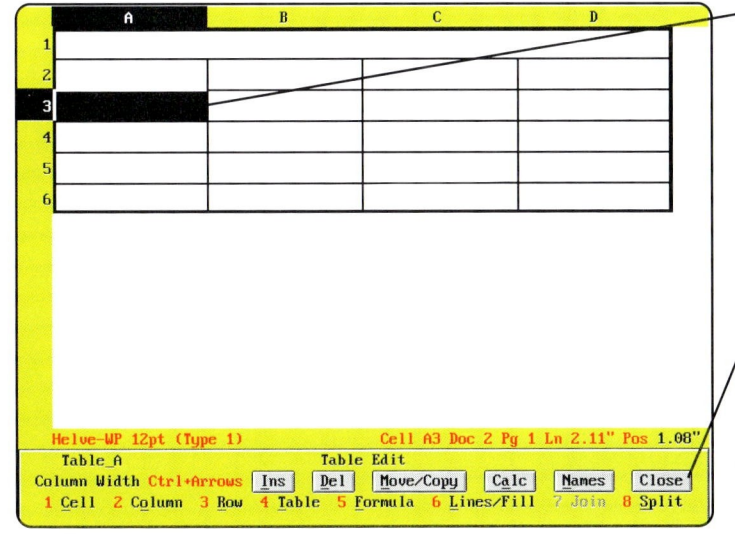

4. Click anywhere on the table to remove the highlight bar so you can see the joined cells in row 1.

You must exit out of the Table Edit mode in order to type in the table.

5. Click on **Close**. The blank table will appear at the cursor spot in your document.

ENTERING TEXT AND NUMBERS IN A TABLE

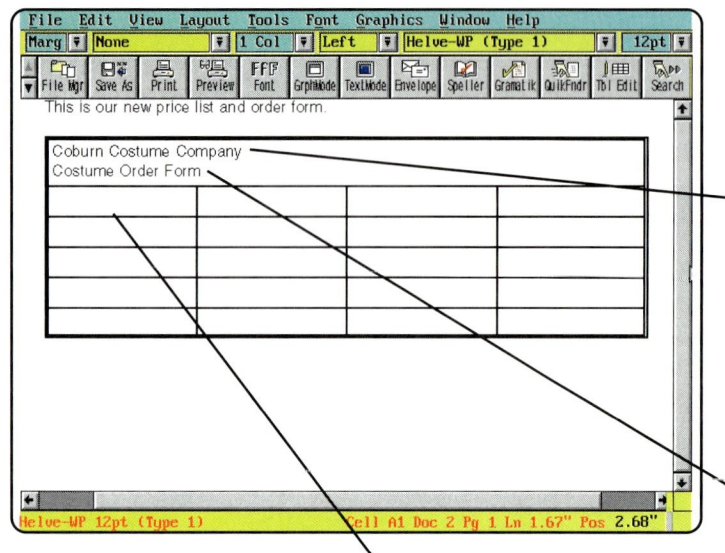

Once the table is in a document, you enter and edit text as you would in the document itself.

1. **Click** on the **first cell** (cell **A1**) if your cursor is not already there. **Type Coburn Costume Company**.

2. **Press Enter**. This will add a line to the cell you are in.

3. **Type Costume Order Form**.

4. **Click** on the **cell in column A row 2** (cell **A2**).

5. **Type Costume** and **press** the **Tab key**. The cursor will move to the next cell (**B2**). If you accidentally press Enter, an extra line will be added to the cell. Simply press Backspace and the extra line will be deleted.

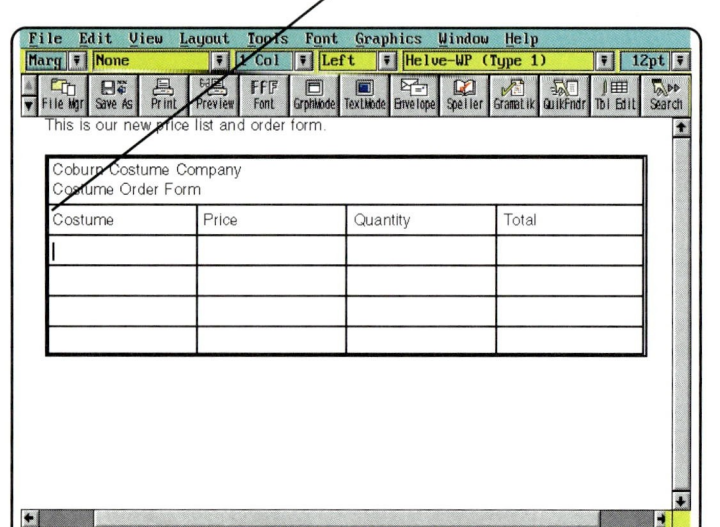

6. **Type Price** and **press** the **Tab key**. The cursor will move to the next cell (B3).

7. **Type Quantity** and **press** the **Tab key**. The cursor will move to the next cell (**B4**).

8. **Type Total** and **press** the **Tab key**. The cursor will move to the next cell (**C1**).

CHAPTER 17: CREATING A TABLE

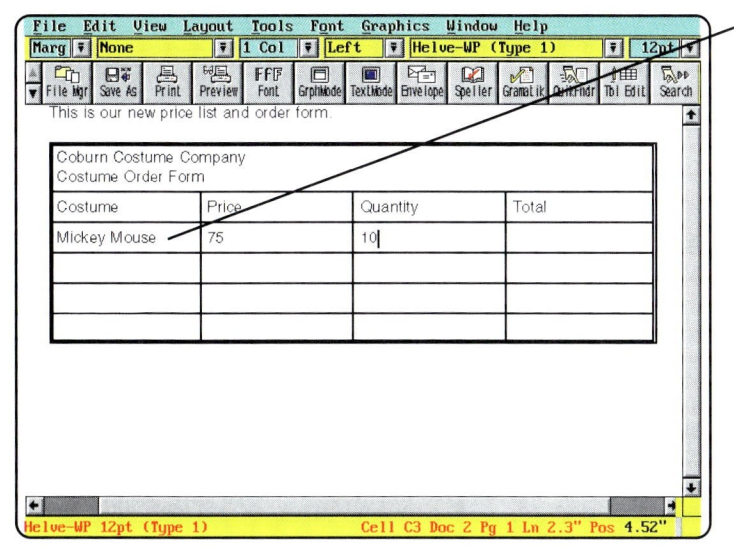

9. **Type Mickey Mouse** in **C1** and **press Tab** to move the cursor to the next cell (**C2**).

10. **Type 75** and **tab** to the next cell (**C3**).

11. **Type 10**.

12. **Click** on the **cell in column A row 4** (**A4**).

13. **Type Catwoman** and **tab** to the next cell (**B4**).

14. **Type 95** and **tab** to the next cell (**C4**).

15. **Type 5**.

Your table will look like the example to the left.

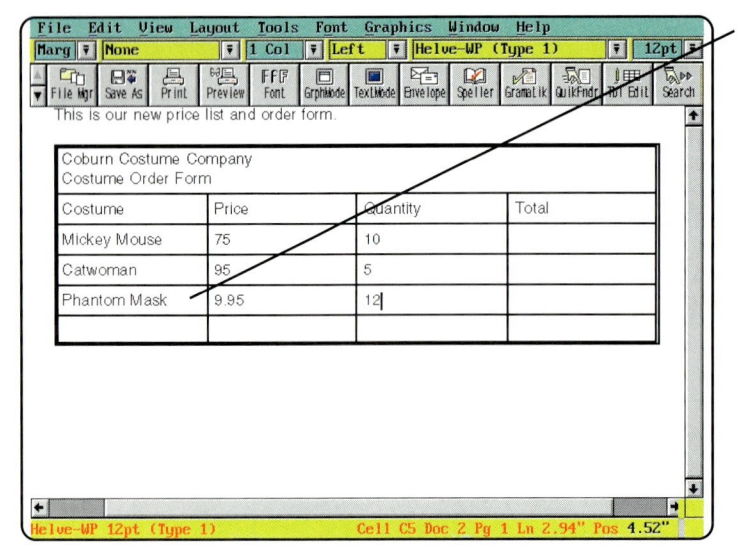

16. Click on **A5**.

17. Type Phantom Mask and **tab** to **B5**.

18. Type 9.95 and **tab** to **C5**.

19. Type 12.

20. Click on **A6** and **type Totals**.

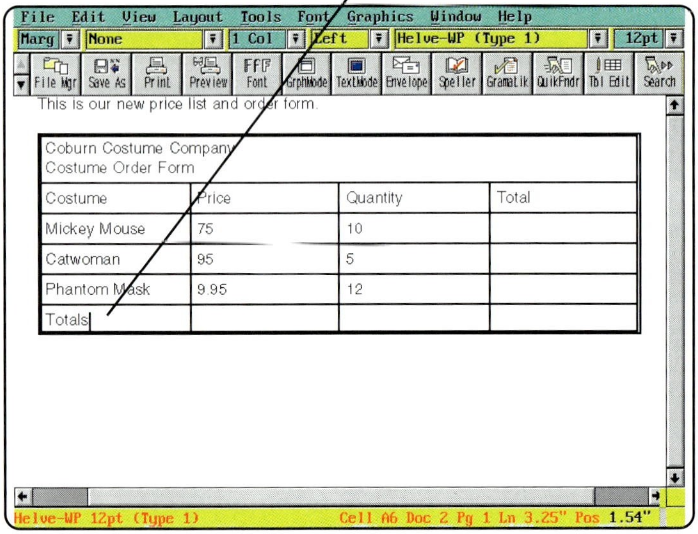

Your screen will look like the example to the left.

Save this table so you can work on it in the next two chapters. If you need help saving a file, see Chapter 2, "Naming and Saving a Document." In the following examples, the file is named ORDERFRM.

In the next chapter you will edit the table.

Editing a Table

Once you have created a table in the Table Edit mode, you enter and edit text and numbers in the document itself. WordPerfect 6 even lets you sort data alphabetically. But if you want to edit the structure of the table by adding a row or column or changing the width of a column, you must go back to the Table Edit mode. In this chapter you will do the following:

- ❖ Sort data alphabetically
- ❖ Sort data numerically
- ❖ Add a row to a table
- ❖ Delete a row from a table
- ❖ Change column widths
- ❖ Format text
- ❖ Change the position of a table so that it is centered across the page

SORTING DATA ALPHABETICALLY

You can sort data while you are in the document itself. If you do not want to sort the entire document you must highlight, the cells you want to sort. In this example you will sort the data in rows 3 through 5 alphabetically by the first cell in each line in the ORDERFRM sample table.

1. Click to the left of "Mickey Mouse" in **A3**.

2. Press and hold the mouse button as you **drag** the highlight bar down to the number "12" in **C5**. All the cells between A3 and C5 will be highlighted.

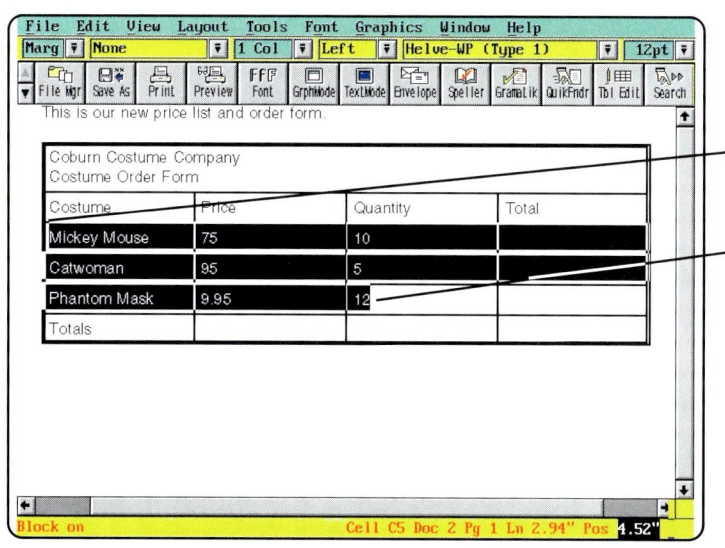

WORDPERFECT 6 FOR DOS: THE VISUAL LEARNING GUIDE

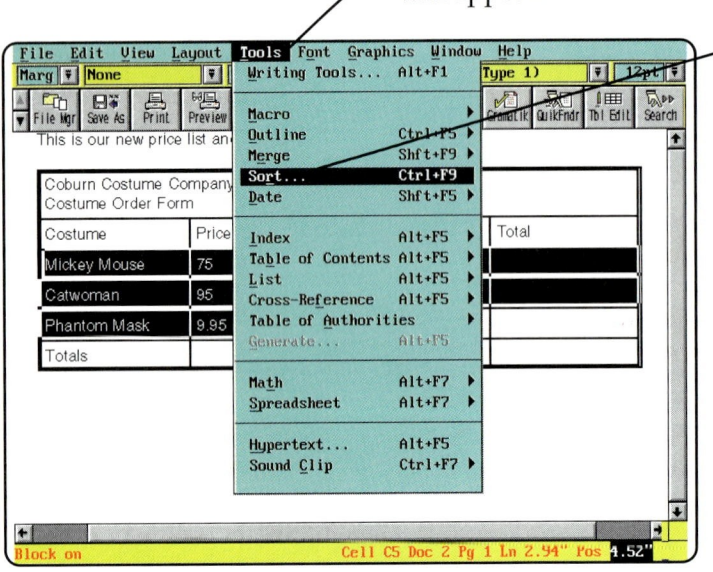

3. **Click** on **Tools** in the menu bar. A pull-down menu will appear.

4. **Click** on **Sort**. The Sort dialog box will appear.

In this example you will use the standard (default) sort settings.

Table is already selected as the Record Type because your cursor was in a table when you chose Sort from the pull-down menu.

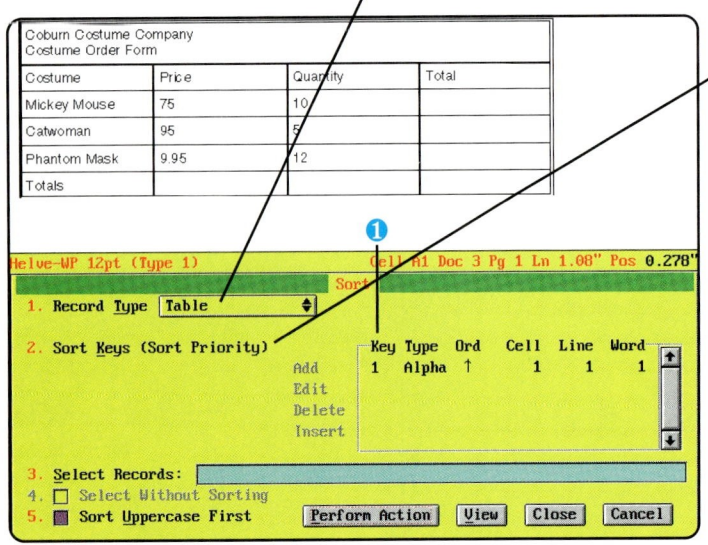

The Sort Keys (Sort Priority) tell WordPerfect how to sort lines, as follows:

❶ **Key = 1** means that you will sort on one criterion. You can sort on up to nine criteria. Consult *WordPerfect 6.0 Reference Manual* for directions on more complicated sorting procedures.

CHAPTER 18: EDITING A TABLE

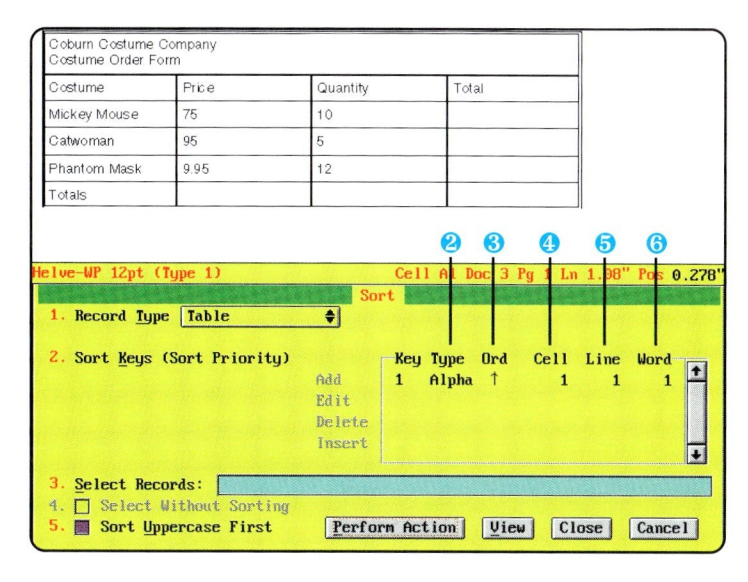

❷ **Type = Alpha** means this will be an alphabetic sort.

❸ **Ord = ↑** means the sort is in an ascending order (from A to Z).

❹ **Cell = 1** means WordPerfect will sort the lines based on the first cell in each line.

❺ **Line = 1** means the sort will be made on the first line in the cell.

❻ **Word = 1** means WordPerfect will sort on the first word in the cell. For example, in "Phantom Mask" the sort will be on "Phantom" rather than on "Mask."

Each of these settings can be changed. You will do a numeric sort on the second cell later in this chapter.

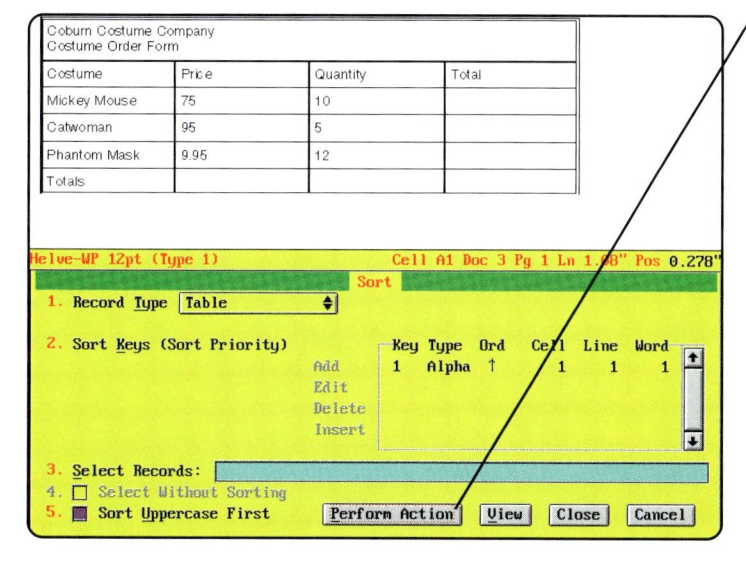

5. Click on **Perform Action** to start the sorting process.

You will see a Please Wait message box and the Sorting Records box will show on your screen. When the sorting is finished, the data in the table will be rearranged on your screen based on the sort priorities you set in the Sort dialog box.

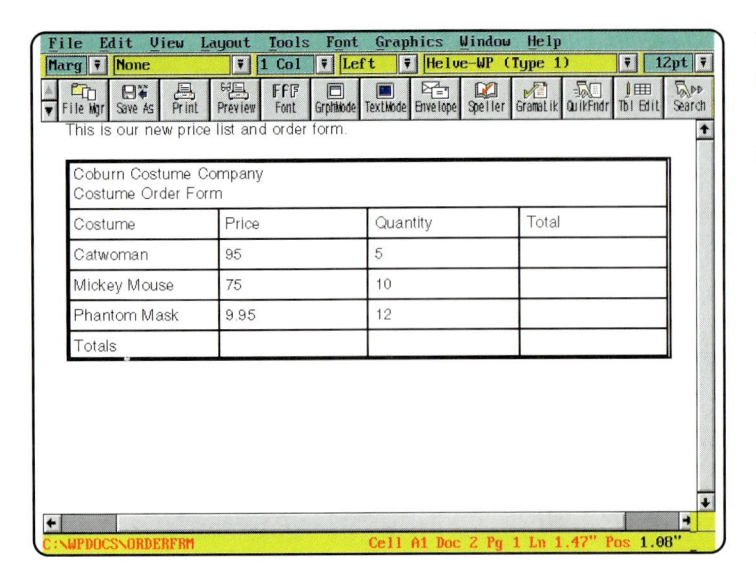

WORDPERFECT 6 FOR DOS: THE VISUAL LEARNING GUIDE

Your screen will look like this.

Pretty neat!

SORTING DATA NUMERICALLY

In this example you will sort the data in rows 3 through 5 based on the price of each costume.

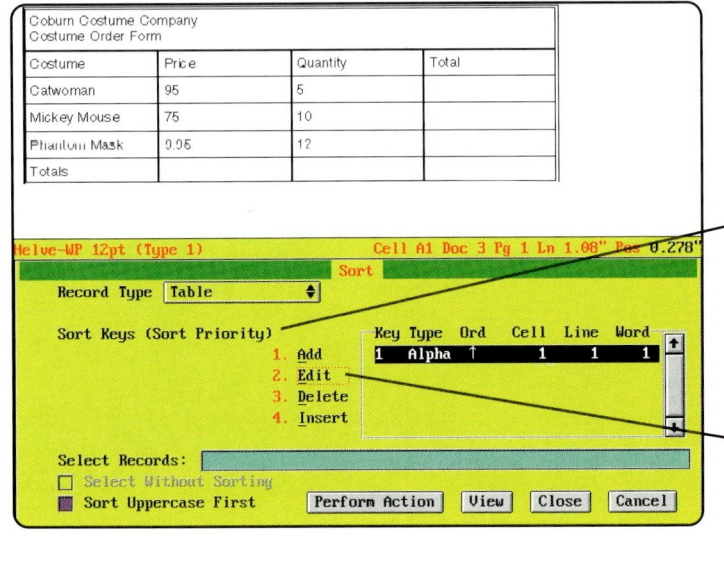

1. Repeat steps 1 through 4 in the previous section to **highlight A3 through C5** and to **open** the **Sort dialog box**.

2. Click on **Sort Keys (Sort Priority)**. The sorting keys to the right will be highlighted and a dotted box will appear around Edit.

3. Click on **Edit**. The Edit Sort Key dialog box will appear.

CHAPTER 18: EDITING A TABLE

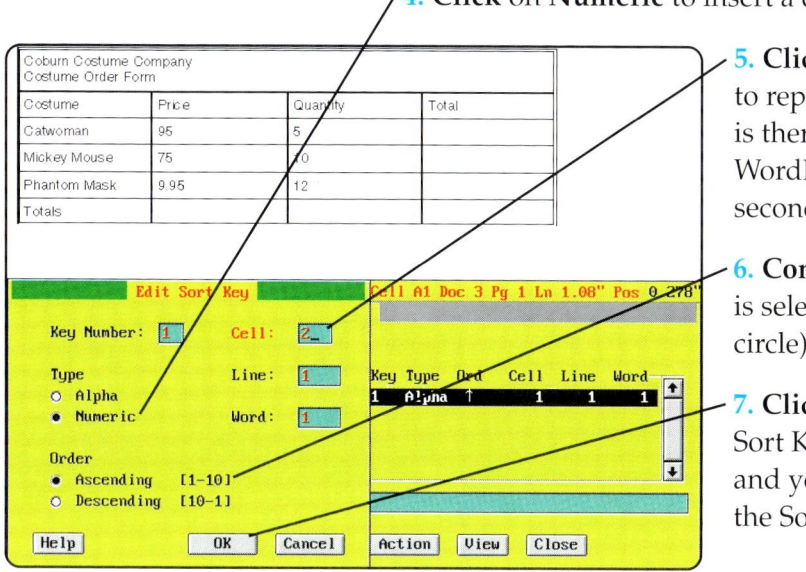

4. **Click** on **Numeric** to insert a dot in the circle.

5. **Click** on **Cell** and **type 2** to replace the number 1 that is there. This tells WordPerfect to sort on the second cell in each line.

6. **Confirm** that **Ascending** is selected (has a dot in the circle).

7. **Click** on **OK**. The Edit Sort Key dialog will close and you will be returned to the Sort dialog box.

Note: If you changed your mind about these sort commands, you could click on Delete. This would return the Sort keys to the default positions you saw in the previous section. Don't do this now unless you're willing to repeat Steps 2 through 7

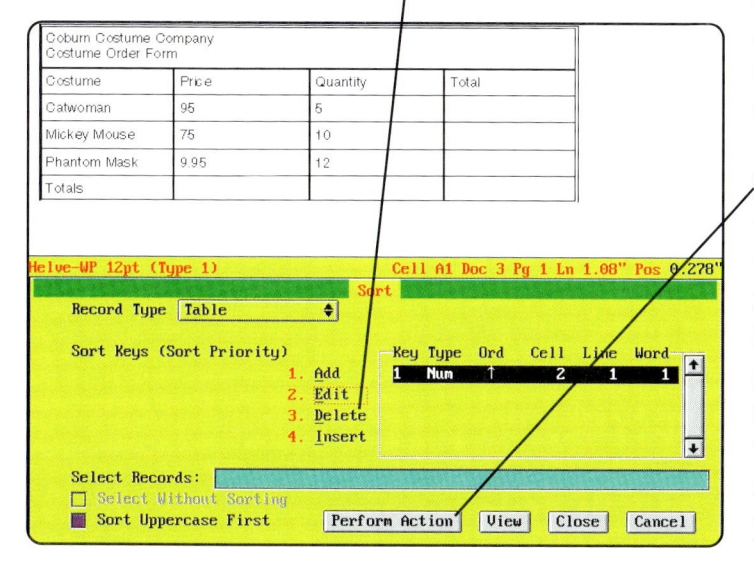

8. **Click** on **Perform Action** to start the sort process. You will see the Please Wait message box and the Sorting Records box will show on your screen. When the sorting is finished, the data will be rearranged numerically with the lowest-priced item listed first.

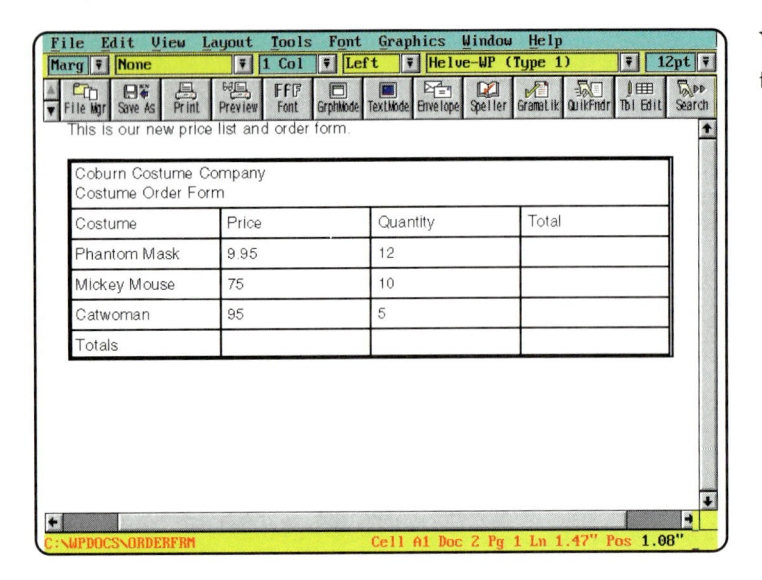

WORDPERFECT 6 FOR DOS: THE VISUAL LEARNING GUIDE

Your screen will look like this.

UNDOING A SORT

You can undo a sort with the click of your mouse. But be sure *not to perform any other function* between the numeric sort and the Undo or else it won't work. In this example you will undo the numeric sort you just did in the previous section and return to the alphabetic sort.

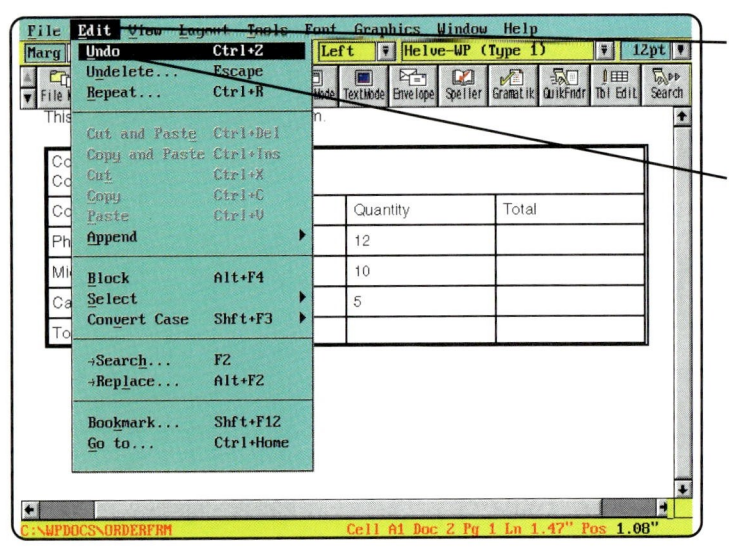

1. Click on **Edit** in the menu bar. A pull-down menu will appear.

2. Click on **Undo**. The last action you performed (the numeric sort) will be undone and you will be returned to the previous sort (the alphabetic sort).

CHAPTER 18: EDITING A TABLE

ADDING A ROW

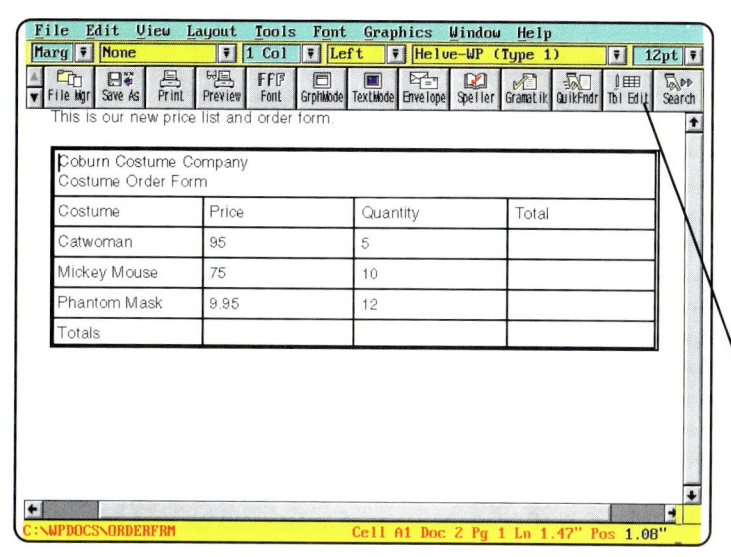

Adding a row changes the structure of the table so it must be done in the Table Edit mode.

1. Click anywhere in the table if your cursor is not already there.

2. Click on the **Tbl Edit button** in the button bar. The screen will change to the Table Edit mode.

The row where your cursor is located will be highlighted.

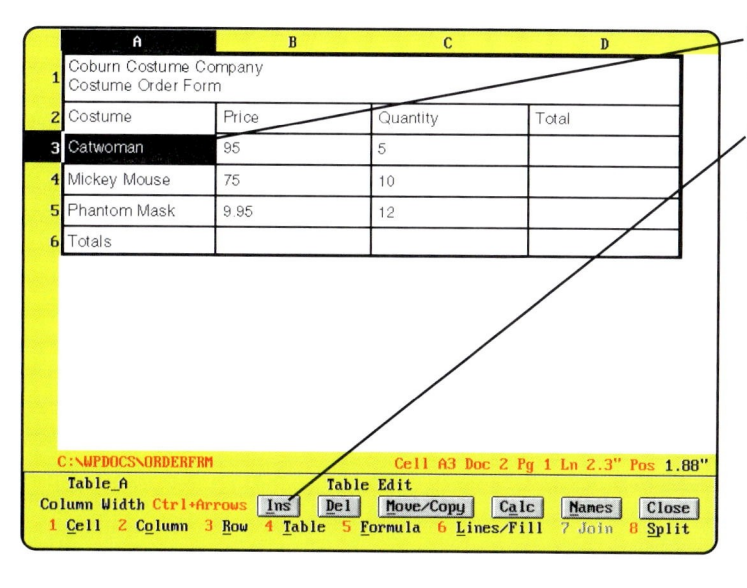

3. Click on "Catwoman" in **A3**. It will be highlighted.

4. Click on the **Ins button**. The Insert dialog box will appear.

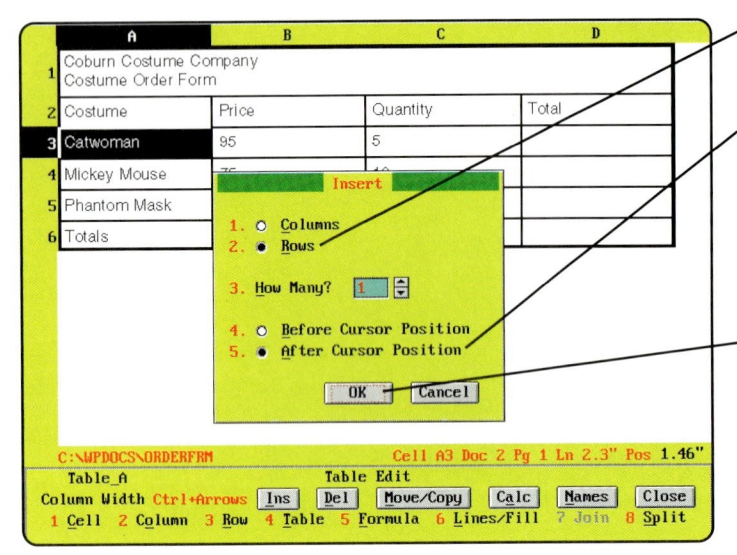

5. Click on **Rows** to insert a dot in the circle.

6. Click on **After Cursor Position** to insert a dot in the circle. This will insert a blank row after the "Catwoman" row.

7. Click on **OK**. The dialog box will close and the edited table will be on your screen.

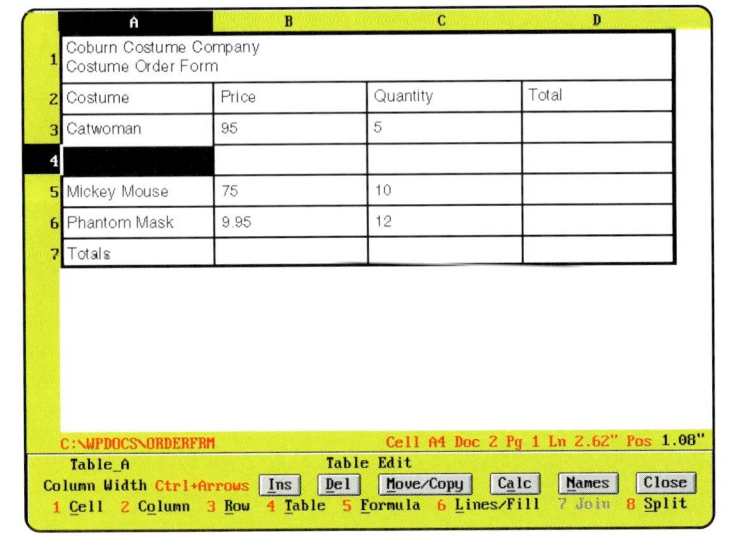

Your screen will look like this.

If you want to follow along with the next section, "Deleting a Row," don't close the Table Edit screen.

CHAPTER 18: EDITING A TABLE

DELETING A ROW

You can delete a row as easily as you added one. If you are not in the Table Edit mode, refer to steps 1 and 2 in the previous section for directions on how to get into the Table Edit mode.

1. Click on the **row you want to delete**. In this example, you will delete the row you just added in the previous section.

2. Click on the **Del button**. The Delete dialog box will appear.

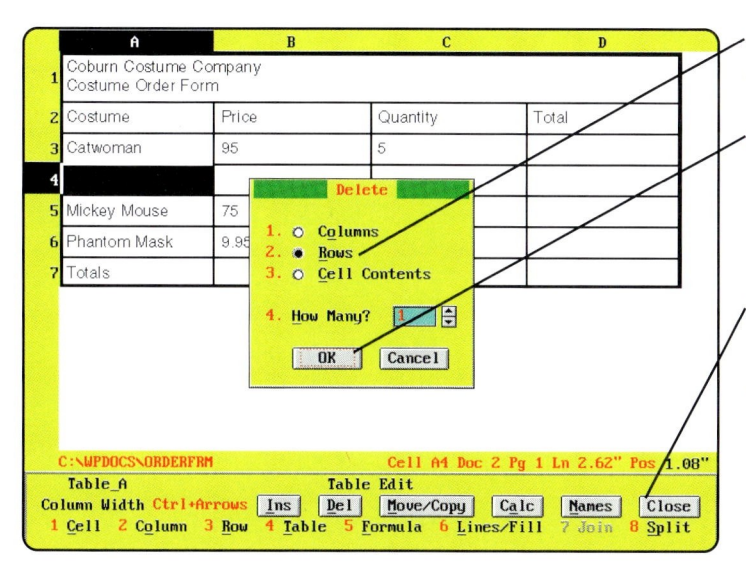

3. Click on **Rows** to insert a dot in the circle.

4. Click on **OK**. The dialog box will close and the edited table will appear on your screen.

5. Click on **Close** to return the edited table to the document.

CHANGING COLUMN WIDTH

Since changing the column width changes the structure of the table, it must be done in the Table Edit mode. In this section you will use the Layout pull-down menu as another way to open the Table Edit screen.

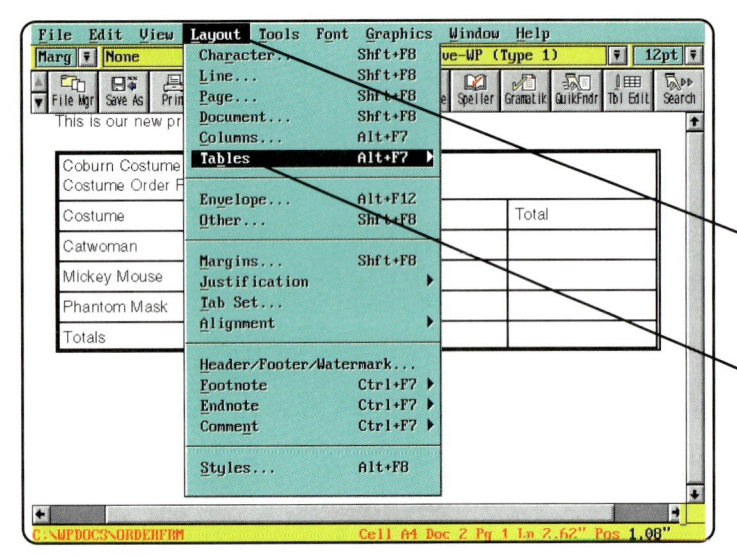

1. Click on **Layout** in the menu bar. A pull-down menu will appear.

2. Click on **Tables**. A second menu will appear.

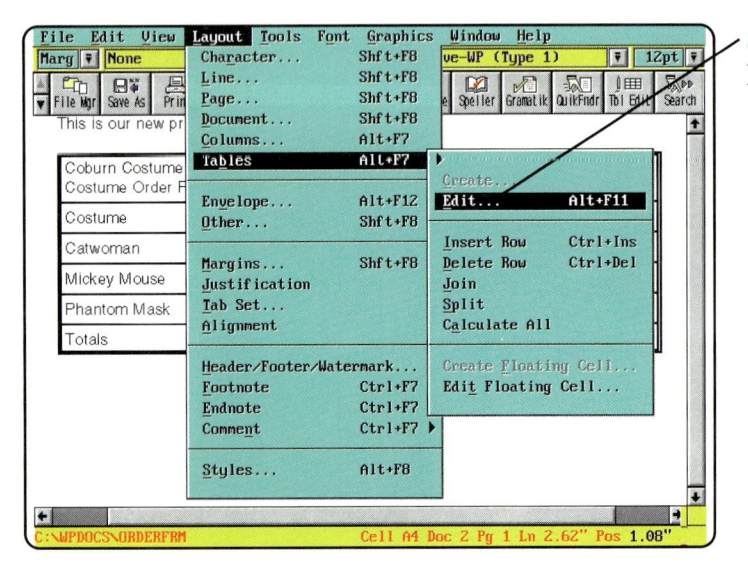

3. Click on **Edit**. The Table Edit screen will appear.

CHAPTER 18: EDITING A TABLE

4. Click on any cell in **column B** (Price).

5. Press and hold the **Ctrl key** as you **press** the ← **key** on your keyboard **seven times** (Ctrl + ←). You will see the column decrease each time you press the ←. (To increase column width, use the → key.)

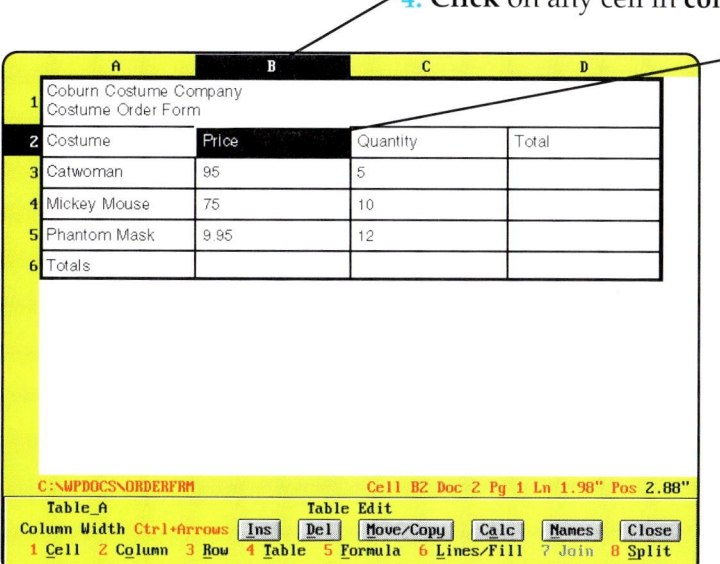

6. Repeat steps 4 and 5 to **decrease the width** of **columns C** (Quantity) and **D** (Total).

7. Click on **Close** to return the edited table to the document screen.

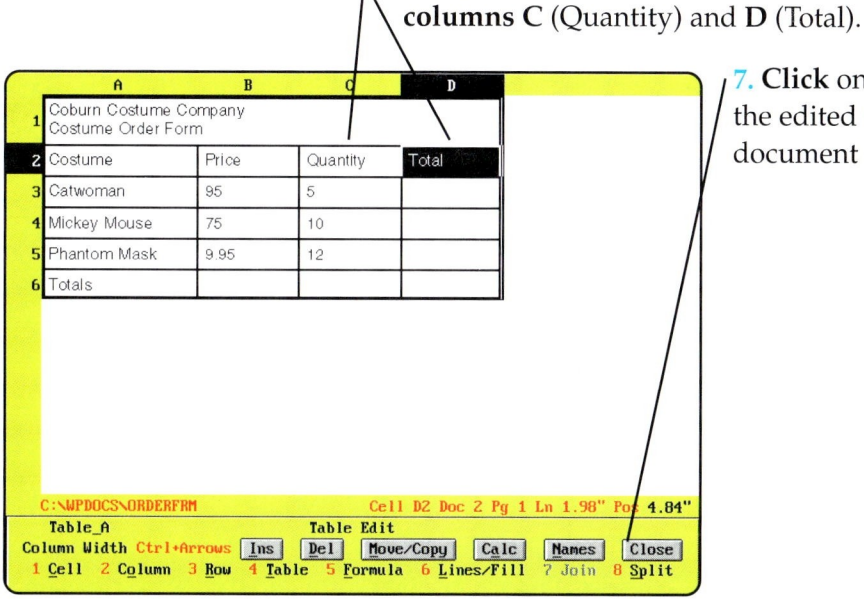

FORMATTING TEXT

You format text in a table just as you would any other text in a document.

Increasing Type Size

1. Click to the **left of "Coburn Costume Company"** in row 1.

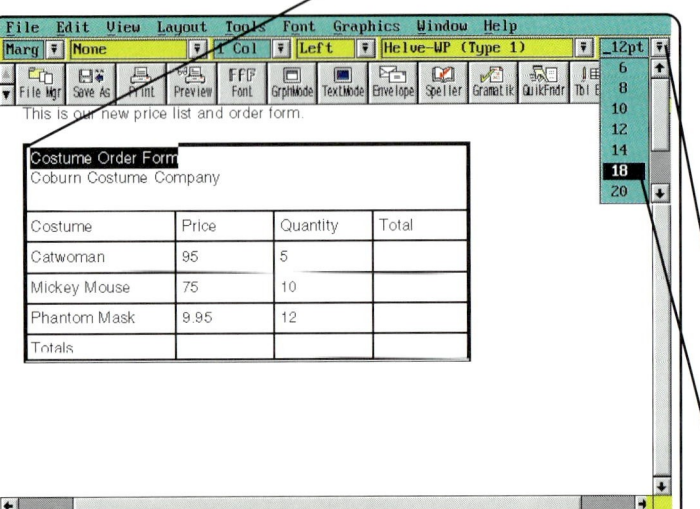

2. Press and hold the mouse button as you **drag** the cursor **over "Coburn Costume Company."** It will be highlighted.

3. Click on the **down arrow** to the **right of 12pt** in the ribbon. A pull-down list will appear.

4. Click twice on **18**. The highlighted text will be changed to 18-point type. (If you are not using the Helve-WP font, you may have different point sizes available.)

5. Repeat steps 1 through 4 to **change "Costume Order Form" to 14-point type**.

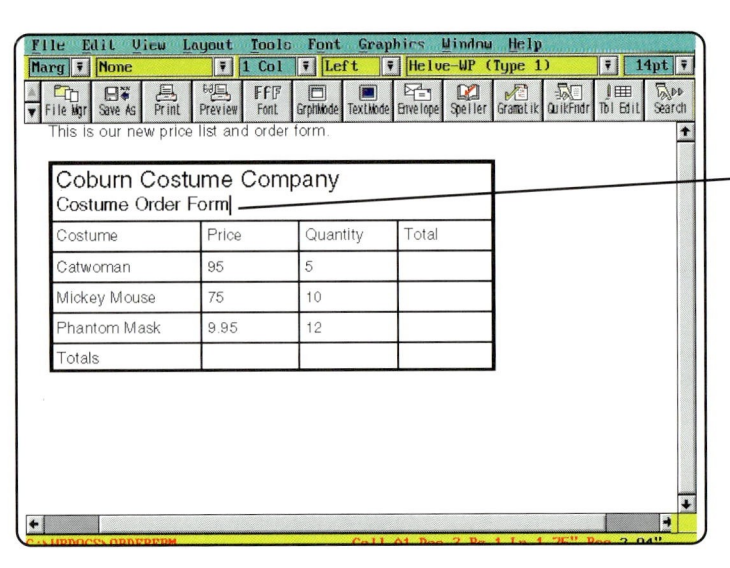

CHAPTER 18: EDITING A TABLE

Changing Cell Formats

You can change formats, such as alignment and font appearance, in one dialog box in the Table Edit mode.

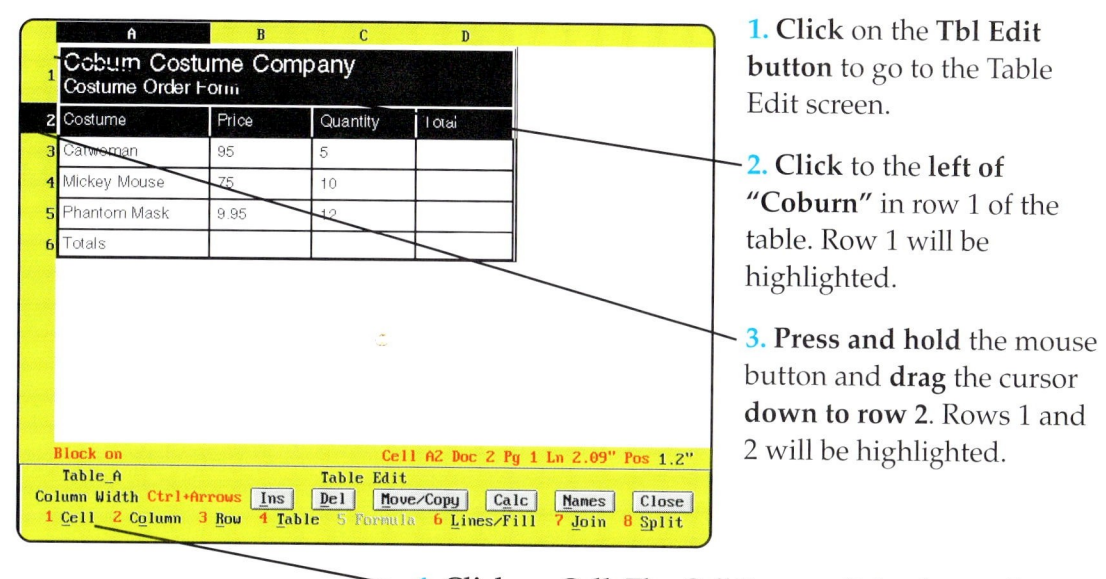

1. Click on the **Tbl Edit button** to go to the Table Edit screen.

2. Click to the **left of "Coburn"** in row 1 of the table. Row 1 will be highlighted.

3. Press and hold the mouse button and **drag** the cursor **down to row 2**. Rows 1 and 2 will be highlighted.

4. Click on **Cell**. The Cell Format dialog box will appear.

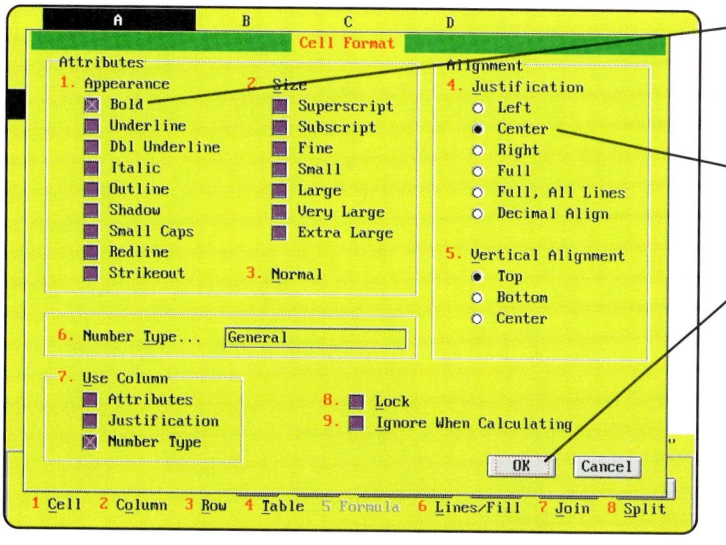

5. Click on **Bold** in the Attributes box to insert an X.

6. Click on **Center** in the Alignment box to insert a dot in the circle.

7. Click on **OK**. You will be returned to the Table Edit screen.

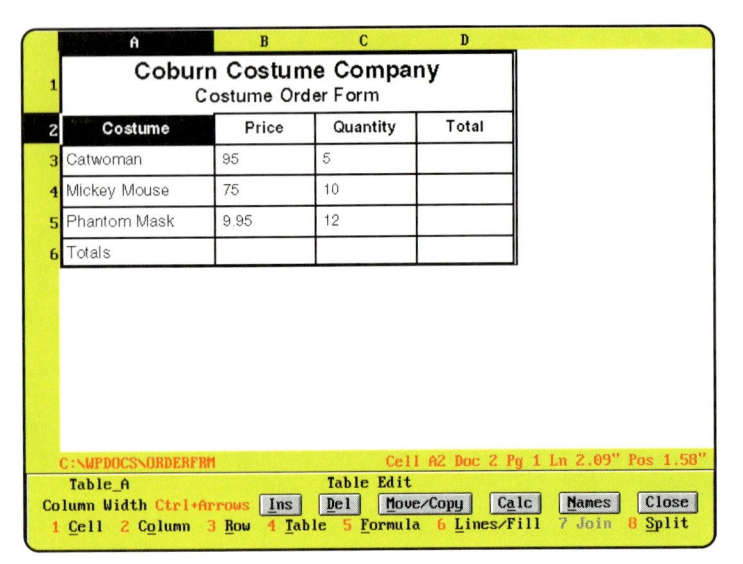

WORDPERFECT 6 FOR DOS: THE VISUAL LEARNING GUIDE

Notice that the text in rows 1 and 2 is bold and the text in each cell in these two rows is centered.

If you want to follow along with the steps in the next section, do not close this screen.

CHANGING TABLE POSITION

When WordPerfect first creates a table, it extends the table the width of the page. When you change column width, WordPerfect keeps the same left margin. This often means that the table is no longer centered across the page. But you can center it very easily.

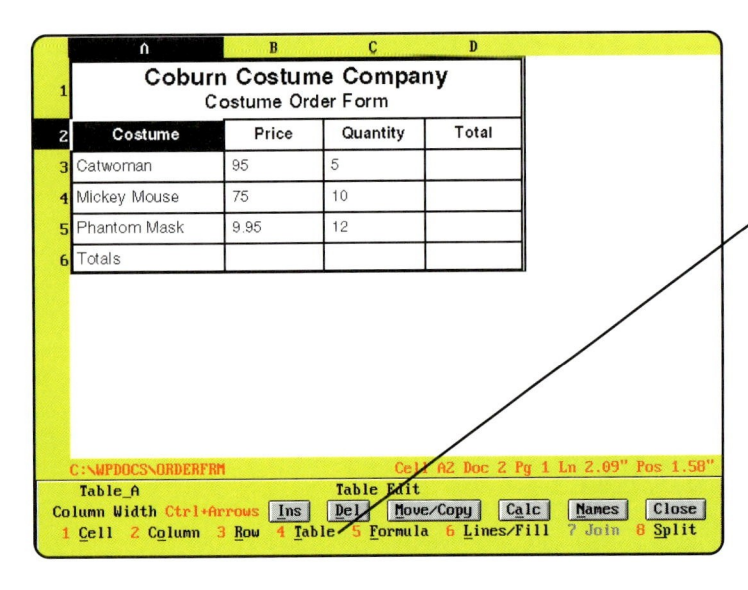

1. Click anywhere in the table and go to Table Edit mode if you are not already there.

2. Click on **Table** at the bottom of your screen. The Table Format dialog box will appear.

CHAPTER 18: EDITING A TABLE

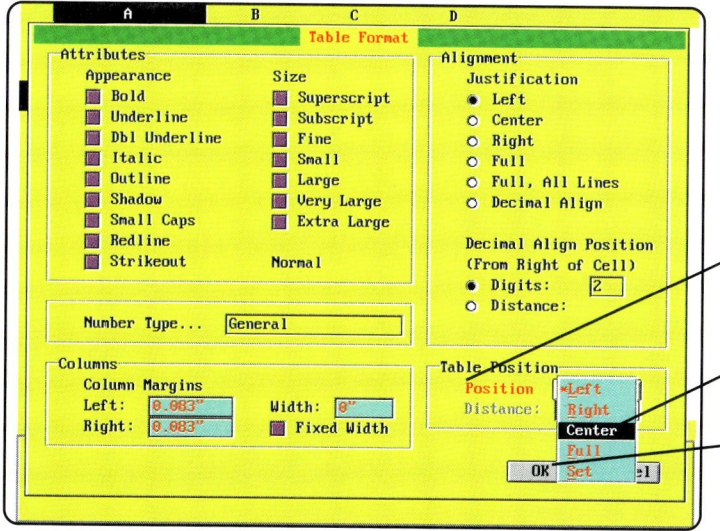

3. Click on **Position**. A drop-down list will appear.

4. Click on **Center**.

5. Click on **OK**. You will be returned to the Table Edit screen.

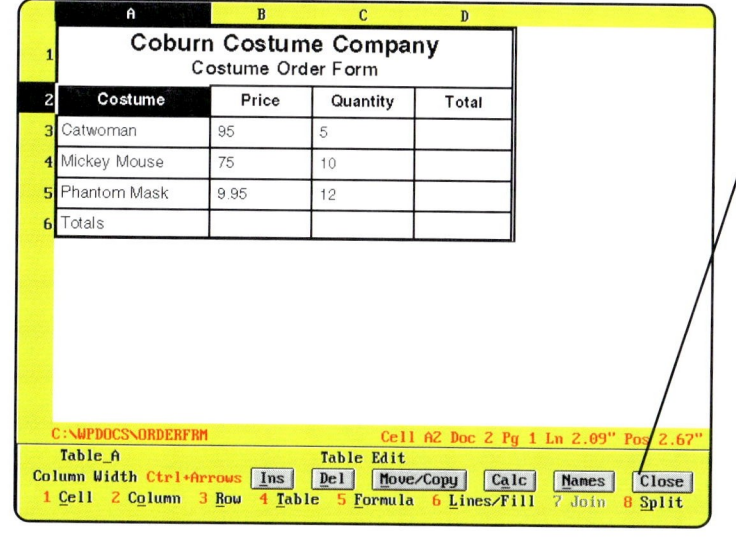

You won't see any difference in the position of the table in the Table Edit screen.

6. Click on **Close**. You will be returned to the document screen.

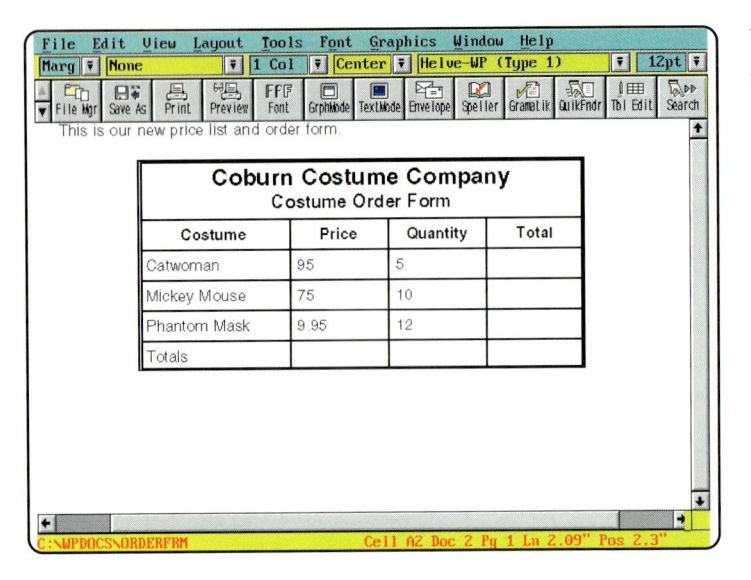

Your screen will look like this.

SAVING THE TABLE

Remember to save your work if you want to keep this file.

1. **Click** on **File** in the menu bar. A pull-down menu will appear.

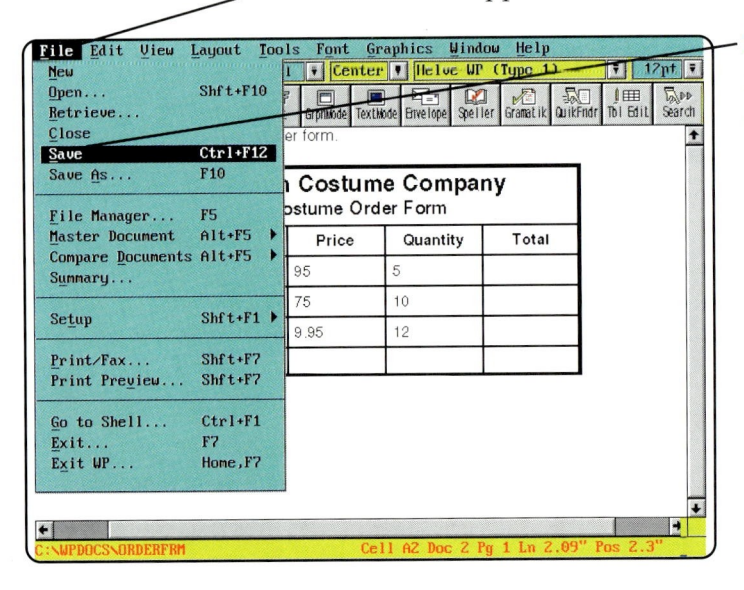

2. **Click** on **Save**. If you plan to follow along with the next chapter, do not close the file.

Formatting Numbers and Writing Formulas

You can format numbers to have decimal places, commas, dollar signs, and a number of other characteristics. You can also write formulas in tables that will perform mathematical functions. In this chapter you will do the following:

- Change the format of numbers
- Write formulas for multiplication and addition
- Delete a table from a document

FORMATTING NUMBERS

Unlike text, you must format numbers in a table in the Table Edit mode.

Formatting Numbers as Currency

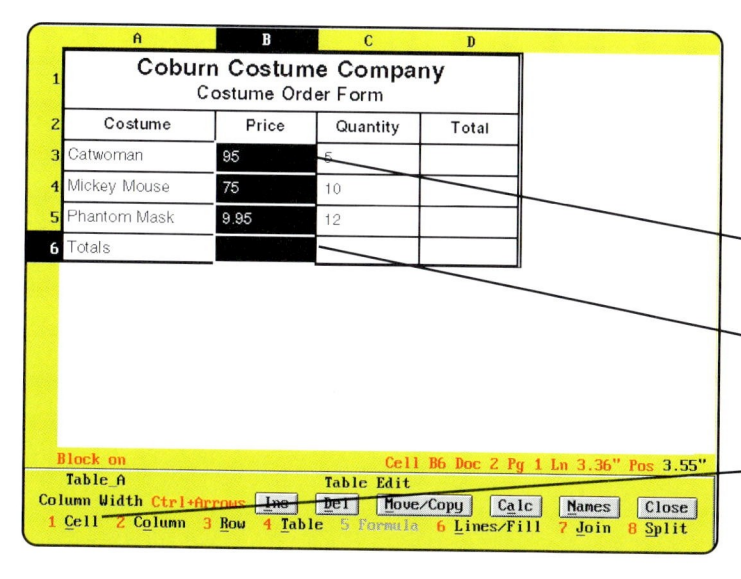

1. **Go to** the **Table Edit mode** if you are not already there. (See the section entitled "Adding a Row" in Chapter 18.)

2. **Click** on "95" in **B3**. It will be highlighted.

3. **Press and hold** the mouse button and **drag** the highlight bar down to **B6**.

4. **Click** on **Cell**. The Cell Format dialog box will appear.

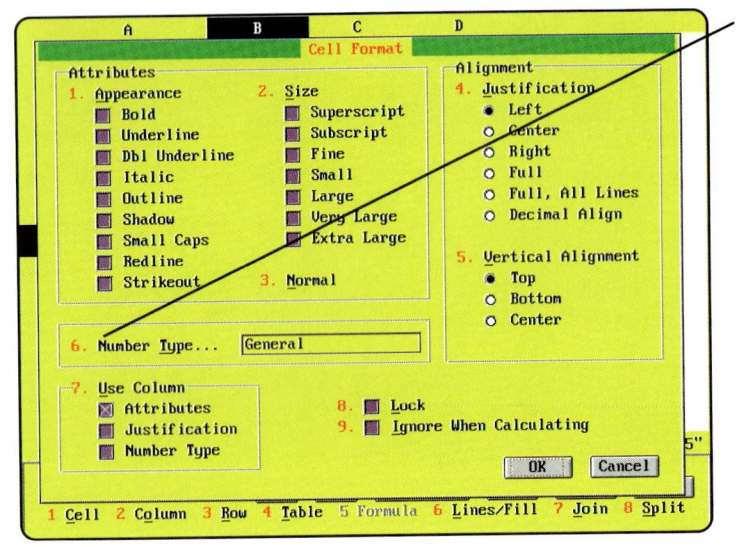

WORDPERFECT 6 FOR DOS: THE VISUAL LEARNING GUIDE

5. Click on **Number Type**. The Number Type Formats dialog box will appear.

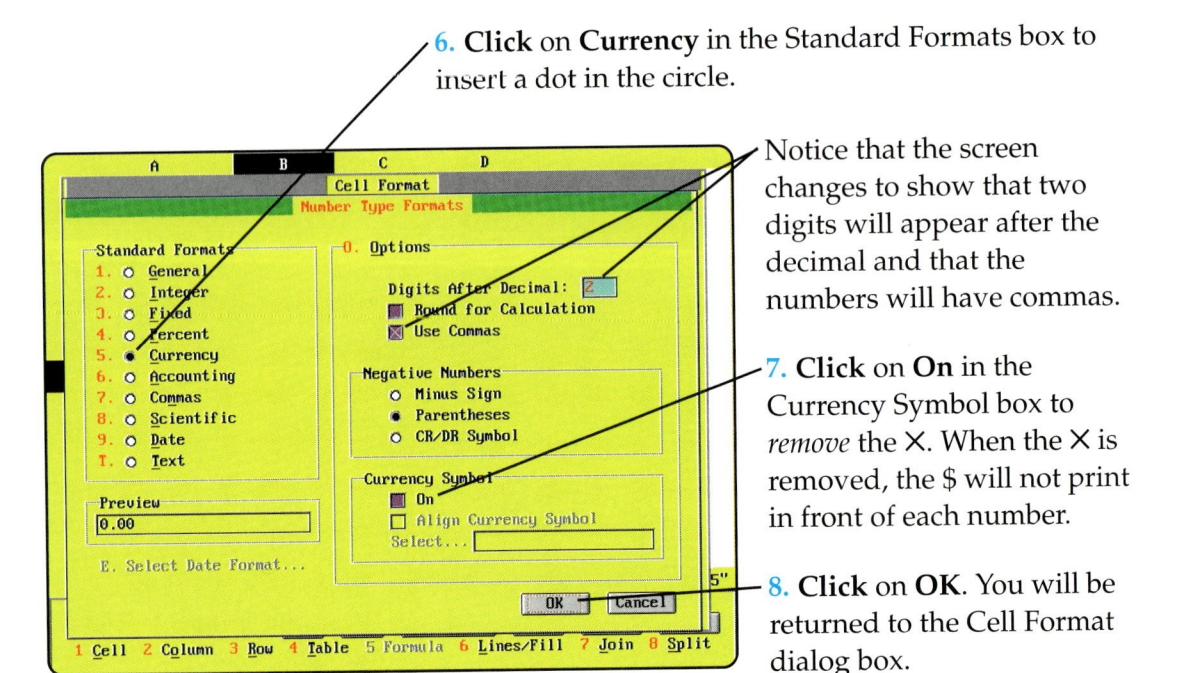

6. Click on **Currency** in the Standard Formats box to insert a dot in the circle.

Notice that the screen changes to show that two digits will appear after the decimal and that the numbers will have commas.

7. Click on **On** in the Currency Symbol box to *remove* the X. When the X is removed, the $ will not print in front of each number.

8. Click on **OK**. You will be returned to the Cell Format dialog box.

CHAPTER 19: FORMATTING NUMBERS AND WRITING FORMULAS

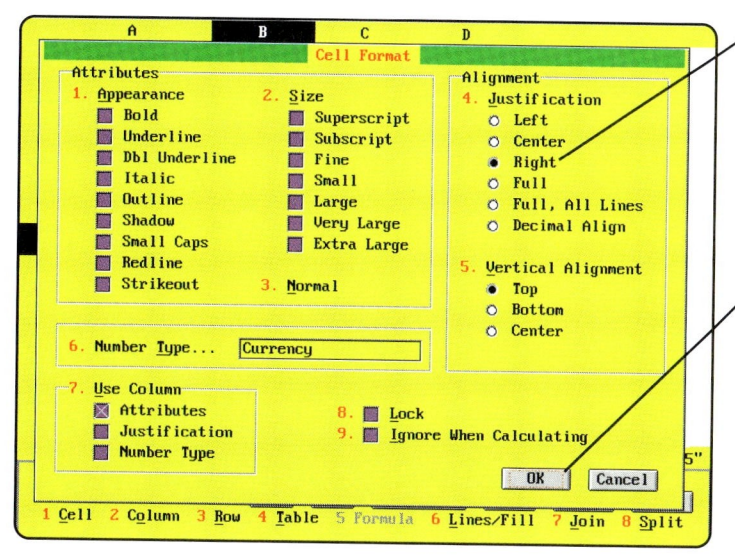

9. Click on **Right** in the Alignment box to insert a dot in the circle. This will position the numbers so that the decimal points will be aligned.

10. Click on **OK**. You will be returned to the Table Edit screen. The numbers will be repositioned in column B, as shown in the next screen.

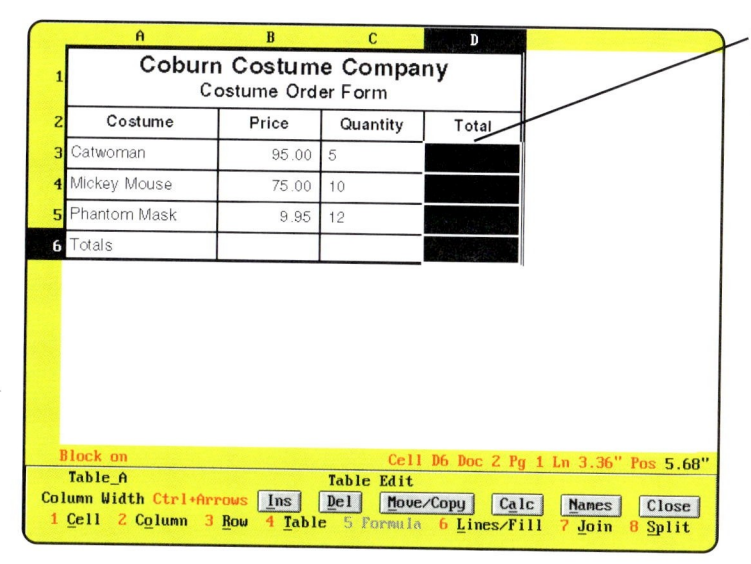

11. Repeat steps 2 through 10 to **format column D** for currency.

Centering Numbers in a Cell

In this example you will center the numbers in column C.

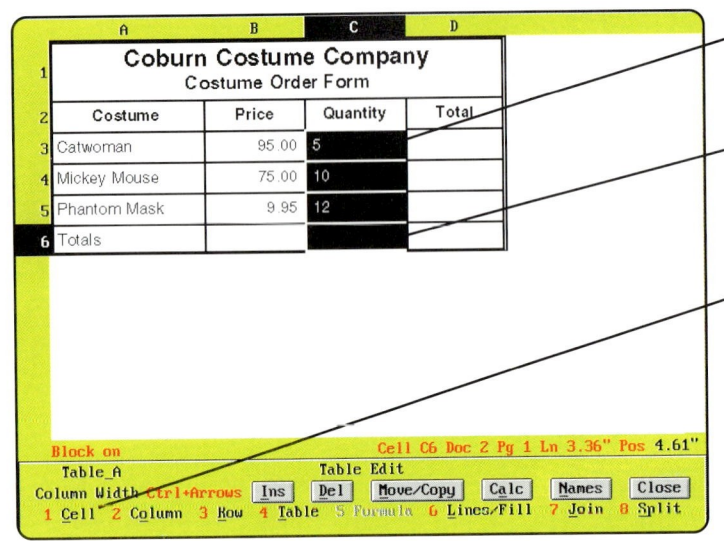

1. Click on "5" in **C3**. It will be highlighted.

2. Press and hold the mouse button and **drag** the highlight bar down to **C6**.

3. Click on **Cell**. The Cell Format dialog box will appear.

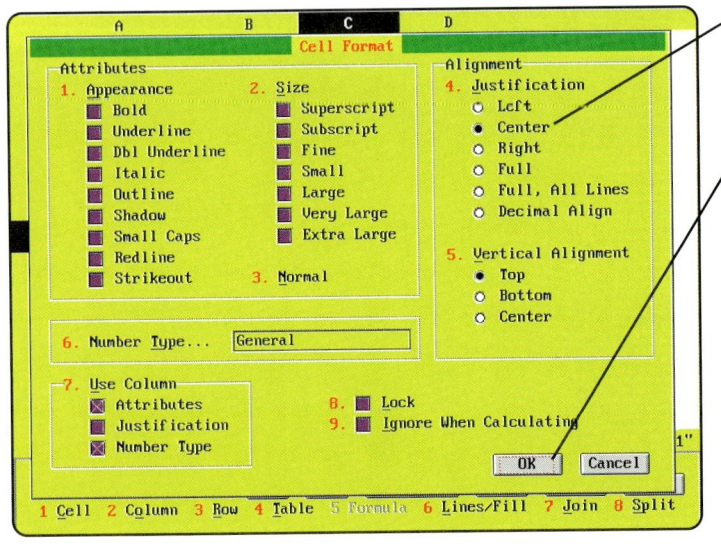

4. Click on **Center** in the Alignment box to insert a dot in the circle.

5. Click on **OK**. The dialog box will close and you will be returned to the Table Edit screen. The numbers in column C will be centered, as shown in the next example.

CHAPTER 19: FORMATTING NUMBERS AND WRITING FORMULAS

WRITING FORMULAS

You can write formulas in your table that will perform mathematical functions. The most common functions and their symbols are as follows:

Function	Symbol	Example
Addition	+	D3+D4+D5
Subtraction	-	B4-C4
Multiplication	*	B3*C3
Division	/	B2/B3

Writing a Multiplication Formula

In this example you will write a formula to calculate the total (column D) by multiplying the price (column B) times the quantity (column C). You will write the formula for row 3, then later in the chapter you will copy the formula to rows 4 and 5. You should be in the Table Edit mode.

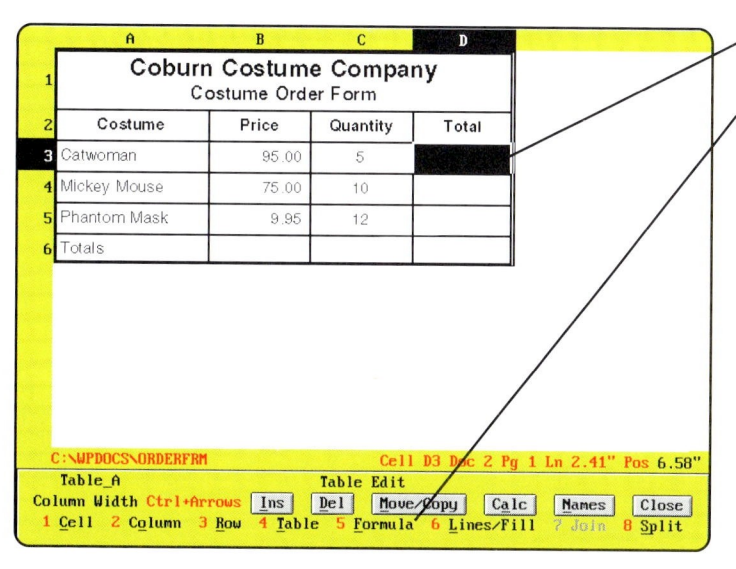

1. **Click** on **D3**.

2. **Click** on **Formula**. The Table Formula dialog box will appear.

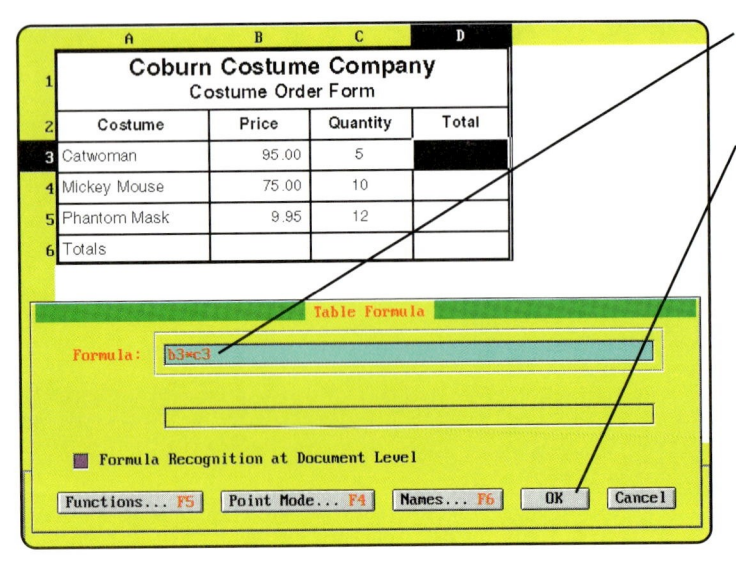

3. Type b3*c3 in the Formula box.

4. Click on **OK**. The number "475.00" will appear in D3. Notice that it is formatted with two decimal places and is aligned at the right.

Copying a Formula

In this section you will copy the formula in D3 to D4 and D5.

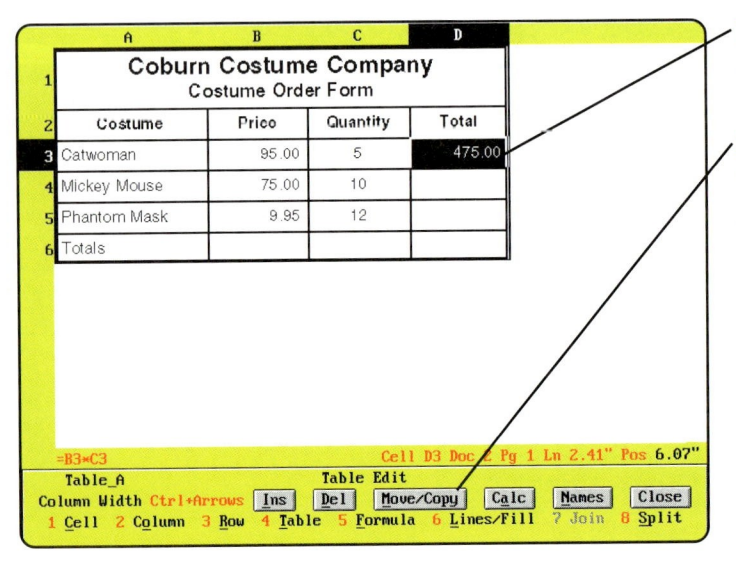

1. Click on **D3** if it is not already highlighted.

2. Click on **Move/Copy**. The Move dialog box will appear.

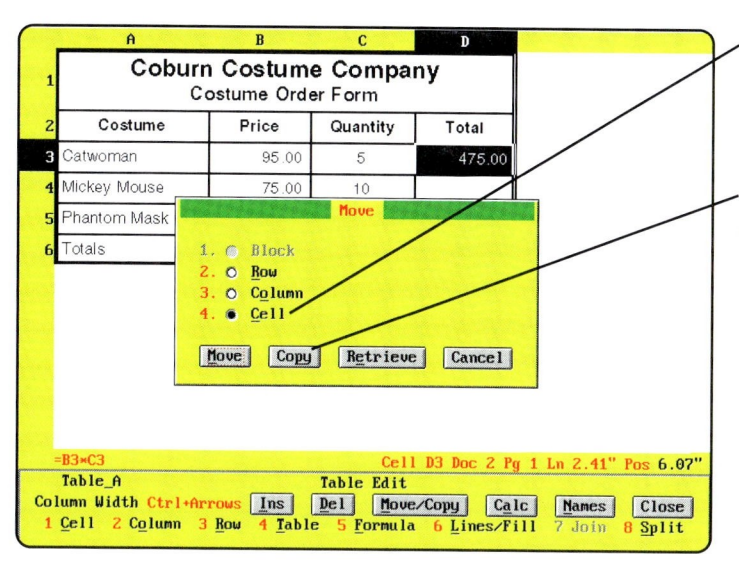

CHAPTER 19: FORMATTING NUMBERS AND WRITING FORMULAS

3. Click on **Cell** to insert a dot in the circle if one is not already there.

4. Click on **Copy**. The Copy Cell dialog box will appear.

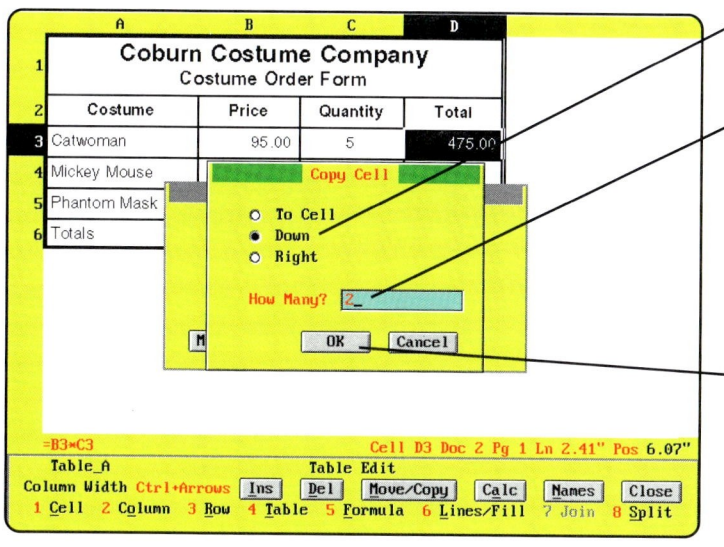

5. Click on **Down** to insert a dot in the circle.

6. Since the number 1 in the How Many? box is already highlighted, **type 2**. This tells WordPerfect to copy the contents of cell D3 down two cells.

7. Click on **OK**. You will be returned to the Table Edit screen. The number "750.00" will be in D4 and "119.40" will be in D5.

Writing an Addition Formula

In this example you will write a formula to add the contents of D3, D4, and D5.

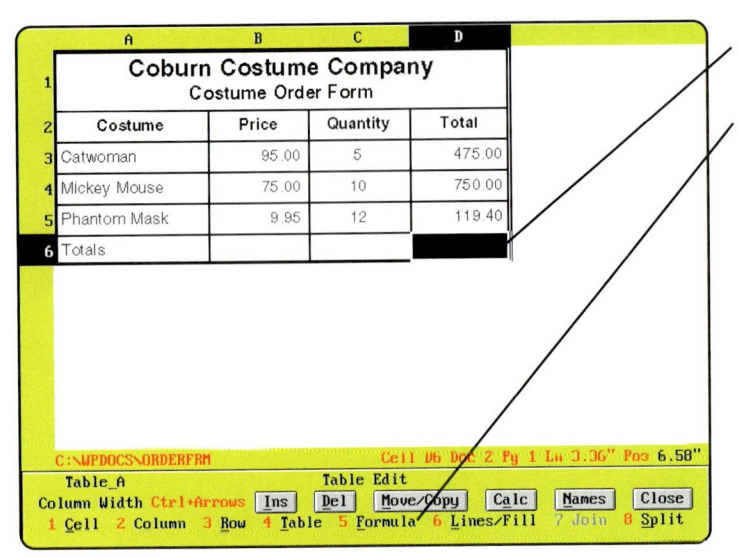

1. Click on **D6**.

2. Click on **Formula**. The Table Formula dialog box will appear.

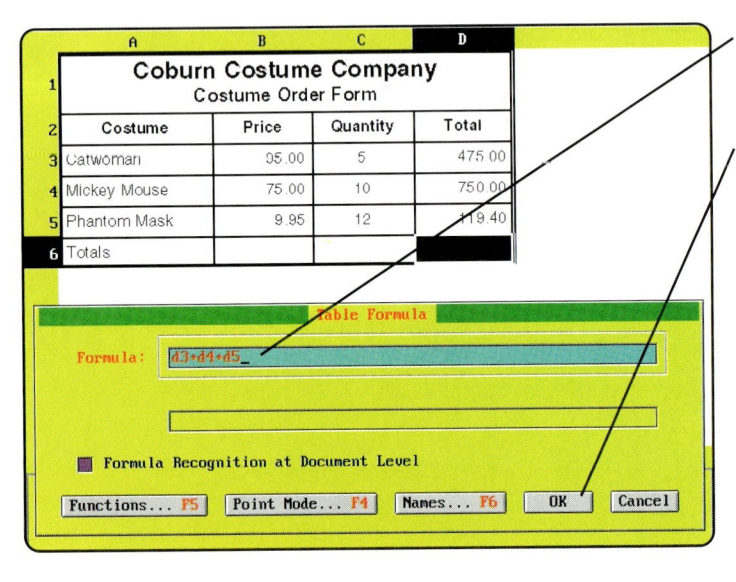

3. Type d3+d4+d5 in the Formula box.

4. Click on **OK**. You will be returned to the Table Edit screen.

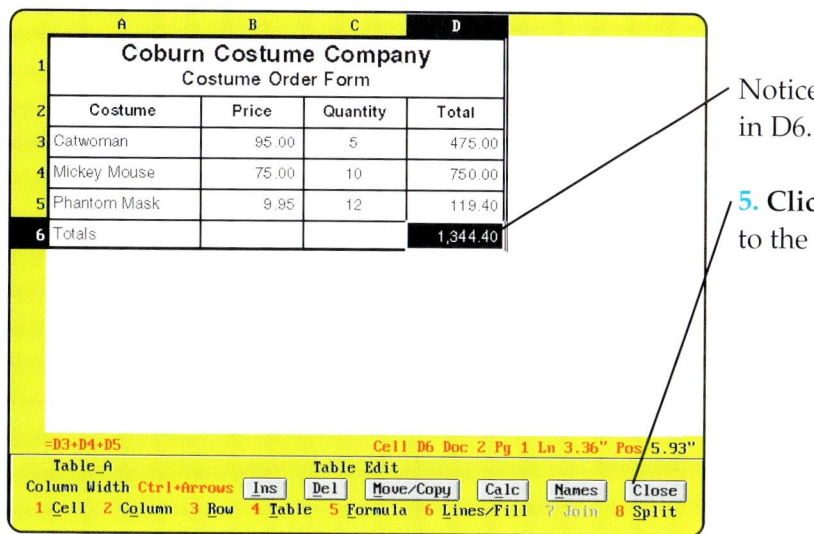

CHAPTER 19: FORMATTING NUMBERS AND WRITING FORMULAS

Notice the total, "1,344.40," in D6.

5. Click on **Close** to return to the document.

DELETING AND UNDELETING A TABLE

Deleting and undeleting a table is as easy as deleting and undeleting text. In this example you will delete the table in the ORDERFRM document.

1. Click on the **line above the table**.

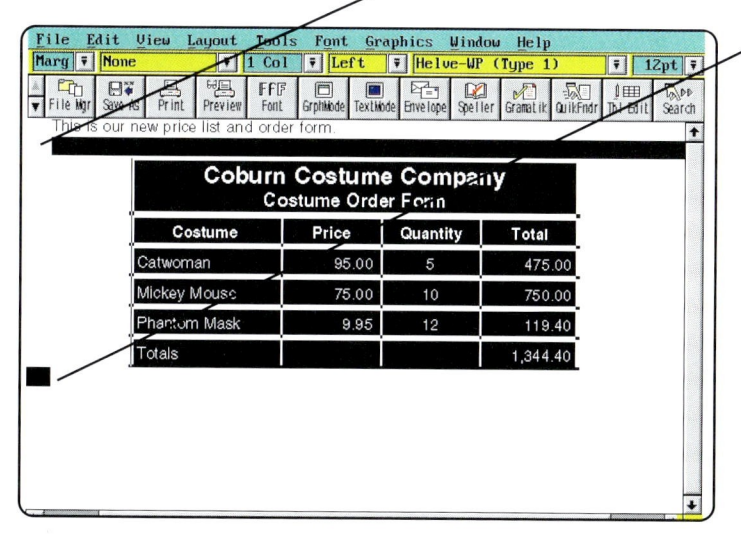

2. Press and hold the mouse button and **drag** the cursor down to D6. Continue to drag the cursor **below the table**.

The line above the table, the entire table, and the line below the table will be highlighted.

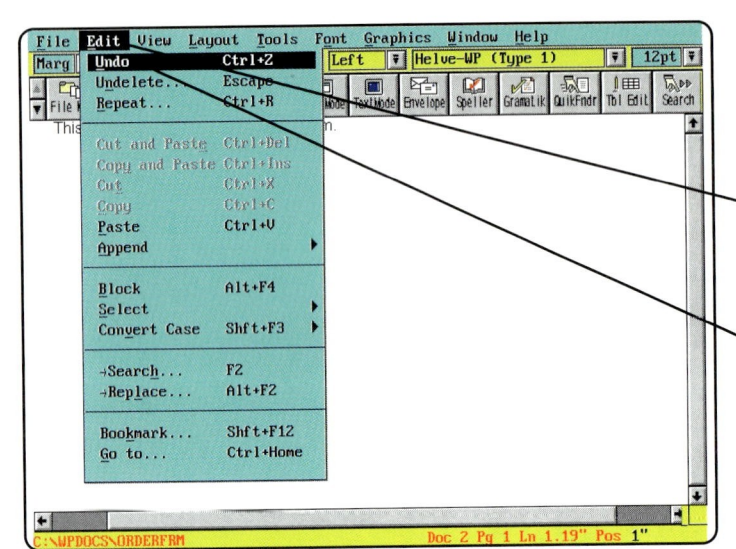

WORDPERFECT 6 FOR DOS: THE VISUAL LEARNING GUIDE

3. **Press** the **Del key** on your keyboard. The table will be deleted.

If you want to restore the table to your screen, use the Undo feature before you do any other function.

4. **Click** on **Edit** in the menu bar. A pull-down menu will appear.

5. **Click** on **Undo**. The table will be restored to your screen.

6. **Save** the changes if you want to keep the table.

File Manager

Part V   Introducing File Manager

Chapter 20: Opening and Printing Multiple Files	Page 232
Chapter 21: Sorting, Moving, and Copying Files	Page 241

Opening and Printing Multiple Files

Managing files in DOS-based programs has always been a nuisance . . . until now. The new WordPerfect 6 File Manager makes keeping track of your files a piece of cake. In File Manager you can perform operations such as opening and printing multiple or single files (Chapter 20) and sorting, looking at, moving and copying files (Chapter 21). In this chapter you will do the following:

❖ Open several files with one command
❖ Print several files with one command

OPENING SEVERAL FILES AT THE SAME TIME

In order to open several files at the same time, each file must first be *marked* with an asterisk (*).

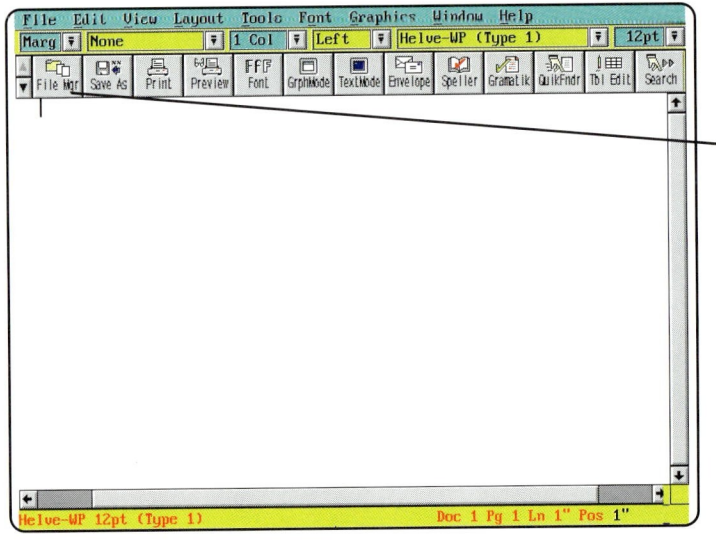

Marking Files

1. **Click** on the **File Manager (File Mgr) button** in the button bar. The Specify File Manager List dialog box will appear.

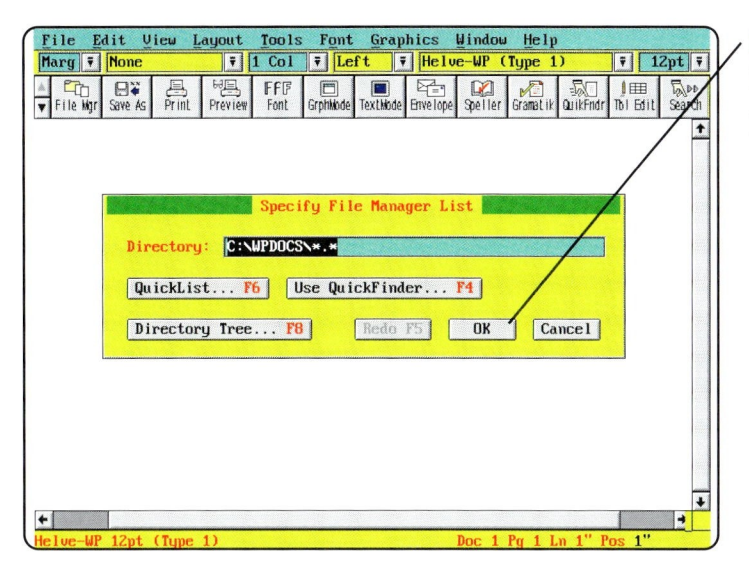

CHAPTER 20: OPENING AND PRINTING MULTIPLE FILES

2. Click on **OK**. The File Manager dialog box will fill your screen.

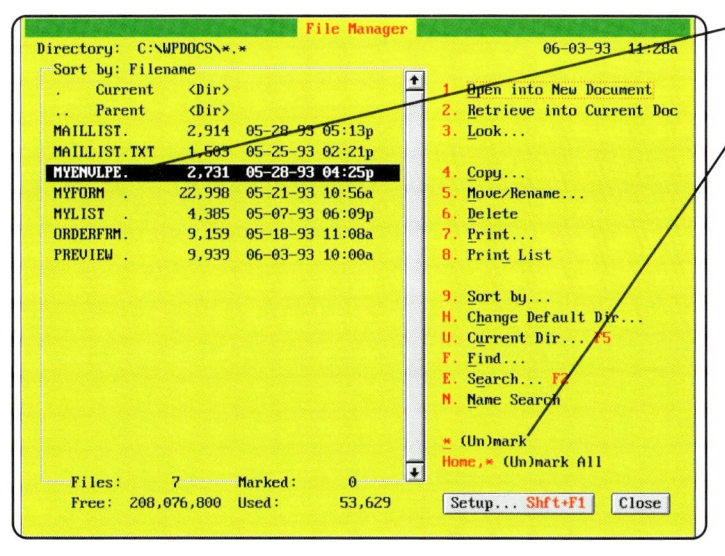

3. Click on **MYENVLPE** to highlight it.

4. Click on **(Un)mark**. An asterisk (*) will appear to the left of MYENVLPE. The highlight bar will move automatically to the next file in the list. (In this case, MYFORM will be highlighted.)

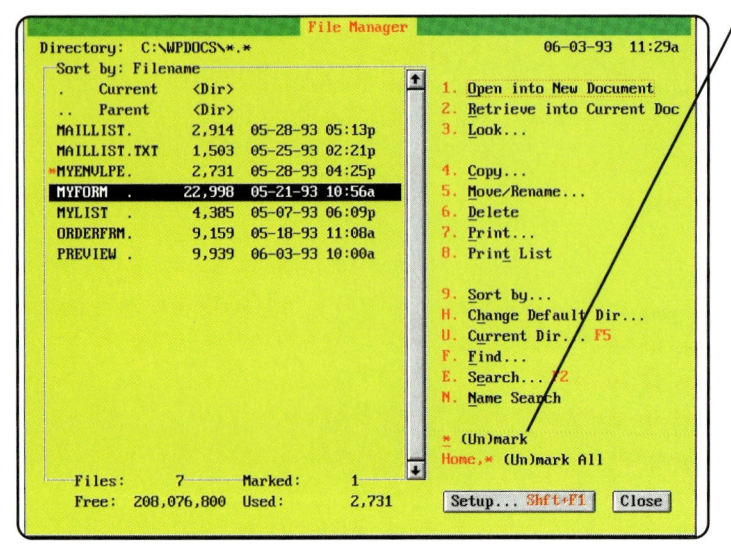

5. Click on **(Un)mark**. An asterisk (*) will appear to the left of MYFORM. The highlight bar will automatically move to MYLIST.

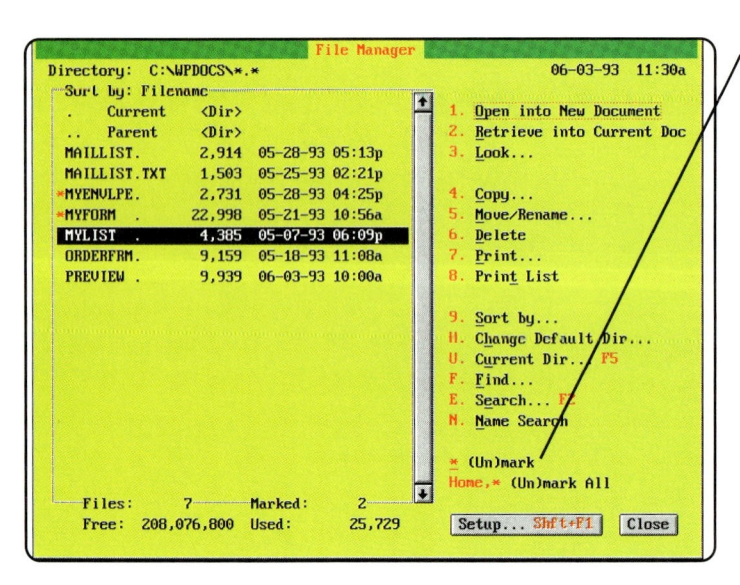

6. Click on **(Un)mark**. An asterisk (*) will appear to the left of MYLIST. The highlight bar will automatically move to ORDERFRM.

CHAPTER 20: OPENING AND PRINTING MULTIPLE FILES

Opening Marked Files

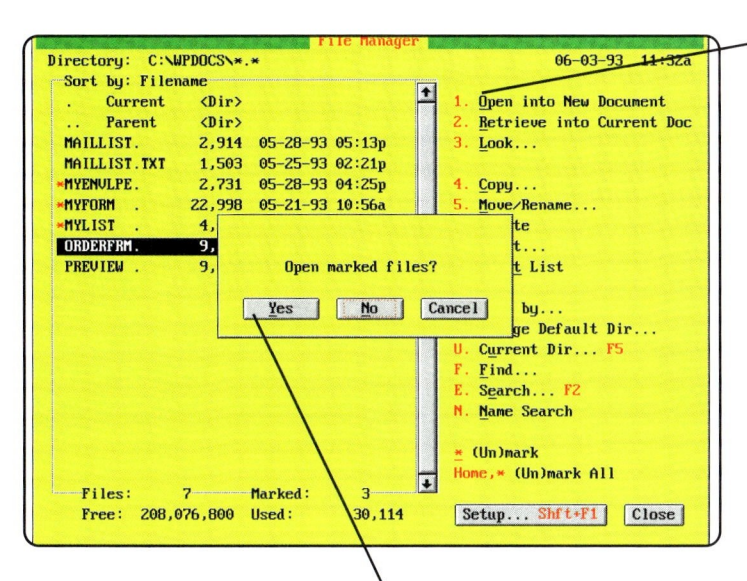

1. Click on **Open into New Document**. The Open marked files? dialog box will appear.

Note that in WordPerfect talk, "Open into New Document" means to open a saved document. "Retrieve into Current Doc," the second choice on the list, means to copy or merge the selected document file into a document you already have opened.

2. Click on **Yes**. A Please Wait message box will appear for a while. The MYLIST document window will appear on your screen. WordPerfect opens marked files from the top of the list to the bottom. Therefore, MYLIST, which was opened last, is the one you see first.

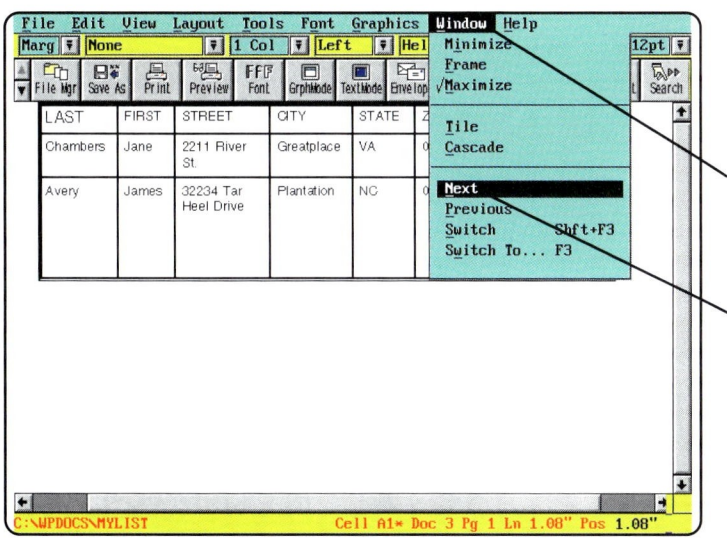

Switching to Another Open Document

1. Click on **Window** in the menu bar. A pull-down menu will appear.

2. Click on **Next**. MYENVLPE will appear.

3. Repeat steps 1 and 2 to switch to each open document in sequence. This will return you to MYLIST.

PRINTING SEVERAL FILES

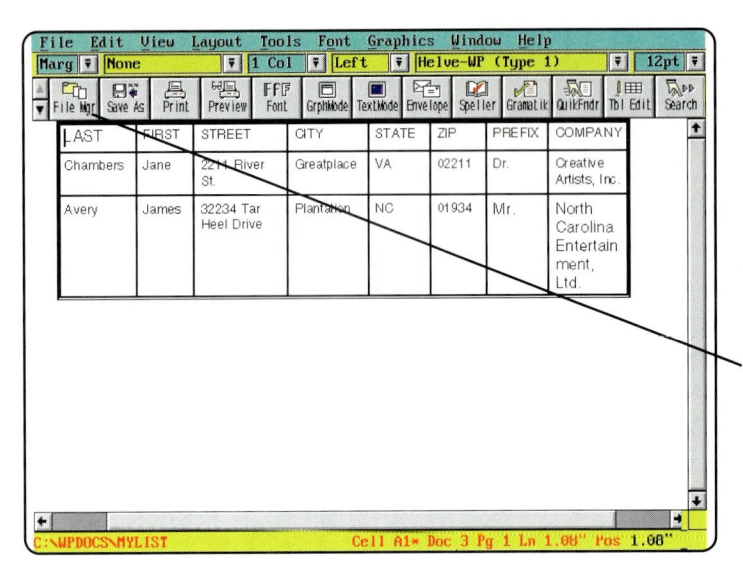

To print several files at the same time, each file must also be marked with an asterisk (*).

Marking Files to Print

1. Click on the **File Mgr button** in the button bar. The Specify File Manager List dialog box will appear.

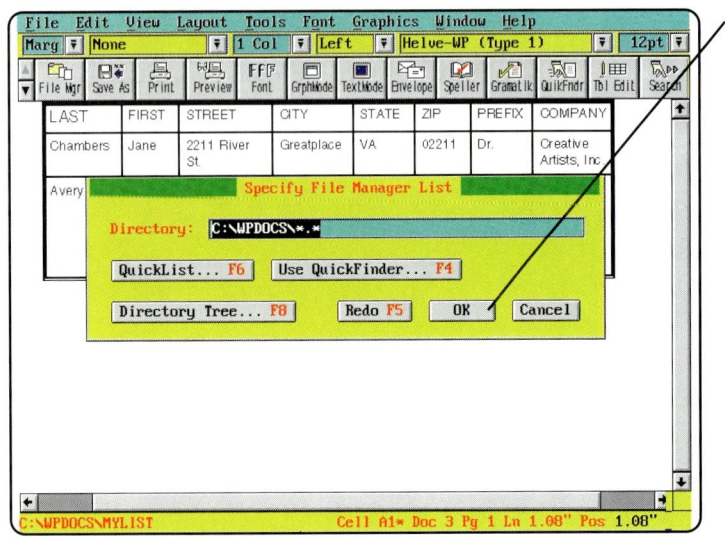

2. Click on **OK**. The File Manager dialog box will fill your screen.

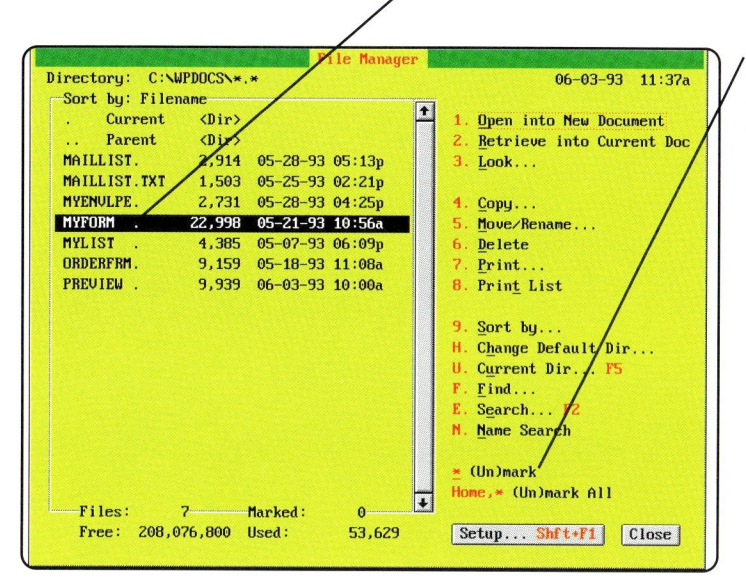

CHAPTER 20: OPENING AND PRINTING MULTIPLE FILES

3. Click on **MYFORM** to highlight the filename.

4. Click on **(Un)mark**. An asterisk (*) will appear to the left of MYFORM.

5. Click on **PREVIEW** to highlight the filename.

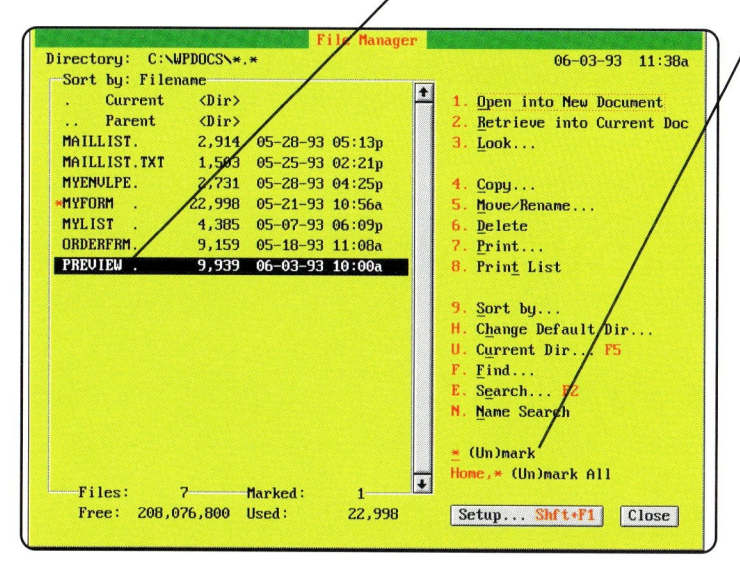

6. Click on **(Un)mark**. An asterisk (*) will appear to the left of PREVIEW.

Printing Marked Files

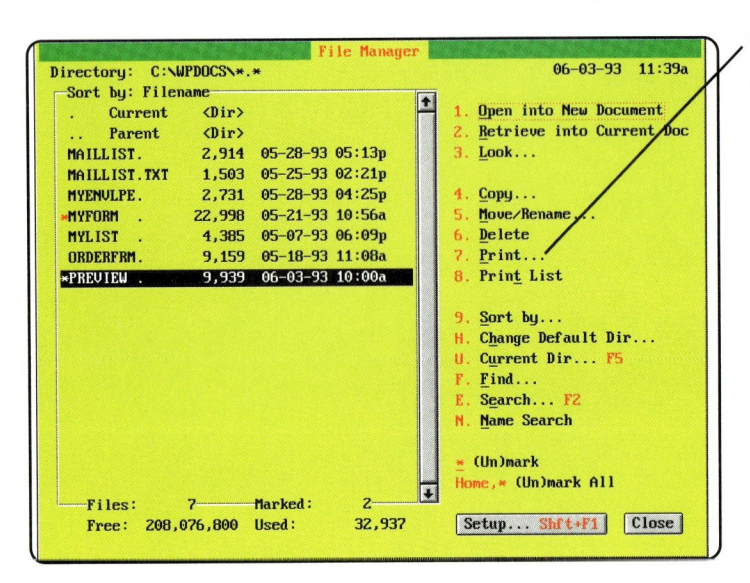

1. Click on **Print**. The Print marked files? dialog box will appear.

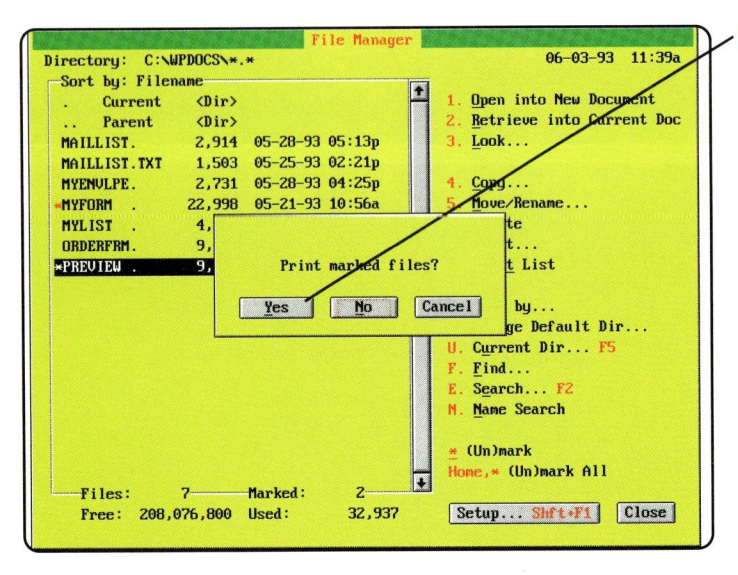

2. Click on **Yes**. The Print Multiple Pages dialog box will appear.

CHAPTER 20: OPENING AND PRINTING MULTIPLE FILES

3. Click on **OK**. A Please Wait message box will appear. The marked files will print.

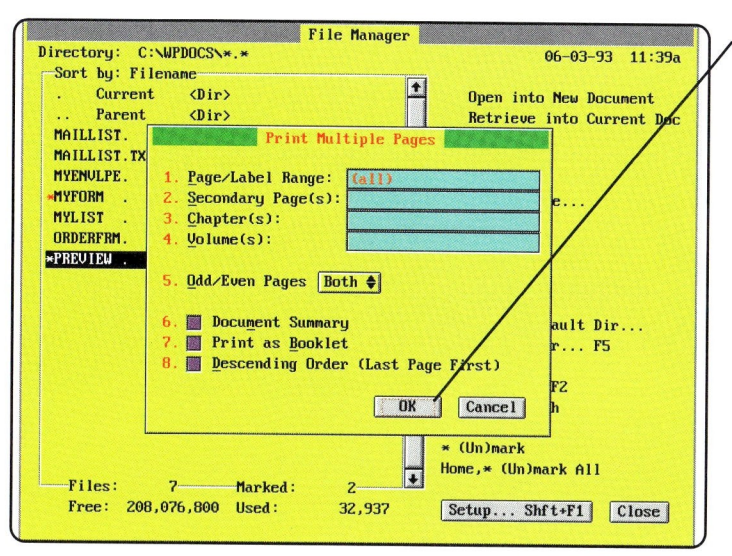

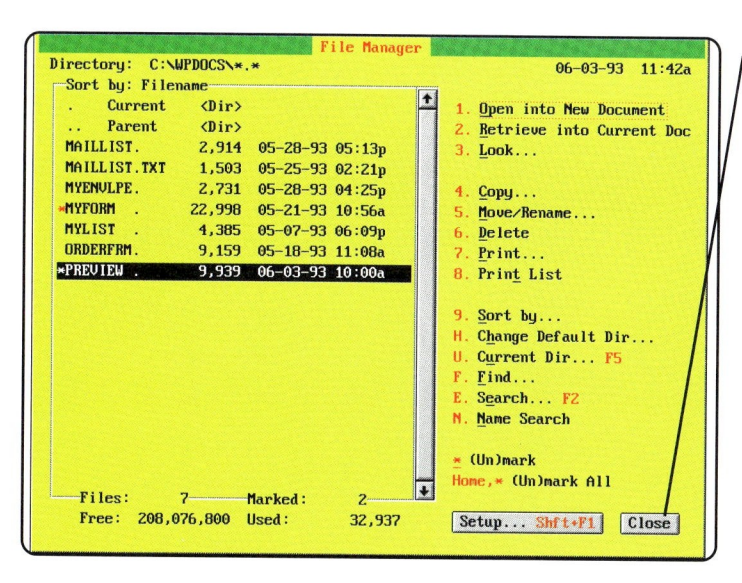

4. Click on **Close**. The opening document screen will appear.

WORDPERFECT 6 FOR DOS: THE VISUAL LEARNING GUIDE

Closing All Marked Files

Ideally, you would be able to close all three marked files with one command without leaving the program. You cannot do that in WordPerfect, but you can close each file, one at a time.

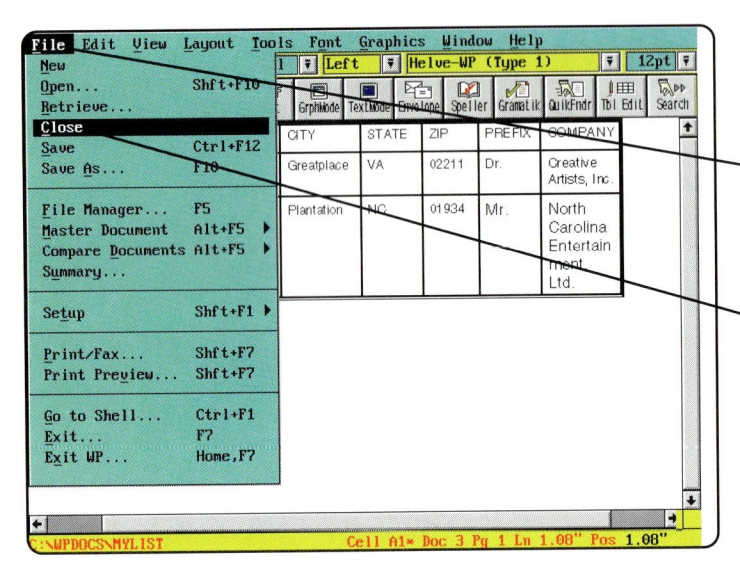

1. Click on **File** in the menu bar. A pull-down menu will appear.

2. Click on **Close**. The MYFORM window will appear.

3. Repeat steps 1 and 2 to close the two remaining marked files.

Sorting, Moving, and Copying Files

In File Manager you can sort, look at and open, copy, move, rename, and delete files. You can also create and delete directories. In this chapter you will do the following:

- Sort files on several criteria
- Look at the contents of a file from within File Manager
- Create a new directory
- Move files to a new directory
- Copy a file to a floppy disk

SORTING FILES IN A DIRECTORY

WordPerfect's File Manager allows you to sort files in a directory by date and time, size, filename, and extension.

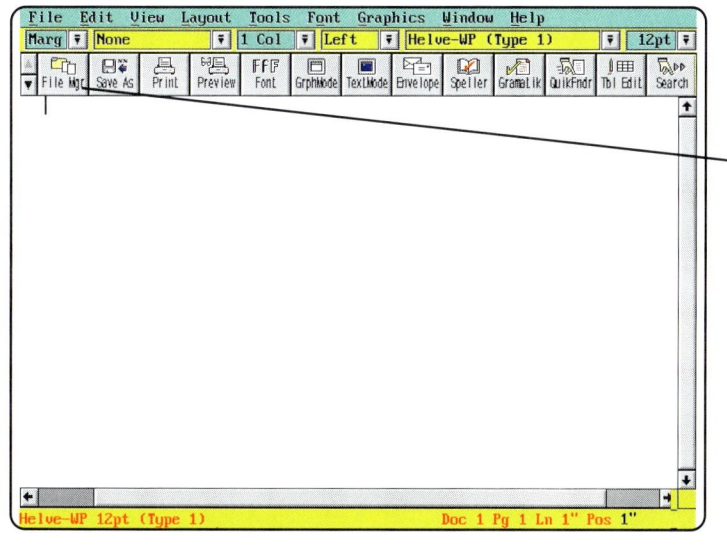

Sorting by Date and Time

1. **Click** on the **File Manager (File Mgr) button** in the button bar. The Specify File Manager List dialog box will appear.

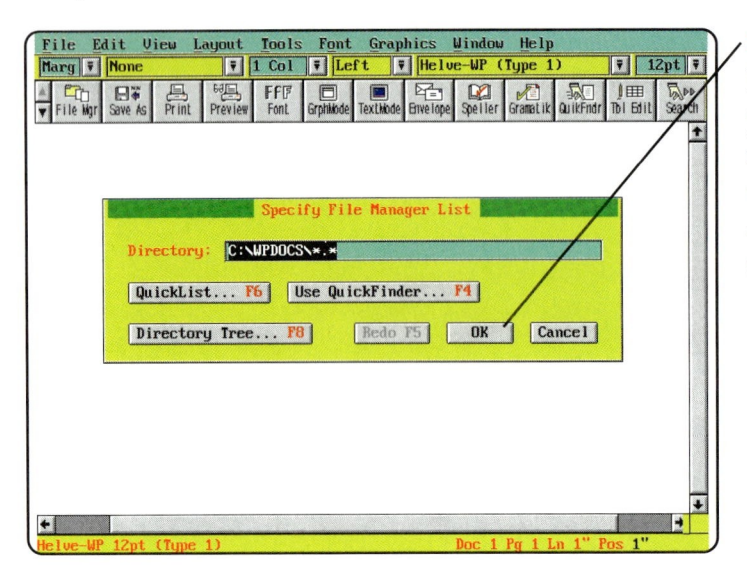

WORDPERFECT 6 FOR DOS: THE VISUAL LEARNING GUIDE

2. Click on **OK**. The File Manager dialog box will fill your screen. The list of files in your current directory (in this example, the WPDOCS directory) will appear in the Sort by: Filename list box.

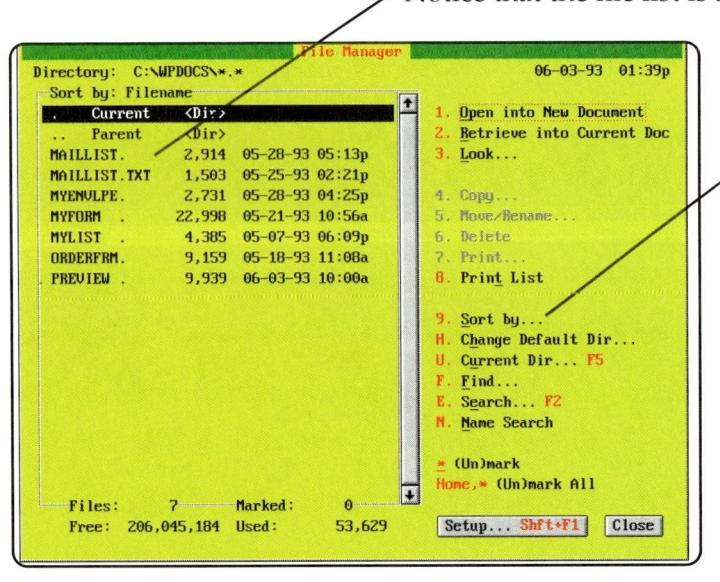

Notice that the file list is sorted alphabetically by the names of the files. This is the standard (default) way WordPerfect sorts files.

3. Click on **Sort by**. The File Manager Setup dialog box will appear.

CHAPTER 21: SORTING, MOVING, AND COPYING FILES

4. Click on **Date/Time** to insert a dot in the circle.

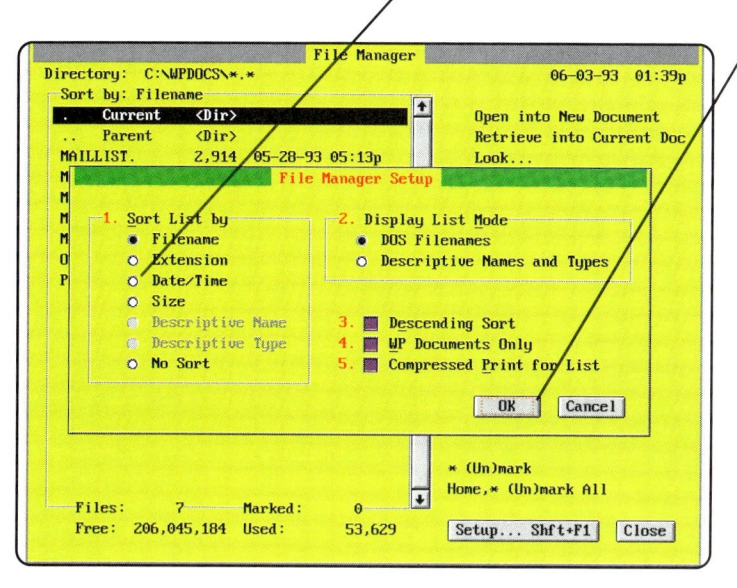

5. Click on **OK**. The File Manager Setup dialog box will disappear.

Notice that the files are now in time and date order with the most recently saved file at the bottom of the list.

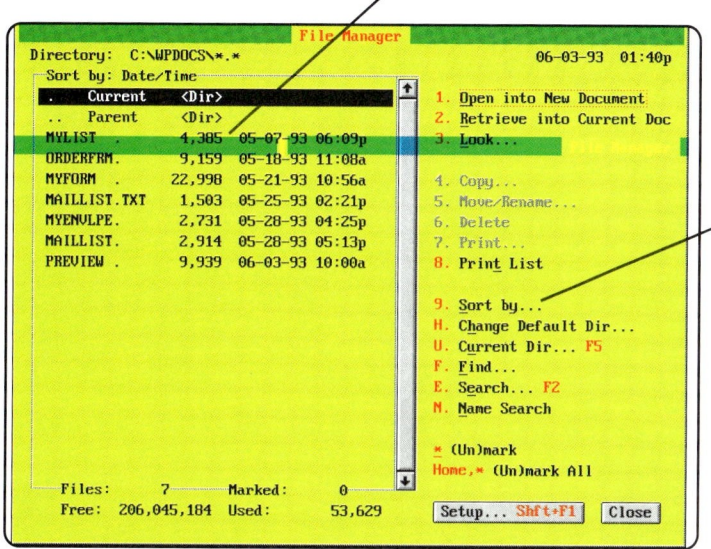

Sorting by Size

1. Click on **Sort by**. The File Manager Setup dialog box will appear.

WORDPERFECT 6 FOR DOS: THE VISUAL LEARNING GUIDE

2. **Click** on **Size** to insert a dot in the circle.

3. **Click** on **OK**. The File Manager Setup dialog box will disappear.

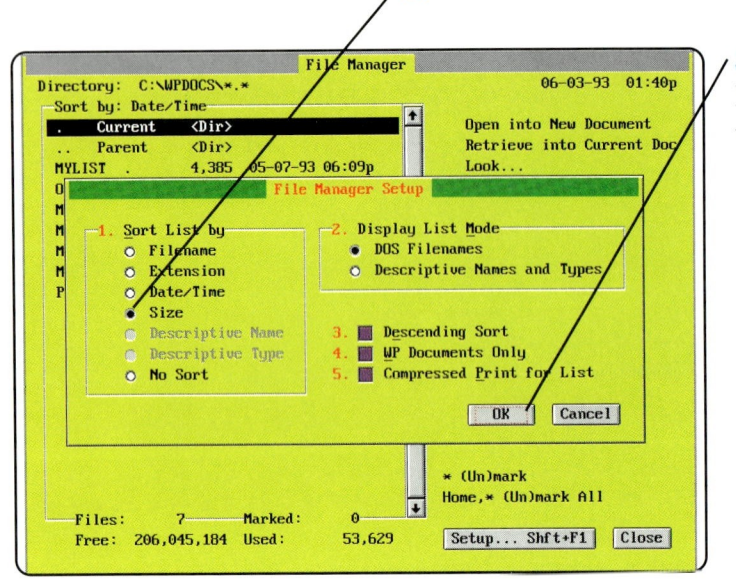

Notice that the files are now in order by size with the smallest file at the top of the list.

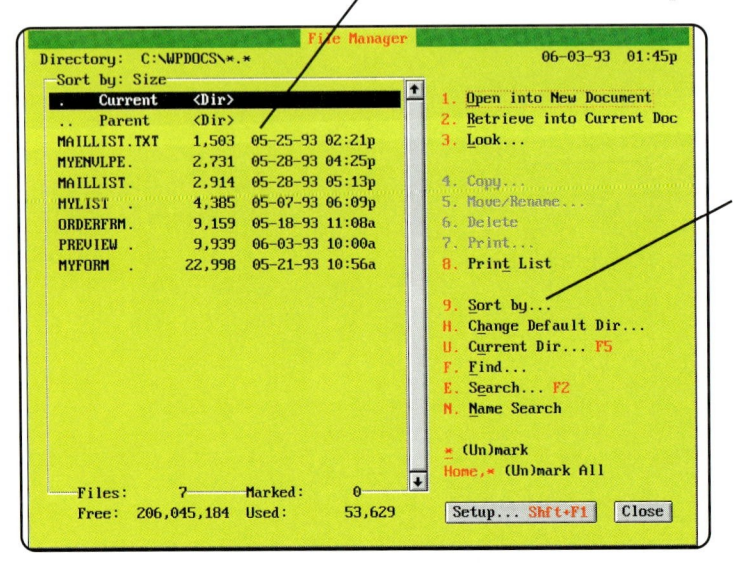

Sorting Alphabetically

1. **Click** on **Sort by**. The File Manager Setup dialog box will appear.

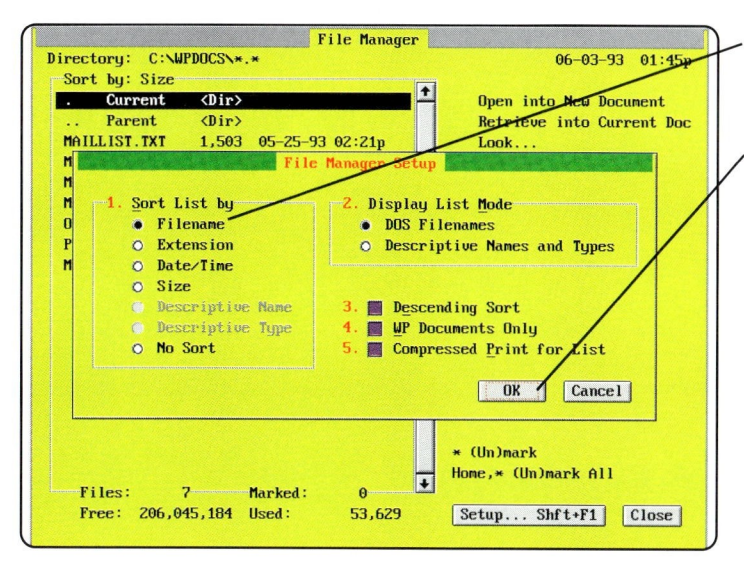

CHAPTER 21: SORTING, MOVING, AND COPYING FILES

2. Click on **Filename** to insert a dot in the circle.

3. Click on **OK**. The File Manager Setup dialog box will disappear.

Notice that the files are now listed in alphabetical order by filename.

VIEWING THE CONTENTS OF A FILE

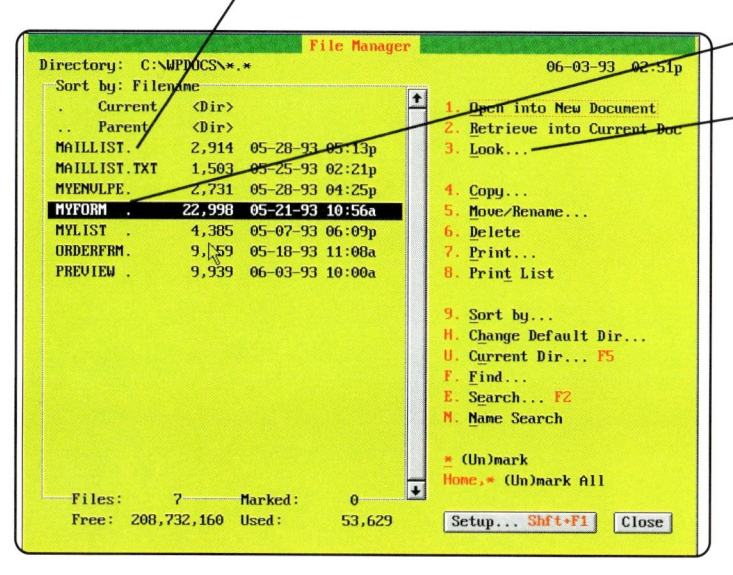

1. Click on **MYFORM**.

2. Click on **Look**. The Look at Document window will fill your screen.

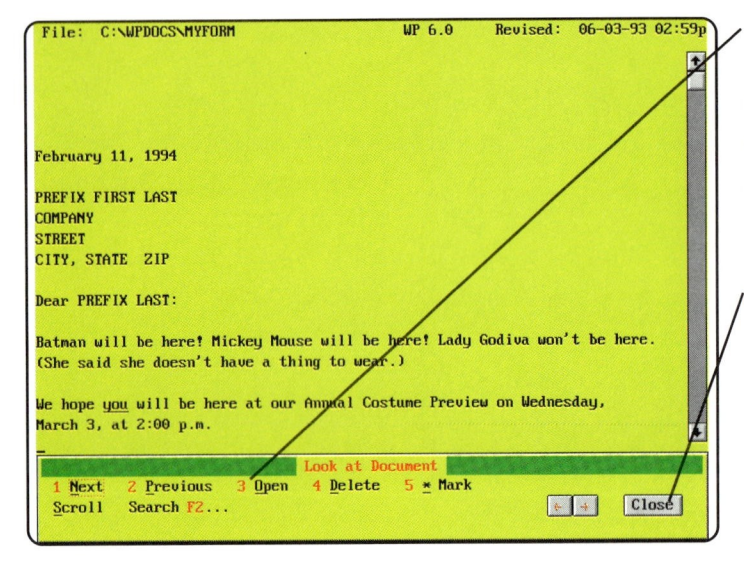

Notice you can open this file by clicking on Open at the bottom of the screen. In this example, you will close this screen and go back to File Manager.

3. Click on **Close**. The File Manager dialog box will appear.

CREATING A DIRECTORY

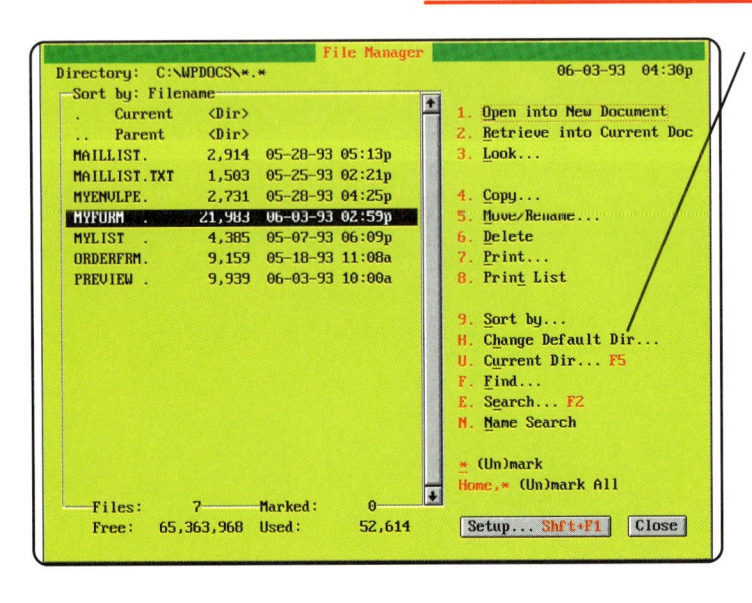

1. Click on **Change Default Dir**. The Change Default Directory dialog box will appear.

CHAPTER 21: SORTING, MOVING, AND COPYING FILES

2. **Click** to the **right of** the directory name C:\WPDOCS to set the cursor.

3. **Type \myforms** to create a subdirectory of WPDOCS. Don't forget to type the backward slash (\) to separate "WPDOCS" and "myforms." Even though you typed "myforms" in lowercase letters, WordPerfect will show the final directory name in all capital letters, as in the screen below.

4. **Click** on **OK**. The Create Directory dialog box will appear.

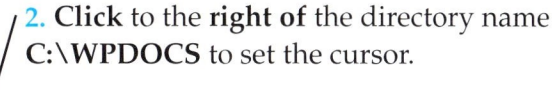

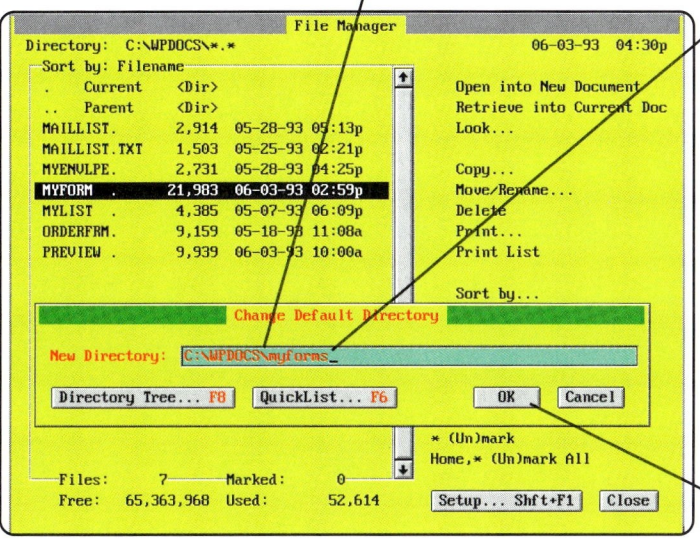

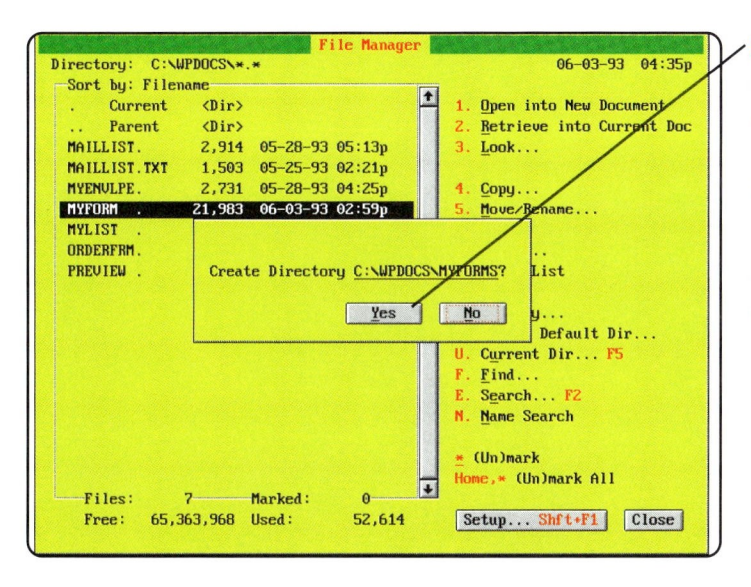

5. **Click** on **Yes**. The Create Directory dialog box will disappear.

Notice that MYFORMS appears at the top of the filename list as a new directory, as shown in the screen in the next section.

MOVING FILES TO ANOTHER DIRECTORY

To move files to another directory, you must mark the files first. In this example, you will move the files MYFORM and ORDERFRM to the MYFORMS directory.

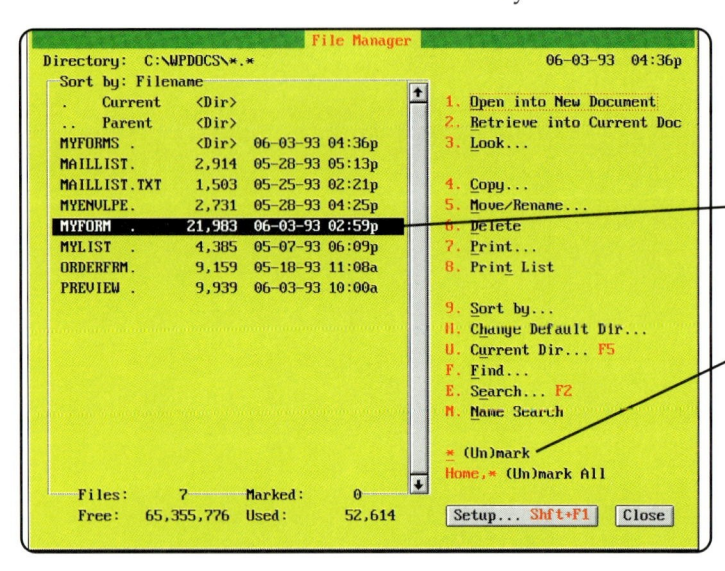

Marking Files to Move

1. Click on **MYFORM** to highlight it if it isn't highlighted already.

2. Click on **(Un)mark** to mark the file with an asterisk. The highlight bar will automatically move to the next file, but that isn't the file you want.

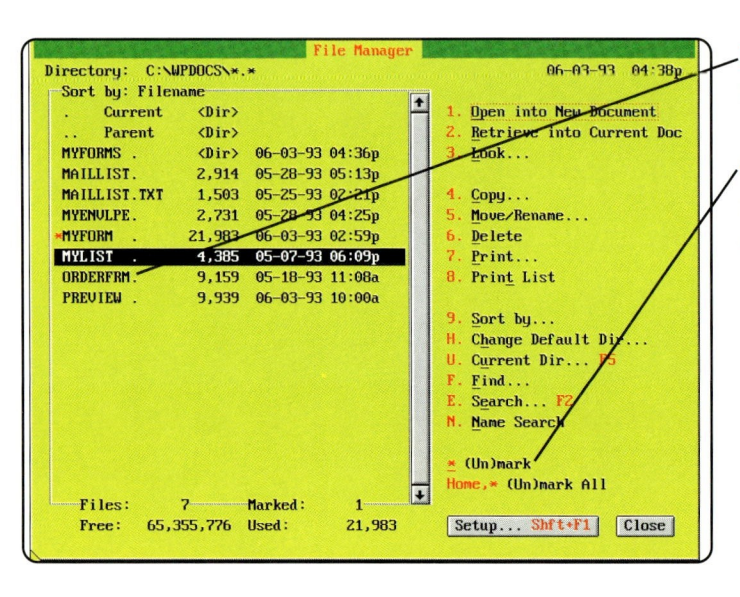

3. Click on **ORDERFRM** to highlight it.

4. Click on **(Un)mark** to place an asterisk to the left of the filename.

CHAPTER 21: SORTING, MOVING, AND COPYING FILES

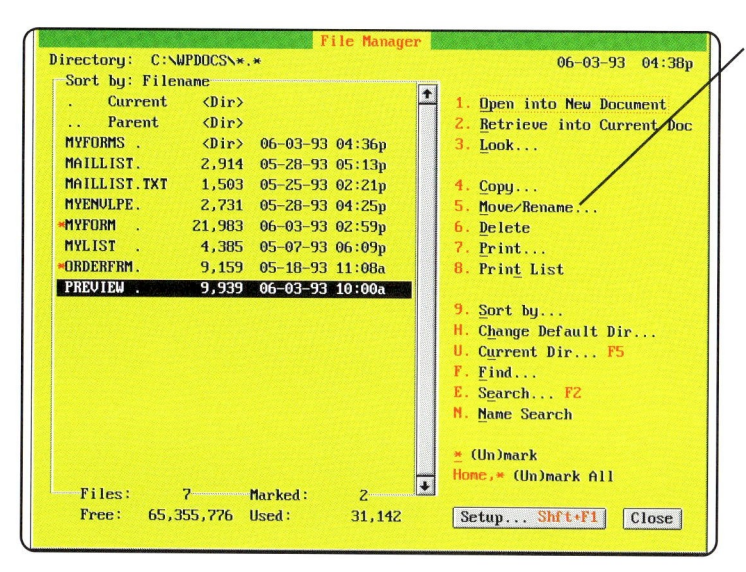

5. Click on **Move/Rename**. The Move marked files? dialog box will appear.

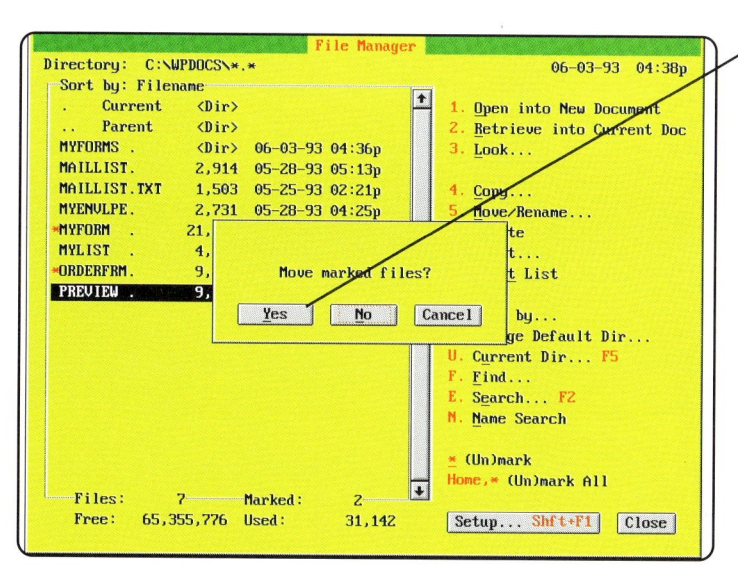

6. Click on **Yes**. The Move/Rename dialog box will appear.

WORDPERFECT 6 FOR DOS: THE VISUAL LEARNING GUIDE

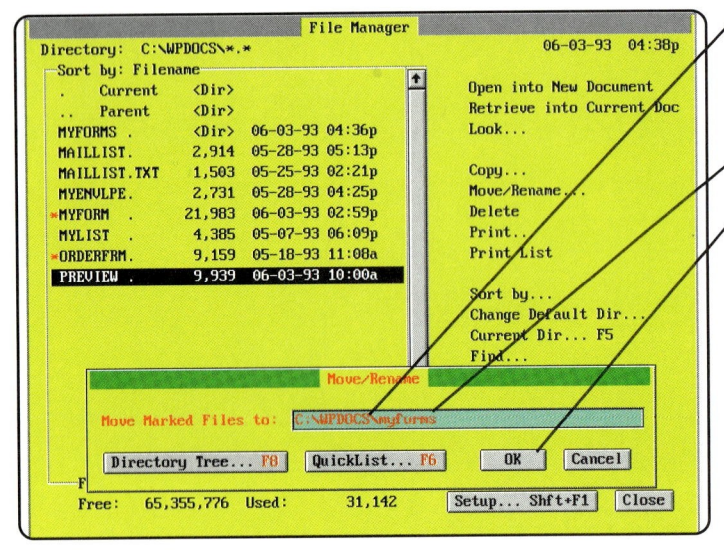

7. Click to the **right of C:\WPDOCS** to set the cursor.

8. Type \myforms.

9. Click on **OK**. The File Manager dialog box will appear. The MYFORM and ORDERFRM files will no longer be in the Sort by: Filename list box. They have been moved to the C:\WPDOCS\MYFORMS directory.

COPYING A FILE TO A DISK

In this example, you will copy a file in the newly created MYFORMS subdirectory to a disk. You'll see how easy it is to access files in another directory.

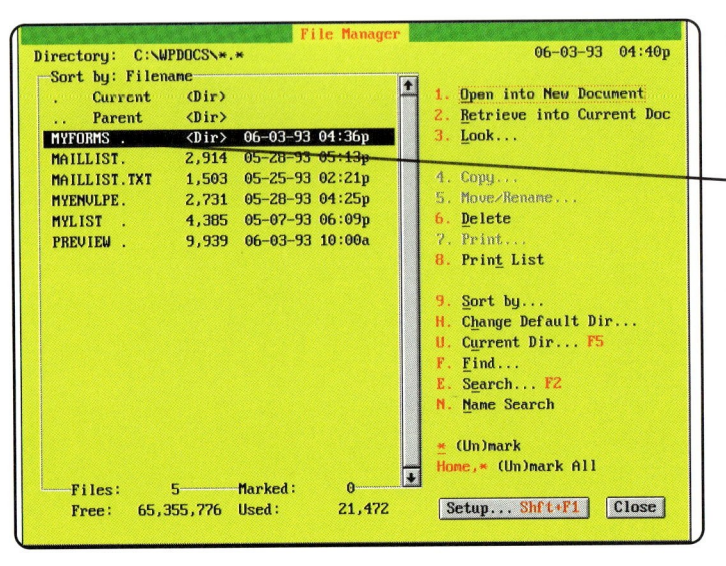

Changing the Directory

1. Click twice on the **MYFORMS directory** (**MYFORMS <Dir>**) in the Sort by: Filename list box. File Manager will show the C:\WPDOCS\MYFORMS directory file list.

CHAPTER 21: SORTING, MOVING, AND COPYING FILES

Copying a File to a Disk

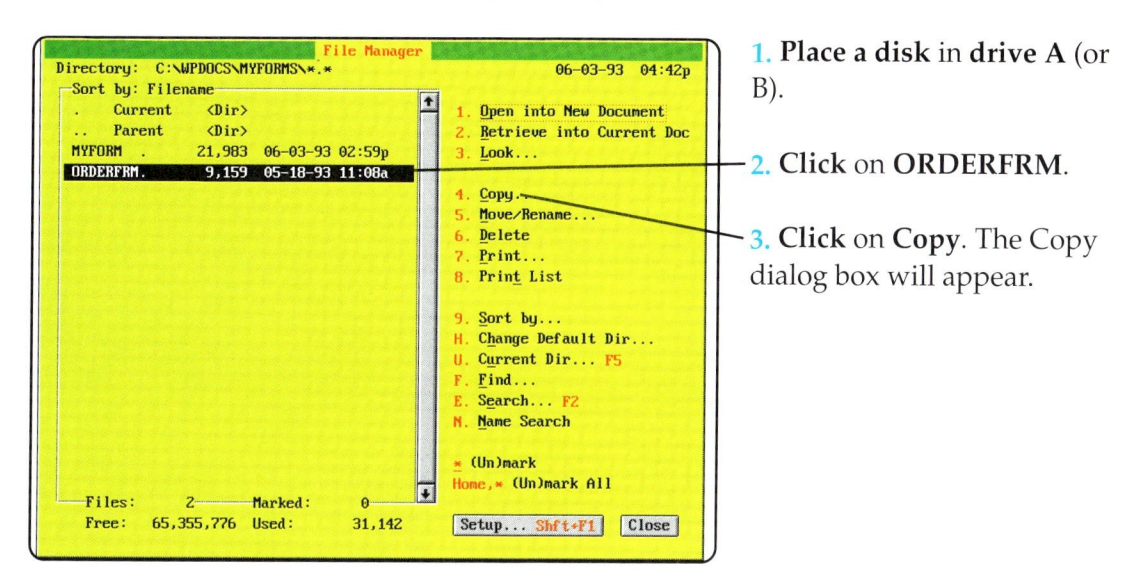

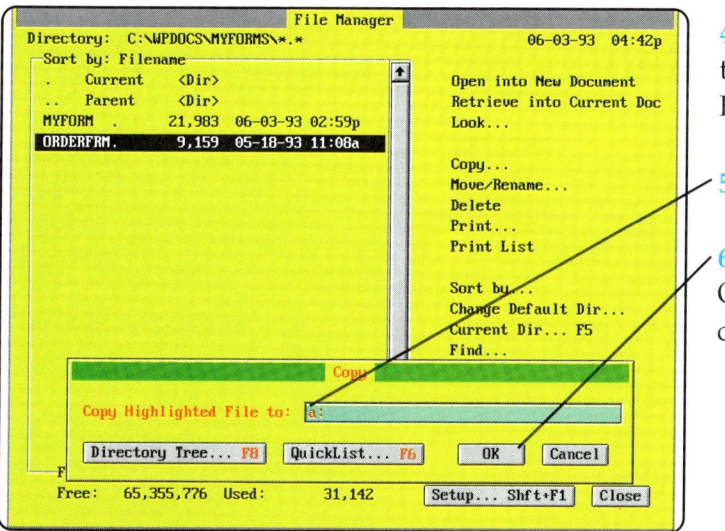

1. **Place a disk** in **drive A** (or B).

2. **Click** on **ORDERFRM**.

3. **Click** on **Copy**. The Copy dialog box will appear.

4. **Press** the **Backspace key** to delete the text in the Copy Highlighted File to text box.

5. **Type a:** (or b:).

6. **Click** on **OK**. The File ORDERFRM will now be copied to your disk.

Returning to the Original Directory

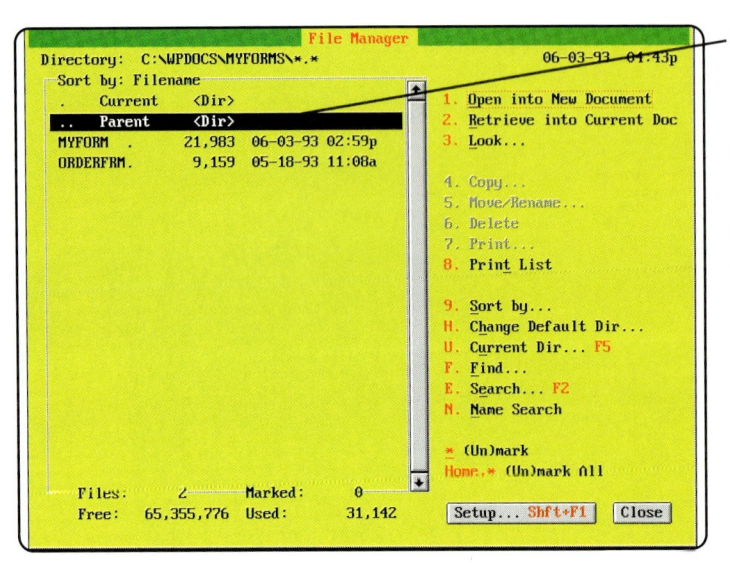

1. Click twice on **Parent <Dir>**. The File Manager dialog box will appear. The files in the directory C:\WPDOCS will be shown in the Sort by: Filename list box.

CLOSING FILE MANAGER

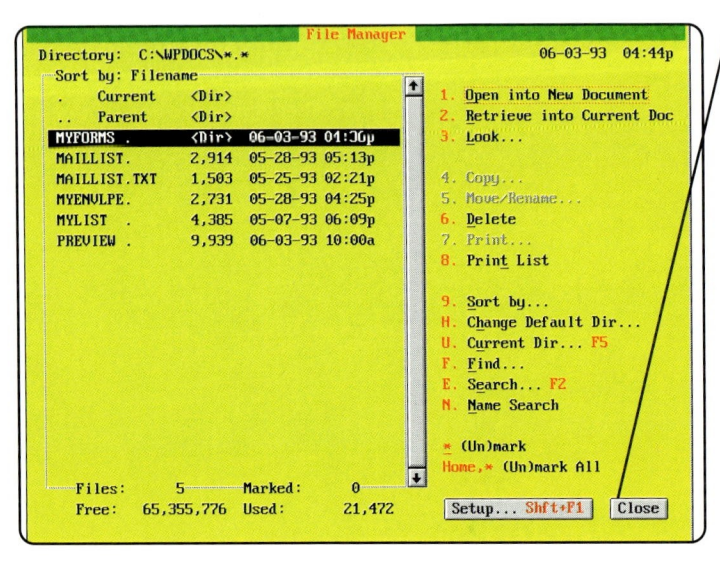

1. Click on **Close**. The opening document screen will appear.

WHAT NEXT?

There are many exciting features of WordPerfect 6 left to explore. We hope this introduction has given you an understanding of its capabilities. We hope, also, that you have gained confidence in your ability to master its complexities.

Experiment! Have fun!

File Manager

Part VI   Appendix

Appendix: Installing WordPerfect 6 for DOS — Page 254

Installing WordPerfect 6 for DOS

This appendix will describe a standard installation. If you want to customize your installation, refer to the *WordPerfect 6.0 Reference Manual*. In this appendix you will do the following:

❖ Install WordPerfect

Before you start, make sure that you have made and are using backup copies of your WordPerfect Install and Program disks. If you need help backing up your disks, see the *WordPerfect 6.0 Reference Manual* for help.

INSTALLING WORDPERFECT 6 FOR DOS

1. **Insert** the **Install 1 disk** into **drive A** (or B).

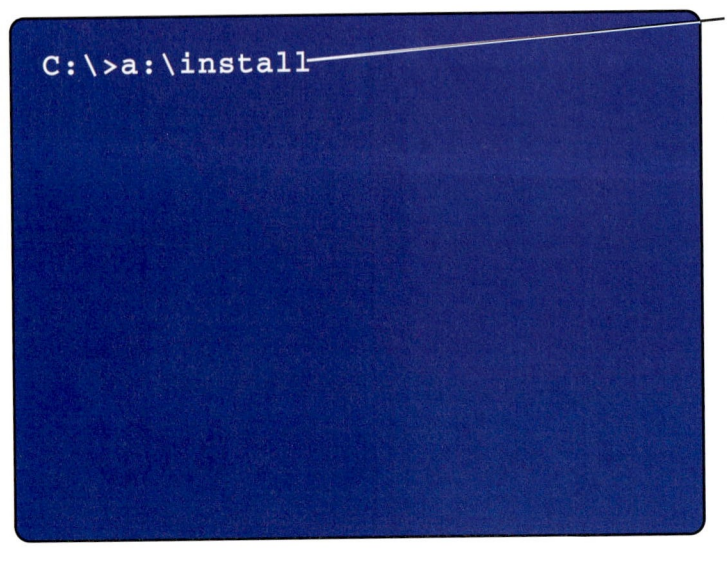

2. **Type a:\install** (or b:\install).

3. **Press** the **Enter key**. After a short pause, the WordPerfect 6.0 Installation screen will appear.

```
C:\>a:\install
```

APPENDIX: INSTALLING WORDPERFECT 6 FOR DOS

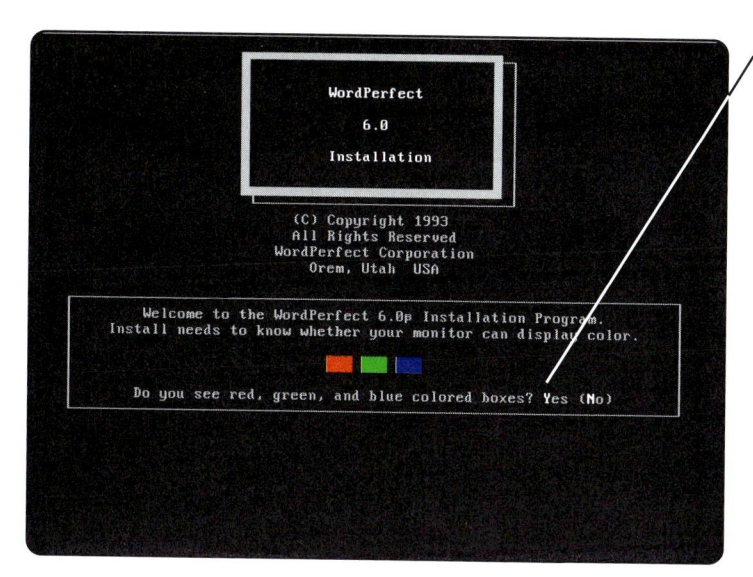

4. Type Y to select **Yes**. (Type N to select No if you do not have a color monitor.) Another WordPerfect 6.0 Installation screen will appear. Standard Installation will be highlighted.

5. Press the **Enter key** to select Standard Installation. A WordPerfect Install dialog box will appear.

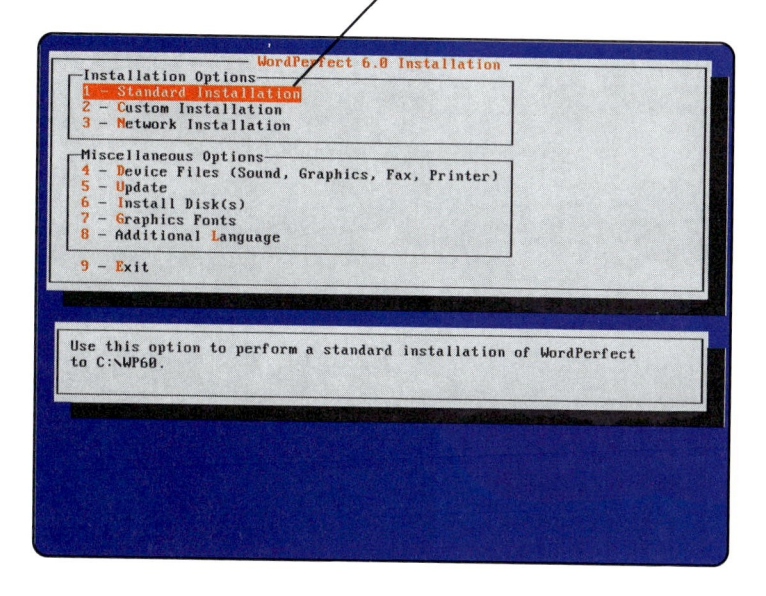

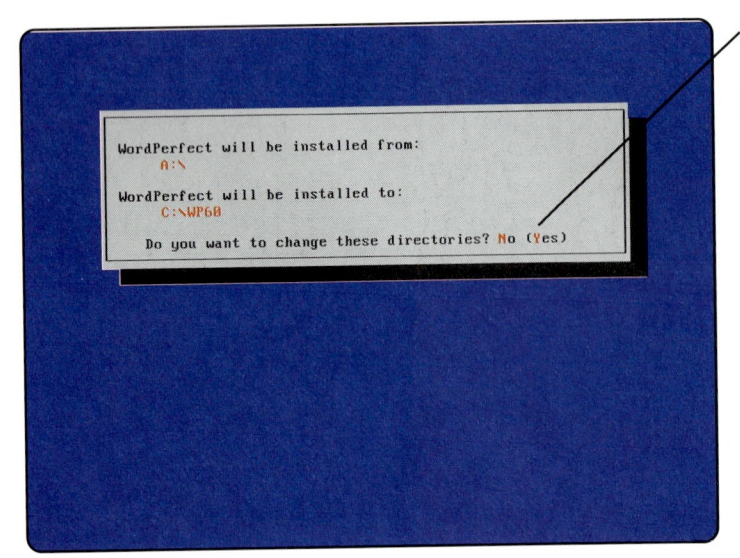

WORDPERFECT 6 FOR DOS: THE VISUAL LEARNING GUIDE

6. Type N to select No. A "Disk Space Recommendations" dialog box will appear.

```
WordPerfect will be installed from:
    A:\

WordPerfect will be installed to:
    C:\WP60

    Do you want to change these directories? No (Yes)
```

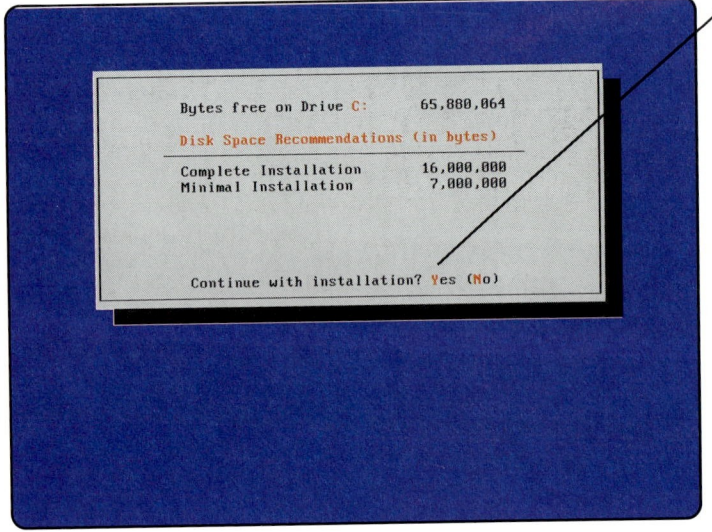

7. Type Y to select Yes to continue with the installation. A "Replace Existing Files Options" dialog box will appear.

```
    Bytes free on Drive C:      65,880,064

    Disk Space Recommendations (in bytes)

    Complete Installation       16,000,000
    Minimal Installation         7,000,000



    Continue with installation? Yes (No)
```

APPENDIX: INSTALLING WORDPERFECT 6 FOR DOS

8. **Press** the **Enter key** for selection 3, Smart Prompting. The Checking AUTOEXEC.BAT File message box will appear. Also the "Add program directory to the path?" dialog box will appear.

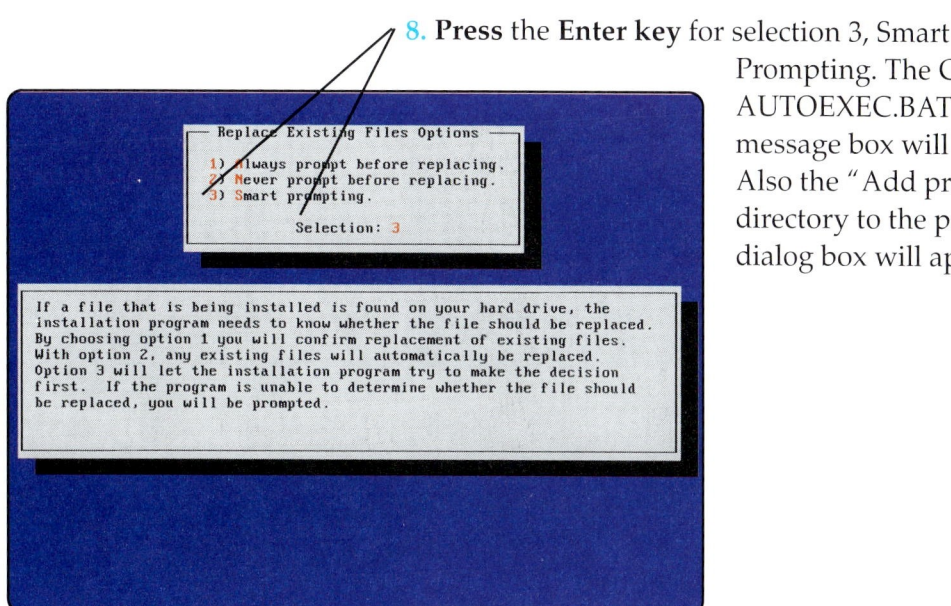

9. **Type Y** to select Yes. You will see a message box, "copying install.exe to C:\wp60." Then the "Do you want to install any additional Graphic Drivers?" dialog box will appear.

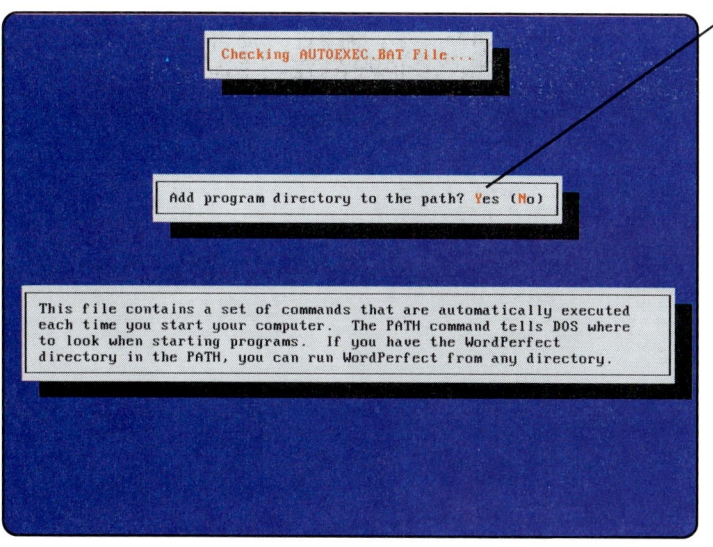

WORDPERFECT 6 FOR DOS: THE VISUAL LEARNING GUIDE

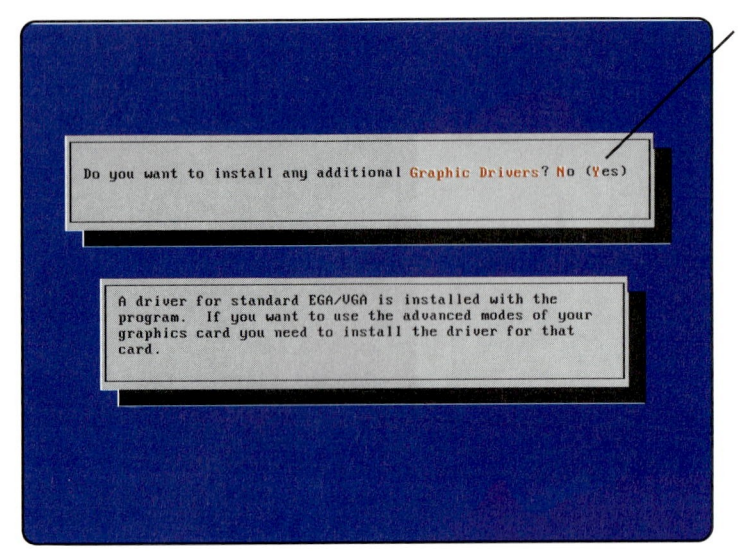

10. **Type N** to select No. The "Do you want to install any Printer Drivers?" dialog box will appear.

Do you want to install any additional Graphic Drivers? No (Yes)

A driver for standard EGA/VGA is installed with the program. If you want to use the advanced modes of your graphics card you need to install the driver for that card.

Installing a Printer

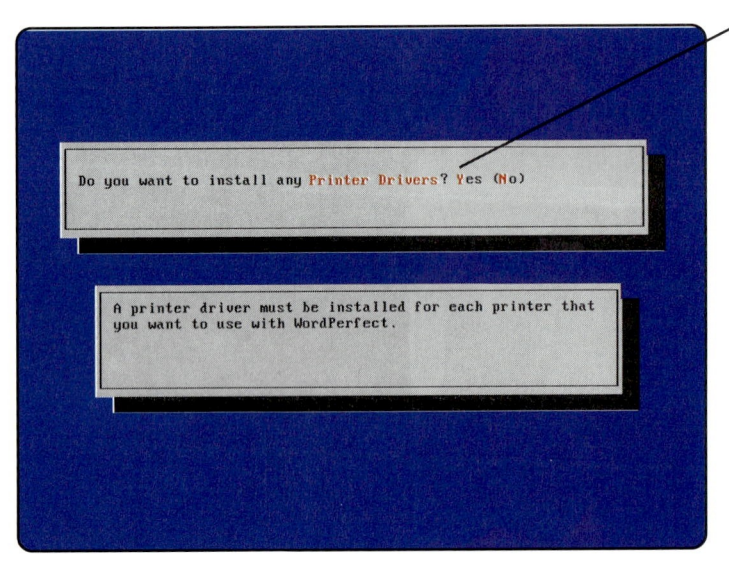

1. **Type Y** to select Yes. A Printer Selection list box will appear with an alphabetic list of hundreds of possible printers.

Do you want to install any Printer Drivers? Yes (No)

A printer driver must be installed for each printer that you want to use with WordPerfect.

APPENDIX: INSTALLING WORDPERFECT 6 FOR DOS

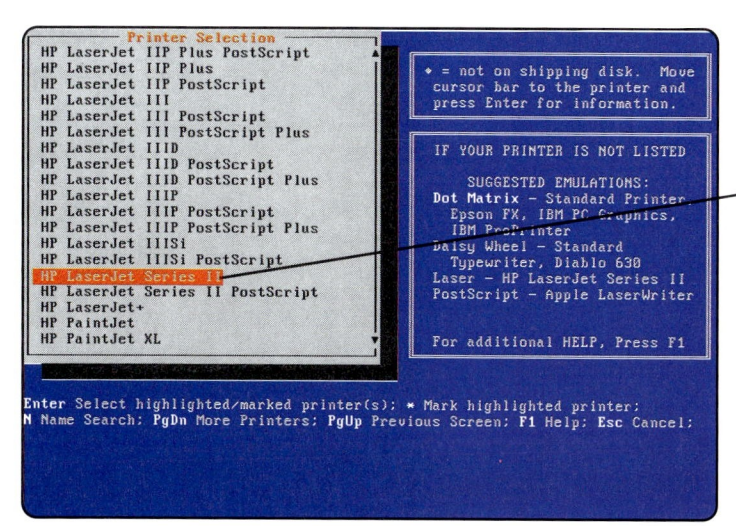

2. Press the **PgDn key** repeatedly until you see your printer.

3. Press ↓ or ↑ on your keyboard until the highlight bar highlights your printer.

In this example we will select the HP LaserJet Series II printer. You can select your own printer from this list.

4. Press the **Enter key** when you have highlighted your printer's name. The "Select printer HP LaserJet Series II?)" dialog box will appear. If you selected a different printer, the dialog box will have your printer's name instead.

Warning: Make certain that the printer listed in the dialog box is the one you wanted. If it is not, type N (No) to return to the printer selection list and select the correct printer.

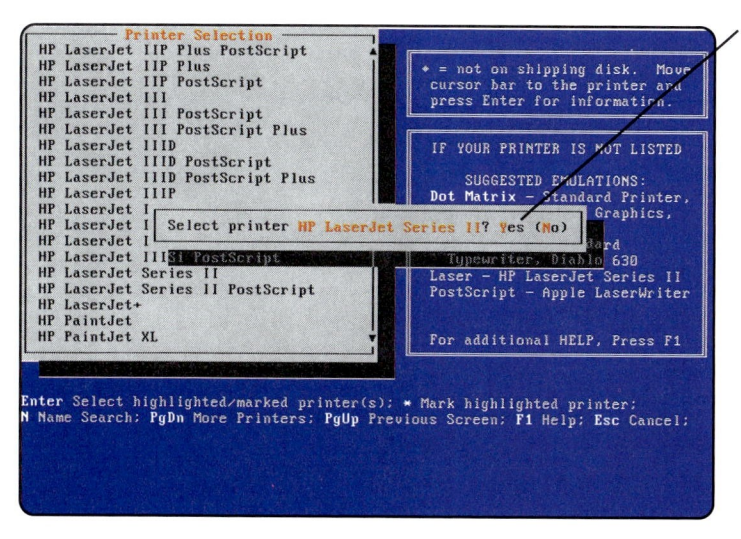

5. Type Y to select Yes. The "Reading Install 1, master diskette" message box will appear.

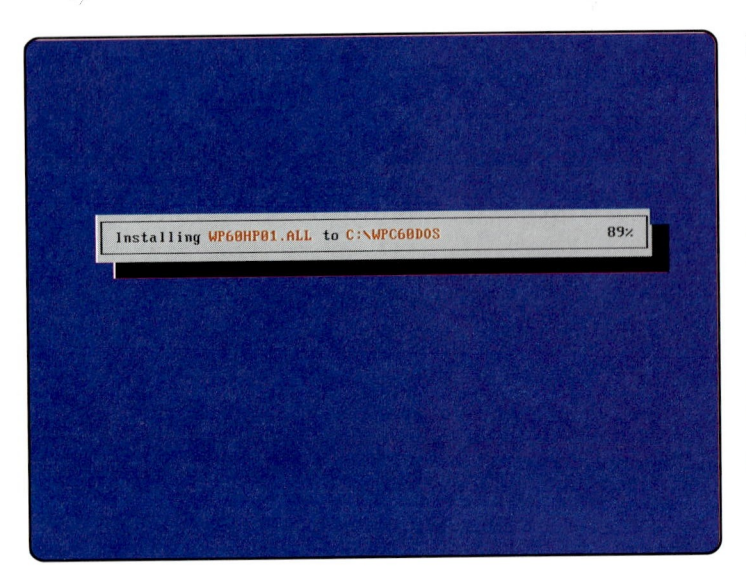

WORDPERFECT 6 FOR DOS: THE VISUAL LEARNING GUIDE

Notice that WordPerfect shows you its progress in percentages as it copies files. The "Do you want to select additional Printer Drivers?" dialog box will appear after WordPerfect has finished copying the necessary files. You will see similar progress percentage dialog boxes throughout the install process.

Completing the Installation

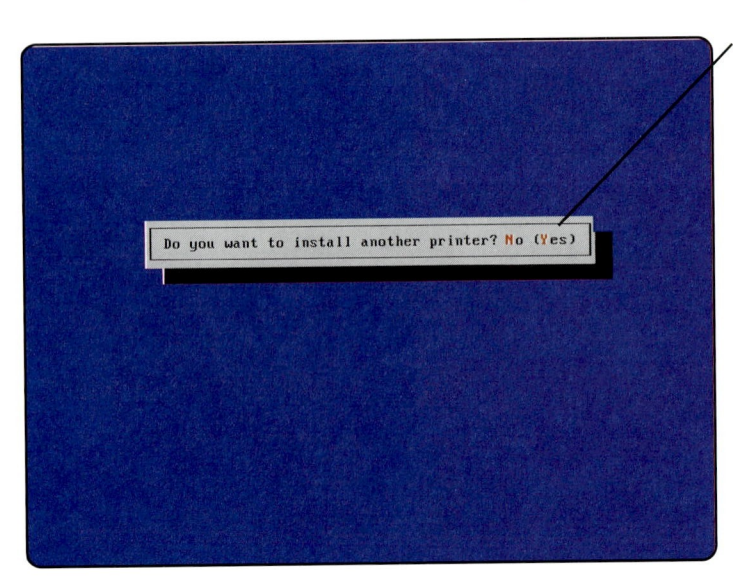

1. Type N to select No if you do not want to install another printer. WordPerfect will continue copying files. You will see the "Reading Install 1, master diskette" message again. Next, the "Insert into drive A . . . Install 2" dialog box will appear.

APPENDIX: INSTALLING WORDPERFECT 6 FOR DOS

2. **Insert** the **Install 2 disk** into **drive A**.

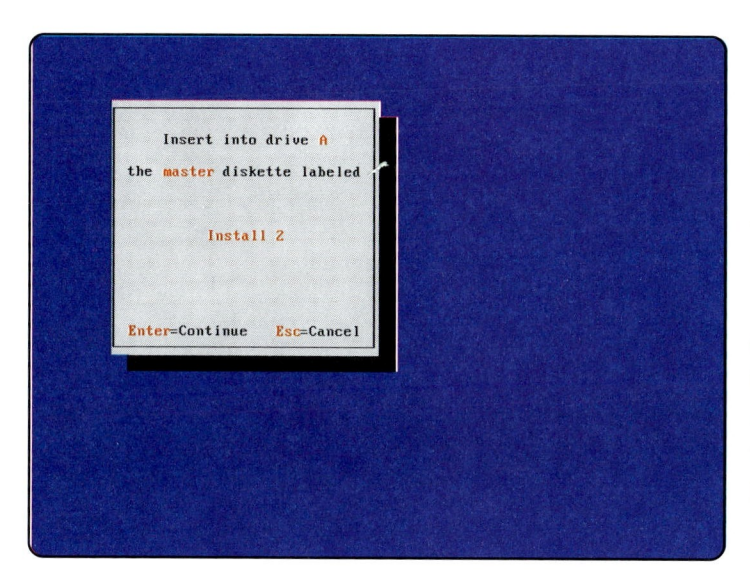

3. **Press** the **Enter key**. The "Reading Install 2 master diskette" message box will show you the percentage of files being copied. Next, the "Insert into drive A...Install 3" dialog box will appear.

4. **Repeat steps 2 and 3** for the **Install 3** and **Install 4 disks**. The "Do you want to install any Fax Files?" dialog box will appear.

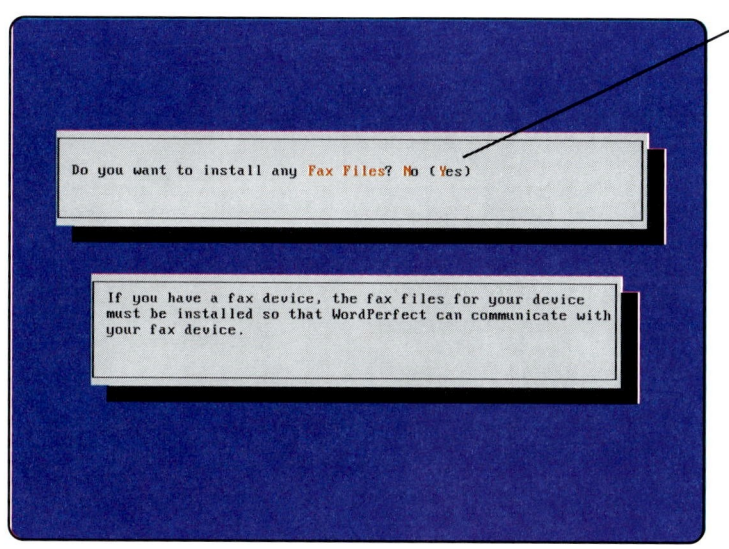

5. **Type N** to select No. The "Do you want to install any Sound Drivers?" dialog box will appear.

WORDPERFECT 6 FOR DOS: THE VISUAL LEARNING GUIDE

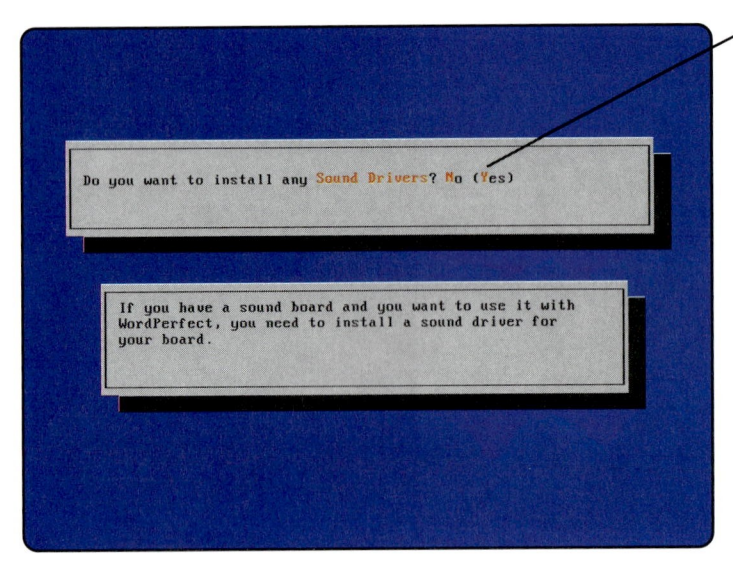

6. **Type N** to select No. WordPerfect will continue copying files. Next, the "Insert into drive A . . . Program 1" dialog box will appear.

7. **Insert** the **Program 1 disk** into **drive A**.

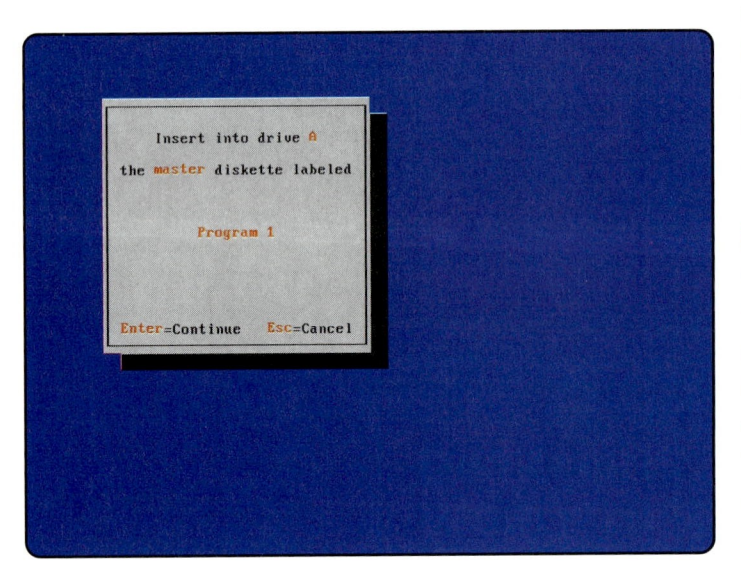

8. **Press** the **Enter key**. WordPerfect will copy the files from the Program 1 disk to the WP60 directory. Next, the "Insert into drive A . . . Program 2" dialog box will appear.

9. **Repeat steps 7 and 8** for the **Program 2** and **Program 3 disks**. You will see several messages as WordPerfect lets you know what it is doing. Then the "Welcome WordPerfect User" registration box will appear.

APPENDIX: INSTALLING WORDPERFECT 6 FOR DOS

ENTERING YOUR REGISTRATION NUMBER

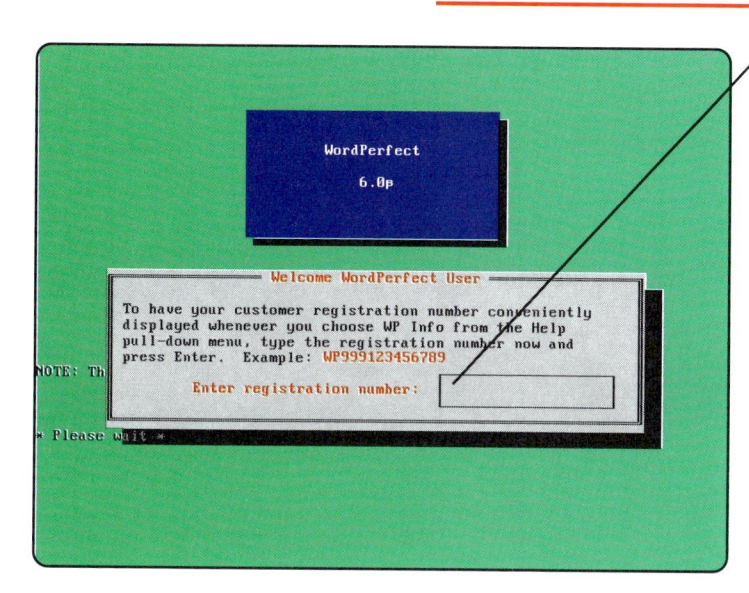

1. **Type** your **registration number**.

2. **Press** the **Enter key**. Several message boxes will flash as WordPerfect completes the installation. A black-and-white WordPerfect information screen will appear.

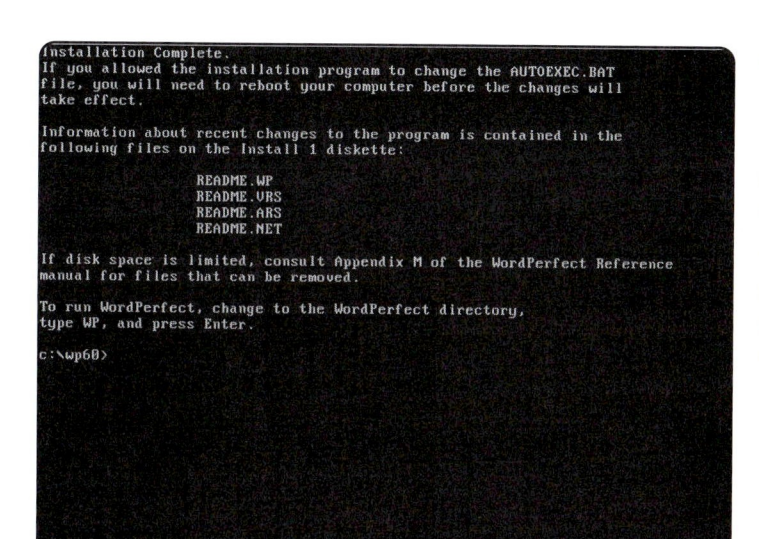

Congratulations! You have successfully installed WordPerfect 6 for DOS. Go to the "Introduction" at the beginning of this book, select your first learning goal, and you can begin learning about and using WordPerfect 6 for DOS now!

Index

A

Absolute tabs, 91
Addition formulas in tables, 225, 228-229
Addresses. *See also* Envelopes
    entering address on letter, 15
Alphabetical sorting
    files, 244-245
    tables, data in, 205-208
Asterisk (*) for marking files, 232-234
Attached envelopes. *See* Envelopes
Automatic page breaks, 17

B

Backspace, error correction with, 16
Backup feature, 25
Backward slash (\), 2, 247
Boldfacing
    envelopes, first line of address on, 126-128
    text, 73-74
Booting up WordPerfect, 2, 35
Borders and shading
    adding borders and shading, 80-83
    deleting borders and shading, 83-84
Box symbols, insertion of, 21-22
Buffer, copying to, 161
Bulleted lists
    deleting bullet, 87
    new bullet styles, 84-85
    other paragraphs, applying style to, 86
    tabs reset for, 89-92
Button Bar
    display of, 5
    Preview tool in, 26

C

Cells. *See also* Tables
    in mailing list, 137
Center-aligned tabs, 88
    setting of, 101
Centering text, 75-78
    customizing text, 78-79
    with layout menu, 77-78
    with the ribbon, 75-77
    table, centering numbers in cells in, 224
Closing
    changes, closing after, 33
    File Manager, 252
    files, 32-33
    marked files, 240
    preview screen, 28
    without saving, 105
Columns and rows. *See also* Tables
    mailing list column widths, adjustments to, 146-148
Combining paragraphs, 53-54

Converting mailing lists. *See* Mailing lists
Copying and pasting
    disk, copying files to, 250-252
    drag-and-drop copying, 65-67
    merge fields, 161
    text, 68-70
Courier 10cpi font, 8
C: prompt, 2, 35
Currency, formatting numbers as, 221-223
Cursor
    and scrolling, 60
    status line information on, 13
Customizing text. *See also* Borders and shading; Bulleted lists
    boldfacing text, 73-74
    centering text, 75-78
    of envelopes, 123-128
    personal goals, xiv
    type size changes, 72-73
    underlining text, 74-75
    undoing alignment of text, 78-79

D

Date
    entering date on letter, 15
    sorting files by time and date, 241-243
Decimal tabs, 88
    setting of, 102
Deleting. *See also* Tables
    borders and shading, 83-84
    bullets, 87
    page breaks, 64
    row in table, 213
    tabs, 99
    text, 51-52

Dictionary. *See* Speller
Directory
    changing directory for copying files to disk, 250
    creating directories, 246-248
    moving files to other directories, 248-250
    original directory, returning to, 252
    sorting files in, 241-245
Disk, copying files to, 250-252
Division formulas in tables, 225
DOS. *See also* Mailing lists
    installing WordPerfect 6 for DOS, 254-258
Dot matrix printers, envelopes printed with, 120
Dotted-line leaders, 93
Drag-and-drop copying, 65-67
Drag-and-drop moving, 61-62

E

Editing, 50-70. *See also* Copying and pasting; Tables
    combining paragraphs, 53-54
    deleting text, 51-52
    drag-and-drop moving, 61-62
    with Grammatik 5, 39-40
    hard returns, 54, 58
    headers, 109
    inserting text, 50-51
    mailing lists, 142-150
    personal goals, xiv
    Replace command, 59-60
    Speller, editing words in document with, 45
    text wrap, 54-58
    undoing edits, 52
Entering text, 14-18

INDEX

body of letter, 16-18
date, address and salutation, 15
letterheads, 14
personal goals, xiv
symbols, insertion of, 18-22
in tables, 202-204
Envelopes. *See also* Mailing lists
    attached envelopes
        closing letter without saving, 132
        printing letter with, 128-131
        printing letter without, 132
    boldfacing first line of address, 126-128
    customizing text of, 123-128
    dot matrix printers, printing with, 120
    envelope button, printing with, 118-120
    envelope tray, printing with, 178-183
    font and point size changes on, 123-126
    HP LaserJet II or III printers, printing with, 119
    omitting and restoring return address, 122-123
    personal goals, xv
    return address
        omitting and restoring, 122-123
        printing of, 121-122
    saving envelope tray setup, 183-184
Exiting WordPerfect, 34

F

Field names. *See* Mailing lists
File Manager
    closing of, 252
    marking files with, 232-234
    opening saved file with, 35-36
    personal goals for using, xv
Filenames, 24
    on exiting WordPerfect, 34
Files. *See also* Marking files
    disk, copying files to, 250-252
    moving files to other directories, 248-250
    sorting. *See* Sorting
    viewing contents of, 245-246
First time, opening WordPerfect for, 2
Fonts
    all documents, changing font for, 10-13
    automatic page break and, 17
    changing fonts, 8-13
    current document, changing font for, 8-10
    envelopes, changing font and point size on, 123-126
    status line information on, 13
    tables, increasing type size in, 216
Formatting. *See* Tables
Form letters. *See* Merge feature
Formulas, 225
    addition formulas in tables, 225, 228-229
    multiplication formulas in tables, 225-227
Forward slash (/), 2

G

Go To command, 69
Grammatik 5, 37-41
    editing with, 39-40
    interactive check with, 38-39
Graphics mode
    Button Bar, 5
    switching from Text mode to, 3-4

H

Hard returns, 54, 58
Headers, 108-110
    adding headers, 109
    creating headers, 109-110
    mailing list, header row for, 137
    print preview, viewing with, 115
    space between text and, 109
    viewing headers, 114-115
Help on installing WordPerfect 6 for DOS, xiii
Helvetica font, 9
Home space, insertion of, 54-57
Horizontal scroll bar, 6
HP LaserJet II or III printers
    envelopes printed with, 119
    installation of, 258-262

I

Iconic Symbols set, 19
    for box symbols, 21
Inserting text, 50-51
Installing
    help for, xiii
    printers, 258-262
    registration number, entering of, 263
    WordPerfect 6 for DOS, 254-258
Interactive check with Grammatik 5, 38-39

L

Layout menu, centering text with, 77-78
Leaders, 88
    dotted-line leaders, 93
    solid-line leaders, 94-96
Left-aligned tabs, 88, 89

Letterheads, 14
Lists. *See* Bulleted lists; Mailing lists

M

Mailing lists. *See also* Merge feature
    adding fields to, 142-145
    cells, 137
    closing envelope file without saving, 188
    column widths, adjustments to, 146-148
    converting mailing lists
        generally, 189-191
        adding field names to converted list, 192-194
        specific program, converting files from, 191
        view, changes to, 192-193
        WordPerfect data file, saving list as, 194-196
    creating mailing list, 137-140
    editing of, 142-150
    envelopes
        closing envelope file without saving, 188
        creating envelopes, 169-174
        entering merge fields for address, 170-173
        envelope tray, printing with, 178-183
        inserting mail merge envelope in document, 173
        marking envelopes to print, 183-188
        saving envelopes, 174
        selected envelope from list, printing of, 183-188
    field names
        converted list, adding field names to, 192-194

INDEX

    entry of, 135-136
    opening data table for, 133-135, 151-154
  header row for, 137
  marking envelopes to print, 183-188
  more data, entry of, 148-149
  personal goals for using, xv
  saving
    generally, 141
    closing envelope file without saving, 188
    editing mailing list, 150
    envelopes, 175
    envelope tray setup, 183-184
    WordPerfect data file, saving list as, 194-196
  setting up data table for, 133-136
  WordPerfect data file, saving list as, 194-196
Margins
  automatic page break and, 17
  changing margins, 106-108
  defaults for, 7-8
  setting margins, 7-8
  for tables, 218-219
Marking files, 232-234
  closing all marked files, 240
  moving to other directory, marking files for, 248-250
  opening marked files, 235
  print, marking files to, 236-239
Merge feature. *See also* Mailing lists
  beginning merge process, 164-165
  closing files, 168
  coding form letter for, 151-163
  copying and pasting fields, 161-162
  deleting merge fields, 158
  inserting merge fields into form letter, 155-160
  opening list of field names for, 151-154

  personal goals, xv
  printing form letter, 166-167
  saving form letters, 163
  selecting form and data file to merge print, 165
Mouse
  clicking with, 4
  drag-and-drop copying with, 65-67
  drag-and-drop moving with, 61-62
  with scroll bars, 6
Multiple files. *See* Several files
Multiplication formulas in tables, 225-227

N

Naming document, 23-24
Numbers. *See also* Formulas; Tables
  formatting numbers, 221-223

O

Opening
  File Manager, opening saved file with, 35-36
  marked files, 235
  new documents, 100
  several files at same time, 232-235
  switching between open documents, 104, 235
  WordPerfect 6 for DOS, 2

P

Page breaks
  automatic page breaks, 17
  deleting page breaks, 64
  inserting page breaks, 63
Page Mode, viewing with, 114-115

Page numbers
    insertion of, 111-113
    print preview, viewing with, 115
    viewing page numbers, 114-115
Pages, printing of. See Printing
Paragraphs, combining of, 53-54
Pasting. See Copying and pasting
Personal goals, xiii-xiv
Position of table, changes to, 218-219
Pre-set tabs, 91
Previewing, 26-28
    closing preview screen, 28
    headers, 115
    multiple pages, preview of, 27-28
    page numbers, 115
    scrolling through pages, 27
    Thumbnail 8 feature, 27-28
Printers
    for envelopes, 119-120
    fonts and, 9
    installing a printer, 258-262
Printing. See also Envelopes
    current page, 29
    documents, 29-31
    entire document, 31
    form letters, 166-167
    marking files to print, 236-239
    selected pages, 30
    several files, 236-239

R

Registration number, entering of, 263
Relative tabs, 91
Replace command, 59-60
Return address, printing of. See Envelopes
Ribbon
    centering text with, 75-77
    display of, 5
    font and point size indicated on, 13

Right-aligned tabs, 88
    insertion of, 92-93
    setting of, 100-101
Rows and columns. See Columns and rows

S

Salutation on letter, entering of, 15
Save As button, 23
Save command, 25
Saving. See also Mailing lists
    after bulleted lists, 87
    attached envelopes, closing letter without saving, 132
    changes to document, closing after, 33
    closing without, 105
    converted mailing lists, 194-196
    envelope tray setup, 183-184
    on exiting WordPerfect, 34
    File Manager, opening saved file with, 35-36
    form letters, 163
    intermittent saving of document, 25
    new documents, 23-24
    shortcut for, 25
    tables, 220
    while working, 79
Scissors symbol, insertion of, 18-21
Scroll bars
    display of, 6
    methods of scrolling, 60
Search
    with Replace command, 59-60
    with Thesaurus, 47
Set Tab command, 96-98
Several files
    opening several files at one time, 232-235
    printing several files, 236-239

INDEX

switching between, 104, 235
Shading. *See* Borders and shading
Solid-line leaders, 94-96
Sorting. *See also* Alphabetical sorting; Tables
    date and time, sorting files by, 241-243
    directory, files in, 241-245
    size, sorting files by, 243-244
Spacebar, use of, 16
Speller, 42-46
    accepting suggested changes, 46
    adding words to dictionary, 43-44
    editing words in document with, 45
    ignoring suggested changes, 44
    skipping words with, 44
Status line, 13
    filenames listed in, 24
Subtraction formulas in tables, 225
Switching between open documents, 104, 235
Symbols, insertion of, 18-22

T

Tables. *See also* Formulas
    adding rows in, 211-212
    addition formulas in tables, 225, 228-229
    cells
        formats of cells, changes to, 217-218
        joining cells in tables, 200-201
        numbers, centering of, 224
    centering numbers in cell, 224
    creating tables, 198-200
    currency, formatting numbers as, 221-223
    deleting
        entire table, 229-230
        row in table, 213
    editing
        adding rows in tables, 211-212
        alphabetically sorting data, 205-208
        deleting rows in, 213
        numerically sorting data, 208-210
        structure of table, 200
        undoing sort, 210
        width of column, changes to, 214-215
    entering text and numbers in, 202-204
    formatting
        numbers in tables, 221-223
        text in tables, 216-218
    joining cells in, 200-201
    multiplication formulas in tables, 225-227
    numbers
        centering numbers in cell, 224
        sorting data numerically in table, 208-210
    personal goals, xv
    position of table, changes to, 218-219
    saving tables, 220
    type sizes in, 216
    undeleting tables, 229-230
    undoing sort, 210
    width of column, changes to, 214-215
Tabs. *See also* Center-aligned tabs; Decimal tabs; Right-aligned tabs
    absolute tabs, 91
    applying tabs, 103
    for bulleted lists, 89-92
    deleting, 99
    left-aligned tabs with mouse, 88, 89
    pre-set tabs, 91
    relative tabs, 91
    with set tab command, 96-98
Text. *See also* Centering text; Customizing text; Editing; Entering text

Text *(continued)*
    copying text, 68
    pasting text, 70
Text mode to Graphics mode, 3-4
Text wrap, 54-58
Thesaurus, 47-49
    replacing word with, 48-49
    search with, 47
Thumbnail 8 feature, 27-28
Time and date, sorting files by, 241-243
Typefaces. *See* Fonts
Type size changes, 72-73

U

Underlining text, 74-75
    for solid-line leaders, 94-96
Undoing
    edits, 52
    redoing undone step, 52
    sort in tables, 210

V

Vertical scroll bar, 6
Viewing
    file contents, 245-246
    headers, 114-115
    page numbers, 114-115

W

WordStar, xv
Word 2, xv
WYSIWYG, 3